THE HEALTHY HEART

Other Publications:

CLASSICS OF THE OLD WEST
THE EPIC OF FLIGHT
THE GOOD COOK
THE SEAFARERS
THE ENCYCLOPEDIA OF COLLECTIBLES
THE GREAT CITIES
WORLD WAR II
HOME REPAIR AND IMPROVEMENT
THE WORLD'S WILD PLACES
THE TIME-LIFE LIBRARY OF BOATING
HUMAN BEHAVIOR
THE ART OF SEWING
THE OLD WEST
THE EMERGENCE OF MAN
THE AMERICAN WILDERNESS
THE TIME-LIFE ENCYCLOPEDIA OF GARDENING
LIFE LIBRARY OF PHOTOGRAPHY
THIS FABULOUS CENTURY
FOODS OF THE WORLD
TIME-LIFE LIBRARY OF AMERICA
TIME-LIFE LIBRARY OF ART
GREAT AGES OF MAN
LIFE SCIENCE LIBRARY
THE LIFE HISTORY OF THE UNITED STATES
TIME READING PROGRAM
LIFE NATURE LIBRARY
LIFE WORLD LIBRARY

FAMILY LIBRARY:
HOW THINGS WORK IN YOUR HOME
THE TIME-LIFE BOOK OF THE FAMILY CAR
THE TIME-LIFE FAMILY LEGAL GUIDE
THE TIME-LIFE BOOK OF FAMILY FINANCE

THE HEALTHY HEART

by Arthur Fisher

AND THE EDITORS OF TIME-LIFE BOOKS

LIBRARY OF HEALTH / TIME-LIFE BOOKS / ALEXANDRIA, VIRGINIA

THE AUTHOR:
Arthur Fisher has written about science and medicine for more than 20 years. He is an editor of *Popular Science Monthly* and has co-authored two books about inventors and inventions. In 1978, he won the Claude Bernard Science Journalism Award for "Slow Viruses: Biological Time Bombs," one of several articles he wrote for the TIME-LIFE *Nature Science Annual*.

THE CONSULTANTS
Dr. Joseph Stokes III is Professor of Community Medicine at the University of California, San Diego. He was a Senior Assistant Surgeon in the Framingham Heart Program of the National Institutes of Health.

Dr. Jeffrey S. Borer is Chief of the Cardiac Catheterization Laboratory and Director of Nuclear Cardiology at the New York Hospital-Cornell University Medical Center in New York City. He served as chief resident and senior investigator in cardiology at the National Institutes of Health.

Dr. Charles L. McIntosh, a specialist in cardiac surgery, has held appointments at the National Institutes of Health and serves as Senior Surgeon, Clinic of Surgery, at the National Heart, Lung, and Blood Institute.

For information about any Time-Life book, please write:
Reader Information, Time-Life Books,
541 North Fairbanks Court, Chicago, Illinois 60611.

Second printing.
Published simultaneously in Canada.
School and library distribution by Silver Burdett Company, Morristown, New Jersey.

Library of Congress Cataloguing in Publication Data
Fisher, Arthur, 1931-
The healthy heart.
(Library of Health)
Bibliography: p. 172
Includes index.
1. Heart—Diseases. 2. Heart.
I. Time-Life Books. II. Title. III. Series
RC 672.F57 616.1'2 80-21587
ISBN 0-8094-3752-X
ISBN 0-8094-3751-1 (lib. bdg.)
ISBN 0-8094-3750-3 (retail ed.)

Valuable assistance was also provided by: Nakanori Tashiro, Asia Editor, Tokyo. The editors also wish to thank: Wibo Van de Linde (Amsterdam); Ed Curran (Belfast); Selwyn Parker (Dublin); Robert Kroon (Geneva); Lance Keyworth (Helsinki); Robert Slater (Jerusalem); Judy Aspinall, Karin B. Pearce (London); John Dunn (Melbourne); Carolyn T. Chubet, Miriam Hsia, Christina Lieberman, Gretchen Wessels (New York); Mimi Murphy (Rome); Carol Barnard (Seattle); Mary Johnson (Stockholm); Eiko Fukuda, Katsuko Yamazaki (Tokyo).

CONTENTS

CHAPTER 1

The great plague of the 20th Century

A pump to fill the Astrodome
When the plumbing breaks down
Waxing and waning of a world epidemic
The heart specialists' wizardry

There is good news about the heart and blood vessels. Their afflictions are coming under control. In much of the world, death rates from these diseases are decreasing. Not in all the world: For reasons no one understands, death rates from some of the diseases are level in some countries, such as England and Wales, and they are rising in others, such as Yugoslavia and Poland. But the rule holds up in most of the industrialized countries, from Japan, which has always had little heart disease, to Finland, which has the world's most.

What is more, the greatest improvement in controlling circulatory afflictions is taking place in the worst ailment: heart attack, in which the victim's heart, starved of blood, dies in part or completely. In the United States, heart attack deaths started to drop in the mid-1960s. During the next decade they dropped by about 25 per cent—the largest decline in the world. And the drop took place in every age group, every race and both sexes.

Good news, indeed—and it came at a time when good news about the heart and its life-sustaining connections was desperately needed. For in the 20th Century, they had fallen prey, suddenly and without explanation, to a disastrous epidemic of disorders. In 1969 the World Health Organization called it "the most serious epidemic facing mankind." And even now, despite all the comforting progress of recent years, such diseases remain the leading cause of death in industrialized nations.

The enormity of the epidemic can be sketched in grim numbers. In France nearly five million people were found to have cardiovascular disease in just one year. In Northern Ireland, with a population of only 1.5 million, approximately 7,500 people have heart attacks each year, and some 3,000 of them die. In the United States more than 40 million men, women and children have something wrong with their hearts or blood vessels. About a million die each year. For every American who dies of cancer, the second-ranking cause of death, three die of heart-related disease. And though the human costs cannot be reckoned, the economic cost—expenditures for medical services, and losses in earnings and production—has been calculated in the United States. It is astronomical: more than $40 billion a year.

These stark statistics make clear the importance of the recent victories over what physicians call cardiovascular ailments. Many explanations have been offered for those victories. Some fatalists suggest that epidemics simply come and go inexplicably, and that this one will disappear as mysteriously as the Black Death of the Middle Ages. More persuasive explanations are based on new knowledge about the heart and blood system and on new methods of fighting or preventing their disorders. Some of these methods are medical—innovations in intensive hospital care, new drugs and sophisticated surgery.

Perhaps most important to the waning of the epidemic, however, are not things that doctors and nurses do, but things that ordinary people—healthy or sick—do for themselves. The new knowledge of the heart and blood vessels has identified certain habits of everyday living—smoking, diet and

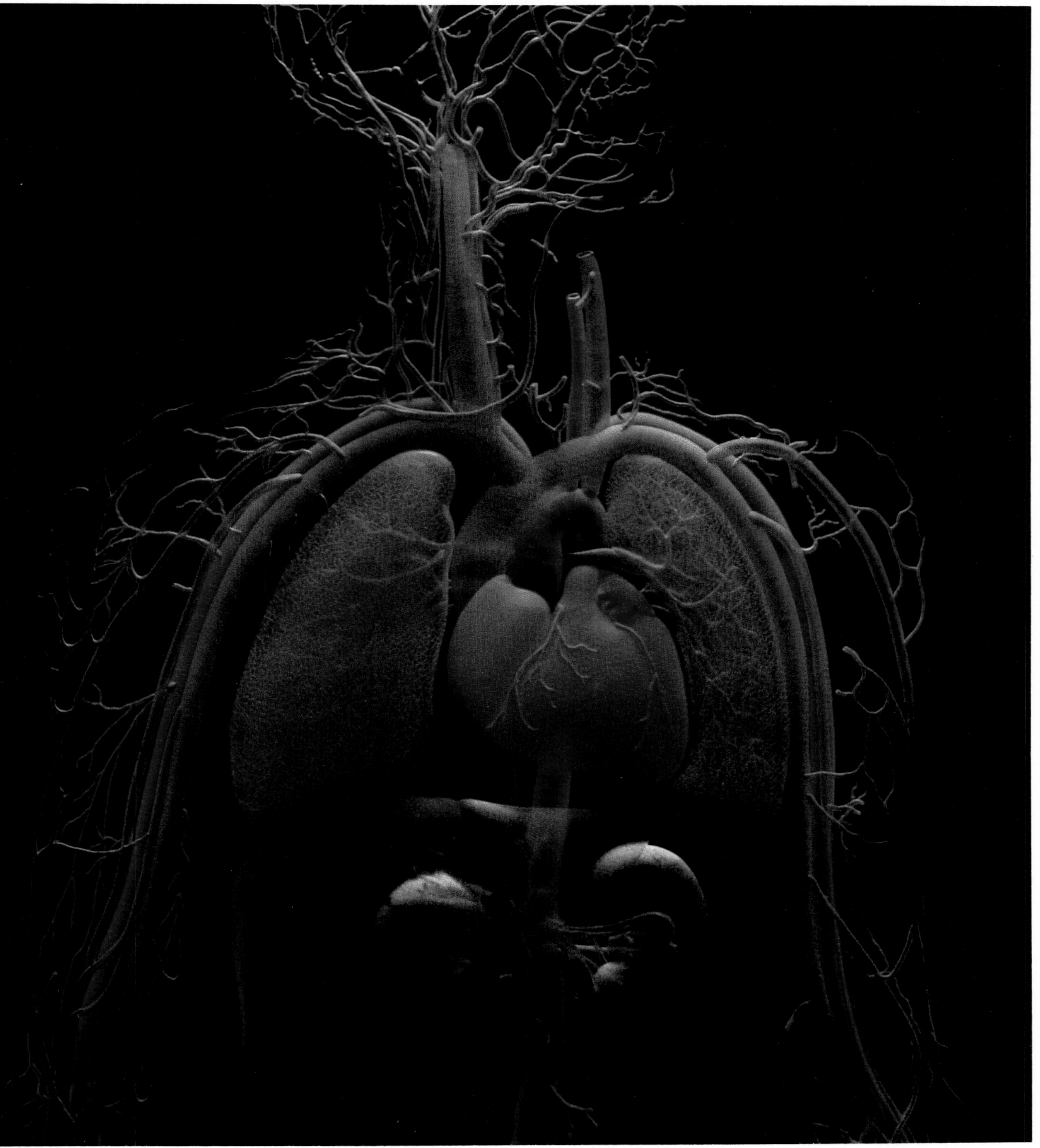

Cradled almost in the center of the chest, the heart is indeed the center of the blood-circulating system that sustains life throughout the body. In this relief map of part of the system, the vessels carrying oxygenated blood from the heart and lungs are colored red; vessels returning depleted blood are blue.

exercise—that affect one's chances of enjoying a healthy heart. From this research have come rules for maintaining a heart-preserving life style. The rules do not guarantee a healthy heart, but overwhelming evidence indicates that they greatly reduce the risk of disease. The rules are simple:

- If you smoke, stop—or cut down as much as you can.
- If you weigh more than the ideal for your age and body build *(page 42),* reduce.
- Eat foods that contain little fat—particularly animal fat—and little salt.
- Exercise regularly and as strenuously as your physical condition permits.
- If you drink, limit yourself to two drinks a day.
- Learn to relax; if necessary, experiment with ancient and modern techniques, such as yoga, meditation and biofeedback, that have helped others.

These new rules for a healthy heart have an oddly old-fashioned ring. They echo the common-sense advice great-grandmother might have given. But great-grandmother's regimen was abandoned by most people in the 20th Century. And the significance of that change in life styles has only recently been perceived. Indeed, most of what is now known about the circulatory system is relatively new knowledge. The epidemic that struck the system is recent; the ailments that make up the epidemic are just beginning to be understood. Even the mechanism of the system—the way heart and vessels work to keep the normal body alive—was discovered by Western physicians only a few centuries ago.

A pump to fill the Astrodome

The idea that the heart is a pump circulating blood through a maze of vessels in the body was known to the Chinese more than 2,000 years ago, but their doctrines had no influence on the West. In the ancient Greek idea of the body, the blood did not circulate at all, and Greek medical ideas dominated the Western view of the heart until the 17th Century. Then King Charles I's court physician, William Harvey, conducted human and animal experiments that revealed the pumping action of the heart, the functions of the blood vessels and the flow of blood out from the heart, through the vessels and back to the heart. In 1628 Harvey published his findings in *On the Movement of the Heart and Blood*—and the age-old picture of the heart system changed forever.

In one sense the new picture was a prosaic one: a pump connected to a network of pipes and valves. But what a pump, and what pipes! Paradoxically, after Harvey the medieval notion that the heart was the noblest of the body's organs, reigning at the core of a human being just as the earth was thought to reign at the center of the universe, retained much of its semimythical force.

Consider the prodigious working of the heart itself. Texas surgeon Denton Cooley described it as "a fist-sized pump that can fill the Astrodome." It is indeed no bigger than a clenched fist, and weighs no more than 11 ounces in an average-sized adult—but it drives the blood through some 60,000 miles of blood vessels to nourish every one of the trillions of cells in the body. Working ceaselessly, the heart beats 100,000 times a day, 2.5 billion times in a full lifetime.

At birth the human heart beats about 120 times a minute. By adulthood the normal contraction—or pulse—rate drops to between 60 and 80 beats per minute when the body is at rest, or sitting or lying down quietly. Mere walking raises the rate 20 to 30 per cent because more blood must be circulated to meet the body's increased demand for energy. Greater exertion raises the pulse rate still further. The rate can be pushed only so far, to what is called the maximum heart rate—normally about 200 beats per minute at the age of 25, and generally declining with age.

Regular exercise, however, can decrease normal pulse rates. It improves the efficiency of the entire circulatory system, so that the heart works less hard to drive blood through the body; accordingly, the pulse rate at all levels of exertion tends to drop. In superbly conditioned athletes the drop may be extraordinary; when tennis player Björn Borg was in his prime, at the age of 20, his pulse rate at rest was an amazing 35 beats per minute.

Whatever the pulse rate, at rest or under stress, the volume of blood pumped out by the heart at each beat is fairly constant. A beat is a contraction of the heart muscle, resembling a clench of the fist; generally, the contraction squeezes about

Listening to telltale throbs of life

In 1816 French physician René Laënnec had to examine a corpulent young woman with puzzling signs of heart disease. He needed to listen to her heartbeat, but it was so muffled by her bulk that his usual technique—his ear against her chest—would not work. Laënnec found a way. Recalling that sound carries through a log, he rolled a sheaf of papers into a tight cylinder and put one end to his patient's chest, the other to his ear. The clarity of sound was startling; even in a single heartbeat the snap of closing heart valves could be clearly heard. Using his improvised stethoscope, which he later modified to a durable, foot-long wooden tube, Laënnec spent two years cataloguing the secret sounds of the heart.

In 1852 Dr. George Cammann of New York perfected the flexible Y-shaped version that remains a basic diagnostic tool. With it a physician can begin to diagnose many ailments: A normal heart goes "lub-dub"; a leaking valve sounds, in Laënnec's words, like "a rasp on wood"; a thick valve produces a sharp click.

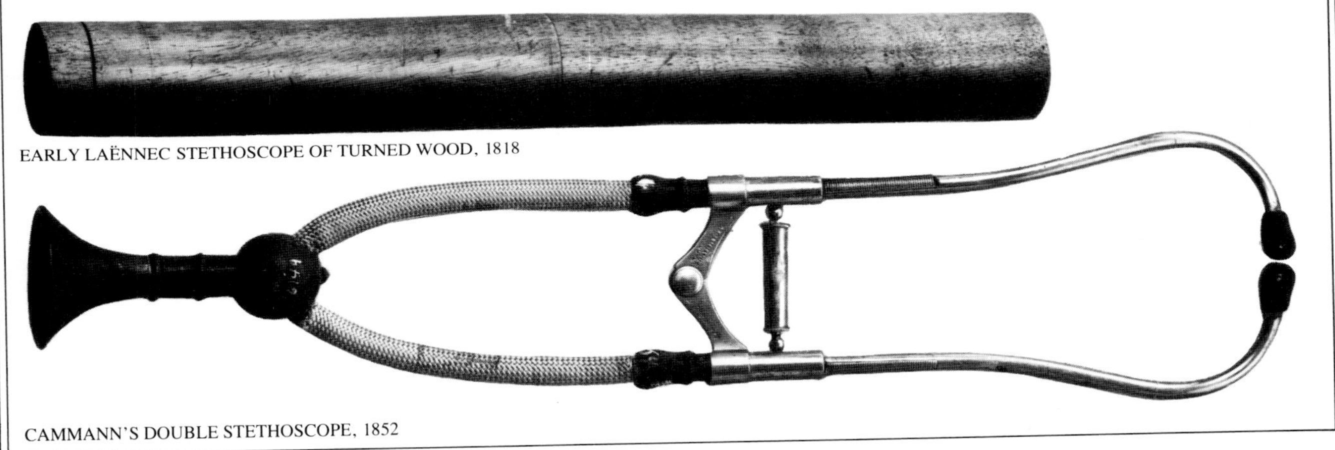

EARLY LAËNNEC STETHOSCOPE OF TURNED WOOD, 1818

CAMMANN'S DOUBLE STETHOSCOPE, 1852

two and a half ounces of blood out of the heart and into the vessels. This is not much, but it totals about 10 pints of blood a minute, and can rise to five times as much during strenuous exercise. An average heart pumps 2,500 to 5,000 gallons of blood in a day, 100 million gallons in a lifetime.

The muscled organ that accomplishes this miracle of pumping is itself a miracle of intricacy and elegance. The human heart—like the hearts of all mammals—contains four chambers: two collecting chambers, called atria, at the top; two pumping chambers, called ventricles, at the bottom. A single heartbeat lasts less than a second, but it is a wonderfully complicated process *(pages 11-14)*. First the ventricles relax and fill with blood, the right ventricle with oxygen-depleted blood collected from the body, the left ventricle with oxygen-rich blood collected from the lungs. Then the ventricles contract: The right ventricle pumps its oxygen-depleted blood into a major blood vessel called the pulmonary artery, which leads to the lungs; the left ventricle pumps its life-giving, oxygen-rich blood into the aorta, a blood vessel that branches off to the rest of the body. With each beat, blood travels through the longest pathways of the body—from the heart to the big toes and back again.

The vessels that make up such pathways, more complex than any network of man-made piping, run to and from every point in the body. Fresh blood leaves the heart through relatively large, thick-walled arteries (the aorta, largest of all, is about an inch in diameter). The blood branches out through smaller arteries into vessels called arterioles, no more than $1/125$ inch thick. Finally, in the last stage of the blood's outward journey, it must squeeze through tubes so tiny that they cannot be seen without a microscope. There are 10 billion of these minuscule capillaries, each one so narrow that a single cell of red blood may distend the flexible capillary wall in order to pass through. It is here that blood gives up its precious cargo of oxygen and nutrients, before picking up carbon dioxide and cell wastes for disposal. Then the return journey to the heart begins: The blood passes from the capillaries into larger vessels called venules, then to the big vessels called veins, which lead back to the heart.

Even the heart itself is the site of such an outward and return journey. Though constantly flooded with blood, it cannot take nourishment from this supply—its walls are too thick and have a liquid-tight lining. The heart muscle needs its own—and crucially vulnerable—network of arteries, arterioles, capillaries, venules and veins. Most important, partly because they are most likely to cause trouble, are the coronary arteries (named from the Latin word for "crown" because they lie over the heart like a lopsided tiara).

All this activity—about five quarts of blood squeezed by a fist-sized pump through 60,000 miles of piping in less than a minute—must not stop; if it does the body dies within minutes. Not only must blood flow continue, it must continue in rhythm. In time with the heartbeat, valves must open, then shut, to keep blood from flowing backward from ventricle to atrium, or from artery to ventricle. The timing of the cycle is triggered by a tiny bundle of nerves, the sinoatrial node, at the top of the right atrium. Electrical signals radiate from here to regulate every split second of the heartbeat. This delicate nerve control is independent of the brain, a fact that, in one sense, makes the circulatory system strangely immortal. It can continue to work normally, nourishing body tissues, for hours and even years after its owner is for all practical purposes dead. But although the heart can survive without the body, the body cannot survive without the heart.

When the plumbing breaks down

Most of the time the pump called a heart and the pipes called blood vessels work together superbly—in fact, better and more reliably than pumps or pipes built by men. But like a man-made plumbing system, the human circulatory system can break down. As in all plumbing, the fundamental causes are simple: The pump or the pipes can clog; they can leak or rupture; their controls can go out of adjustment. Some disorders result from a single cause, but most arise from combinations of these defects.

Some forms of heart leakage may exist at the moment of birth. About eight in every thousand children are born with defective heart valves, with holes in the wall between the ventricles, or more drastically, with arteries connected to the wrong ventricles. Subtler leakages can develop later in life: Rheumatic fever, a disease that generally attacks children between the ages of five and 15, can scar heart valves so that they never quite close.

Other problems, however, are ailments of the aged. One of these is failure of the heart's electrical controls. After many years of keeping the heart beating in perfect rhythm, the natural pacemaker in the right atrium often begins to miss the timing of the heartbeats—to open and close valves at the wrong times—or to trigger extra ones.

More common than simple leaks or worn-out electrical controls are defects in the pipes of the circulatory system. For any of a variety of reasons, arteries become thickened and inelastic—less able to expand and contract. The popular term for the general condition is hardening of the arteries; the medical term, arteriosclerosis. In a form of arteriosclerosis called atherosclerosis, the lining of the arteries is thickened and roughened by deposits of fatty material. Not only do the arteries themselves become less flexible, but the passageways through them become narrower and narrower as the fatty deposits build up and harden.

Atherosclerosis alone can completely obstruct an artery; even before that happens, the deposits can cause a clot of blood at the site. Normally, the cells of the blood will not adhere to the inner walls of an artery—but certain blood cells, called platelets, pile up and die on the fatty deposits of atherosclerosis. On the surfaces of the dead platelets, thread-like structures called fibrils are formed, and the platelets and matted fibrils grow into a hardened, solid mass. This blood clot may become enlarged until it plugs the artery, or it may break loose and be carried through the body in the blood-

A maze of tubing and a wondrous pump

The human circulatory system is a maze of more than 60,000 miles of assorted tubing and a wonderfully powerful pump that weighs less than a pound. All this plumbing, depicted in simplified form in models on the following pages, exists to serve one purpose: circulating the blood that brings life-giving nutrients to every cell in the body and takes away wastes.

Three types of blood vessels—arteries, veins and capillaries—make up the tubing. Blood colored crimson by oxygen is pumped out one side of the heart through the largest artery, the aorta, and then into arteries serving the head, limbs and internal organs. Arteries branch into smaller arterioles, which link up with the smallest vessels of all, the capillaries. Less than a tenth the thickness of a human hair, the capillaries have walls so thin that nutrient molecules filter through from the blood's red cells into surrounding tissues, and waste products filter the other way; the red cells ordinarily never leave the capillaries.

From the capillaries, spent blood (now colored blue) flows into narrow veins called venules and then into veins for the journey back to the heart. From the heart, blood is pumped to the lungs to pick up fresh oxygen, then back to the heart for another round trip.

The longest round trip—from the heart to the big toe and back—takes less than a minute. All along the route, the design of the tubing expedites circulation. Muscles and elastic tissues of arteries regulate pressure; one-way valves in veins prevent backward flow. But the efficiency of the system depends mainly on its pump *(following pages)*. Squeezing out about two and a half ounces at every beat, it daily pumps at least 2,500 gallons of blood, which weighs 20 tons.

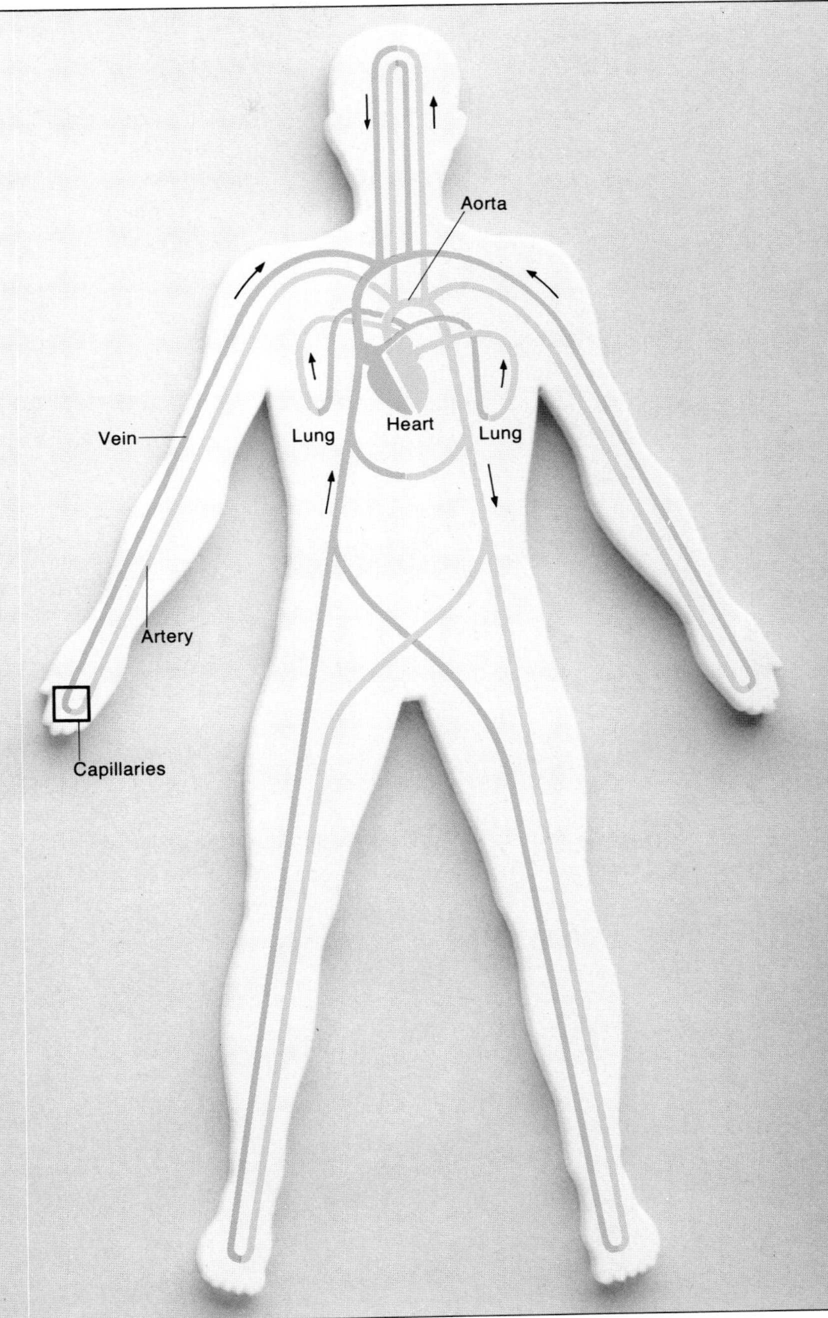

A MAP OF THE BLOOD SYSTEM
In this model, arrows indicate blood flow out of the heart in arteries and back in veins. At loops connecting the two, invisibly small capillaries handle the exchange of nutrients and wastes between fresh blood (red) and spent blood (blue).

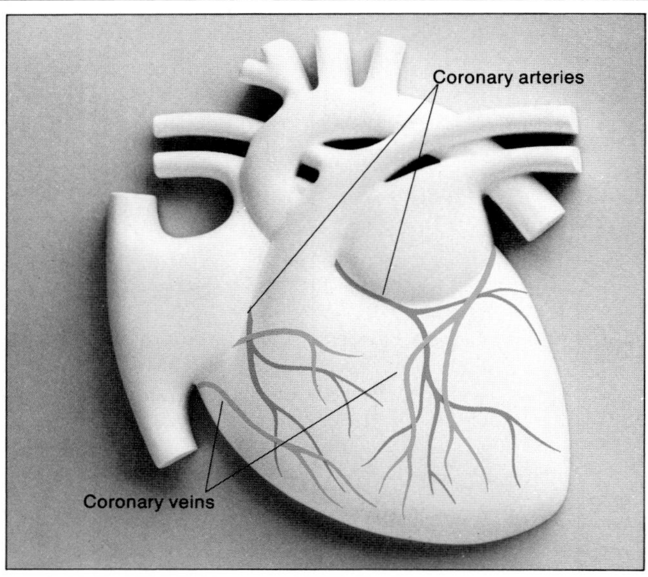

THE HEART: OUTSIDE
This exterior view shows how the pump is fed. Coronary arteries branch from the aorta to nourish heart muscles with fresh blood (red), and veins return spent blood (blue). Blood flowing through the pump cannot nourish it—its lining is liquid-tight.

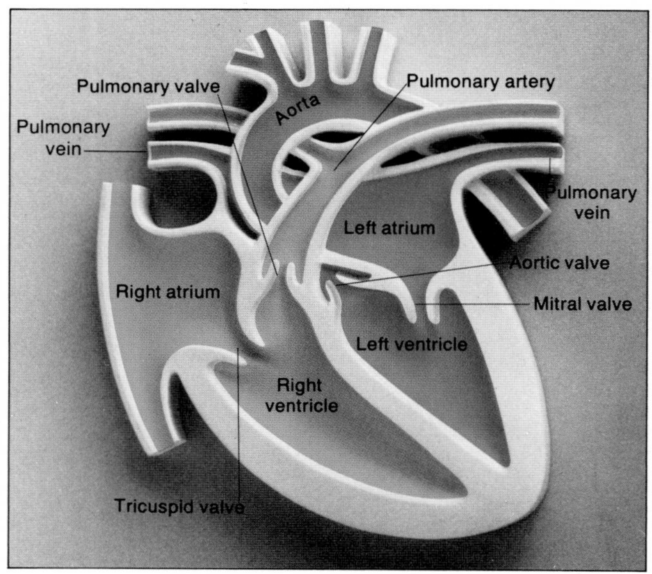

THE HEART: INSIDE
This cutaway identifies parts of the pump, shown blood-filled and stopped. It is seen head on; right and left parts are transposed. The veins bring blood—spent (blue) or oxygenated (red)—to the atria, which supply the ventricle pumping chambers.

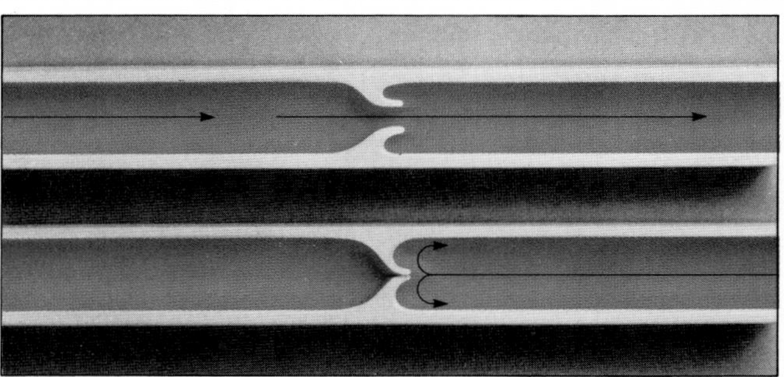

HOW THE AUTOMATIC VALVES WORK
Pressure from blood flowing in one direction forces the hinged flaps of the valve open (top). Pressure from the opposite direction closes the flaps to block backflow (bottom).

THREE STAGES OF A SINGLE HEARTBEAT

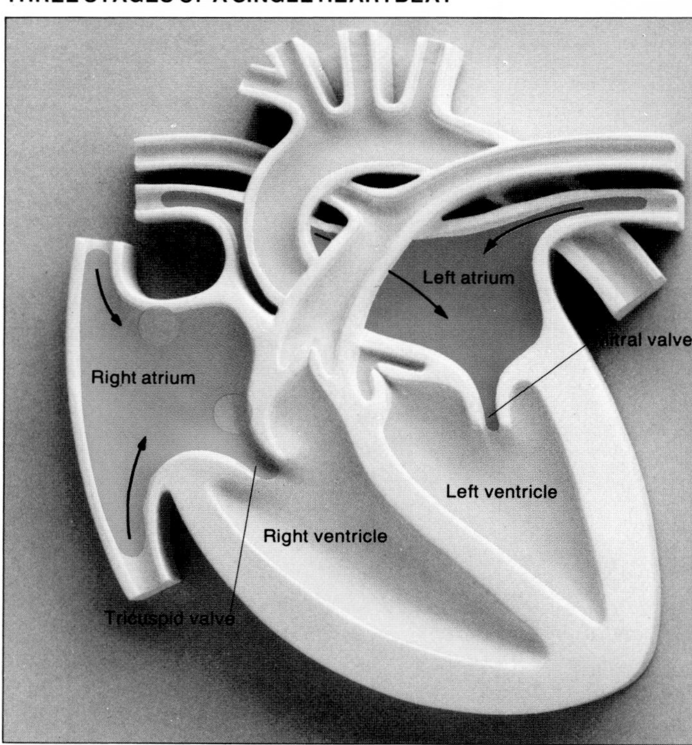

FILLING AT REST
In the stage called diastole, the heart is relaxed, its controls (yellow) electrically negative. Blood from the body and lungs (dark colors) fills the atria, forcing the tricuspid and mitral valves partially open and starting blood flow to the ventricles.

Nerves, muscles and valves coordinated to beat "lub-dub"

The heart is a self-contained pump—it has its own power supply, valves and control system—that is remarkably simple in design and amazingly durable. In a normal life span it operates more than two billion times without ever stopping.

The energy to keep it running is supplied by blood from the heart's own network of arteries, veins and capillaries *(far left)*. The valves are elastic, overlapping flaps of tissue *(left)*. They can be pushed aside to let blood flow in one direction but will not open the other way, blocking reverse flow. The control system—which can carry on without any prodding from the brain but also responds to certain brain signals—consists of two nerve centers called nodes. Signals coming from these nodes activate the pumping muscles.

The pumping part of this machine has no pistons or cylinders but has four flexible chambers. Like rubber bulbs, they fill with blood when expanded, then squeeze blood out when contracted, as illustrated below.

The process involved in a single heartbeat—chambers filling and emptying, nodes firing signals, and valves operating—can be heard through a physician's stethoscope as a rhythmic "lub-dub," the sounds made by the two pairs of valves snapping shut in precise sequence. With the body at rest, such a beat occurs about 70 times a minute. But when emotional stress or physical exercise makes extraordinary demands for extra blood, the brain signals the control system, and for short periods the heart may pump as fast as 200 lub-dubs per minute.

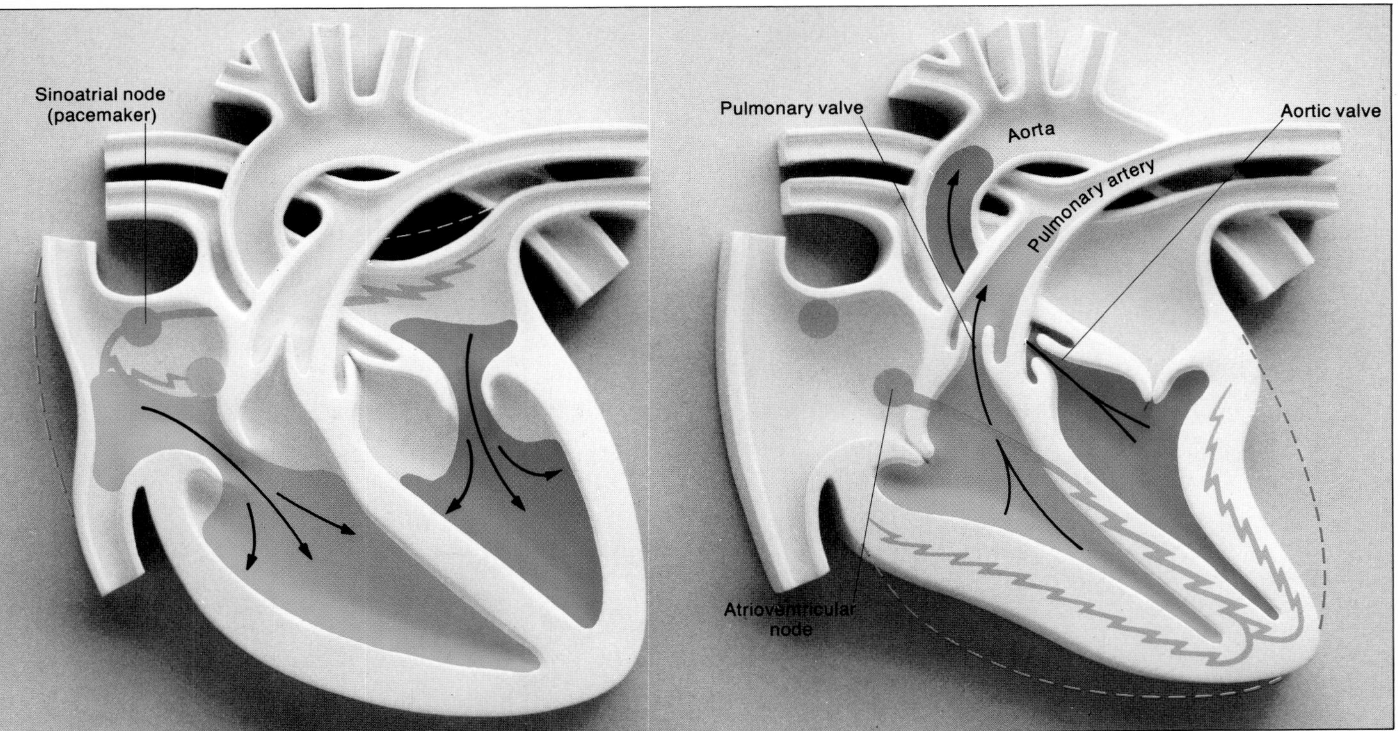

STARTING A SQUEEZE
The sinoatrial node, or pacemaker, fires an electrical impulse (green) that makes the muscles of both atria contract from their expanded shape (dotted lines) for the atrial systole stage. This squeezes blood through completely open valves into the ventricles.

FORCING OUT THE BLOOD
In ventricular systole, the pacemaker signals the atrioventricular node, which waits .08 to .12 second for the mitral and tricuspid valves to close, then signals (green) the ventricles to contract from their relaxed position (dotted lines) and force out the blood.

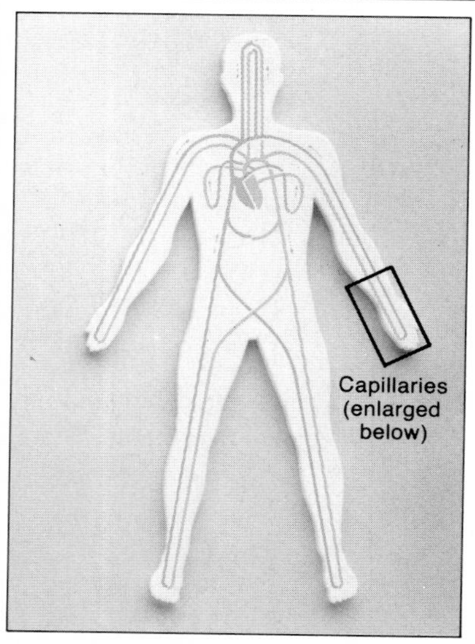

A pay-off in the tiniest pipes

The pay-off for the heart's prodigious labors takes place in 10 billion capillaries that web the body. They provide the vital connection between the arterial system, which carries blood away from the heart, and the venous system, which returns it.

Unlike arteries and veins, capillaries have very thin and porous walls, made up of a single layer of cells. Nutrients seep from the blood through the cell walls to nourish surrounding tissue. Likewise, wastes pass from the tissue into the blood, to be pumped to the lungs and other organs where they will be traded for fresh cargo.

Vein
Venules
Capillaries
Arterioles
Artery
Oxygen-depleted blood cells
Oxygen-rich blood cells

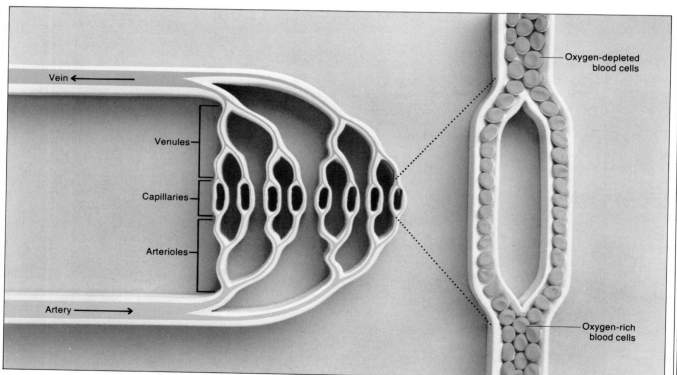

A WEB OF INTERCONNECTIONS
A magnified detail from the model at top diagrams the network of blood vessels that connect an artery and a vein. From the artery, small arterioles branch out to the still-smaller capillaries; from the capillaries, venules merge into the vein.

A CAPILLARY IN ACTION
Blood cells—red with nutrients, blue with wastes—pass single file through the capillaries. This detail from the drawing at left is enlarged 40 times life size.

stream, eventually to obstruct a narrower vessel elsewhere.

Clogging and loss of flexibility, often accompanied by malfunctioning in certain chemical controls, can result in the most common circulatory ailment, high blood pressure—the liquid pressure exerted by blood pulsing through the arteries is higher than normal *(page 70)*. Afflicting perhaps 250 million people worldwide (and, mysteriously, a disproportionately large number of black Americans), high blood pressure has been called the silent killer because it generally shows no symptoms until it has been developing for decades. Even then its symptoms tend to arise not so much in the blood vessels as in organs such as the kidneys, after they have been damaged by it. But high blood pressure always does harm to the circulatory system itself as well. The heart, pumping against high pressure in the blood vessels, has to work harder to move the blood. If the pressure gets very high, a vessel may burst, producing leakage.

Both leakage and extreme clogging in a blood vessel are serious problems, and for exactly the same reason. Either one will reduce or cut off entirely the blood flow to body tissue. And even a partial loss of the blood supply can kill the tissue. If the loss occurs in the brain, the result is a stroke, with effects that range from temporary loss of speech or vision to paralysis or death. The disease is tragically common everywhere in the world but it is unaccountably more prevalent in Asia than elsewhere—each year stroke kills almost 170,000 people in Japan.

If the loss of blood supply occurs in the heart, the result is coronary heart disease, the greatest single killer of the modern world. In a typical case, coronary arteries are gradually narrowed by atherosclerosis, reducing the flow of blood. Because the heart muscle is then malnourished, the heart functions inefficiently, and often in pain. But there is worse to follow. If the build-up of fatty deposits in the coronary arteries continues unchecked, one artery or another becomes blocked, rather than merely narrowed. In an instant the part of the heart served by that artery is without a blood supply; within five minutes it may suffer severe damage or death. This is a heart attack.

Many heart attacks are sudden, without any previous sign of coronary heart disease, but almost all develop from long-standing atherosclerosis. Generally, the warning signs exist in plenty: In the United States, more than four million people have a history of previous heart attacks or of a chest pain called angina pectoris, a sign of developing coronary heart disease. These are the survivors, who can fight the disease with a changed life style or with therapy. But of the millions of people around the world who suffer heart attacks—over 4,000 each year in London alone—more than half die, and over half of them before they can reach a hospital. In the United States, heart attack is not only the greatest single killer; it is also the most common cause of premature death, that is, of death before the age of 65.

The 20th Century epidemic

Heart attacks and the other diseases of the heart and blood vessels—all these have surely struck at mankind from ancient times. What has changed is their prevalence—with its terrible climax in the epidemic of the first half of the 20th Century—and man's awareness of them.

As late as 1900, medical records did not even indicate heart attack as a cause of death (although many whose death certificates read "acute indigestion" must have succumbed to it). The symptoms of heart attack were not medically described until 1912. Until the late 18th Century the ailment called dropsy, an accumulation of fluid in the tissues due to a malfunctioning heart, was not linked to the heart—and the final proof of the linkage did not emerge until the 1930s.

One reason there was so little awareness of circulatory diseases was their comparative rarity in the past. One scientist, Dr. John Farquhar of Stanford University, has attempted to reconstruct the heart disease picture since 1850, and his conclusions are generally considered valid. Before 1900, he found, "there was very little coronary heart disease. And it's likely that the incidence of heart attack in the 40-to-70 age group was only a fifth as bad in 1910 as it is now. I date the incidence as increasing markedly from 1940 to 1967." In Japan, for example, the death rate from heart disease jumped roughly 20 per cent during the period.

A theory has been developed to account for this surge, and

it is applicable not only to ailments of the heart but to many other circulatory ailments, such as stroke and high blood pressure. This theory is not universally accepted, and there are anomalies and contradictions that it does not completely explain, but it represents the consensus of heart experts. According to the theory, the heart disease epidemic developed in industrial nations because in these nations a high technology and increasing affluence combined to create the life styles that favor heart disease. "When mass disease occurs," said Dr. Jeremiah Stamler of Northwestern University, "things are out of joint"—and what throws them out of joint is the way people live in their society.

Dr. Stamler compared heart disease with tuberculosis, the white plague that swept through the cities of the industrial world during the Industrial Revolution. In those teeming cities families were large; food was meager; populations were overcrowded; and men, women and children labored long hours for low pay in unsafe and unsanitary conditions. All in all, the setting was ideal for the spread of an infectious disease that preys on the tired, the weak and the undernourished. The result, commented Dr. Stamler, was inevitable: "Tuberculosis went wild."

Dr. Stamler contended that, just as tuberculosis was the typical epidemic disease of an infant industrial society, so coronary heart disease is the typical disease of a mature industrial society. The 19th Century city created the conditions in which tuberculosis thrived; the 20th Century world has produced a life style in which the risk factors leading to circulatory disorders have been on the increase.

As the term is used medically, a risk factor is anything that contributes directly or indirectly to the probability of contracting a disease. The key word in the definition is "probability." Researchers armed with statistics, experimental findings and informed guesses heatedly debate the roles and even the existence of specific risk factors. But a clear consensus has identified such factors as smoking, obesity and the lack of physical exercise as probable causes of many circulatory diseases. And all of these factors became more prevalent between 1900 and 1967.

Take cigarette smoking for an example. According to Dr. Farquhar, "If smoking had never become a common habit, one half the heart disease problem would be eliminated." Cigarette smoking became widespread, he said, because of two developments. The first was the technique, introduced in the late 19th Century, of flue-curing tobacco; soon afterward the technique was applied to mixtures of relatively mild tobacco. The fumes of these mixtures can be inhaled into the lungs, where tobacco starts to do its damage; before flue curing, tobacco smoke had been too acrid and offensive to be inhaled. The second development was mass distribution, made possible by mass-production machinery and mass-advertising methods.

Changes in diet can be traced to similar causes. Industrialization and the affluence it brought enabled people to enjoy a rich diet—to live, in the old metaphor, off the fat of the land. Refrigeration and sophisticated processing made it possible to store fatty foods, which in earlier times would soon have turned rancid. With more money to spend, the average man could, in any season, eat foods that were once available only to the wealthy. It is not surprising that he took advantage of the opportunity. "We all came from cultures of poverty," remarked Dr. Farquhar, "where only the rich could afford to eat white flour, white sugar, and meat and dairy products." Now almost anyone could eat them, and the industrialized peoples responded eagerly to their new feast.

The foods that made up the feast are, it now turns out, dangerous foods. They are high in various animal fats and in a special kind of fat called cholesterol, found only in animal products. Eaten in large quantities, these fats turn into compounds that create the arterial deposits of atherosclerosis. The rich foods are also high in calories, a measure of the energy content of food—and of its capacity to add weight to the eater. At the same time they are low in fiber—the roughage of whole grains and fresh vegetables—and in complex carbohydrates, the starches of potatoes and pasta. Fiber and complex carbohydrates make an eater feel full, and they discourage overeating; meat and dairy products do not. A combination of high calories, little fiber and few complex carbohydrates favors overeating and leads to excess weight.

In most of the industrialized countries, obesity is widespread; a survey in East Germany found 42 per cent of the women overweight. Even worse is the preponderance of people who, while not technically obese, ''weigh more than is good for them''—a description that one study applied to 60 per cent of British men and 53 per cent of British women in the 40-to-49-year-old age group. The fat baby, only a century ago a heartwarming symbol of health and well-being, has now become a cause for worry. Concern about excess weight is greatest in the United States, and justifiably so. ''For the first time in human history,'' commented Dr. Stamler, ''and still unique to the United States, obesity in the first and second decades of life, let alone the third, fourth and fifth, is a common phenomenon.''

Physical inactivity, a third probable cause of heart-related diseases, comes naturally to an affluent, mechanized society. The automobile eliminated much of the exercise people once took as an everyday routine. Automation has replaced thousands of strenuous jobs with desk sitting and button pushing. This reduction in physical effort has two effects, both bad for the heart. Inactivity weakens muscles, apparently including

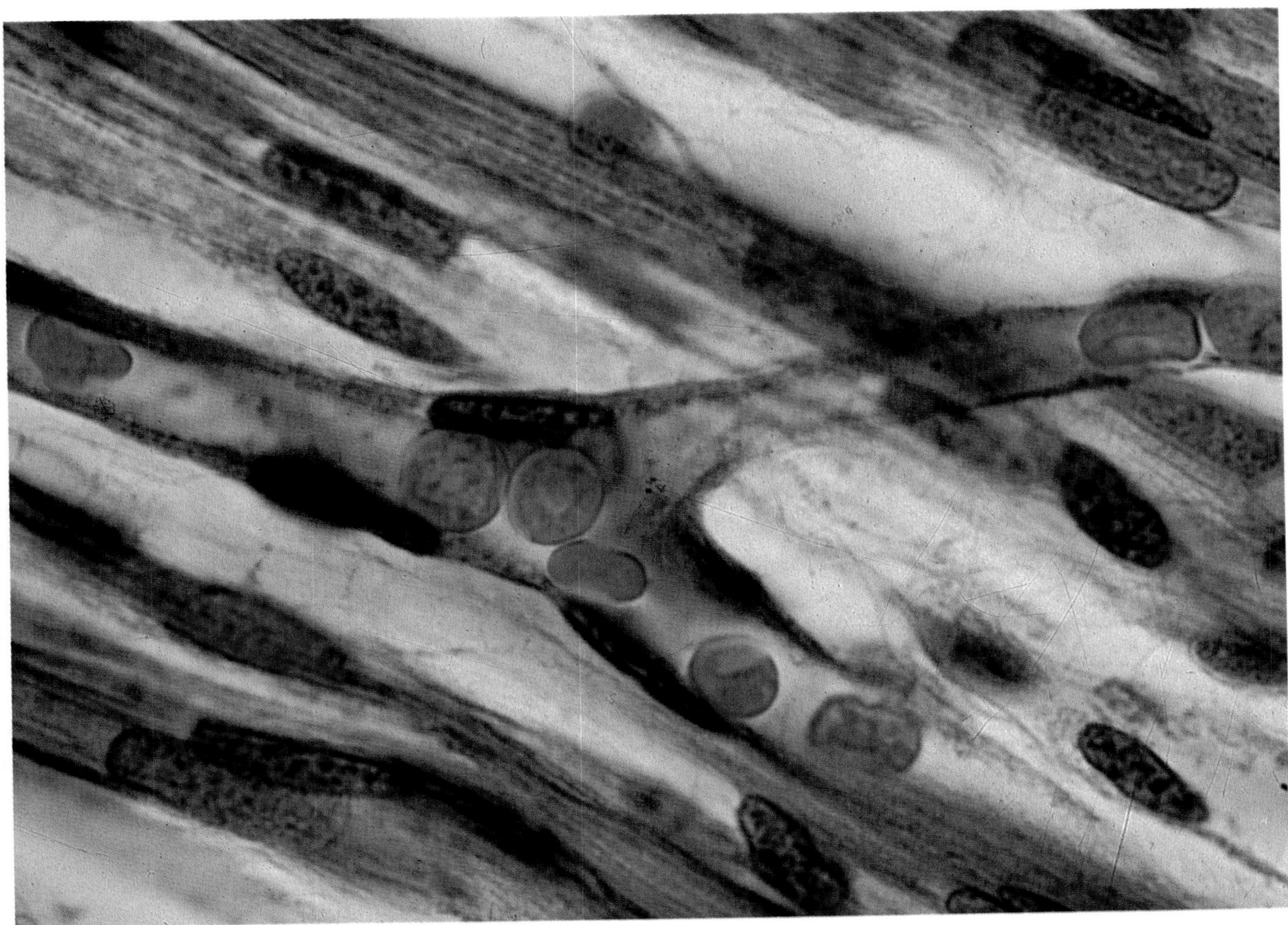

Twisting and turning, red blood cells tumble through a capillary embedded in a muscle; because capillaries are less than 1/10 the thickness of a hair, the cells must travel single file in order to squeeze through. At top, a red blood cell forced out of the capillary by injury floats free in the surrounding tissue.

those of the heart. It also reduces the consumption of energy provided by food; unless food intake is reduced to make up for lessened activity, the excess energy remains as fat, increasing body weight.

As a matter of record, people of 1900 took in more food calories than their descendants do today, but they weighed less because they worked the calories off in daily activities. To compensate for the difference—and to reduce the risk of heart disease that arises from inactivity—modern men and women must seek out opportunities to push their bodies hard. As Dr. Farquhar observed, "It's a paradox. We used to rest in our leisure time because we worked so hard on the job. Now we earn our livings on our rear ends and have to exercise in our leisure time."

If changes in life style caused the rise in circulatory diseases, then reversals of those changes—along with improved medical care—must have played a part in the decline. In the years after 1967, smoking decreased among adult males. In some industrial countries, changed diets lowered blood cholesterol levels and reduced weight. Combinations of diet and drugs brought blood pressure down.

The evidence is not clear-cut, and many puzzles remain. For example, the effects of stress and loneliness, as opposed to calm and loving care, intrigue and baffle investigators. In an animal experiment at The Ohio State University, one group of rabbits was fed a high-fat diet; a second group received an identical diet but was also petted and cuddled for at least an hour a day. The first group developed three times as many atherosclerotic deposits as the second. ("This is one of those gee-whiz experiments," commented the leader of the research team, Dr. Robert Nerem. "We don't have any mechanism to explain it.") On the human level, British researchers reported that recently widowed men suffer far more heart attacks than married men.

Even more puzzling are anomalies in the large-scale statistical studies on which research into the heart attack epidemic is generally based. Women have been smoking more heavily since 1967, yet their rate of heart disease has decreased even more sharply than that of men. In Japan the consumption of the fats linked to heart disease increased as much as 200 per cent between 1954 and 1965, but the Japanese shared a decline in heart disease with the other industrial nations. In Israel, heart disease is declining among men but not among women; in the United States, inexplicably, the sharpest decline of all is among black women. Facts such as these do not fit the prevailing theory about the heart disease epidemic; presumably, they do not fit because influences yet to be isolated are at work.

Still, the theory stands up well on the whole. In general, smoking, cholesterol levels and high blood pressure contributed to the rise in circulatory diseases after 1940. Wherever they declined, the epidemic waned—and the rise and wane are consistent with the theory. The exercise boom that began in the late 1960s probably arrived too late to account significantly for the decline of heart disease—but if the theory is sound, the influence of the boom will sooner or later show up in the statistics.

Early warning

Anyone can work to avoid heart-related diseases, by abandoning the dangerous modern life style in favor of great-grandmother's habits of moderation. But if disease does strike, early detection and treatment can generally stem its course. Checking for disease is primarily your responsibility, not the doctor's. Though there are some forms of trouble that do not give clear symptoms in their early stages, most do; it is up to you to learn what the early warning signs are and to report them to the doctor.

Chest pain during physical exertion, for example, may be a sign of coronary heart disease, in which one or more coronary arteries are partially clogged and blood supply to the heart is reduced. If you experience such a pain, make an appointment to consult your doctor. The case histories of fatal and near-fatal heart attacks show that many victims ignored this clear danger signal, sometimes for years, or explained it as "just indigestion." (There are even accounts of men who refused assistance during a heart attack—and did push-ups, in agony, to prove they were not having one.)

Another kind of signal warns of the danger of stroke, the loss of blood supply to a part of the brain. A brief episode of

Encouraging trend in deaths: down

After an appalling increase in the first half of the 20th Century, heart-related ailments began to decrease in industrialized countries—but the manner of their fading away is inexplicably variable, as the chart below indicates. It graphs the drops in death rates from the major circulatory diseases in 14 countries over the decade beginning in 1963. Switzerland's heart mortality declined the most—almost 30 per cent—despite massive increases in Swiss consumption of the fatty foods that are blamed for heart disease. The Australian rate declined the least, but again no one knows why.

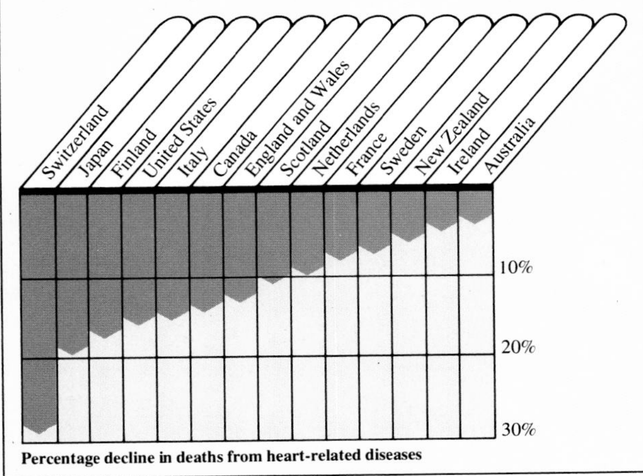

Percentage decline in deaths from heart-related diseases

dizziness, numbness or disturbed vision may be what doctors call a transient ischemic attack (the term "ischemia" indicates a shortage of blood in a localized area). Report even the possible signs of any such attack at once to a physician. He can test for a blockage in one of the neck arteries leading to the brain and can generally clear the vessel. Untreated, a blocked neck artery presents a constant threat of stroke.

The heart specialists' wizardry

If warning signals are confirmed, your outlook is probably far better than you might imagine. In the years since the great turnaround of the middle 1960s, new methods of diagnosis, drug treatment, emergency and hospital care, and surgery not only have saved lives but have promised pain-free and reasonably normal futures for many of the victims of circulatory ailments.

The diagnosis of a living heart used to be a fairly primitive exercise: A doctor could listen to the heart through a stethoscope, and do very little more. Compare this with the combination of techniques, first widely used in the 1940s, that goes by the long names of catheterization and angiocardiography.

To begin the process, the doctor inserts a long, thin plastic tube—the catheter—into a blood vessel of the patient's arm or leg. He pushes the catheter along the vessel to the heart, through the heart valves and directly into a chamber of the heart, tracing the progress and final position of the tube with X-rays. Once it is in the heart, the catheter can draw samples of blood for diagnostic purposes. At a later stage of the procedure, the doctor can inject a liquid that shows up on X-rays, then make an X-ray movie (called a cineangiogram) as the liquid flows through the heart and into the coronary arteries; the movie clearly reveals any damage in the heart valves, defects in the structure of the heart or clogging in the arteries.

The procedure entails some discomfort and a modest degree of risk. Some alternative techniques make the workings of the heart visible without penetrating the body at all. In one, the doctor injects a radioactive compound into the bloodstream, then follows its progress with a scanning device that is sensitive to radioactivity; a computer helps convert the scanning data into a color-coded movie of the heart at work. In another, developed from the sonar used to detect submarines and schools of fish underwater, sound waves are bounced off the walls of the heart and the echoes create an image of the pumping heart on a viewing screen.

Drug therapy has made equally dramatic progress. As recently as the 1940s pharmacologists could offer little beyond a tonic called digitalis, which strengthens the heartbeat, and an emergency drug, a variant of the explosive compound nitroglycerin, which eases the pain of angina pectoris. Today, by contrast, a huge arsenal of medicines controls or modifies almost every heart-related disease. Anticoagulant drugs keep blood clots from forming and existing clots from enlarging. Diuretics help the body and bloodstream excrete excessive fluid, to lighten the load on the heart. Antibiotics overcome or prevent the ravages of rheumatic fever and other infections. Most important of all, a whole battery of different medicines, with different actions, controls high blood pressure; these compounds, which save more lives than all the others, have been called the most significant drug advance since the 1960s.

In the case of one disease, the most serious form of heart attack, new types of emergency treatment save thousands of lives every year. Many attacks stop the heart completely; unless it can be restarted within about five minutes, the victim dies. A set of on-the-spot techniques called cardiopulmonary resuscitation (CPR) enables anyone trained in its use to work this miracle, seemingly bringing the dead back to life. The American Red Cross and other agencies began training people in CPR in the 1970s; within a decade, more than 12 million firemen, ambulance crews and ordinary citizens had been certified *(pages 85-87)*.

Although CPR can prevent sudden death, long-term survival of a heart attack victim depends on what happens to him next. At a hospital he now enters a coronary care unit, where automatic monitoring machines watch over his heartbeat, blood pressure and other vital signs 24 hours a day. At the slightest danger signal in these functions, the machines trigger an alarm, bringing the full resources of the hospital into play in the dramatic action often depicted in the television serials. The TV versions do not exaggerate: Doctors and nurses race through the corridors with lifesaving equipment. Drugs reduce a soaring blood pressure almost immediately; powerful electrical devices revive a stopped heart, or restore the steady beat of a heart whose controls have ceased functioning.

The last resort of the modern hospital is surgery, but it is a kind of surgery utterly different from any known before. As recently as the 1940s, cutting into a living heart was essentially impossible. Any interruption of the heart's pumping would have stopped the flow of blood to the entire body and consequently killed the patient. Today surgeons perform such operations every day, as a matter of course. The key to the change is the heart-lung machine *(page 111)*, perfected in 1953, which makes the impossible possible. Today a surgeon can literally disconnect the heart and lungs from the rest of the body, and set a heart-lung machine to take over their jobs. For hours on end, if need be, the machine breathes for the patient and pumps his blood, while the surgeon cuts into the heart and arteries.

With this new tool at their command, heart specialists developed an astonishing repertory of operations that repair or replace defective parts of the heart and its arteries. Plastic valves take the place of leaky ones. Congenital heart defects are patched up. In one relatively common operation, the electrodes of an artificial electronic pacemaker are surgically implanted in the heart. The device generates electrical signals that override those of a defective natural pacemaker, and thus regulate the heartbeat.

In the arteries, surgery now clears or bypasses the blockages that cause pain or disability and threaten to bring on heart attacks or strokes. In one type of operation, the surgeon opens an artery and scrapes away the fatty deposits that obstruct it; this is the treatment used to clear the blocked neck arteries that foretell a stroke.

A more radical technique deals with coronary heart disease through a coronary bypass *(pages 122-137)*—an operation once controversial but now safe and common. To perform it, the surgeon cuts out a section of vein from a limb of the body, generally the leg, and grafts it as a detour around a blocked stretch of a coronary artery. The new pathway restores the blood supply to the heart muscle, relieving the pain of angina and often extending the life of the patient.

As the fight against coronary heart disease scores more and more victories, it produces a larger and larger population of recovered heart attack victims. Four out of five of these survivors can return to their jobs and lead full, productive lives. In fact, modern medical opinion calls for a fuller life for the recovered patient than it did in the past. Only a few years ago the survivor of a heart attack spent weeks or even months in complete bed rest—some were not even permitted to brush their teeth or feed themselves—and avoided exercise indefinitely. Today he may begin an exercise program, under medical supervision, before he leaves the hospital.

The progress of a fairly typical exercise program, fitted to the severity of a heart attack and the rate of the patient's recovery, shows a new relationship between doctor and patient. While still in a specialized coronary care unit, a patient, closely watched by a doctor or nurse, may be encouraged to move his limbs through their full range of motion. Most patients begin walking, with assistance if necessary, when they are transferred out of the coronary care unit. Gradually, activities increase. Some patients practice stair climbing while still in the hospital, particularly if they will have to climb stairs at home.

The recovering patient may leave the hospital with a detailed, written-out set of exercise prescriptions—for walking or light calisthenics, perhaps—from his doctor. His progress is observed; as he improves, the doctor prescribes additional kinds and amounts of activities. But the patient's role in the choice and variety of his physical activities steadily increases, while the doctor's role decreases. In six weeks, on the doctor's advice, a recovering heart patient may be ready to return to sedentary work; within three months, still under the doctor's consultation but without day-to-day supervision, he may be running, swimming or playing basketball. Even sexual activity, which was once forbidden to heart patients, now is considered not only permissible but desirable.

The object of such advice is to put the patient back in charge of his own life as quickly as possible. Once the cardiologist and the coronary care unit have done their work, the patient shares the responsibility for regaining his health. More than most, he must hold to the life style that maintains a healthy heart—weight reduction, good diet, the conscious avoidance of stress, no smoking. A doctor may prescribe such a way of life, but he cannot impose or enforce it. That responsibility is the patient's; to prevent a recurrence of the heart attack that hospitalized him in the first place, the patient must become his own doctor. ❋

From potion to prescription

In 1785, English physician William Withering analyzed a secret potion—a tea concocted by an elderly Shropshire woman and used as a tonic and stimulant. Among its more than 20 components he isolated a powder from the leaves of the popular garden plant foxglove *(Digitalis purpurea, right)* as the active ingredient. For centuries this folk medicine had been prescribed as a cure for dropsy, or swelling of the legs and tissues, but Withering went further in his research and speculation. Convinced that dropsy was a symptom, not a disease, and that its underlying cause lay elsewhere, he deduced that digitalis "has a power over the motions of the heart."

Not until the 1930s did scientists confirm Withering's deduction. Digitalis does indeed cure dropsy—or, to use the modern term, edema—by causing the heart to beat more steadily, more slowly and with greater force, relieving congestions of blood and fluid in the body. Today, refined in its constituents and made precise in its dosage, it is an essential weapon in a doctor's arsenal of medicines. But its target is no longer a swelling of limbs or tissue; instead, digitalis is the first step in the standard treatment for congestive heart failure.

A fantastic journey through the heart

The hidden world within the heart is a place of eerie beauty—and a marvel of engineering. Each of the chambers, valves and vessels is a model of elegant simplicity, its design perfectly suited to a particular task.

The right ventricle, for example, which pushes spent blood to the lungs for fresh oxygen, pumps at low pressure—about one fifth that of the left ventricle—because the short connections between heart and lungs offer little resistance to flow. It is designed for low-power operation and is shaped like an old-fashioned bellows, with broad sides that push a large volume of blood with little movement. By contrast, the left ventricle, which must pump at high pressure to drive blood throughout the body, has walls three times as thick and is cylindrical—a more powerful design.

The shape of the valves matches their function in much the same way. Between the atria and ventricles, the tricuspid valve *(opposite)* in the right side of the heart and the mitral valve in the left must seal tightly against the pressure and turbulence generated by ventricular contraction, so they have multiple reinforcements. At the ventricular outlets, the simpler, lighter pulmonary and aortic valves serve to seal against relatively low pressure.

The sum of all these parts is a pump that far surpasses any man-made device of similar size. The heart is so powerful that with each beat the body recoils slightly—so that, when someone stands motionless on a sensitive scale, the needle oscillates rhythmically.

Until recently, not many people outside the medical profession had seen a human heart, let alone looked inside. Swedish photographer Lennart Nilsson changed that. Using modern electronics and fiber optics, he painstakingly threaded flexible wands tipped with tiny lenses—some are no larger than a grain of rice—through hearts from cadavers, to show how they actually look inside. In the dazzling photographs on the following pages, he traces the path blood ordinarily would follow, dramatically revealing the intricate machinery of this remarkable pump.

Photographer Nilsson in his laboratory studio

Within the right ventricle, tabs of muscle and a glistening web of some 120 tiny cords tie down the leaves of the tricuspid valve (in shadow at top and located by the dot in the diagram at left), through which spent blood comes in from the right atrium to be pumped to the lungs. This network holds the leaves as pressure from the ventricle's contraction snaps the valve shut; without the cords, the pliable valve leaves would flap like a tent in the wind, ruining the seal. The highlighted areas are the heart wall.

PHOTOGRAPHS BY LENNART NILSSON

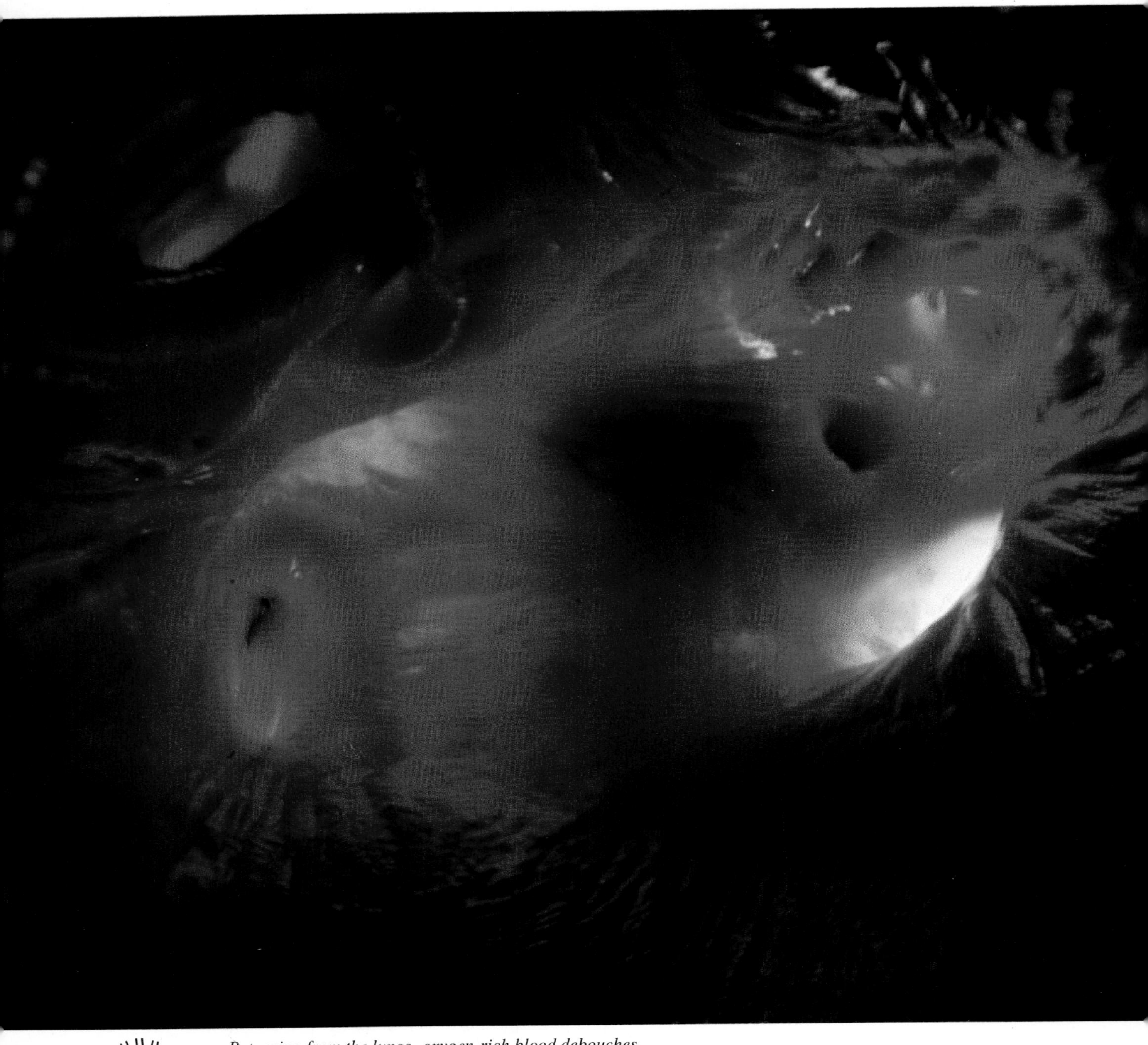

Returning from the lungs, oxygen-rich blood debouches through the ceiling of the left atrium (diagram at left) from four pulmonary veins—at upper left, lower left, right center and, faintly defined, at lower right. Though these veins are open-ended, lacking valves, the sleeves of muscle around their ends (dark red) may pinch them partially shut when the atrium contracts.

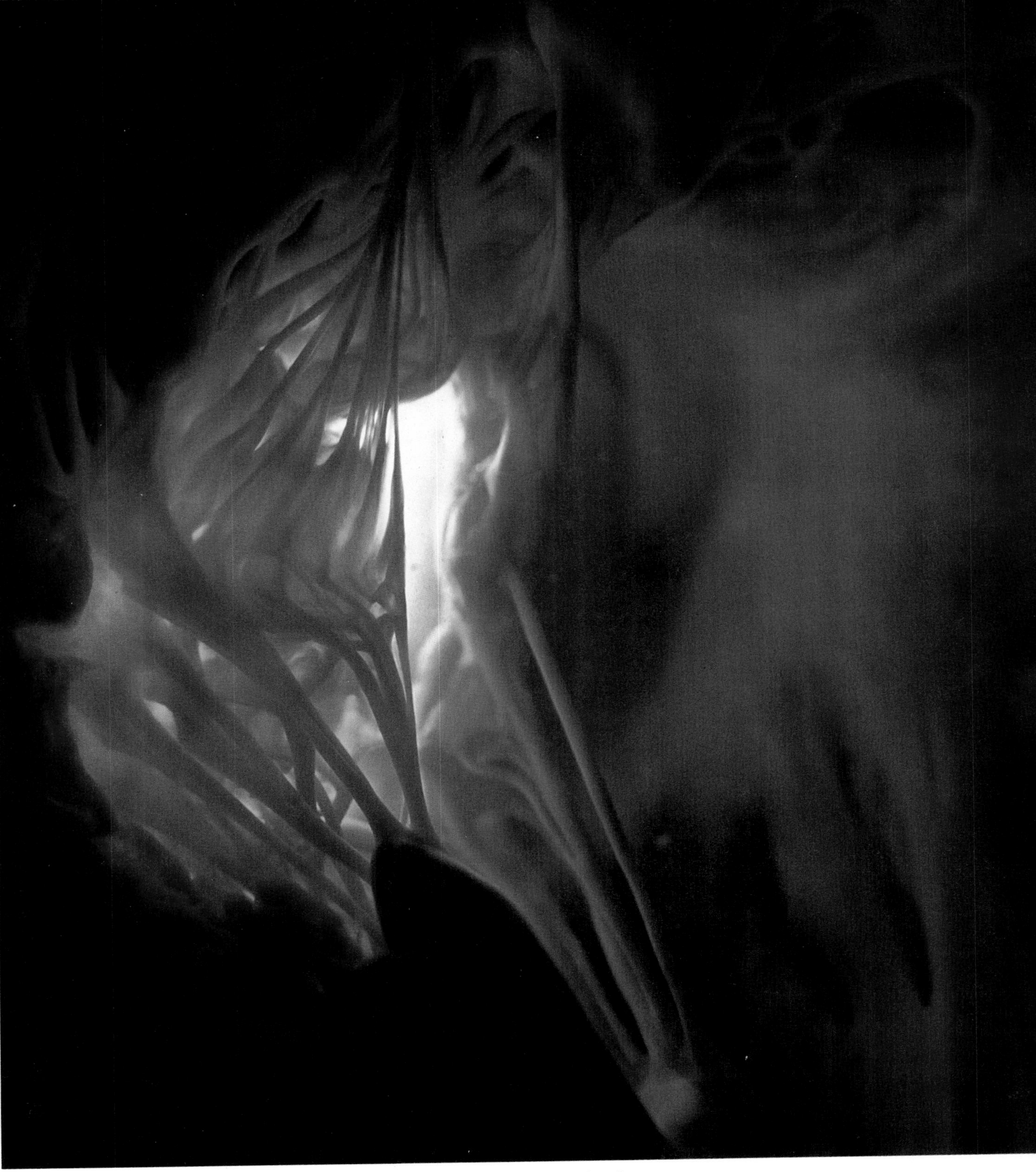

The open leaves of the funnel-shaped mitral valve, barely visible behind the lacy cords inside the left ventricle, channel blood from the left atrium to the bottom of the left ventricle (diagram). These cords serve the same function as those of the tricuspid valve in the other ventricle: Both prevent flapping of the translucently thin leaves when the valve is closed.

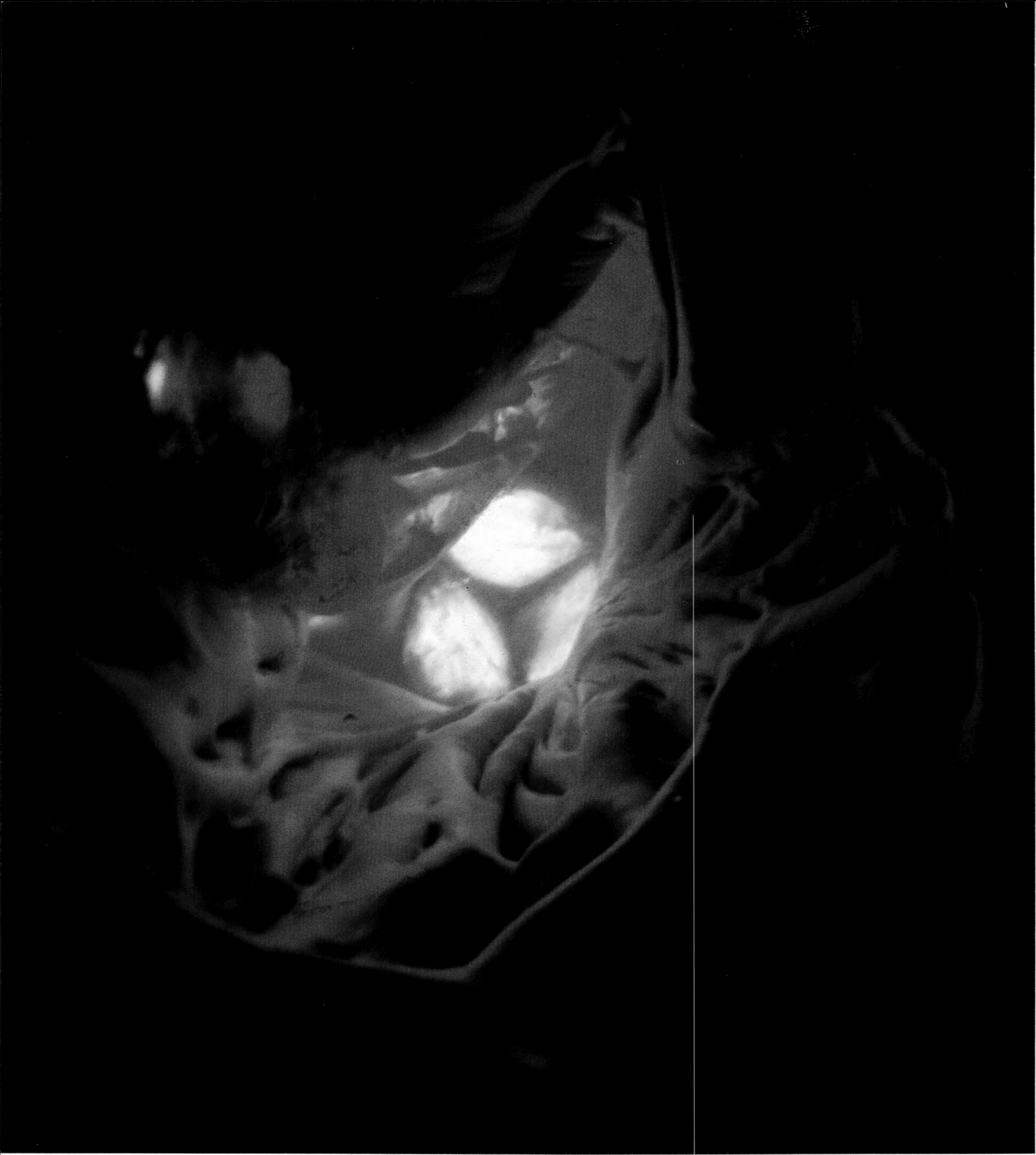

Above the striated walls of the left ventricle, in the center of this photograph, are the three gossamer leaves of the aortic valve (diagram), the outlet for blood flowing from the heart into the aorta, the body's central artery. The leaves, here seen overlapping in the closed position, are membranes shaped like teacups, with their convex bottoms facing the ventricle.

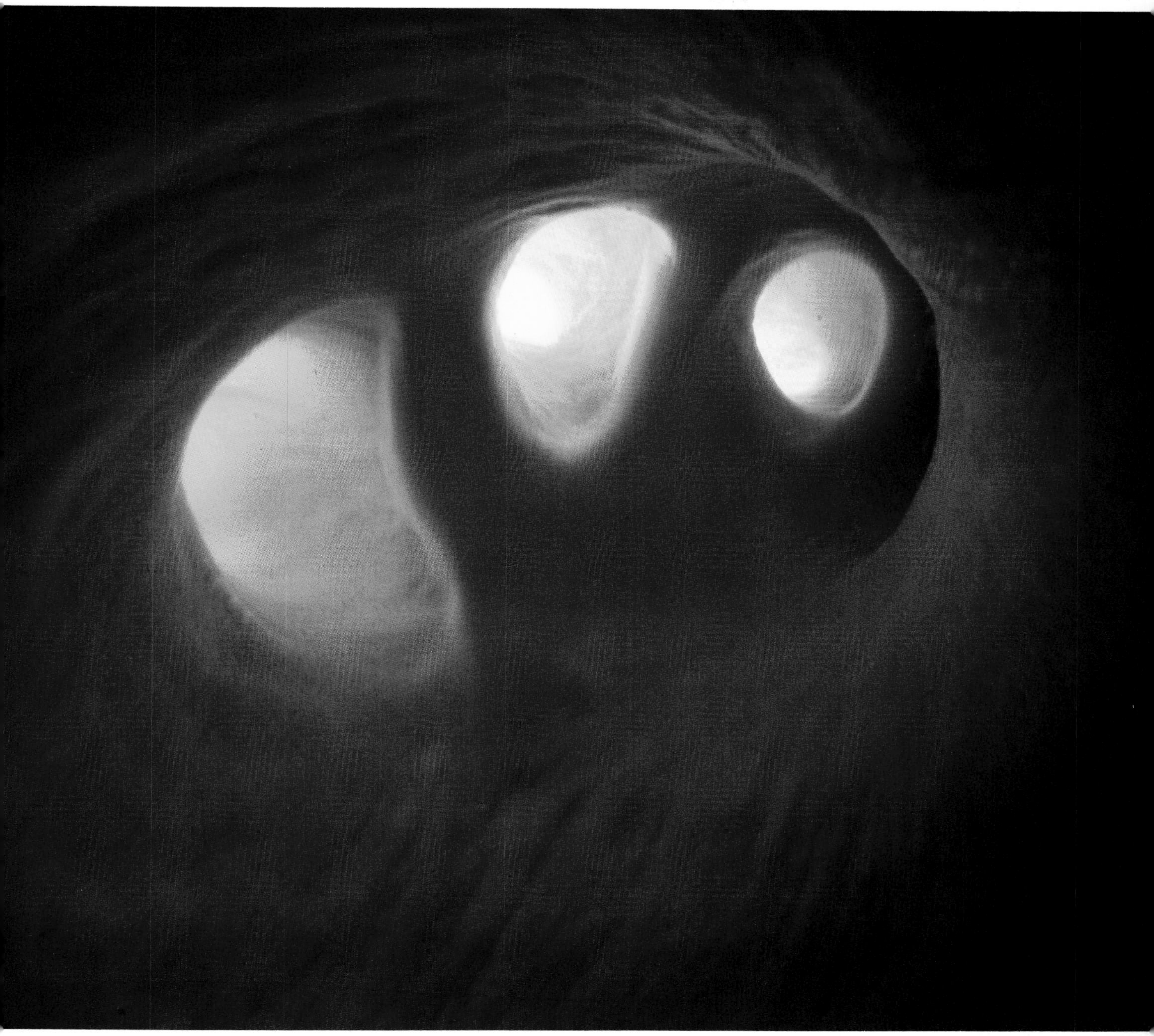

Inside the aorta, in the arch (diagram) sweeping over the heart, are highlighted openings where the three major arteries of the upper body branch off: The large branch at left supplies the right arm and the right side of the chest, head and brain; the center branch supplies the left side of the head and brain; and the branch beginning at right supplies the left chest and arm.

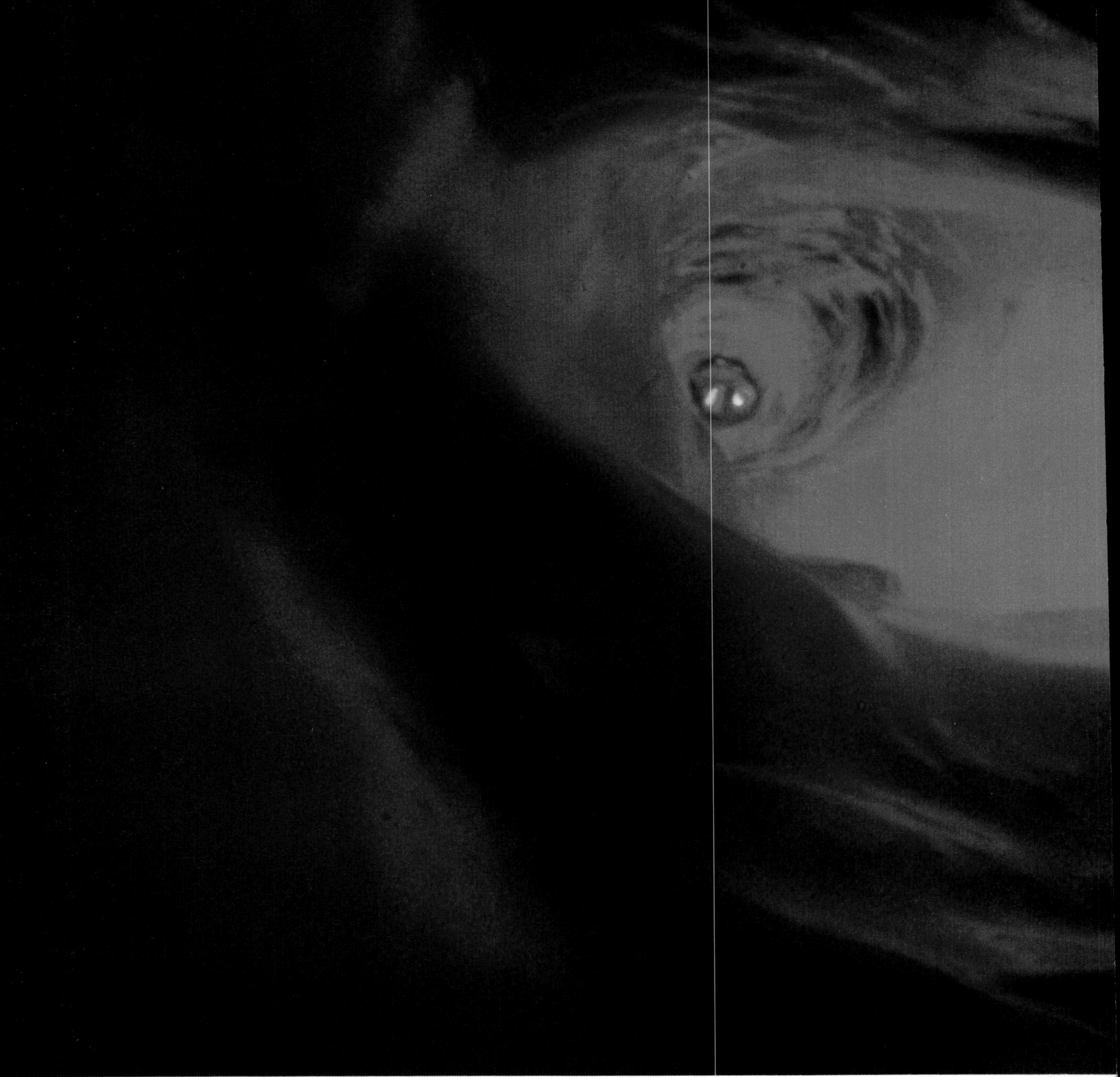

In this downward view, the undulating red tunnel of the aorta (diagram) descends through the chest and abdomen, supplying branch arteries (dark spots at left center) for the stomach, liver and kidneys, among other organs. Behind the belly button it divides into the two iliac arteries—the bright spots at the end of the tunnel—which supply blood to the pelvis and legs.

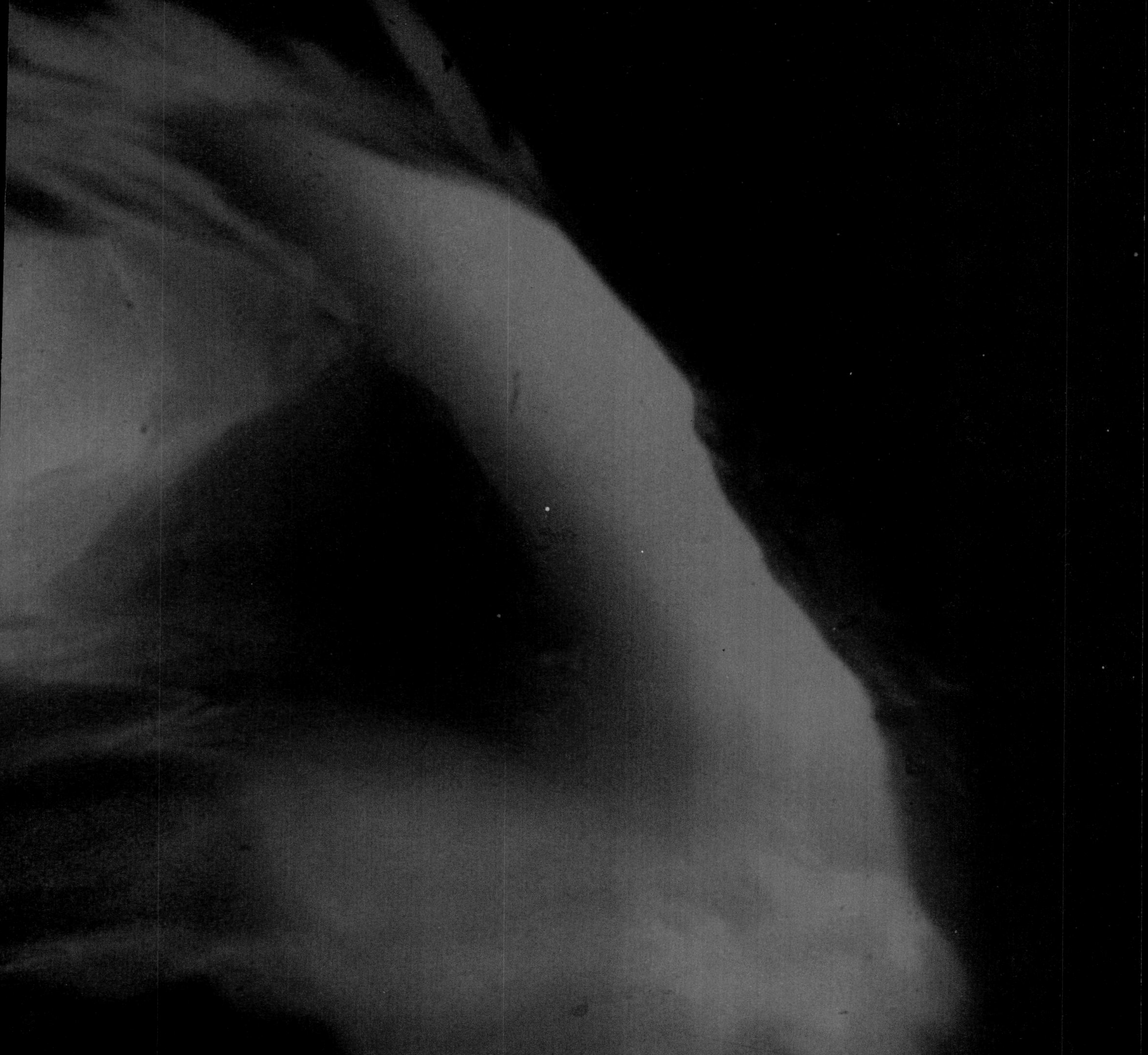

CHAPTER 2

How not to get heart disease

The nicotine habit
The perils of pressure
The many benefits of exercise
Protection from your diet

Framingham, Massachusetts, population 68,000, is an average sort of town 20 miles west of Boston. Some of its citizens commute to white-collar jobs in the city, some work farms, and others labor in industrial and commercial enterprises. Thousands of runners—some from as far away as Finland and Japan—know Framingham as Mile 7 on the annual 26-mile pilgrimage called the Boston Marathon. What most of the perspiring pilgrims do not know is that this otherwise unremarkable town is famous for another kind of marathon—the world's longest-running large-scale investigation into the nature and causes of heart-related diseases.

The Framingham Heart Disease Epidemiology Study began in 1948 and quickly became known as the Framingham study or simply Framingham. It focused on stroke and heart failure, the most common and serious of circulatory ailments. Its doctors hoped to chart the history of these killers by starting with healthy subjects and asking: Is there a way to predict which ones will develop circulatory disease?

To find the answer, the doctors began to follow the health of every other Framingham man and woman between the ages of 30 and 60 who had no signs of heart disease—5,127 people. Before long, children of some of the original subjects were included. As people were enrolled in the group, they were given physical examinations and measured for characteristics that might later prove to relate to the onset of circulatory disease. Every two years they were remeasured.

After several decades, the Framingham subjects began to fall into two groups: those who had suffered a stroke or a heart attack and those who had not—yet. The doctors then looked to the growing mountain of statistics to find what the victims had in common. From these faceless numbers, the painstaking detectives at Framingham drew a vivid profile. The subjects struck by heart attack or stroke smoked more, suffered more emotional stress, weighed more, were physically less active, had higher blood pressure and had greater amounts of the fat compound called cholesterol in their blood. "The average person headed for a premature heart attack or stroke is no mystery," said Framingham's medical director, Dr. William P. Castelli. "With a few simple office tests, any physician can identify these people."

These telltale characteristics—probable causes of diseases of the heart and blood vessels—are habits or the results of habits you can control. Other probable causes, or risk factors, are beyond your control: age, sex, susceptibility to certain diseases such as diabetes, genetic inheritance and possibly race. And not all physicians agree that the controllable factors have to be controlled. The danger attributed to cholesterol has been challenged, and its role is only slowly being explained *(Chapter 3)*. Even the risks of smoking are strangely variable. The Seven Countries study, directed by Dr. Ancel Keys of the University of Minnesota, examined heart-related diseases among 12,763 men, aged 40 to 59, over a 10-year period in seven countries. The investigators found that, while heavy smokers in northern Europe and the United States were about four times as likely to die of heart disease as nonsmokers, heavy smokers in Japan had the same

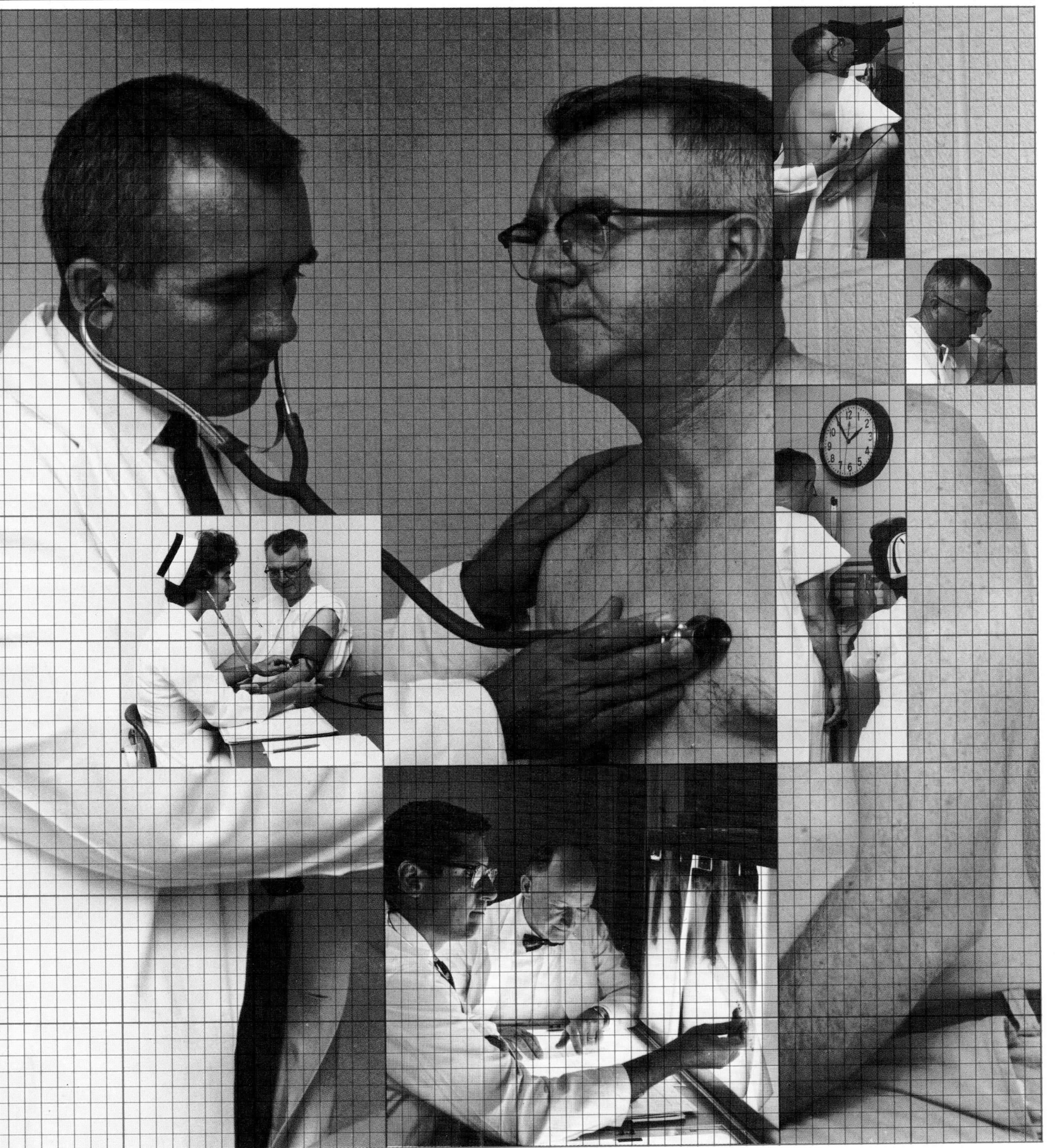

By 1961, when these photographs were made, the search for causes of heart ailments among residents of Framingham, Massachusetts, had compiled statistics on more than 5,000 subjects. Recording heart sounds (large picture), blood pressure (center left) and chest X-rays (upper right and bottom), this continuing study implicates diet, smoking and lack of exercise.

Gauging risk—and cutting it down

This self-scoring test, based on the Framingham study *(page 30),* lists six factors that affect your risk of suffering a heart attack or stroke. To use it, find the number that fits your life style or physical characteristics in each category. (You will have to ask your doctor for your cholesterol level—and, unless you measure blood pressure yourself as explained on pages 73-76, that as well.) Then add your numbers to gauge your total risk at the bottom of the list.

Unlike age, sex, race and heredity—factors that also affect risk but cannot be modified—the factors listed here are all within your control. If the score shows an average or above-average risk, most physicians recommend a program of diet, exercise or medication. The best programs deal with all six categories.

RISK FACTOR	
SMOKING	**0** Nonsmoker **2** Less than 20 cigarettes a day **4** 20 cigarettes or more a day
WEIGHT	**0** Desirable *(page 42)* **2** Up to 10 per cent over **4** More than 10 per cent over
SYSTOLIC BLOOD PRESSURE	**0** Less than 120 **2** 120 to 140 **4** Over 140
CHOLESTEROL LEVEL	**0** Less than 150 **2** 150 to 250 **4** Over 250
PHYSICAL ACTIVITY	**0** Regular vigorous exercise **2** Moderate exercise **4** Sedentary
STRESS AND TENSION	**0** Rarely tense or anxious **2** Feel tense two or three times a day **4** Extremely tense
TOTAL RISK	**0 - 4** Low **5 - 9** Below average **10 - 14** Average **15 - 20** High **21 - 24** Very high

heart-disease death rate as nonsmokers, and heavy smokers in southern Europe a death rate only slightly higher.

Most of the results of the Framingham study, however, have been confirmed by other research. And they lead to clear recommendations for preventing heart-related diseases. If smoking, stress, excess weight, inactivity, high blood pressure and cholesterol are linked to disease, you should be able to prevent disease by avoiding them.

The nicotine habit

The most important risk you can control seems to come from cigarette smoking. It also seems the easiest to control. After all, it is not a natural habit but one that must be learned; you should be able to unlearn it. As all smokers are aware, doing so can be painfully difficult—for all its importance.

Most people are well aware of the connection between cigarette smoking and lung cancer. They might be shocked to learn that smokers in the United States run a risk of developing fatal heart disease three times as great as their risk of dying from lung cancer. All other things being equal, the average smoker has more than twice as much chance as the nonsmoker of having a heart attack—and twice as much chance of dying from it. Furthermore, although the evidence is not conclusive, many doctors believe that the risk of stroke is 50 per cent higher for smokers than for nonsmokers.

The risk goes up with the number of cigarettes smoked. The statistics indicate that men aged 45 to 54 who smoke more than about 40 cigarettes a day have a death rate from coronary heart disease 10 times as great as their nonsmoking counterparts. Pipe and cigar smokers, perhaps because they do not inhale, seem to suffer less. A study of Canadian military veterans indicated that cigar and pipe smokers have no greater risk of heart disease than nonsmokers. But a Swiss study reported that pipe and cigar smokers do incur more risk—half again as much as nonsmokers.

Women who smoke run roughly the same risk of heart attack as men, the figures show, with one important exception. Women who use oral contraceptives and also smoke increase their risk as much as 20 times.

In both women and men, cigarette smoking also contributes to a range of circulatory diseases—especially to arteriosclerotic peripheral vascular disease (PVD), which affects the arteries of the legs. Addressing the Third World Conference on Smoking and Health in 1975, Dr. William B. Kannel, then head of the Framingham study, cited persuasive evidence: Nearly 90 per cent of patients undergoing surgery for narrowed arteries in the legs are smokers.

At least some of the dangers of cigarette smoking are known. More than 90 per cent of cigarette smoke is made up of about a dozen hazardous gases, carbon monoxide being the most important. The rest consists of particles—about a billion in a cubic centimeter of inhaled smoke—of which nicotine seems the most dangerous to the heart.

Nicotine is a poison so lethal that if you were to swallow the amount extracted from five cigarettes, you would die within three minutes. Inhaled in cigarette smoke, nicotine blocks certain nerve impulses, creating an imbalance between stimulating and relaxing impulses. This imbalance forces the smooth muscles of the small blood vessels to constrict, leading to increased resistance to blood flow—and to increased blood pressure. Simultaneously, nicotine raises the heart rate. This one-two punch comes after smoking just one or two cigarettes, and lasts 15 or 20 minutes.

Nicotine also interferes with the liver's ability to dispose of blood fats after a meal. The fats are left to circulate in the system and possibly to contribute to arterial clogging.

The effects of nicotine may be worsened by carbon monoxide, which interferes with the blood's oxygen-delivery system. The danger of carbon monoxide lies in its chemical lust for a vital molecule in blood—hemoglobin. It is the hemoglobin molecule in red blood cells that picks up oxygen from the lungs and carries it through the arteries to every part of the body. If you inhale carbon monoxide, a deadly contest ensues, for hemoglobin can also bind with carbon monoxide. Invariably, carbon monoxide wins—hemoglobin's affinity for carbon monoxide is 250 times as strong as its affinity for oxygen. Heavy cigarette smokers may lose as much as 15 per cent of the oxygen-carrying capacity of their red blood cells.

The loss of oxygen from smoking has a number of unpleasant consequences. The heart muscle itself receives less oxygen—just as if the coronary arteries were not delivering enough blood. This is obviously dangerous for someone whose arteries are already partially blocked by atherosclerosis. Then, because the rest of the body's tissues also are getting inadequate oxygen, the laboring heart must pump faster to circulate blood through the lungs more quickly. If the oxygen starvation continues, the body will produce more hemoglobin-laden red blood cells than normal to try to deliver more oxygen to the system. But the extra cells make the blood thicker. Thicker blood has an increased tendency to clot—a dangerous tendency in already narrowed arteries.

Less directly, carbon monoxide in heavy doses may upset the chemical activity of the cells of the inner lining of the coronary arteries. The gas increases the permeability of this lining and thereby lets cholesterol pass more easily into the artery walls, perhaps to trigger the growth of a plug of fat.

Low-tar-and-nicotine cigarettes offer no protection. Carbon monoxide levels seem independent of tar and nicotine levels. Heavy smokers, even of low-tar-and-nicotine cigarettes, inhale carbon monoxide at levels eight times as high as those deemed safe in factories. As long as you smoke, your risk of heart disease, cancer and other illnesses remains high.

However, if you stop smoking, your chances improve dramatically. The impact of smoking on the heart and blood vessels is reversible over a period of time: About two weeks are required for the red blood cells to be purged of carbon monoxide. According to the Framingham study, within two years, ex-smokers cut their risk of heart disease in half. Within 10 or 15 years, their chances of having a fatal heart attack are no greater than those of nonsmokers. Clearly, no one should begin smoking; anyone now smoking should stop.

Unfortunately, this prescription is, for many, too hard to follow. In the United States more than 30 million smokers quit within 15 years of the Surgeon General's report on the dangers of cigarette smoking—but more than 54 million continued. The number of women smokers actually rose by 11 per cent. Adult smoking declined overall but teenagers, particularly girls, took up the habit. There was a 50 per cent increase in smoking among American teenage girls in little more than a decade. Smoking in Great Britain, Canada and

Sweden has followed the American trend. In Germany, by contrast, smoking is rising among men and women alike.

Nine out of 10 adult smokers in the United States would like to quit. Many—in the United States and elsewhere—have tried and failed. The Pan American Health Organization studied eight Latin American cities and found that about 40 per cent of the smokers had tried unsuccessfully to quit. Why is it so hard to stop smoking once you have begun? One important reason is the smokers' dependence on nicotine, that substance so lethal in concentrated doses. In the smaller doses inhaled by smokers, nicotine leads to physical dependence—addiction. Giving up an addictive drug causes withdrawal symptoms. Withdrawal from the nicotine in tobacco produces anxiety and intense irritability in many smokers. Others suffer a feeling of great lethargy.

Such symptoms do not seem unbearable, yet nicotine apparently holds a tighter grip on its addicts than other drugs often considered more dangerous. Many users of alcohol, marijuana and even heroin are occasional users. By contrast, only one half of one per cent of cigarette smokers could be classified as casual or occasional users. In fact, addicts hooked on both nicotine and either heroin or alcohol find it harder to give up cigarettes than the heroin or alcohol.

Yet it is possible to stop smoking. A variety of techniques have been worked out, none certain but all at least partially effective in most cases; descriptions of them can be obtained from the many voluntary health associations concerned with heart disease and cancer, and from a number of government agencies, such as the Office of Cancer Communications of the National Cancer Institute, Bethesda, Maryland 20014.

Many of these ways to stop smoking adopt techniques of behavior modification. They lead you to change a number of the habits you associate with smoking so that eventually you eliminate smoking itself. For example, to break the habit of automatically reaching for a cigarette, become aware of each one you take: Put the package in an unfamiliar location, perhaps where you must pick it up with the hand opposite the one you ordinarily use. If you normally smoke after meals, interrupt this habit by doing something else after you finish eating: Go for a walk instead. Some programs suggest finding substitute objects to be held in the hand or mouth in place of cigarettes. These techniques of self-directed change, according to Dr. John W. Farquhar of Stanford University, are more successful than attempts that rely on will power alone.

Smoking is so important because it is what physicians call a primary risk factor. Smoking, like high blood pressure or elevated cholesterol levels, seems to increase the danger of circulatory disease by itself. Other hazards—stress, excess weight, inactivity—are considered risk factors principally because they interact with one another and with the primary risk factors to increase the chance of heart disease. Stress, for example, may affect circulatory disease directly, but its interactions with excess weight, lack of exercise and elevated blood pressure are equally important.

The perils of pressure

It has long been known that stress, physical or mental, can trigger a cardiovascular "episode" such as stroke or heart attack. The danger of physical stress is obvious: It overloads the system. Not so obvious is the hazard of mental stress.

"There's no doubt that a coronary episode can be provoked as much by a stressful argument as by climbing two flights of stairs," said Dr. Robert I. Levy, head of the National Heart, Lung, and Blood Institute. The explanation lies in a protective reaction that evolved eons ago in all animals—man included. Danger—or a powerful emotion such as anger—summons the fight-or-flight response, an involuntary mustering of physiological changes that help combat harm. The adrenal glands produce a rush of chemical messengers, hormones such as noradrenalin, aldosterone and renin. These increase blood pressure, heart rate, breathing rate, metabolic rate and blood flow to leg and arm muscles—enhancing reflexes, strength and speed. Your body is poised to do battle or run. But these automatic responses place extra demands on the circulatory system. If any part of it is weak or damaged, the additional load can cause a breakdown.

More dangerous than occasional overload is frequently repeated overload. The emotional stresses of the modern world—work deadlines, traffic jams, arguments with the boss, economic worries—can lead to recurrent stimulation

The adaptable heart: good news from space

Before the three Skylab missions that began in 1973, one of the great uncertainties of space exploration was its effect on astronauts' hearts. Free of gravity, muscles, including the heart, would work less and might weaken—indeed, the first men in space had trouble standing up after reentry. But fears about the heart were unfounded. The Skylab flights, lasting up to 84 days, proved the heart is amazingly adaptable.

To forestall weakening muscles, the astronauts, orbiting in their spaceship laboratories almost 300 miles above the earth, exercised *(right)* on a stationary bicycle similar to those in health clubs. They checked the effectiveness of this exercise by placing their legs in a negative-pressure device—a chamber that reduces air pressure to make blood accumulate in the leg vessels, simulating the downward pull on the blood normally created by earth gravity. If the heart had weakened so that it could not counter this pull, the man would soon have felt very dizzy. None did.

In addition, other aspects of the circulatory system were monitored during flight. The astronauts' hearts shrank a bit and blood pressure changed slightly. But soon after splashdown these abnormalities disappeared, and researchers concluded that the heart can probably endure even longer gravity-free trips.

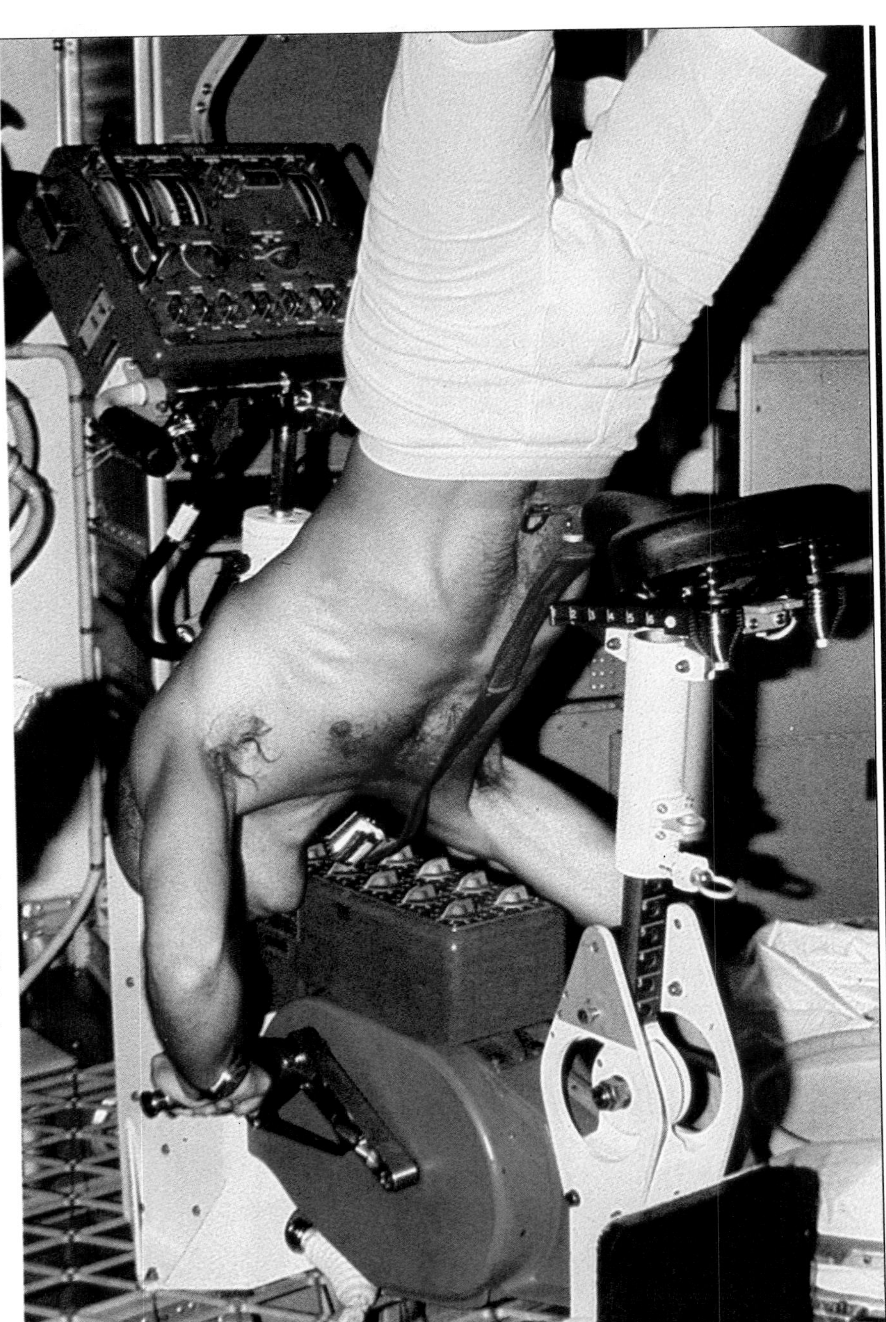

Suspended weightless—and apparently upside down—in the Skylab II cabin, Commander Charles Conrad Jr. pedals an exercise bicycle with his hands. Largely because of such exercises, Conrad did not suffer from any reduction in heart efficiency after his return to earth.

of the fight-or-flight response. In susceptible individuals, this can produce chronically high blood pressure—the hypertension that is a primary factor in heart disease.

One of the most revealing studies of stress-induced hypertension monitored air-traffic controllers. It is hard to imagine a job involving more intense and more constant stress. At busy airports, where planes are taking off and landing one a minute, a mistake can kill hundreds of people. The three-year study of 416 air-traffic controllers found that two to three times as many of them developed hypertension as did other men of similar age from their communities.

The kind of stress that seems to cause hypertension in air-traffic controllers—or, as other research found, in prisoners who had to sleep in group cells instead of in single cells—is brought on by what researchers call "sustained vigilance under threatening conditions." Investigators have also identified another precursor of high blood pressure: low socioeconomic status. Poor people, with little education, menial occupations and low pay, are more susceptible to high blood pressure and hypertensive heart disease.

The connection between poverty and high blood pressure helps explain why black Americans—most of whom are much poorer than their white compatriots—run an almost 50 per cent greater risk of developing high blood pressure. Hypertension-related deaths occur six to seven times as often among blacks under 50 as among whites the same age. Race—genetic inheritance—may be a contributing factor, but the continuing stress under which this minority group lives in the United States is also blamed.

Such stresses of society are suffered by everyone once in a while. When they are chronic—as they are in certain occupations and classes—they seem to induce permanent hypertension. Stress hormones are released so often that blood levels of these hormones remain high. This causes the baroreceptors—the hormone-sensitive artery-wall cells that regulate blood pressure—to adjust to a higher setting.

Reducing or avoiding stress certainly seems desirable. Stanford's Dr. Farquhar believes that stress is the most pervasive of all risk factors for circulatory disease, and that it often prevents people from altering harmful habits such as smoking and overeating. Ways to reduce stress are numerous, but not always easy.

Many individuals have changed their careers, finding occupational stresses intolerable and believing it worthwhile to trade some income or status for a degree of tranquillity. More and more marriages are dissolving in order to free partners from highly stressful relationships. But even these presumably beneficial changes can, at least for a time, increase rather than decrease stress, as people adjust to new lives.

For those unable to change jobs, their marriages or any of the other aspects of the real world that can induce stress, there is one other solution: Learn to cope. Hitting a golf ball every weekend may be a valuable way to vent hostilities. Venting such tension is one way of coping. There are many others. Regular exercise is one of the best methods of relieving stress. Equally important are rest and constructive use of leisure. Even a warm glass of milk at bedtime can help.

Beyond these coping techniques is a new recognition of some ancient remedies. According to Dr. Herbert Benson of Harvard Medical School, everyone is able to combat "overstress" through the physiological opposite of the fight-or-flight reaction; he named this ability the relaxation response.

This response does what its name suggests: forces the body to relax. Unlike the stress reaction, which is involuntary, the relaxation response is voluntary, regulated by conscious mental effort. Somehow the mind gains control over bodily characteristics that ordinarily are beyond conscious control, including blood pressure, heart rate and blood flow. Methods for attaining the relaxation response have been known in Eastern traditions for centuries: yoga, Zen Buddhism and Transcendental Meditation are taught all over the world. After centuries of skepticism in the West, they are now recognized as effective, medically valuable techniques.

Benson and his colleagues conducted a number of experiments with practitioners of Transcendental Meditation and later with volunteers who had high blood pressure. Most of them felt a sense of calm or well-being after meditation. Regardless of the subjective reactions, Benson detected physiological changes. The hypertensive subjects significantly lowered their blood pressures so long as they practiced relaxation methods twice a day. But when some of the subjects stopped the sessions, their blood pressures returned to the initial hypertensive levels within four weeks.

Another method, apparently related to meditation and the relaxation response, employs modern electronic devices to help the user moderate the effects of stress on himself. He is hooked up to a biofeedback machine *(below),* which measures some characteristic such as blood pressure and signals its value with lights or beeps. The patient responds by thinking thoughts that he believes will change the characteristic. The machine constantly feeds back the results of his efforts so that he can tell when he is achieving the desired goal.

The success of any of these schemes for relieving stress—daily jogging, meditation or even abandonment of the rat race—depends greatly on personality. One type of person may have a hard time controlling his reactions to heart-damaging stress. This is the "Type A" personality, first described by Drs. Meyer Friedman and Ray H. Rosenman of Mount Zion Hospital and Medical Center in San Francisco. The Type A is very time-conscious, competitive, impatient, hostile and often short-tempered—the kind of person who does two things at once, such as shaving while reading.

Drs. Friedman and Rosenman found that people with those characteristics are prone to circulatory disease. In sharp contrast, personalities they identified as Type B—who put off work and decisions, seem to be under no time pressure and are low-keyed—are free of heart troubles.

Although still controversial, a link between Type A personality and heart ailments has been found in several studies, most notably in the Western Collaborative Study in the United States. Healthy persons with Type A characteristics were found to have a greater incidence of heart disease. In the

Electrodes taped to his forehead to measure muscle tension, a patient trying to lower his blood pressure listens to tones emitted by the device on the table. By visualizing a pleasant scene, for example, the subject hears tones indicating a drop in tension and blood pressure—a technique called biofeedback.

Framingham study the impact of personality was strikingly greater for women than for men. For women under the age of 55, coronary heart disease in Type A's was eight times as prevalent as in Type B's. Although the effect seems to diminish with age, Type A women 65 to 74 were still twice as prone to heart disease as their Type B peers.

Whether Type A individuals can shift mental and emotional gears enough to reduce their risk of heart disease is not certain. Twenty minutes of meditation twice a day may be simply beyond them. On the other hand, 20 or 30 minutes of tennis may be more to their liking as a way to relieve stress.

The many benefits of exercise

Exercise reduces stress because it lowers the levels of hormones that speed up the heart rate and increase blood pressure. But it has many other effects on the body. If certain types of exercise are performed regularly, these effects seem to work together to provide general protection against circulatory disease. Research in Tanzania, Great Britain, Italy, Israel and the United States demonstrated that people who regularly exert themselves physically—for recreation or work—are strikingly free of circulatory disease.

Dr. Ralph S. Paffenbarger of Stanford University examined groups of San Francisco area longshoremen over more than 20 years. He found that the men doing hard physical labor had only half as great a chance of a sudden-death heart attack as those with lighter chores. When labor-saving machinery was introduced to the San Francisco docks following World War II, heart attacks among longshoremen increased. Dr. Paffenbarger also studied the health and leisure activities of the men who entered Harvard University between 1916 and 1950 and found that those who engaged in strenuous

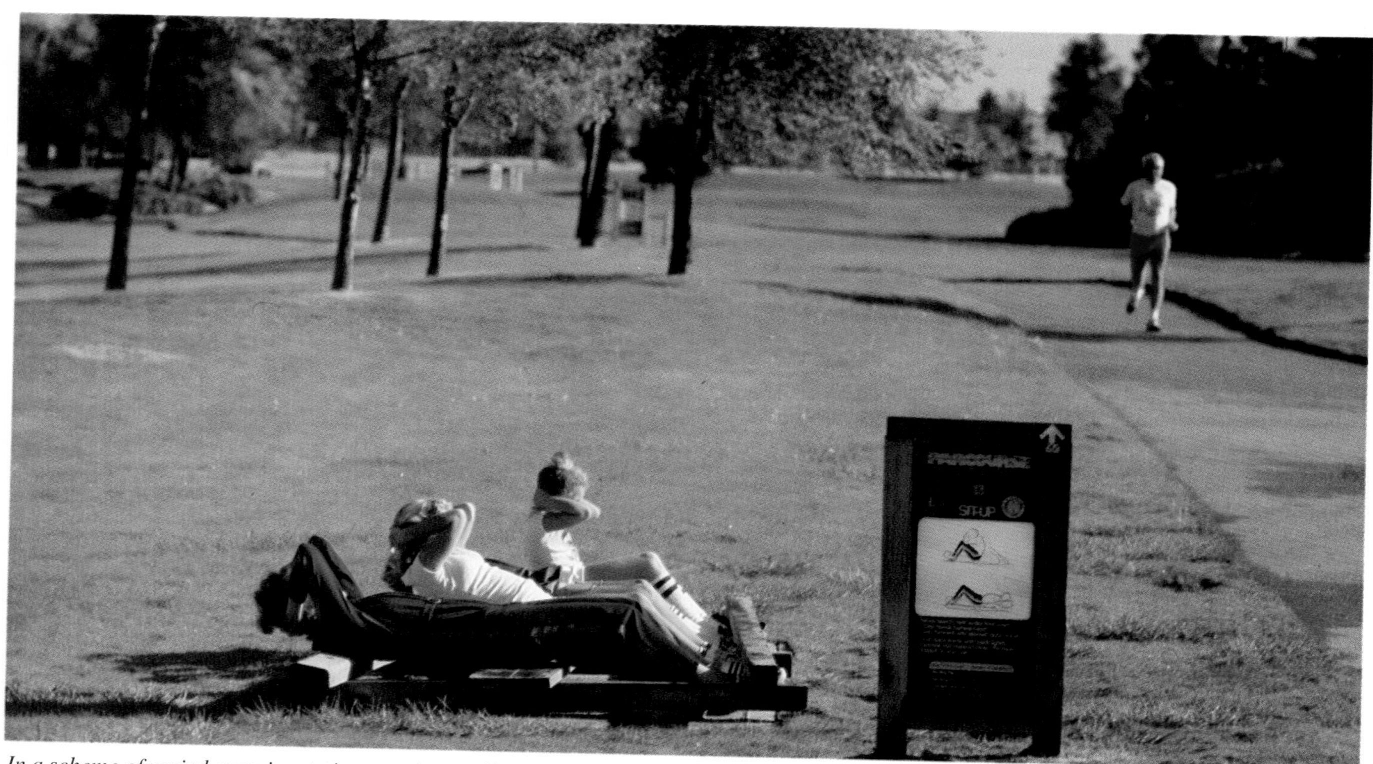

In a scheme of varied exercises to improve heart efficiency, four participants do sit-ups at one station on an exercise trail in Foster City, California, while another (background) jogs.

activities for at least three hours a week had one-third fewer heart attacks than their less active classmates.

Not all research confirms the value of exercise, however. The Seven Countries study of Dr. Ancel Keys could discover no consistent relationship between physical activity and heart disease, a finding that confounds many authorities. Keys found, for example, that one group of physically active American railwaymen—switchmen—die from heart disease about as often as the less active rail clerks and ticket agents. (By contrast, Dr. Keys discovered that physically active Italian railwaymen do indeed have a lower death rate from heart disease than their more sedentary co-workers.)

Some of the ways that exercise acts to protect the circulatory system are fairly obvious—it helps control weight, for one thing. Exercise also seems to increase the body's ability to dissolve blood clots. A clot can be fatal if it blocks an artery to the heart or brain. Normally, the body responds to the presence of a clot with a biochemical process called fibrinolysis, which breaks down the obstruction. After 10 weeks of jogging half an hour three times a week, volunteers at Duke University exhibited fibrinolytic activity significantly greater than before they began exercising. Their physical activity, the Duke study discovered, also increased their levels of HDL, a blood substance that seems to counter the impact of cholesterol in heart disease.

One of the reasons that exercise is good for your circulatory system is simple. The heart becomes more efficient the more it is used. It beats more slowly and pumps more blood with each beat. Moreover, this training effect of exercise is felt throughout the circulatory system. All muscles involved in the exercise make more efficient use of the blood passing through them. Being more efficient, they require less blood when laboring, and demand less increase in blood pressure and heart rate during exertion than in an untrained person.

To provide the training effect that increases efficiency of the circulatory system, an exercise must involve movements of large body muscles, it must tax you continuously for at least 20 to 30 minutes, and it must be repeated regularly.

The sustained movements of large muscles increase the flow of blood to the heart. This kind of exercise is called aerobic (from the Greek for "air"), because during such exercise, the blood continues to supply the working muscles with all the oxygen they need for as long as the activity continues. The more oxygen the muscles receive, the stronger they get and the larger their network of blood vessels grows, permitting them to do more work without strain.

The importance of sustained effort makes certain exercises more effective than others. Brisk walking, jogging, bicycling, cross-country skiing and swimming meet this requirement. Some competitive sports—golf, bowling, tennis doubles and softball, for example—do not, because they involve relatively long periods of inactivity between short bursts of strenuous exertion. Such exercises, although useful in relieving stress, offer little or no aerobic benefit.

Aerobic exercise must be not only sustained but, paradoxically, also limited in the effort it requires. It must be strenuous enough to require your blood to flow faster than it does when you are not exercising; otherwise there is no training effect. But it must not be so strenuous that your heart cannot pump fast enough to keep up with the demands for oxygen. When the muscles require more oxygen than they can get, they switch to a different method of extracting energy, one that burns their principal fuel, a carbohydrate called glycogen, without oxygen. Such "anaerobic" effort—required of sprinters, for example—can be continued only briefly; the heart reaches its maximum output, then chemical byproducts generated by the anaerobic energy production accumulate in the tissues, and the sprinter becomes exhausted.

Each individual has a maximum attainable heart rate, beyond which the heart simply cannot beat any faster, no matter what demands are made on it. The average maximum heart rate of a healthy 20-year-old is 200 beats per minute. The rate declines steadily with age, to about 175 for a 45-year-old and about 155 for a 65-year-old. (There is a great variation from the average, however; a well-trained athlete can do more strenuous exercise at a slower heart rate than an untrained person.) A rough formula for figuring your own maximum heart rate is to deduct your age from 220.

The training effect takes place when the exercise gets your heart beating at about 70 to 85 per cent of your maximum

How to take your own pulse

Everyone should know how to measure pulse rate, which tells how fast the heart is beating. This is not just for the rare emergencies when detecting a dangerously faint or rapid pulse can be vital. You need to be able to measure your own pulse so you can pace yourself properly in performing heart-strengthening exercises *(page 47)*. And if you have a record of heart trouble, your doctor may want you to check your own pulse from time to time.

Taking a pulse—your own or someone else's—is easy once you know where to feel for the light throb that the blood makes as the heart pumps it through the body. The best spots are at the wrists and neck, where major arteries run just below the skin *(right)*. Place your index and middle fingers lightly over the artery. Too much pressure can obstruct the flow and make it difficult to feel. To count the throbs, which correspond exactly to the beats of the heart, use a watch or clock that indicates seconds. For accurate measurement when at rest, maintain the count for 60 seconds; when pacing exercise, count beats for 10 seconds, then multiply the count by six.

Counting heartbeats and interpreting their rate are two different matters. To begin with, normal pulse rates, taken at rest—that is, when sitting quietly—range between 60 and 80 beats per minute; excitement or exertion can speed the rate, up to a perilous 200 beats per minute. Normal resting rates also vary widely: Healthy people can have resting pulses as high as 100 beats per minute and as low as 35. Only your doctor can tell if departures from the average rates indicate illness.

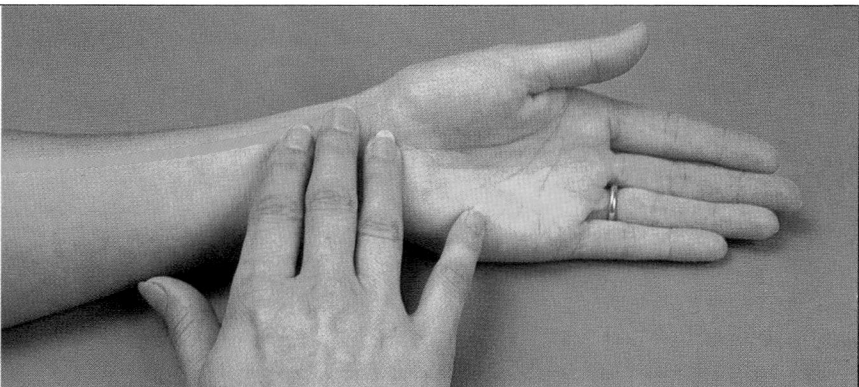

FINDING THE PULSE AT A WRIST
Use the fingers of one hand to find the knoblike wristbone nearest the base of the thumb of the other hand, then slip the finger tips toward your palm and down your wrist, onto a soft pocket of flesh. Move the tips in a circle to detect the throb in the artery (red).

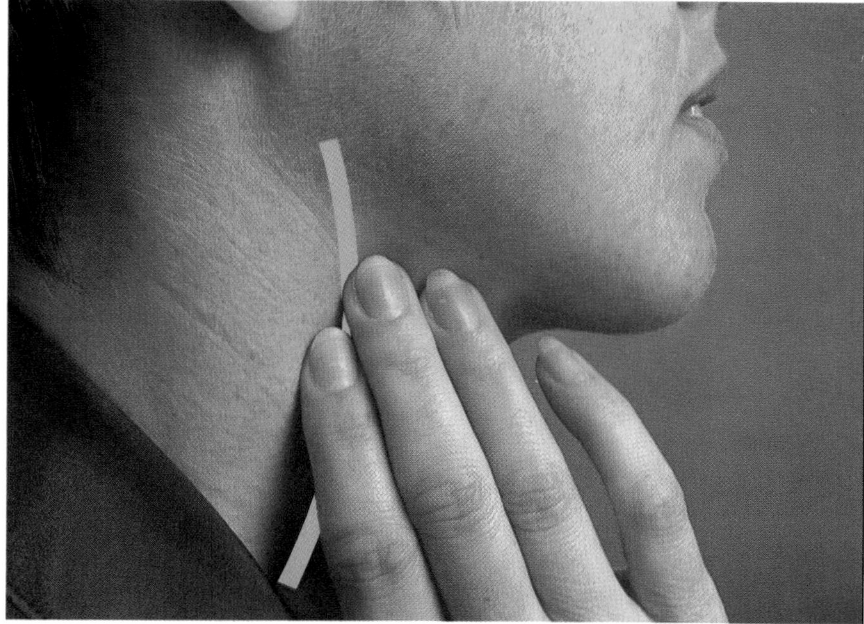

FINDING THE PULSE AT THE NECK
Place your finger tips gently on one side of your neck, below the jawbone and halfway between your main neck muscles and windpipe; locate the pulsing artery. Do not take a pulse on both sides of the neck at once; you may cut off the circulation.

heart rate, the "target zone," as determined from your pulse *(left)*. The exercise must be sustained in the target zone for 20 to 30 minutes at least three times a week, with no more than a two-day lapse between exercise days. More time out than that, and the benefit begins to fade.

The harsh effort of aerobic exercise—driving the heart close to its maximum capacity for 20 or 30 minutes nearly every other day—makes a healthy heart more efficient, but it can damage one that is not so healthy. There may be considerable danger if strenuous exercise is undertaken by sedentary people. Therefore it is probably wise to consult your doctor before beginning a regular exercise program. Many authorities recommend a medical examination. And for some people, a so-called exercise stress test may be required.

Such a test requires you to perform some kind of exercise—usually pedaling a stationary bicycle or walking on a motorized treadmill—while a device called an electrocardiograph *(pages 94-95)* monitors electrical signals emitted by your heart. At the same time, your blood pressure, heartbeat and perhaps the amount of oxygen you use are measured. The intensity of exercise is increased until your maximum heart rate, or something close to it, is reached—unless some sign of heart disease, such as chest pain, intervenes.

Not all authorities believe an exercise stress test is necessary. The test is costly and not totally reliable. Individuals who have narrowing of the coronary arteries may be pronounced healthy; others who are perfectly healthy will be cautioned against strenuous exercise. Dr. Lenore R. Zohman, a noted exercise cardiologist, believes the stress test is optional but desirable for any apparently healthy but sedentary person under age 35; she considers it mandatory for those with high cholesterol levels, more than 20 pounds of excess weight, high blood pressure, or a family history of heart attack before the age of 60. It is certainly indicated for anyone with chest pain or a record of heart disease.

If you decide to have an exercise stress test, you should also give some thought to where to have it done; the test itself poses some danger—slight but not negligible. The test should be conducted by a physician, preferably a cardiologist, rather than a medical technician or a nurse, and emergency equipment—including a defibrillator and appropriate drugs—should be at hand.

Such careful medical preparation is necessary only for aerobic exercise. For less arduous exercise, you can judge your capabilities on your own. Even mild exercise is helpful. Although it may not strengthen the circulatory system as aerobic exercise does, it relaxes tension and aids weight control, both of which are crucial to the health of your heart.

Simply walking an extra four miles a day at a pace of two miles an hour consumes about 200 calories of energy. That is a leisurely stroll (vigorous, aerobic walking is three and a half to four miles an hour). A daily amble may seem trivial—one hamburger adds 250 calories. But remember, those are 200 calories a day more than were consumed before. The 200 calories burned off every day for a year—assuming food intake is not increased—will take off 20 pounds and reduce the risk of cardiovascular disease.

Diet and your heart

As this example shows, exercise alone can help you lose weight. But in the fight against cardiovascular disease, it is more efficient and more healthful to combine exercise with proper diet. Eating right is crucial because it affects a whole cluster of the factors linked to heart disease: not simply weight, but also blood pressure and cholesterol.

Excess weight is endemic in many industrialized countries. More than two thirds of West Germans weigh 5 per cent more than the weight that doctors recommend, and one out of six weighs more than 15 per cent above the optimum. In Great Britain, one fifth of all men over 30 exceed their ideal weight by 20 per cent or more; in Holland, an estimated one out of five men is obese. In the United States, overweight is at least as prevalent—if not more so. Statistics show that one out of three American men and one out of seven women are at least 10 per cent overweight. Even this excess—15 pounds, more or less, for the average person—increases the risk of circulatory disease, according to some research, and greater excess weight worsens the hazard sharply.

The Framingham study, for example, reported that the risk of suffering from angina rises significantly as weight rises. It

Finding your healthiest weight

Only extremes of healthy weights are given in this table, a listing of wide ranges recommended for men and women by height. To tell if you are overweight, compare your poundage with the table, but also apply a test for excess fat *(text, right)* and look in the mirror for fat in the abdomen and—especially in women—arms, buttocks, thighs and legs.

HEIGHT	MEN'S WEIGHT	WOMEN'S WEIGHT
6 ft. 4 in.	164 - 204 lb.	
6 ft. 3 in.	160 - 199 lb.	
6 ft. 2 in.	156 - 194 lb.	
6 ft. 1 in.	152 - 189 lb.	
6 ft.	148 - 184 lb.	138 - 173 lb.
5 ft. 11 in.	144 - 179 lb.	134 - 168 lb.
5 ft. 10 in.	140 - 174 lb.	130 - 163 lb.
5 ft. 9 in.	136 - 170 lb.	126 - 158 lb.
5 ft. 8 in.	132 - 166 lb.	122 - 154 lb.
5 ft. 7 in.	128 - 161 lb.	118 - 150 lb.
5 ft. 6 in.	124 - 156 lb.	114 - 146 lb.
5 ft. 5 in.	121 - 152 lb.	111 - 142 lb.
5 ft. 4 in.	118 - 148 lb.	108 - 138 lb.
5 ft. 3 in.	115 - 144 lb.	105 - 134 lb.
5 ft. 2 in.	112 - 141 lb.	102 - 131 lb.
5 ft. 1 in.		99 - 128 lb.
5 ft.		96 - 125 lb.
4 ft. 11 in.		94 - 122 lb.
4 ft. 10 in.		92 - 119 lb.

also discovered that the chance of sudden death from heart attack is more than three times as great for subjects who are 20 per cent over their ideal weight. The Seven Countries study, however, found no relation between overweight and risk of heart disease if age, blood pressure, cholesterol and smoking were excluded from the calculations. But British researchers have suggested that overweight may help boost blood pressure and cholesterol levels, working through those two risk factors to increase the risk of heart disease.

Despite conflicting research, the safest policy—as shown by insurance statistics compiled over more than a century—is to stay within 20 per cent of your ideal weight. "There is a small group of people whom weight doesn't affect adversely—very small," noted Framingham's Dr. Castelli. "Most people who gain much weight get into trouble."

An easy way to find your ideal weight is to refer to a chart like the one at left. How helpful such charts are is open to question—they list broad ranges rather than specific figures because ideal weight depends not simply on height but also on bone structure. Thus, even if you find your weight lies within the range recommended for your height, you may still have excess fat. Most physicians refer to the charts but do not rely on them. One of the world's leading cardiologists, pressed to explain how he decides whether or not a patient is overweight, replied, "I look at the patient." However, he looks at particular places, those that are known to be significant indicators of excess fat: in men, the abdomen; in women, the abdomen, buttocks, thighs, arms and legs.

Precise measurement of body fat requires fairly elaborate techniques, but there are one or two simple tests you can use to detect excess fat. One is the ruler test. Lie on your back and place a ruler lengthwise along the midline of your body. Your abdomen should be flat between the bottom of your rib cage and the top of your pelvis. If the ruler points upward at the midsection, it indicates excess fat. Another test measures the fat located directly under the skin—the "pinch test." Grab a fold of skin with your thumb and forefinger, at the stomach or the back of the upper arm. If the fold is much more than one inch thick, you have some fat to lose.

There is only one way to lose weight: Consume fewer calories in the food you eat than you burn up with exercise. The first step is to add up the calories you eat in a day—charts listing the caloric contents of common foods are widely available. Also available are charts listing the calories consumed by various exercises, from the 200 calories of a slow four-mile walk to the 225 calories of a 30-minute jog. To reduce, you can cut down on your calories, or you can exercise more, or—best of all—do both.

Optimum weight may be the first goal of a proper diet, but it is not the only one. The ingredients of your diet affect other factors associated with heart disease. Debate continues over the exact constituents and precise proportions of an ''ideal'' diet. But there is a broad consensus: Most people eat too much fat, salt, cholesterol and sugar. Cutting down on these could help cut down on heart-related disease.

Salt is a principal villain. Salt is sodium chloride, 40 per cent of which is sodium, an element essential to the body. But sodium also boosts blood pressure. It makes the body retain fluids; greater fluid retention boosts total blood volume and this increase raises blood pressure. Where salt is used freely, a large proportion of the population develops chronic high blood pressure, the hypertension that is a primary factor in coronary heart disease, stroke and disorders of the leg arteries. Farmers in northern Japan traditionally preserve their food with salt. They consume as much as six teaspoons a day—and 40 per cent of them have high blood pressure. Among the Eskimos of Greenland, however, who consume little salt, high blood pressure is almost unheard of.

The body of an adult needs only about 200 milligrams of sodium a day—the amount in 500 milligrams, or 1/10 of a teaspoon, of salt. But the average American consumes about 12,000 milligrams, or more than two teaspoons, of salt a day—which supplies 24 times as much sodium as necessary; Germans consume an average 5,300 milligrams of salt a day.

A sharp reduction is recommended by authorities everywhere—to about 8,000 milligrams of salt per day for healthy people. For those who already suffer from hypertension, the normally suggested maximum is about 2,000 milligrams per day; more drastic restrictions—to about 200 milligrams—are required in special cases. So little salt makes food almost insufferably bland for most Americans and Europeans, and some physicians prescribe as a replacement seasoning potassium chloride, which tastes salty but contains no sodium. However, extremely heavy use of potassium—unlikely because of its unpleasant taste in large doses—can cause death. Hence, the substitution of one chloride for the other should be undertaken only on the advice of a doctor.

When you set out to reduce your salt intake—and almost everyone should—you quickly find that the taste of unsalted food is not the only obstacle. Most of the excess sodium is not added at the table, where control can be easily exercised. An average day's meals supply about 3,000 milligrams of salt that are naturally present in common foodstuffs *(pages 58-59)*. And if any of the foods are commercially processed—such as canned vegetables or soups—there is much more.

Many of these salted foods do not even taste salty. Two slices of white bread contain more sodium than an ounce of salty potato chips, while an ounce of corn flakes has twice as much sodium as an ounce of salted peanuts. The amounts involved can be sensationally high: One popular American fast-food hamburger contains about 500 milligrams of sodium, about a sixth of the total recommended for a day.

Although salt seasoning is the greatest source of sodium, other compounds also supply large amounts. One example is the synthetic sweeteners used by people who are avoiding sugar in an attempt to reduce calorie intake and lose weight. Saccharin, the most common artificial sweetener, contains no calories but much sodium. For this reason, the consumption of synthetically sweetened, low-calorie desserts and soft drinks, particularly by children, concerns health authorities. Even commonly used medicines—antacids and laxatives—include sodium compounds, and they must be used with caution by anyone with high blood pressure.

Salt is one of the principal and most difficult ''don'ts'' of a diet intended to protect the heart. Fortunately there are some ''do's'' that many people find pleasing. The complex carbohydrates in rice, spaghetti and potatoes—foods that have been shunned because their caloric content makes them potentially fattening—are now viewed as preferable alternatives to the meats, fats and sweets that dominate many diets. And alcoholic beverages—traditional accompaniments to food and traditional target of reformers—are also beneficial, if consumed in moderation (no more than two whiskies or glasses of wine per day). Just how alcohol helps prevent heart disease is not entirely clear, but it seems to increase the body's production of blood proteins that counter the effects of cholesterol, the special fat implicated in damage to the coronary arteries. How dangerous cholesterol is, and how far anyone should go to avoid it, are the subjects of one of the sharpest controversies about the circulatory system.

An early alert to safeguard the young

"Early Birds," proclaimed the perky yellow T-shirts of a group of children at John F. Kennedy Elementary School in West Babylon, Long Island. The words had a double meaning. Three times a week, for 20 weeks, these children came to school at 8 a.m., an hour before other students. But they were Early Birds in another, more important, sense: These 10-year-old fifth graders participated in a program intended to keep their hearts healthy when they grew up. They began learning early to lower their blood pressure and control their weight through exercise and diet—and thus to reduce the risk of developing heart-related diseases.

This pioneering program grew out of the discovery that heart problems are not limited to adults. Signs of atherosclerosis, the artery blockage that leads to heart attack and heart failure, were found in 10-year-olds, and a study of Michigan school children revealed that almost half were affected by one or more of the probable causes of heart ailments. These facts are not really surprising. Nowadays, children often do not get enough exercise—they are shuttled to and from school, and they watch TV for hours on end—and they consume great quantities of fatty, salty food. This rich, indolent life style makes them high-risk candidates for heart trouble.

Determined to help such children, Jerome Schiffman, the principal at John F. Kennedy, had his fifth grade take a six-minute run. Students who could not run half a mile in that time were given blood-pressure tests. Those with high readings, and any who were overweight, went into the Early Bird program.

It proved a startling success. Factors that indicate risk of heart disease were controlled. Over the 20-week period the Early Birds' blood pressure dropped an average of 12 points, their rate of weight gain decreased by half and the blood-pumping efficiency of their hearts increased by a third. The children themselves were enthusiastic—about the exercises, about losing weight and, as one said, "because it makes me feel like I'm special."

An Early Bird watches the gauge as her blood pressure is checked for effects of diet and exercise. Everyone in the group had his blood pressure taken every other week.

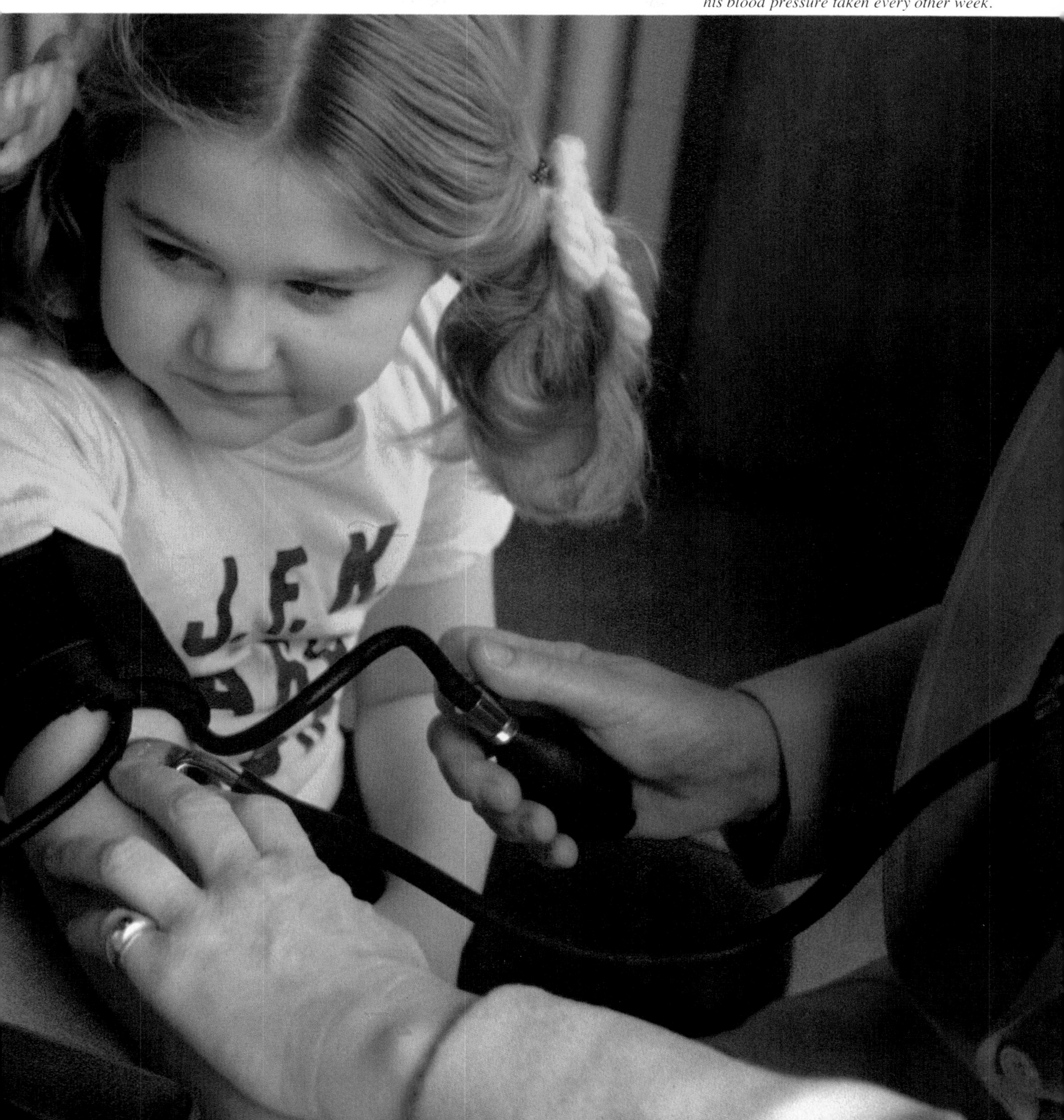

Monday morning measurements for signs of progress

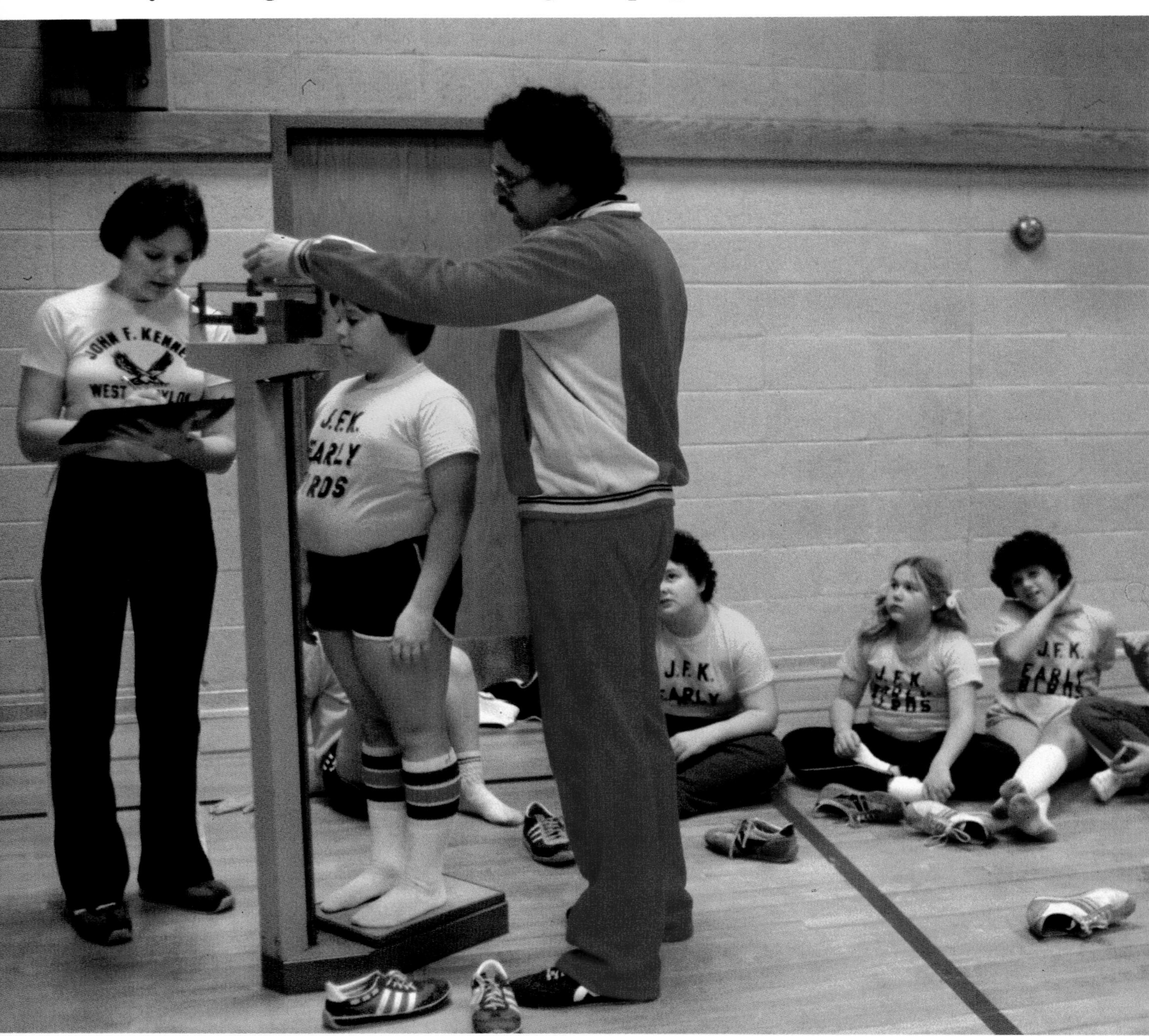

Lilka Lichtneger and Richard Rowcroft, two physical-education instructors who helped design the Early Birds program, record a boy's height and weight, as they do every Monday morning for the entire group. Before the program started, the students' average weight had been increasing more than a pound a month; at the end of the program, the monthly gain was half a pound.

Early Birds take their own pulses—the two boys check their wrists, the girl her neck—before the morning's exercises. Over a period of time, lowered pulse rates indicate that the exercises are making the heart pump more efficiently. Fifth graders were selected as Early Birds partly because they were old enough to learn to check their own pulses and record the results.

Keeping it lively with a variety of exercise

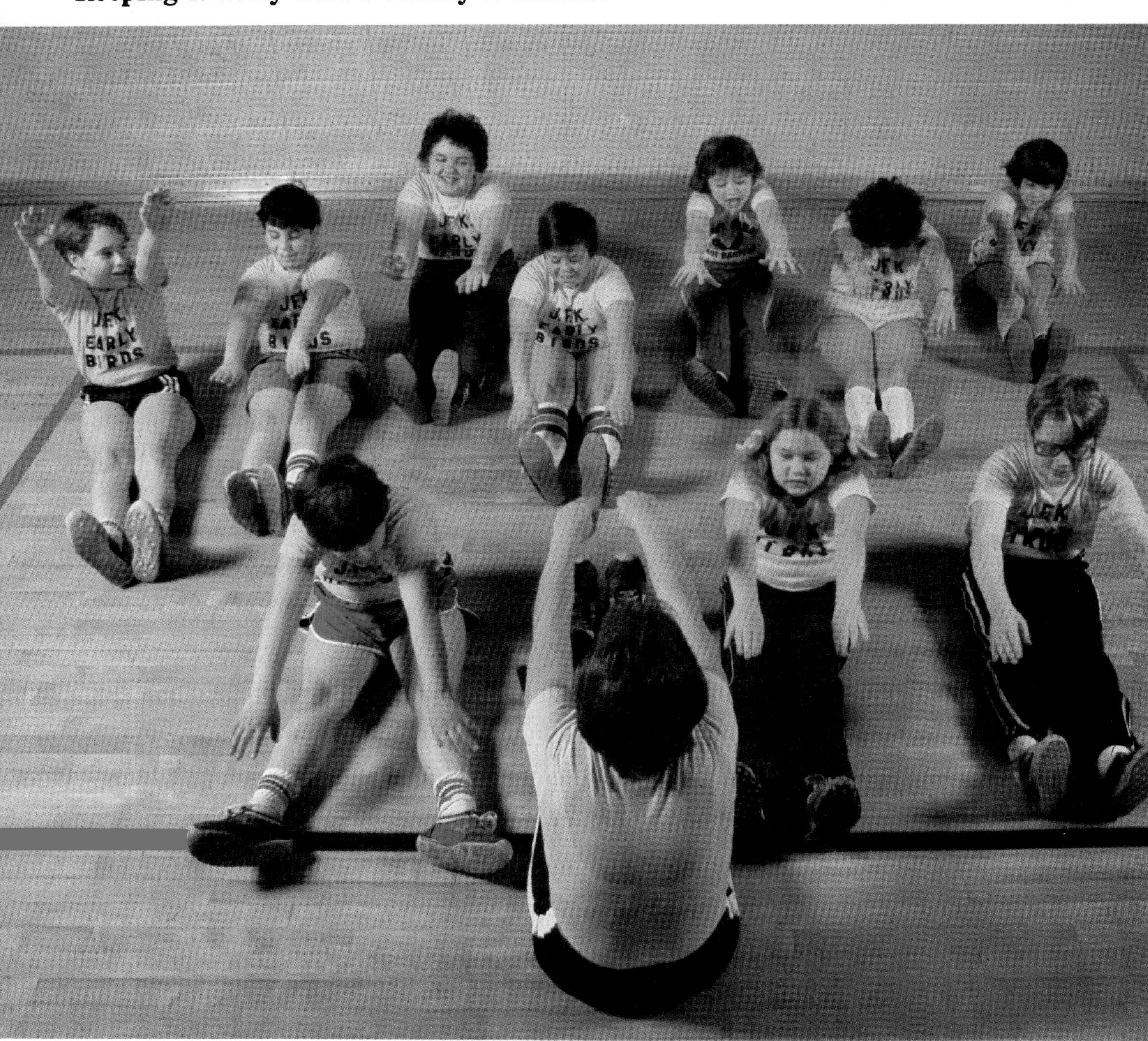

Lilka Lichtneger leads the Early Birds in 10 minutes of stretching, a warm-up before strenuous exercises (opposite). The Early Birds were tested before beginning the program to determine their "training" heart rates, that is, the speed at which each child's heart should beat during periods of exercise if the exercise is to provide optimum physical conditioning.

Early Birds puff through the hoops and past the pylons of an obstacle course set up in the school gym. Such heart-expanding "aerobic" exercises, varied to relieve boredom, included jogging, running up and down stairs, swimming and pedaling an exercise bicycle.

A jolly fifth grader pumps away on an exercise bicycle, watching her speed on the dial of the machine. The pedals are adjusted to be hard enough to work so that, at her required speed, the effort brings her heart to her own training rate.

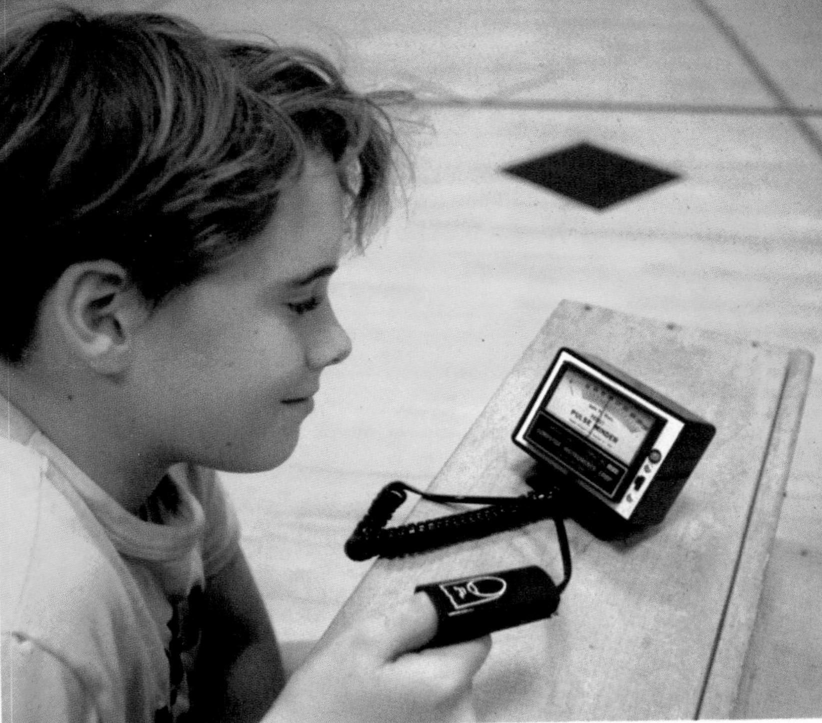

Pressing an electronic gauge, an Early Bird monitors his pulse in an exercise break. This reading checks the training heart rate during an exercise. Another shows how far the rate drops one minute after exertion, an indicator of conditioning—the faster the recovery rate, the more efficient the heart. Early Birds' one-minute readings dropped from an average of 138 to 108 beats.

Learning how to eat for future well-being

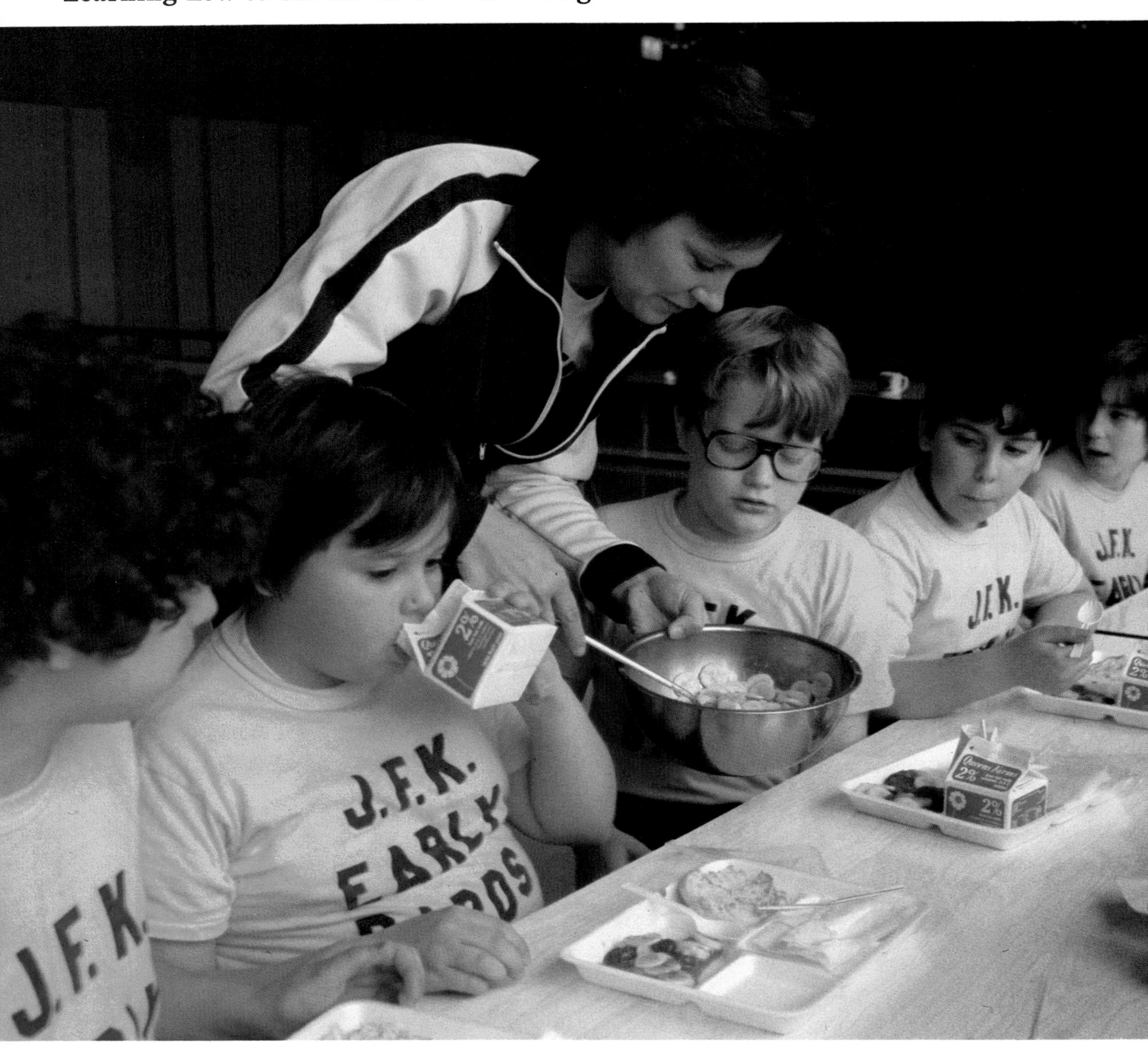

After exercises and a cool-down period, the Early Birds have a breakfast of low-fat milk and low-sugar cereal with fruit or juice; for variety, they are served eggs and English muffins. Special breakfasts, along with discussions of their other meals (opposite), are intended to instill eating habits conducive to good health.

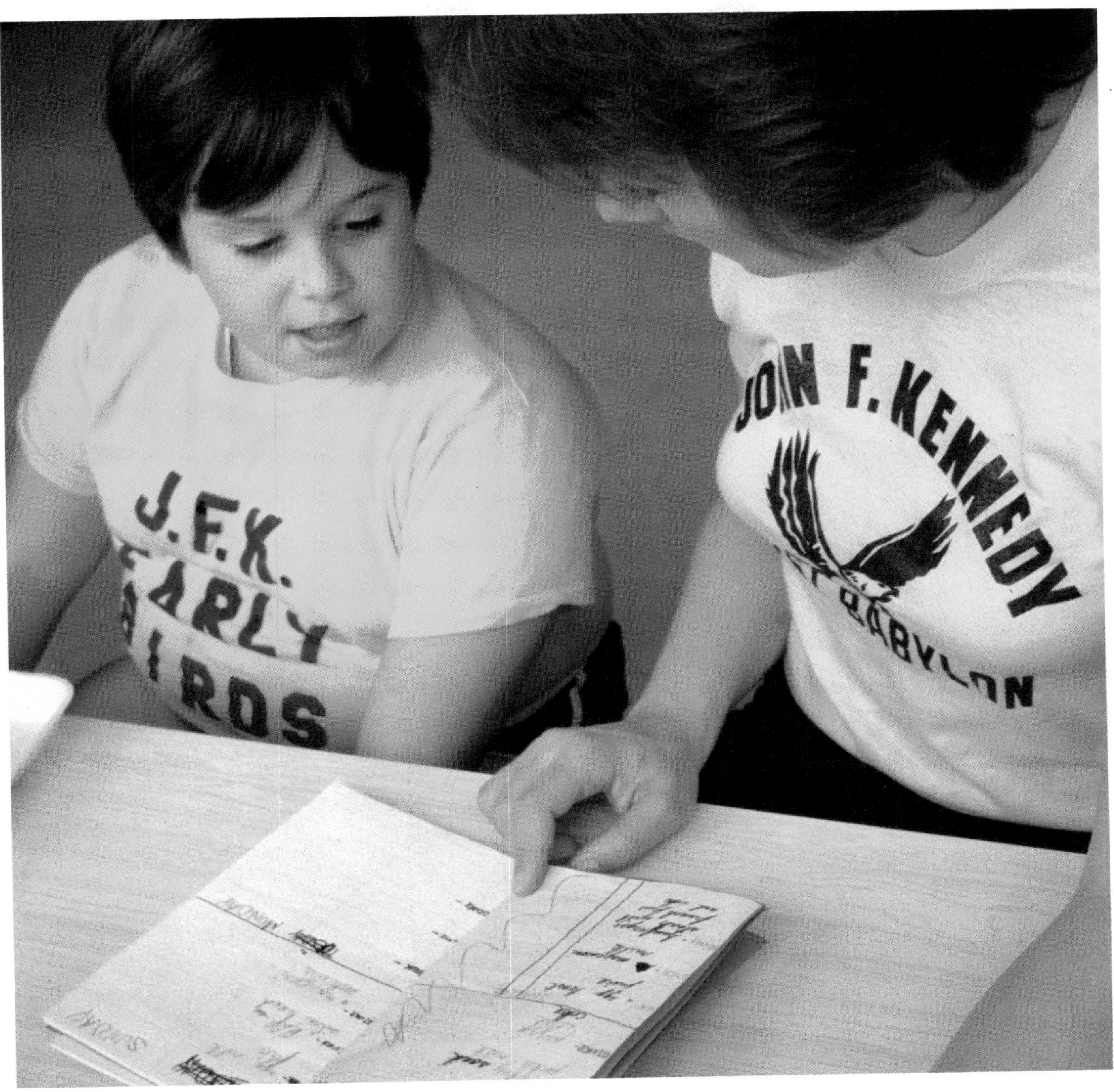

Instructor Lichtneger goes over a diet diary with one of the fifth graders, who, like every Early Bird, keeps a record of what he eats at home. This diary is reviewed periodically with one of the instructors to watch for eating that exceeds the recommended calorie count: 1,000 calories a day for a 100-pound child.

JOHN F. KEN
ELEMENTARY S

Romping in delight, six Early Birds take to the outdoors as principal Schiffman and the instructors watch from the school steps. The children became physically fit—three finished a six-mile marathon—and more alert and successful in class.

CHAPTER 3

Tracking down the cholesterol connection

Cholesterol from fats
How fat clogs arteries
The diet controversy
Looking for cause and effect
The other suspects
Not cholesterol, but HDLs

In 1973 doctors at Detroit's Wayne State University performed a bizarre operation: an autopsy on a man dead some 2,100 years. The man was an aristocrat of ancient Egypt whose mummified remains, nicknamed Pum by researchers, had been resting in the University of Pennsylvania for years. Now they were unwrapped and dissected to serve medicine.

The post-mortem findings were provocative. Pum, who was between 35 and 40 years old at his death, had, the report said, ''large and small plaques in portions of the aorta''—the arterial clogging called atherosclerosis. Clearly, this precursor of heart attack and stroke was no stranger to antiquity.

The discovery that atherosclerosis is such an ancient condition intensifies a controversy that, two millennia after Pum's death, embroils medical scientists. Atherosclerosis is clearly linked to heart attack and stroke, among the most deadly diseases of the 20th Century world. But what causes atherosclerosis? Although there is evidence connecting the clogging to the fats in the bloodstream—and thus to the fats that people eat—this evidence is circumstantial. Still, it is so persuasive that it has convinced many scientists that the diets of industrialized countries should be modified to lower the fat levels. Most physicians accept this view.

Not all scientists agree. On the other side, an array of experts insists that circumstantial evidence for the theory linking diet and heart disease is inadequate—after all, Pum did not eat a fat-laden 20th Century diet, but he had atherosclerosis anyhow. These experts maintain that it is disruptive and possibly dangerous to impose drastic changes of diet on large numbers of people if the changes are not necessary.

Like most great scientific debates, the diet controversy is also a great detective story. All over the world researchers are hunting clues to answer a basic question: Does changing diet reduce fat levels in a way that reduces cardiovascular risk? The search for the answer begins with the fat that has been the main suspect in the atherosclerosis mystery—cholesterol.

Cholesterol is a waxy, white, odorless, tasteless substance made up of three elements: carbon, hydrogen and oxygen. The chemical formula for a single molecule is $C_{27}H_{45}OH$—and that complex molecule has been called in *The New England Journal of Medicine* ''one of the most enigmatic molecules in human biology.''

Cholesterol is an essential ingredient of every organ of your body, for it is a structural part of every cell wall. It is also part of myelin, a white sheath that surrounds and insulates certain nerve strands. It helps to form bile acids for digestion and to produce the chemical messengers called hormones. On the other hand, cholesterol is implicated in gallstones and anemia as well as atherosclerosis.

Some cholesterol is present in common foods—the average Briton daily gets over 530 milligrams (about 1/60 ounce) from his diet, the average Frenchman just less than 500 milligrams, but the average Japanese only about 130 milligrams. In addition, the liver makes about 600 milligrams of cholesterol every day. Cholesterol from both sources circulates in the bloodstream. (The concentration of cholesterol in the blood is measured as the number of milligrams of cholesterol

The beauty of this pure crystal of cholesterol, shimmering in colors created by special lighting, belies its deadly effect. This one was obtained from a 42-year-old man whose artery was clogged with the substance. Body cholesterol is normally white and waxy but sometimes occurs in the pure form pictured.

in every 100 milliliters [about one-fifth pint] of blood. Thus when doctors specify an individual's cholesterol level as 200, for example, they mean his blood contains 200 milligrams of cholesterol per 100 milliliters.)

The cholesterol in food all comes from animal sources, such as meat, poultry, eggs, butter, milk and cheese; there is none in plant foods, such as cereals, vegetables, fruits and nuts. The amount of cholesterol in animal foods varies widely. One large egg yolk (all the cholesterol of an egg is in the yolk) has about 252 milligrams. Organ meats are rich in cholesterol: Calf sweetbreads have 396 milligrams in a three-ounce serving; beef liver, 372; calf brains, a huge 2,668. Beef, pork and processed luncheon meats are fairly high in cholesterol; shellfish, such as clams, oysters and scallops, somewhat less so; fish and poultry, still less.

Cholesterol from fats

But foods containing cholesterol are not the main cause of cholesterol in your blood. How much cholesterol—from any source—ends up in your bloodstream depends not just on the cholesterol you eat but also on other fats you eat. The quantity affects cholesterol level, but so does the kind of fat. There are three chemical types of fat: saturated, monounsaturated and polyunsaturated. Saturated fats have carbon atoms filled with all the hydrogen atoms they have room for; monounsaturated fats contain two carbon atoms that each have room for one more hydrogen; polyunsaturated fats contain more than two carbon atoms having vacancies for hydrogen atoms.

The saturated fats occur mostly in animal foods that already are high in cholesterol, such as beef, ham, pork, butter, whole milk, eggs and cheese, but they also appear in a few plant products, notably cocoa butter and palm and coconut oils. These fats contribute to a rise in blood cholesterol levels; if cholesterol is included in the food you eat, more of it will show up in your blood if you eat more, rather than less, of the saturated fats. Monounsaturated fats—olive oil and peanut oil are the most common—have no significant effect on cholesterol level. Many researchers believe that polyunsaturated fats, including corn oil, safflower oil, sesame oil and soybean oil, help reduce the cholesterol in the blood—up to a point. They are about half as effective in lowering the level as saturated fats are in raising it. Why these three kinds of fats change blood cholesterol level in three different ways is unknown, although the effect presumably is tied to the variations in hydrogen atoms in their molecules.

Most foods contain a combination of the three types of food fats, though one may predominate. Butter, for example, is about 80 per cent fats; about two thirds of the total is saturated, less than a third monounsaturated and only four per cent polyunsaturated. Ordinary margarine is only about one-fifth saturated fat and the fats in liquid safflower-oil margarine are almost entirely polyunsaturated. A three-ounce serving of lean beef contains about a quarter ounce of fats, about half saturated, half monounsaturated and only a trace polyunsaturated. By contrast, a similar serving of broiled codfish or other lean fish contains .02 ounce fats, of which only 24 per cent is saturated while 21 per cent is monounsaturated and 55 per cent polyunsaturated. The fat contents of other common foods are listed on pages 58-59.

The study of such fat analyses interests many people who are seeking to lower their blood cholesterol levels by eating foods low in cholesterol and saturated fats. If you choose this course, you will find that selecting low-fat foods may be complicated, particularly in the case of packaged foods. Their fat contents are seldom listed clearly. In addition, food processors often treat the oils used in some products—baked goods and margarines are examples—by hydrogenation, a chemical method that hardens vegetable shortenings and helps them resist spoilage. Hydrogenation works in part by turning unsaturated fats into saturated ones, altering the original mix of fats in the shortening. The label on a box of cake will tell you whether the oil in the recipe was partially hydrogenated, but not to what extent—and the more hydrogenated an oil, the higher its saturated-fat content.

Avoiding saturated fat thus becomes a tricky business, and it is made trickier by the fact that—in the words of W. S. Gilbert—"things are seldom what they seem, skim milk masquerades as cream." Coffee drinkers who buy nondairy creamers to avoid the saturated fats in dairy cream actually increase their intake of those fats because the cream substitutes are made from coconut oil, one of the most saturated fats in nature. In light dairy cream about 50 per cent of the fats are saturated, in the nondairy products about 75 per cent.

How fat clogs arteries

The reason these numbers and proportions attract so much interest, of course, is the intimate connection between cholesterol and atherosclerosis, and thus between cholesterol and heart and blood-vessel disease. The link was detected more than a century ago by the German biologist Rudolf Virchow, the founder of the modern science of pathology, the study of the effects of disease. Virchow examined the plaques, or plugs, taken from the diseased arteries of autopsy subjects. He found them to be fibrous material heavily impregnated with a cheesy, fatty substance. Chemical analysis showed that most of the substance was cholesterol.

Virchow knew that plaques can clog an artery as a plug of hair and grease can clog the drain of a sink. He knew, too, that plaques can eventually obstruct an artery completely, or form sticking points where traveling blood clots lodge and hold fast. But he could not discover how a plaque gets started—and indeed, a final explanation has yet to be found.

Virchow suggested that an injury to the inner wall of a blood vessel triggers the formation of a plaque. Somehow, he thought, the injury is associated with the deposition of cholesterol, and it results in an inflammation. Remarkably, the key element in Virchow's notion—the idea of an "insult" to the thin layer of cells, called endothelial cells, that line the inside of an artery—is part of the most widely accepted modern hypothesis. Proposed in 1976 by Dr. Russell Ross and Dr. John Glosmet of the University of Washington School of Medicine, the modern concept takes this form:

The endothelial cells are a shield, protecting the main part of the artery wall from infiltration by the blood that courses through the vessel—blood laden with fatty compounds containing cholesterol. This protective lining can be damaged by various agents and processes. Among the suspects are: the turbulent flow of the blood through the artery; a substance called a glycoprotein antigen, a chemical derived from cigarette smoke; high blood pressure, which forces the blood in the artery to strike the walls with unusual force; a high concentration of the blood fats; and viral or bacterial infection.

Whatever the cause, the result is the same: a breach in the endothelial shield. Blood fats get into the space opened up within the artery wall. So do platelets—very small blood cells involved in blood clotting—and the platelets secrete chemicals that induce an extraordinary change in the artery itself. Smooth-muscle cells, which ordinarily form the elas-

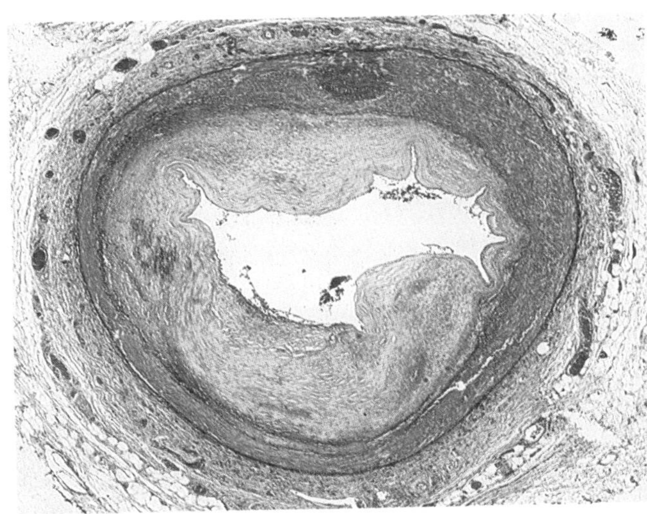

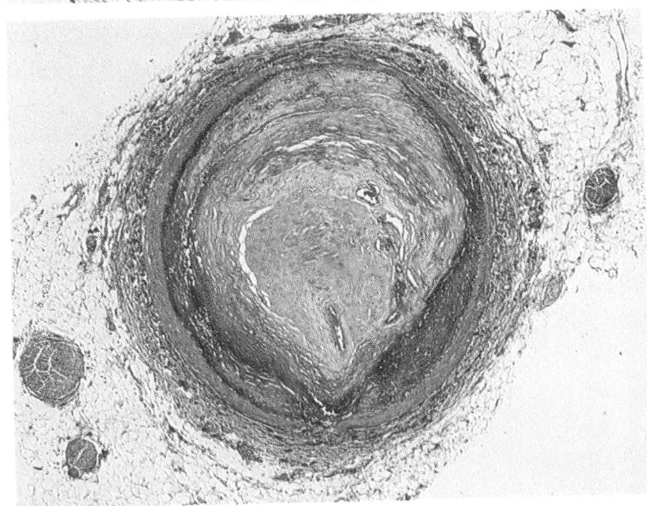

How cholesterol blocks an artery to cut off blood flow and cause a heart attack or stroke can be seen in these photographs of laboratory specimens, reproduced here 600 times actual size. In the cross section at top, the pink-and-yellowish fatty plaque—fibrous tissue mixed with cholesterol—partially chokes the artery; the artery in the lower picture is completely plugged.

tic walls of the artery, migrate to the site of the breach—and there they multiply. In turn, the muscle cells produce connective tissue and elastic fibers. A lesion, or plaque, takes shape—a bump composed of fiber, misplaced muscle cells and cholesterol-rich fats, by connective tissue.

If this injury is a one-time affair, the lesion may shrink and remain small, producing no symptoms of disease. But if the victim smokes heavily, if he has untreated high blood pressure, if he has chronically high cholesterol levels—or worse, if he combines such insults to the artery wall—then the lesions grow and multiply. Eventually they block the artery, possibly with fatal results. Dr. Levy of the Heart Institute described the doctor's helplessness in the face of such events: "It is a terrible frustration that in about a quarter of heart attack victims, the first clinical sign of atherosclerosis is also the last and terminates in sudden death."

The fatty deposits that play a crucial role in the formation of a plaque are apparently laid down inside arteries practically from birth. They form yellowish fatty streaks in the arteries of quite small children, but these streaks are not full-fledged atherosclerotic plaques. For many years atherosclerosis was considered a disease condition that developed with age, appearing only in later life.

Then came a stunning revelation. When autopsies were performed on American soldiers killed in action in the Korean War, doctors were shocked to find that over 77 per cent of the men, whose average age was only 22, had coronary arteries narrowed by atherosclerosis. In a later study of Americans killed in Vietnam, the situation was better, but not much: About half these young men had cholesterol-filled plaques. The arteries of soldiers in the opposing forces—young Koreans and Vietnamese—showed no such damage.

One other difference could be noted between the Americans and the Asians: the cholesterol levels of their blood. American levels were far higher. Subsequently, in studies of the average cholesterol levels in country after country, one conclusion emerged: In general, the higher the country's average cholesterol level, the higher its heart attack rate.

Consider, for example, a comparison between men in southern Japan with men in eastern Finland. The Japanese

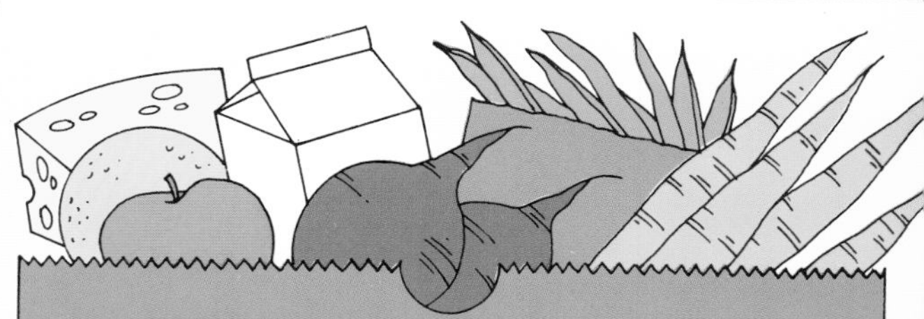

Eating to avoid heart trouble

The controversies over the connection between diet and circulatory disorders are arguments over degree. Most experts agree that you should limit the fatty food you eat *(Chapter 3)* and reduce the sodium—mainly in salt—you consume. The table at right lists weights of cholesterol, sodium and fats in average servings of common foods—three ounces of meat, for example. Fats are specified in grams, cholesterol and sodium in milligrams (thousandths of one gram).

Of these nutrients, sodium may prove the most difficult to control. A maximum of 3,300 milligrams per day is recommended—an allowance you can consume almost unknowingly. (One pickle contains 928 milligrams of sodium.)

Regulating consumption of fat and cholesterol can be just as hard. Suggested limits are stringent: 300 milligrams a day of cholesterol, and for men about 30 grams a day of each type of fat, for women 22 grams. In choosing most foods, the main consideration is how much cholesterol-producing saturated fat each contains; the quantity of cholesterol is secondary. So much saturated fat may be present that the cholesterol it later produces in the body overshadows the cholesterol already in the food—butter has 180 times as much saturated fat as cholesterol. (Monounsaturated fat is believed less harmful, polyunsaturated fat still less so.)

Thus chicken, low in saturated fat, is recommended over beef despite the fact that they have similar cholesterol contents. Eggs, on the other hand, are so rich in cholesterol that doctors recommend avoiding them despite the relatively slight amount of saturated fat they contain.

FATS, CHOLESTEROL AND SODIUM in average food servings

	Saturated fats (grams)	Monounsaturated fats (grams)	Polyunsaturated fats (grams)	Cholesterol (milligrams)	Sodium (milligrams)
DAIRY PRODUCTS					
CHEESE: American	4.7	2.8	.3	25	322
Cottage	5.7	3.4	.3	48	561
CREAM, light	1.7	1.0	.1	10	6
MILK: Whole	4.7	2.8	.2	34	122
Low-fat	2.7	1.6	.1	22	150
ICE CREAM	7.8	4.7	.4	53	84
SHAKE, chocolate	5.0	2.0	.2	29	329
MEAT, POULTRY, EGGS AND FISH					
BEEF, roast	5.5	5.0	.2	77	59
CHICKEN: Dark meat (skinless)	1.7	2.1	1.1	77	74
Light meat (skinless)	1.4	1.5	.9	67	56
CLAMS	.2	.2	.2	43	175
EGG	1.8	2.5	.4	252	61
FLOUNDER, broiled	.2	.2	.3	53	83
FRANKFURTER	5.6	6.5	1.2	34	627
HAM: Cured	2.7	3.2	.7	75	770
Fresh	3.1	3.6	.8	75	62
HAMBURGER	8.0	7.3	.3	77	49
LIVER, fried	2.9	3.8	1.4	372	94
PORK, roast	4.4	5.1	1.1	75	56
SAUSAGE	4.2	4.8	1.0	23	250
SHRIMP	.1	.1	.4	128	119
TUNA: In oil (drained)	1.7	2.1	2.6	56	324
In water (drained)	1.3	1.2	1.0	56	299
TURKEY: Dark meat (skinless)	2.0	3.0	1.5	86	84
Light meat (skinless)	1.0	1.4	.7	65	70
VEGETABLES					
CARROTS: Fresh	Trace	Trace	Trace	0	26
Canned	Trace	Trace	Trace	0	183
POTATOES: Baked	Trace	Trace	Trace	0	6
French fried	1.7	1.4	3.3	0	5
Mashed with milk and butter	2.5	1.5	.2	35	348
FRUITS					
APPLE	Trace	Trace	Trace	0	1
GRAPEFRUIT	Trace	Trace	Trace	0	1
ORANGE	Trace	Trace	Trace	0	1
BREADS AND CEREALS					
BREAD: French	.2	.5	.3	0	203
White	.2	.4	.2	0	134
DEVIL'S FOOD CAKE	4.9	5.3	1.5	32	233
BREAKFAST CEREALS: Bran flakes	Trace	Trace	Trace	0	207
Corn flakes	Trace	Trace	Trace	0	251
Oatmeal	.5	.8	1.0	0	523
FATS AND OILS					
BUTTER	6.3	3.8	.3	35	140
MARGARINE	2.1	5.9	3.1	7	140
MAYONNAISE	2.0	2.4	5.6	10	84
COOKING OIL: Corn	1.4	3.8	7.2	0	0
Olive	1.5	10.3	.9	0	0
NONPRESCRIPTION DRUGS					
ANTACID: Sodium bicarbonate	0	0	0	0	89
Effervescent	0	0	0	0	276
LAXATIVE	0	0	0	0	250
SLEEP AID: Effervescent	0	0	0	0	544

had an average cholesterol level of 140, appreciably lower than the world average of 160 to 170, and they had the world's lowest rate of heart attacks. The Finns had the highest cholesterol levels in the world, averaging about 280—twice the Japanese level—and they had the world's highest heart attack rate; it was 10 times the Japanese rate.

After Finland, one of the highest heart attack rates was found in the United States, where the cholesterol level resembled that of the Finns. For middle-aged American men, the average was about 225. For years many physicians considered such a reading normal, not worth worrying about. But "normal" meant "average," and there is a difference between "average" and "desirable." For the typical American heart attack victim, the average level is dangerous. According to Dr. William Castelli, director of the great Framingham study of heart disease, 75 per cent of American heart attack victims have cholesterol levels within normal limits. "Go to any hospital in America," he said, "stand at the coronary care door, and listen to the men who come out. Many of them say, 'My doctor doesn't know why I got a heart attack—my cholesterol was normal.' "

The average cholesterol level of the 700 men in the Framingham study who got heart attacks was 244. "So you might say that's one of the most dangerous levels there is," said Dr. Castelli. "It's associated with more heart attacks than any other. But how many doctors do anything for people with this cholesterol level? Yet the world average is 160 to 170. Only a few other regions have cholesterol levels like ours—Scandinavia, Britain, northern Europe, Australia and New Zealand—and they all have major cardiovascular problems."

The diet controversy

Even Dr. Castelli, vehement as he was about the role of blood cholesterol in circulatory ailments, did not label cholesterol level a "cause" of disease. Like most other experts, he cautiously "associated" it with heart attacks. There is no longer much argument about going that far toward indicating at least one villain in the mystery.

The consensus among medical scientists is: Most victims of heart attack and stroke have arteries plugged with cholesterol, and the amount of cholesterol available in the blood for creating such plugs can be influenced by the fats in food. This does not prove that a high cholesterol level causes disease, or that fat consumption is crucial in determining cholesterol level. Many other influences could be at work. Culture, which affects the kinds of activities people engage in, could protect or endanger some peoples. Inherited genetic characteristics, varying widely among the ethnic and racial groups of the world, could be at work. Until those factors are ruled out, any real nationwide change of diets seems unlikely.

The research designed to settle these crucial questions has produced contradictory and confusing results. Two different lines of investigation have been followed. One studies and compares groups of human beings with differing diets, or follows a single group whose diet undergoes a change. The other, by contrast, experiments with animals to explore the mechanism by which diet may induce atherosclerosis.

One of the most wide-ranging studies on national differences in diet and their connection to disease is the Seven Countries coronary disease study, organized by Dr. Ancel Keys of the University of Minnesota. The countries compared were the United States, Finland, the Netherlands, Italy, Yugoslavia, Greece and Japan. The study found clear connections in each country between heart attacks and the average blood-cholesterol level. Just as important, it showed ties between cholesterol level and the amount of saturated fat in a country's diet.

The Seven Countries study found that the Japanese, with the lowest heart attack rate, ate the lowest amount of saturated fat among the seven countries—about 3 per cent of all calories in the diet. The Finns, with the highest heart attack rate, ate the greatest amount of saturated fats, about 20 per cent of their total calories, from record consumption of butter, cheese, milk and sausage. These facts once again implicate diet but do not rule out racial or cultural influences. There is evidence that race—inherited characteristics—may not matter. This evidence comes from people who have abandoned their national diets, wholly or partly.

When someone from a low-risk population migrates to a high-risk country, he generally begins consuming the high-risk diet common in his new home. If that is the only change in his life style and if some strong, nondietary factor—such as racial origin—is really the critical cause of heart disease, his risk of contracting disease should not change. But it does change, as studies of a variety of peoples have demonstrated. One group of researchers traced Japanese who moved to California—and found that they suffered 10 times as much coronary heart disease as their countrymen did in Japan. Similar studies followed Irish who joined their compatriots in Boston, Italians who moved to New York and Yemenite Jews who went to Israel. In each case the move from a relatively low-risk area to one of high risk was accompanied by a rise in the incidence of heart disease.

Observations of certain small groups pointed in the same direction. These groups were native inhabitants of high-risk countries but adhered to diets that were not typical of their regions. Dr. Castelli singled out one such group in the United States. "We tend to scoff at vegetarians," he said, "yet we should remember that certain groups like the Seventh-day Adventists, who live on a vegetarian diet, have less than half the heart-attack rate of American men on the average."

How much a vegetarian diet can affect cholesterol level was revealed in a survey led by Dr. Edward Kass of Harvard Medical School. He and his team rang doorbells all over Boston to find patterns of high blood pressure in vegetarian families and to spot young children with elevated pressures. During this survey he singled out 18 small communes of vegetarians for closer study. The blood pressures of the men in these groups were amazingly low, an average 110/62, compared with the American average of 131/83. "These people's cholesterol levels," said Dr. Castelli, "were incredible—an average of 125, lower than the Japanese average and about half the American average."

This kind of evidence corroborates other indications that people living on low-fat diets have low blood-cholesterol levels and few heart attacks; but it goes further. It shows that if they switch from low-fat diets to high-fat ones, both cholesterol and disease levels rise. Still more convincing would be examples of the reverse: people who switched from high-fat to low-fat diets and thereafter had lower cholesterol levels and less disease. Some such examples have been found; none is conclusive. This sort of switch, of course, is given credit by some experts for the worldwide drop-off in heart-related diseases that began in the 1960s. But a more dramatic and persuasive example was provided by World War II.

The war in Europe forced dietary changes on whole areas that were occupied or attacked by the German armies. The inhabitants of those areas suffered severe food shortages; their intake of fatty foods such as meat and dairy products declined radically. At the same time atherosclerosis declined sharply among these people. In Norway, one of the best-documented cases, there was a corresponding fall in the death rate from heart disease—a decline so rapid that physicians could hardly believe it. A generation later, Norway, its fat-laden peacetime diet restored to it, was among the countries afflicted with the highest mortality from heart disease.

Looking for cause and effect

All of these observations on the diets and health of population groups led to conclusions by inference. The studies did not yield direct, cause-and-effect proof that diets produced high cholesterol levels, or that those high levels produced atherosclerosis and heart attacks. But certain experiments gave indirect support to the diet theory, establishing cause-and-effect proof that some diets could indeed cause atherosclerosis—at least in animals.

The earliest of these experiments was performed in 1913 by the Russian pathologist Nikolai N. Anitschkow. Seeking to produce the kind of cholesterol-filled plaques analyzed by Rudolf Virchow, he fed rabbits a diet loaded with such cholesterol-rich foods as animal fats. Normally these vegetarian animals never develop atherosclerosis, but on Anitschkow's abnormal diet they soon had the telltale plaques.

Since Anitschkow's time, many experiments have proved that high-fat, high-cholesterol diets can induce atherosclerosis in animals that are much closer to man than rabbits. In monkeys, scientists have stopped the progress of atherosclerosis, and even reversed its course, by changing diets.

One group of pathologists from The University of Iowa and the University of Oregon ran a long series of experiments with adult rhesus monkeys, whose normal cholesterol level is about 140. For 17 months they fed the animals a cholesterol-rich diet, driving their cholesterol levels up to about 700. Then the investigators killed and dissected the monkeys, and found that their main coronary arteries had been narrowed some 60 per cent by atherosclerosis.

To find whether these effects were reversible, the experimenters placed a second group of monkeys on the same 17-month diet, then switched them to a normal diet for 40 months. When these monkeys were sacrificed, they had two-thirds fewer atherosclerotic plaques than the first group.

Scientists cannot, of course, sacrifice human subjects to study changes in their diet. But direct, not just circumstantial, evidence of the reversibility of atherosclerosis in humans now exists, based on the examination of arteries in living patients. The changes are detected by angiography *(pages 100-101)*, in which dyes opaque to X-rays are injected into human arteries and a sequence of X-ray pictures is made.

In one study at the University of Southern California, Dr. David Blankenhorn used diet and drugs to lower abnormally high fat levels in the blood of patients who had detectable plaques in their leg arteries. Angiograms taken about 13 months apart showed a reduction of plaques. In another study, headed by Dr. David T. Nash of the State University of New York, atherosclerosis in some coronary heart disease patients was halted, and in at least one case reversed, by drugs, such as colestipol, that lower blood fats.

Pieces that do not fit

From all of these observations and experiments, a mosaic of evidence has been assembled, a mosaic that most cardiologists consider a fairly accurate picture of the relationship between diet, cholesterol, atherosclerosis and circulatory disease. But there are still gaps in the mosaic, chinks that remain to be filled in. And there are pieces left over, pieces that do not fit the pattern at all. These discrepancies have made some experts cautious of—or even hostile to—any large-scale changes in dietary patterns.

One critic of the diet thesis is the English cardiologist Sir John McMichael. In a broadside in the *British Medical Journal,* McMichael wrote that he flatly did not subscribe to the view that atherosclerosis is "a nutritional disorder caused by faulty dietary habits." He added, "The time has come to reject advice to substitute polyunsaturated fats for animal and dairy fats in the nation's diet."

Part of Sir John's objections are based on population studies that do, in fact, present difficult puzzles. In Israel, for example, the records of two ethnic groups seem to defy prevailing cholesterol theory. Jewish Israelis eat a greater proportion of polyunsaturated fats than most peoples in the Western world, yet their death rate from coronary heart disease is very high, about three quarters that of the United States. The Bedouins of the Israeli desert have singularly little heart disease in their own environment, where the fats in their diet, mostly from meat and milk, are generally saturated. But when they move to Israeli towns and share in a diet higher in polyunsaturated fat, they become more—not less—prone to coronary heart disease. Obviously, neither race nor fat consumption can explain these facts.

Other puzzlements arise within a single people. In a study of the Maoris of New Zealand and nearby Polynesian islands, those with the lowest cholesterol levels turned out to have the highest death rate from heart disease. The Japanese heart attack death rate, already low, declined during a period when the consumption of saturated fat increased by 200 per cent. In Sweden the death rate rose by 6 per cent at a time when it fell rapidly in the United States, though saturated-fat consumption declined in both countries.

A persistent American critic of the diet-disease theory, Dr. George Mann of Vanderbilt University, cited the case of the Masai, a tribe of East African cattle herders, as another piece of evidence that does not fit the theory. The Masai live primarily on fermented cow's milk, rich in saturated fats, yet they are among the world's healthiest people, with virtually no heart disease. One possible answer to this puzzle is exercise, which, according to many studies, lowers the cholesterol level. Masai herdsmen walk an average of 26 miles a day—then, for amusement, compete in leaping straight up in the air. But Dr. Mann showed that the more milk the Masai drank, the lower their cholesterol levels got. One explanation for this finding may be the fermentation of the Masai's milk. At Harbor General Hospital of the University of California at Los Angeles, researchers showed that large amounts of yogurt—which is made from fermented milk—lowered blood cholesterol levels.

Contradictions to the diet-disease theory from research on the Masai or Maoris might be shrugged off. There are weightier reasons for doubt. They come from clinical trials that resemble laboratory experiments, which physicians consider more reliable than statistical evidence. In some of these trials, continued for as long as 12 years, selected groups of men and women were carefully kept on diets low in saturated fats. Their cholesterol levels and death rates were compared with those of other groups on diets differing only in fat content. Such studies were carried out in London, Oslo, Helsinki, New York City and Los Angeles. The outcome was disappointing. The subjects on the low-fat diets had lower cholesterol levels than those in the control groups. But the difference in death rates between the paired groups was insignificant. The low-fat diets and lowered cholesterol levels did not seem to forestall heart-related diseases.

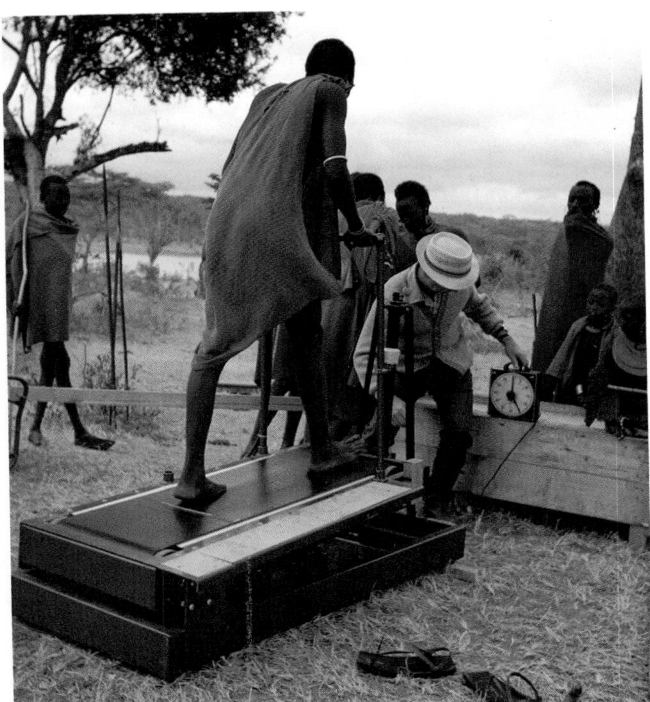

His spear and sandals hastily discarded nearby, a Masai warrior paces briskly on the motorized treadmill that Vanderbilt University's Dr. George Mann (adjusting timer) used to measure endurance, a sign of heart health. The average tribesman, toughened by extensive walking, could keep up with the treadmill 23 minutes, nine more than the average U.S. college man.

Similar results were obtained from an allied type of research involving 15,000 men over six years in Prague, Edinburgh and Budapest, and 8,000 men over five years in the United States. They were given drugs that eliminate cholesterol from the blood. The drugs did this, but not much else—the effect on disease was unimpressive.

The other suspects

The general response to anomalous studies is precisely that they are anomalies, outweighed by the bulk of the evidence. Yet alternative theories abound, exonerating dietary cholesterol and implicating other agents in heart-related disease.

At Cornell Medical College Dr. C. Richard Minick and his colleagues found that a virus called herpes induced atherosclerosis in chickens, suggesting that infection rather than diet was a cause. However, even in his experiments, diet appeared to be a factor. Birds injected with the virus and put on high-fat diets got more plaques and more severe ones than chickens subjected to the virus alone.

Another proposal, by Dr. Kilmer McCully at Harvard University, indicted a shortage of vitamin B_6 in the body. Dr. McCully believes the vitamin converts a dangerous metabolic by-product called homycysteine, which has induced atherosclerosis in laboratory animals, into a harmless substance.

One possible cause of disease remains genetics. Despite the statistics compiled from population studies, the differences among individuals cannot be ignored. Human beings vary widely in their responses to identical diets. In some the level of cholesterol in the blood remains about the same, even if the amount they consume changes drastically from meal to meal. In another group, called the responders, a fat-rich meal leads to a sharp rise in cholesterol level. The difference between the two groups is probably inborn.

Genetic make-up, for example, may make you respond to a diet by maintaining a higher cholesterol level than most other persons eating the same foods. Following a typical American diet, you might develop a cholesterol level of 260, while your neighbor, eating exactly the same, might have a level of 220. But this range of responses occurs in every population, with every kind of diet. On a Japanese diet you would be on the high end of the cholesterol levels for Japanese—perhaps 180, against the Japanese average of 140.

Such alternatives to the diet theory provoke sharp arguments. Dr. Castelli brusquely dismissed the vitamin B_6 proposal: "If people think they can go out and eat all the hamburgers they want and then be safe by taking vitamin B_6, they're crazy." Controversy can get heated even over something so seemingly simple as eggs. No less an authority than the great heart surgeon Dr. Michael DeBakey once said, "There is nothing wrong with having an egg breakfast every morning." But Dr. Castelli, noting that the cholesterol is all in the yolk, suggested "three fried egg whites, an excellent source of protein, for breakfast." And Dr. Jeremiah Stamler

Lipoproteins: molecules that counter cholesterol

Studies of six ethnic groups, pulled together for the first time in the charts below, help explain why cholesterol, a substance long known to clog arteries, cannot be a simple cause of heart disease. Eskimos, for example, have the highest cholesterol levels of all the groups but the lowest disease rate.

It has been found that it is not cholesterol itself but the compounds carrying cholesterol, called lipoproteins, that influence risk. One type, high-density lipoprotein (HDL), counteracts the bad effects of cholesterol. The upper chart indicates total cholesterol level *(yellow)* and HDL level *(orange)*. The ratio of total cholesterol to HDL level, indicated in the lower graph, seems to be a good measure of heart disease risk—the Eskimos, with the lowest ratio, have the fewest heart attacks, while the California Japanese, with the highest ratio, have the most.

What increases the heart-protecting HDLs may be different in each case. For the Eskimos it is probably a diet that, although high in fat, is low in saturated fat. For the Georgia blacks and Swedes it may be exercise. And the California Japanese, like most Americans, having forsaken their ancestors' spartan regimen, suffer presumbably because of a fatty diet, cigarettes and sedentary habits.

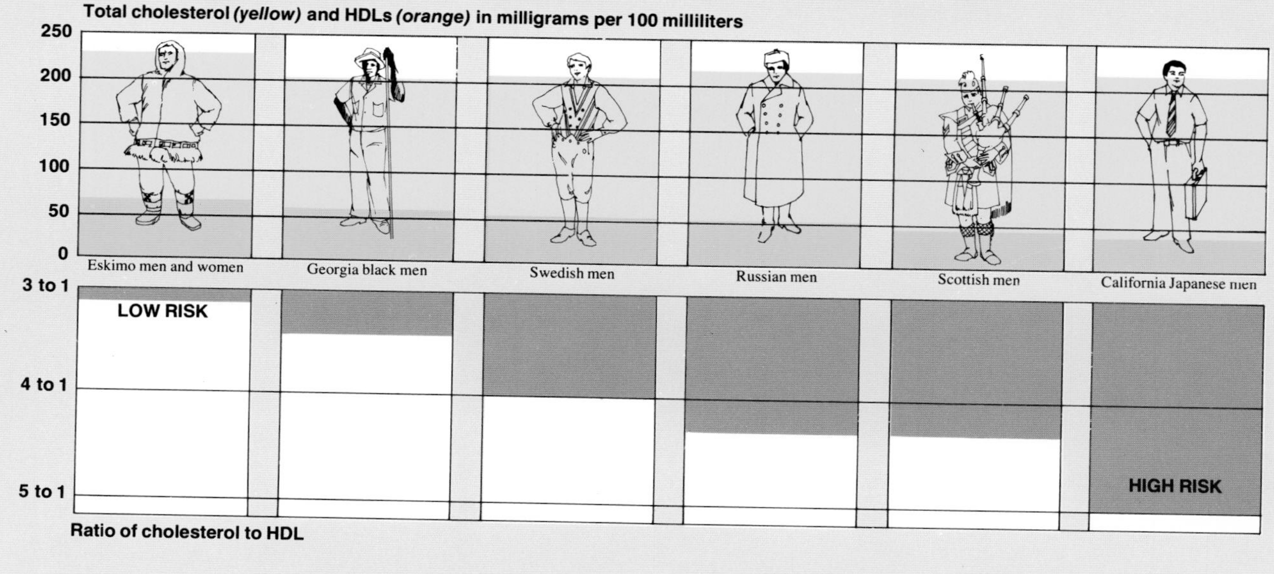

of Northwestern University went further: "I think we should restore the egg to its original function, making chickens. As far as I'm concerned, the fewer eggs eaten the better. And none isn't bad."

Not cholesterol but HDLs

Although most experts are quick to dismiss alternatives to the cholesterol theory of heart disease, they do not deride a refinement of it that almost amounts to an alternative. This modified view comes from the discovery that some types of cholesterol may actually be good for you. The findings may help to dispel the contradictions in the diet theory.

The modified diet theory is based upon new knowledge about all fats in the blood—not only cholesterol but also substances called triglycerides, which make up 98 to 99 per cent of the weight of food fats. Neither cholesterol nor the triglycerides dissolve in water; in their unaltered form these essential compounds cannot travel in the bloodstream, which consists mainly of water. In the human body the blood fats are linked with proteins to form molecules that are soluble in water. These "freight" molecules, which carry fats in the blood, are called lipoproteins.

Researchers have known for years that the lipoproteins fall into four major groups, classified according to density. The lightest (that is, those of the lowest density) pick up triglycerides from food fats. They consist of up to 95 per cent triglycerides, with a small cargo of cholesterol.

Next in weight come VLDLs, an abbreviation for very low density lipoproteins. They carry only 15 per cent of the cholesterol moving in the blood.

Heavier still are LDLs, or low-density lipoproteins. These are rich in cholesterol, transporting about 65 per cent of the cholesterol in the blood.

Heaviest of all are the HDLs, the high-density lipoproteins, which carry only about 20 per cent of blood cholesterol. Their cholesterol content, however, is less important than the fact that they are apparently heroes in the cholesterol drama. The villain has turned out to be not cholesterol alone, but cholesterol in LDLs.

As early as 1951, Dr. David Barr of Cornell University found that men with coronary heart disease generally have lower than average HDL levels; later studies showed that men with the high total-cholesterol levels linked to heart disease also have high LDL levels. Apparently LDLs are the major source of the cholesterol deposited in the plaques of atherosclerosis. But the role of HDLs was virtually ignored for over two decades.

Then, starting in the mid-1970s, statistics began to show that low levels of HDL were actually a warning sign of heart attack. The populations studied were diverse. Among them were male civil servants in Albany, New York, blacks and whites of a rural community in Georgia, men of Japanese ancestry living in San Francisco and Honolulu, and the faithful participants in the long-term Framingham study. All the studies seemed to show that HDLs protect against heart disease—that is, the higher the HDL level, the lower the risk.

One widely accepted theory holds that HDLs act as scavengers, gathering cholesterol from cells and tissues and returning it to the liver. Another theory suggests that HDLs interfere with the absorption of LDL cholesterol within cells.

Whatever the explanation, the facts are clear. Among the Framingham subjects, for example, the average man has an HDL level of 45 (measured in milligrams per 100 milliliters), the average woman 55. The discrepancy may help to account for the lower rate of heart attack in women. For every five points HDL level falls below the 45 mark, the risk of coronary heart disease increases by 25 per cent. On the other hand, very high HDL readings seem to confer longevity. Families have been found with HDL levels over 75—apparently inherited—and members of these families live into their eighties and nineties relatively free of atherosclerosis.

In the light of such facts, Framingham's Dr. Castelli believes that HDL levels must be worked into new calculations of heart disease risk. Instead of gauging risk by the total cholesterol level, as in the past, he proposed an index number based on the ratio of total cholesterol to HDL. Statistical analysis of the Framingham subjects showed that this index is a more accurate predictor of the risk of coronary heart disease than either HDL or total cholesterol alone.

The index assigns standard, high and low risks. For men a

ratio of about 5 is the standard risk of getting coronary heart disease; for women, about 4.5. A ratio of about 10 for men means twice the standard risk.

Life styles and HDLs

The new knowledge of HDLs is directly useful because you can take advantage of it on your own to change your HDL level and possibly reduce your risk of disease. Several ways to improve the ratio of cholesterol to HDL are fairly well established. Diet remains important—eating less cholesterol and saturated fat may change the ratio in your favor. But also important are smoking, drinking and exercise.

The value of exercise is most clearly established. Considerable evidence indicates that men who run regularly have significantly better HDL levels than inactive men. One of the first to detect the link between HDLs and exercise was Dr. Peter D. Wood of the Stanford University Heart Disease Prevention Program, himself a lifelong marathon runner.

Dr. Wood's work on HDL levels began with observations of his own body. Finding that his HDL level was unusually good, he set up a blood-testing program involving runners and sedentary men and women. The middle-aged subjects he chose had each run at least 15 miles a week for the previous year (most of them had averaged about 40 miles per week). Comparisons of their blood fats with those of inactive subjects from the same area of Northern California were striking. The average ratio of cholesterol to HDL among the runners was 3.1, among the sedentary control subjects 4.9.

These comparisons do not prove the relationship between HDLs and exercise. Wood's intensive runners, like most long-distance runners, were thin, and thin people have good HDL ratios. Runners may have better HDL ratios than other people because they are leaner to begin with, not because they exercise more. Only large-scale studies can tell whether sedentary, overweight people can, after participating in exercise programs, improve their HDL levels.

Other methods of modifying HDL levels are less certain. Many studies suggest that alcohol can improve HDL ratios, but Dr. Wood found only small differences between drinkers and nondrinkers in his experimental groups. Moreover, the improvement that moderate drinking—usually defined as two drinks a day—can bring is limited, and more drinking risks liver disease, cancer and heart-muscle damage.

There are some things not to do—smoking, for one, is clearly bad for the HDL pattern. A study of more than 5,000 men and women by the National Heart, Lung, and Blood Institute found that men who smoked 20 cigarettes a day were poorer in HDL levels than nonsmokers by 11 per cent; women smokers averaged 14 per cent poorer than nonsmokers. The difference appears even in adolescence. An investigation of Cincinnati school children 12 to 19 years old showed that those who smoked had HDL levels 11 per cent worse than their nonsmoking schoolmates. Coffee seems to intensify the effect of smoking on HDLs, worsening the ratio still more, reports Dr. Siegfried Hayden of Duke University.

It is easy to see how a growing understanding of the role of lipoproteins may help to resolve contradictions in the cholesterol controversy. The Masai, for example, who live on saturated fats yet have low cholesterol levels and little heart disease, may owe their good health to their continual walking, which seems to improve HDL levels.

A similar paradox involving the Eskimos may also be explained by HDLs. Heart disease is very rare among these people, though they eat a great deal of fat and have cholesterol levels even higher than the United States average. Among the foods comparable to those favored by Eskimos are scallops, oysters and red caviar—all laden with cholesterol. But more than 20 per cent of this seafood consists of an unusual, highly unsaturated fat called eicosapentaenoic acid. It may be connected with another characteristic of the Eskimos, one that presumably explains their freedom from disease: Their average HDL ratio is only 3.2—almost two full numbers better than the standard risk. (The journal *Medical Tribune* greeted the news about the Eskimos with a gleeful headline: "Bring On the Oysters and Caviar.")

A prudent course

What is now known about HDLs may clarify the connection between diet and circulatory ailments, but it also indicates how complex that connection is. The chain of evidence is long, stretching from acute disease to visible plaques of cholesterol in arteries, cholesterol in the blood, saturated fats, lipoproteins and finally to food habits, genetic inheritance, exercise, drinking and smoking. What is more, every link in that chain is circumstantial; there is no direct proof that one leads inevitably to another. They are associated one with another, like people noted as present at the scene of a crime. Like those people, they could be innocent bystanders or they could be guilty of the crime.

The circumstantial nature of the evidence against fatty foods makes some authorities reluctant to act on it. The action called for is drastic: a radical change in the balance of foods eaten by people in the industrialized world. If you were to follow exactly the diet recommended by the most fervent apostles of the diet theory, you would have to do more than cut down on fat consumption. You would have to cut out many of the foods that are traditional favorites of Europeans and Americans. For example, you could eat no butter, no whole milk, and no eggs at all. You could eat no more than one small serving of red meat—one hamburger or one slice of beef—per week. No one can predict the side effects on health that might accompany such a change if it were applied to everyone, old and young, healthy and sick. The social and economic effects are foreseeable—and enormous.

"Are you a no-cholesterol doctor or are you one of those no-cholesterol-is-all-bosh doctors?"

Drawing by Stan Hunt; © 1959 The New Yorker Magazine, Inc.

Yet the circumstantial evidence seems overwhelming. With few exceptions, people of all races in all parts of the world are less prone to circulatory disease if they eat little fat, particularly saturated fat. Their low-fat diets do not seem to bring about other health problems.

These facts lead to a consensus. In the United States, official public-health agencies have urged everyone to reduce the consumption of fatty foods; however, a few semi-official agencies would limit this advice to those who show such signs of susceptibility to heart disease as excess weight or high blood pressure. Elsewhere in the world, official opinion has been practically unanimous. In the United Kingdom, Germany, Sweden and Finland, governmental agencies have campaigned vigorously for diets lower in fat content.

Changing your diet is up to you. If you wish to protect yourself against heart-related disease, the recommended course is simple: Eat much less meat, fewer eggs, and little or no butter or whole milk. Eat more fish and chicken. Get more of your diet from fruits and vegetables. And, of course, exercise a lot, drink only moderately and do not smoke.

No one can guarantee that such a combination of diet and life style will prevent disease. Some authorities doubt that medical science will ever resolve, once and for all, the controversy over the diet-disease theory. But even in their resignation these doubters strike a positive note. Dr. Donald Fredrickson, Director of the National Institutes of Health, put it this way: "We've more or less adjusted to the fact that we probably never will be able to get the kind of ideal proof that we want." But he added, "The weight of the evidence seems to be strong enough so that we can now direct people toward a set of guidelines." ❋

CHAPTER 4

A spectrum of ills and remedies

The dangers of high blood pressure
Stroke: an accident inside the brain
Angina pain from a starved heart
When the pump fails
Valves damaged by childhood fever

"The treatment of hypertension is a difficult and almost hopeless task in the present state of our knowledge." In 1931 those despairing words from the eminent cardiologist Paul Dudley White painted a bleak—but accurate—picture for people with the most common disease of the heart and blood vessels: high blood pressure, the condition in which the blood presses against the walls of the arteries with unusual force. Indeed, in Dr. White's day little was known of hypertension, and less could be done to correct it.

In the decades since, medical understanding of hypertension and other diseases that attack the heart and blood vessels has grown exponentially. Improved diagnostic techniques have enabled doctors to spot trouble before irreparable damage is done. New drugs and ingenious surgical techniques have given physicians the tools to prevent or at least ameliorate most heart and blood-vessel ailments, including high blood pressure, and have turned Dr. White's words of frustration into relics of a seemingly distant past.

To a great extent these encouraging advances depend on recently acquired knowledge of the circulatory system and its ills. This new understanding has brought more efficient control of the most formidable cardiovascular killers, which usually strike the middle-aged and elderly: high blood pressure; stroke, in which part of the brain dies for lack of blood; heart attack, in which part of the heart muscle dies; and congestive heart failure, in which the heart pumps too weakly.

Young victims of heart disease can look forward to brighter futures, too. Thanks largely to antibiotics, the incidence of rheumatic fever, a childhood illness that can damage the heart, has plunged since the 1940s. Most structural malformations present at birth, the dreaded congenital heart diseases, can be repaired surgically if they cannot be treated or cured with medicines.

Of all the serious circulatory ailments, the one that has been put under long-term control most successfully is high blood pressure, or hypertension. It is not merely the most prevalent heart and blood-vessel disease—though it certainly is that, afflicting an estimated 8 to 18 per cent of adults in the industrialized world. It is perhaps the most dangerous, usually striking without symptoms and often abetting a host of other cardiovascular killers. One of its most frequent consorts is stroke; the brain's blood vessels roughen and wear out as blood pounds their walls with extra force. Paradoxically, high blood pressure is probably the least understood circulatory disease. Many people even misinterpret its medical name, believing "hypertension" means "nervous tension." Make no mistake: Calm people, too, suffer hypertension.

In everyone, hypertensive or not, the force that blood exerts against the walls of the arteries varies during each heartbeat. When the heart contracts, the blood pressure rises to its highest level, the systolic pressure; when the heart relaxes, the pressure drops to its minimum, the diastolic pressure. What distinguishes the ill from the healthy is their levels of both systolic and diastolic pressures.

A complex combination of bodily actions determines these limits. Some of the factors are purely physical: the volume of

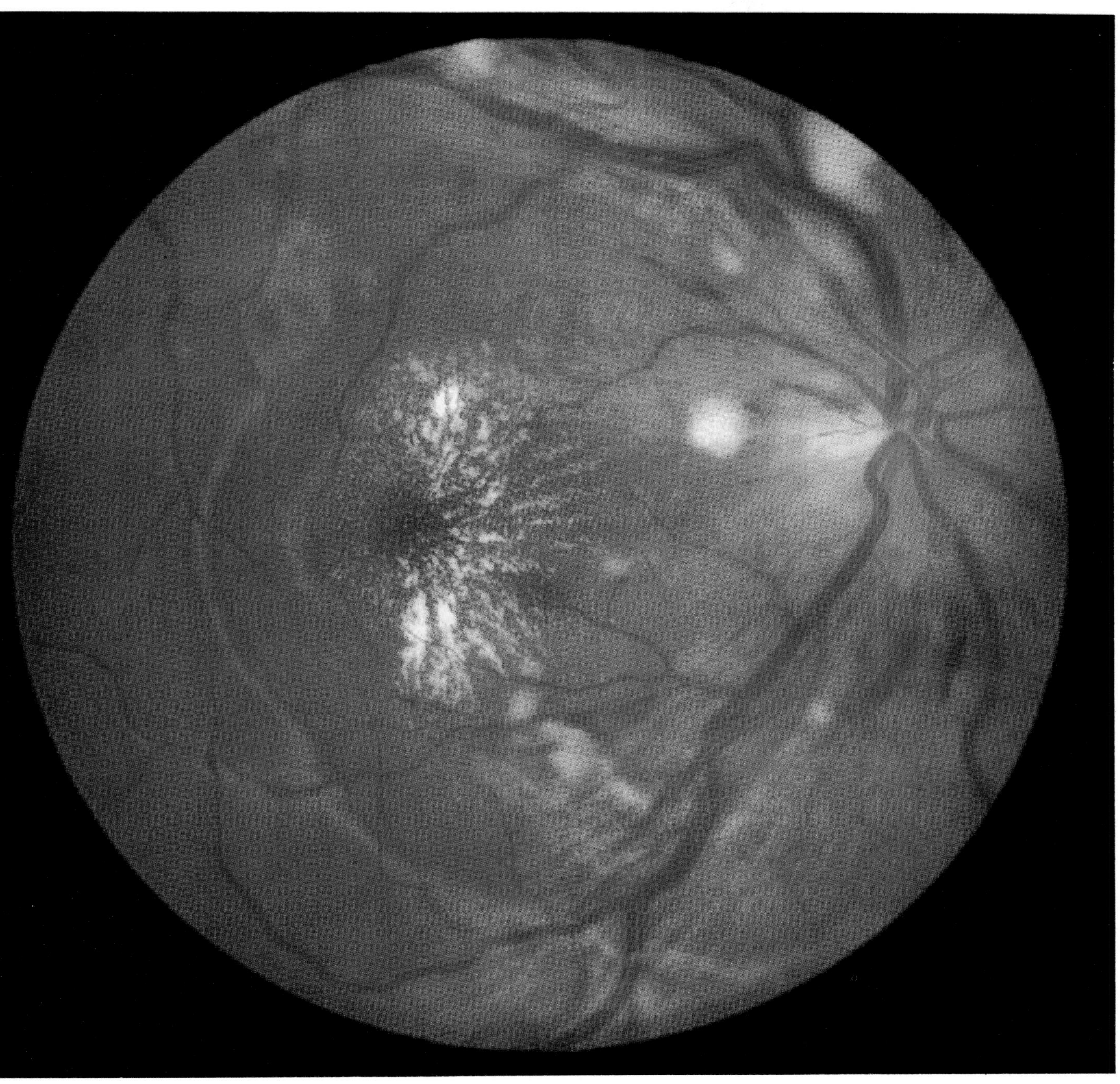

The only parts of the circulatory system that are readily visible are blood vessels in the retina of the eye (wavy red lines, above)— they can be seen by looking through the pupil. What the doctor watches for is a macular star (left of center), produced by fluids from vessels damaged by dangerously high blood pressure.

blood in the body, the amount that can be expelled by the heart with each beat, the resistance the blood meets as it is pumped into the aorta and then squeezed into progressively smaller blood vessels.

A second group of actions is strictly chemical. Certain glands and organs produce compounds that are released into the bloodstream, altering the circulatory system. The adrenal glands, located above the kidneys, give off adrenaline and noradrenaline. These hormones stimulate the heart to pump harder and they cause certain blood vessels, particularly the smaller arteries, to constrict. Another adrenal hormone, aldosterone, makes the body retain salt and water, boosting blood volume and thus changing blood pressure. The kidneys produce yet another enzyme, renin, which reacts in the bloodstream with other chemicals to create two new substances—angiotensin I and angiotensin II—that produce cardiovascular changes.

A third set of pressure regulators is part of the autonomic nervous system, which controls such involuntary functions as breathing, heartbeat and digestion. Like thermostats detecting heat in a house, nerve cells called baroreceptors monitor blood pressure. When pressure varies greatly, baroreceptors sense the change and emit electrical impulses that tell the heart and blood vessels to return to normal.

When any one of the regulators malfunctions, blood pressure changes—and the change is usually an increase rather than a decrease. Among physical regulators are the arteries, which may become hardened and narrowed with fatty deposits, increasing resistance to blood flow and thus boosting pressure. In addition, some people are born with an aorta that is pinched, and their blood must be pumped at higher pressure to pass the bottleneck. Affecting the chemical regulators may be tumors of the adrenal glands, which may cause the glands to secrete abnormal amounts of adrenaline, noradrenaline or aldosterone, elevating pressure. Or diseased kidneys may release more renin than usual, raising pressure downstream.

Finally, the nerve regulators may fail. The baroreceptors may, in effect, reset and tell the body that pressure is normal when it actually is high. These specific causes of hypertension are readily identifiable, but they occur so rarely that they are considered secondary causes. In about nine out of 10 cases, doctors cannot tell which of the regulators is malfunctioning, or why. Such high blood pressure is labeled "essential," a medical euphemism for "of undetermined origin."

Fortunately, measuring the magnitude of high blood pressure is easier than determining its cause. In the 18th Century, an inquisitive English parson named Stephen Hales made the first attempt to measure blood pressure directly—in a horse. He inserted a long glass tube into the neck artery of the animal and discovered that the blood rose to a level of seven and a half feet—which Hales decided was normal blood pressure for a horse. This was not a practical method for learning human blood pressures—seven horses

High pressure, high risk of stroke

The message from one scientific study after another is clarion: To avoid stroke, avoid high blood pressure. This goes for people of all ages, and for those in whom either of the two numbers used to specify blood pressure is considered elevated. The chart below, based on the Framingham heart study, shows that for people aged 45 to 74 the incidence of stroke increases more than fourfold as blood pressure rises from normal, through borderline, to hypertensive.

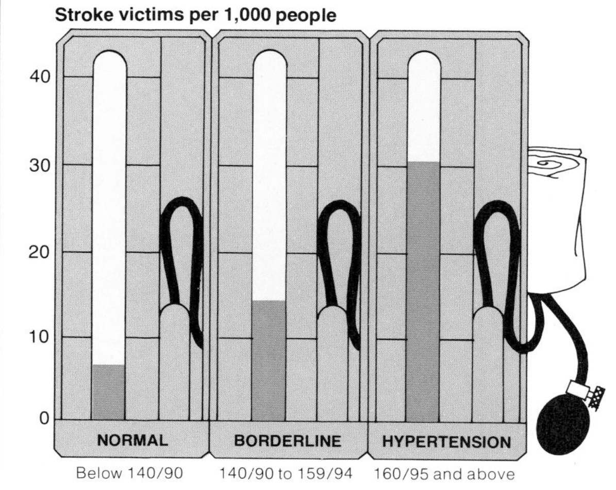

died in the course of the Reverend Mr. Hales's experiments.

Medically minded inventors persisted over the years, however, devising and refining gauges that led to the modern sphygmomanometer *(pages 73-76)*. This device compares pressure inside the brachial artery—the major artery in the arm—with air pressure generated in an inflatable cuff. The numbers in a blood pressure reading correspond to the height (in millimeters) of a column of mercury that the air in the cuff can raise in a tube. If your blood pressure is 120/80, it means that the systolic pressure in your arteries is sufficient to support a column of mercury 120 millimeters high; the diastolic pressure, 80 millimeters.

Different doctors, hospitals and research studies categorize blood pressure levels in different ways: What one doctor considers normal, another may view as elevated. But a strong medical consensus has emerged suggesting that blood pressure of 120/80 is normal and desirable for a healthy adult. A reading of 140/90 generally is regarded as the threshold of hypertension—the level at which many doctors elect to place a person under medical care—while values significantly higher than the threshold level, especially those higher than 160/95, are almost universally classified as dangerously hypertensive. Values in between are considered borderline. Very low readings may indicate illness, although highly conditioned athletes will sometimes have readings somewhat lower than normal.

The dangers of high blood pressure

Definitions of normal, borderline and high blood pressure are far from arbitrary. Pressures higher than 120/80 mean that the heart must pump unnaturally hard to circulate blood. Over time, the muscle may fail from the added strain. High pressures encourage fatty plaques to build up abnormally fast in the coronary arteries. This may clog the arteries completely, starving the heart of its supply of blood. High blood pressure injures and weakens blood vessels in the brain, the kidneys and the eyes. This can lead in turn to strokes, kidney failure and blindness.

Although high blood pressure affects different people in various ways, its ravages are matters of medical fact. For example, the Framingham study *(Chapter 2)* showed that risks of death or disability from stroke, coronary artery disease or kidney failure rose sharply as soon as blood pressure exceeded 120/80.

Insurance companies' actuarial tables make an even more convincing case for keeping blood pressure normal. One table stated that a 35-year-old man with a blood pressure of 120/80 can expect to live an additional 41½ years, but that a man of the same age with a blood pressure of 140/95 can expect to live only 37½ years more. Raise the numbers only slightly and the stakes go up significantly. The 35-year-old man who has a blood pressure of 150/100 has a life expectancy of only 25 more years.

Clearly, then, there is no safe level above normal. If you are told you have high blood pressure, follow your doctor's instructions for lowering it. In contrast to the situation of the 1930s, doctors today know how to reduce blood pressure to nonthreatening levels in about 85 per cent of the cases. Sometimes the treatment is remarkably simple—steps that you take on your own.

If you are overweight, the first step in your treatment will probably be to reduce *(page 42)*. Obesity imposes an added burden on the heart because blood volume increases with body weight. To circulate the extra blood through an extra-large body, the heart must pump at higher pressure.

If you smoke, you may be told to stop. The nicotine in tobacco smoke is widely believed to constrict blood vessels and boost blood pressure.

You may be told to cut down on your salt intake. The sodium contained in salt makes the body retain fluid. Increased fluid retention raises the total volume of blood flowing through the circulatory system and hence raises the blood pressure. In about one out of every three cases of hypertension, a diet that stringently restricts sodium intake leads to some lowering of blood pressure. This means eliminating or sharply curbing your consumption of such salty foods as dill pickles, luncheon meats, corned beef, bacon, ham, canned soups, cheeses (except dry cottage cheese), bakery goods and many commercially canned or frozen vegetables *(pages 58-59)*. Many seasonings—ketchup, relishes, soy sauce and, of course, table salt—should be avoided altogether.

Medically supervised exercise programs can help reduce blood pressure, too. So can learning to relax for short periods of time during the working day, at night and on weekends. Blood pressure drops as you relax, and it reaches a daily low while you sleep.

Many doctors now advocate specific relaxation techniques as a means of treating high blood pressure. Some of these methods, such as yoga and meditation, have their roots in ancient religious rituals. Others, such as biofeedback *(page 37),* employ the latest technology. One noted experiment, conducted by Dr. Herbert Benson of Boston's Beth Israel Hospital, showed that relaxation techniques, including biofeedback, can help many borderline hypertensives reach normal blood pressure levels.

For many other hypertensives, however, it is not enough to lose weight, stop smoking, eliminate salt from the diet, exercise or learn to relax. These people need active medical treatment that must be prescribed by a physician and usually includes antihypertensive drugs.

For years, medical science struggled to discover compounds that lowered blood pressure. Doctors in many cases prescribed sedatives such as phenobarbitol for hypertensive patients, but the results were disappointing. Then, in the 1950s, a variety of potent pressure-reducing drugs became available *(pages 79-81).*

At first, doctors were somewhat reluctant to prescribe these new medications—particularly for mild or borderline hypertension. They were afraid that drug therapy was not worth the bother, the expense and the possible side effects. These can include weakness, sleepiness, digestive upsets, lethargy and sexual problems. Some antihypertensive medicines have produced fainting episodes in their users, caused by sudden drops in blood pressure to very low levels when posture changed abruptly.

But the evidence favoring drug therapy has come to outweigh most such reservations. Results of the Veterans Administration Cooperative Study, published in 1967 and 1970, showed that for 500 middle-aged American men who had moderate or severe hypertension, drug therapy reduced significantly the incidence of other forms of cardiovascular disease and death.

Still, many physicians remained hesitant to prescribe drugs for patients with mild or borderline hypertension. Then, at the end of the 1970s came overwhelming scientific evidence that aggressive drug therapy could prove a lifesaver even for mild hypertensives.

In a five-year study called the Hypertension Detection and Follow-up Program, the National Heart, Lung, and Blood Institute screened almost 159,000 Americans between the ages of 30 and 69. Using an arbitrary dividing line—diastolic pressure above 90—the researchers selected almost 11,000 subjects as having some degree of hypertension, and divided that group into three categories: those with diastolic pressures between 90 and 104, those with pressures between 105 and 114, and those with pressures above 115. About half of the patients in each group then were referred to their physicians or local clinics for care. The remaining half of the patients in each group were treated with drugs designed to bring diastolic pressure below 90. If one drug failed to work, another was added, until some patients received as many as four drugs simultaneously.

The results were persuasive for every high blood pressure group designated in the study. After five years, 17 per cent fewer hypertensives had died in the drug-treated half than in the group referred to private doctors and clinics. There were almost 45 per cent fewer deaths from stroke and 26 per cent fewer from heart attack.

More astonishing, drugs reduced the death rate among mild hypertensives—those with diastolic pressures of 90 to 105—by 20 per cent overall. Deaths from stroke dropped 45 per cent and from heart attack 46 per cent. "For the first time," said Dr. Jeremiah Stamler, a member of one of the study's data-evaluation committees, "we have clear evidence of the efficacy of therapy in so-called mild hypertension." He estimated that 66,000 lives per year could be saved in the United States if physicians would treat mild hypertensives with drug therapy.

To these initial findings was later added more proof that people with mild hypertension can benefit from drug ther-

How to take your own blood pressure

High blood pressure is not only serious in itself; it threatens greater danger: heart attack, heart failure or stroke. To follow its course, or the course of a medication program designed to control it, your doctor may want your blood pressure measured regularly, perhaps every day. You need not go to his office to have these readings made. With the kit at right—part homemade, part available at a pharmacy or a medical supply house—you can take someone else's blood pressure or your own without the help of an assistant.

The most difficult part of the job may be pronouncing the name of the basic instrument: a sphygmomanometer, which consists of a manometer (a pressure gauge) and a cuff that is wrapped around your arm and inflated to stop briefly the flow of blood in a main artery. (This interruption causes a throbbing—hence *sphygmo,* Greek for "throb.")

There are several types of sphygmomanometers. The easiest to use, though costly, is electronic, flashing a light or sounding a beep when you are to note a measurement; however, some physicians question its accuracy. The traditional instrument requires that you recognize the sounds of blood flow through a stethoscope, a skill that takes practice to acquire. For such an instrument, most doctors prefer the type with a mercury-tube gauge, but the simpler and cheaper dial type at right is recommended for home use. All are available with any of three cuff sizes: regular, for normal adults; undersized, for children and thin adults; and oversized, for large arms.

To use a nonelectronic sphygmomanometer, put the cuff on your upper arm, inflate it, then deflate it while noting pressure readings and listening with the stethoscope for the stopping and starting of the sounds of blood flow *(following pages).*

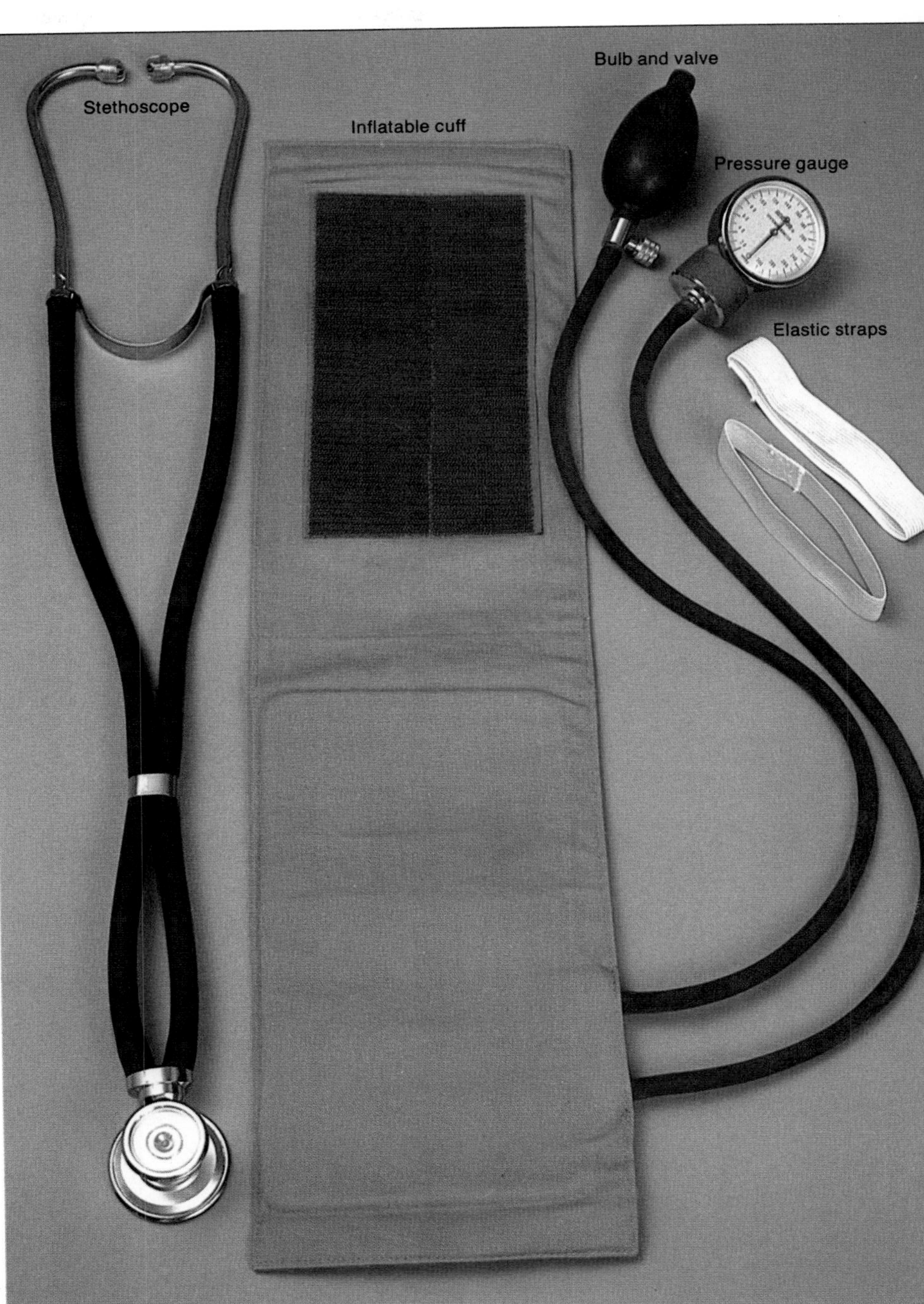

A BLOOD PRESSURE KIT
To monitor blood pressure, you need a stethoscope for detecting blood flow and a sphygmomanometer—an inflatable cuff with a pressure gauge. The two small straps at right, which hold the stethoscope on your arm, are homemade from stretch fabric (not rubber bands). They should fit snugly but not tightly.

Using the blood pressure kit

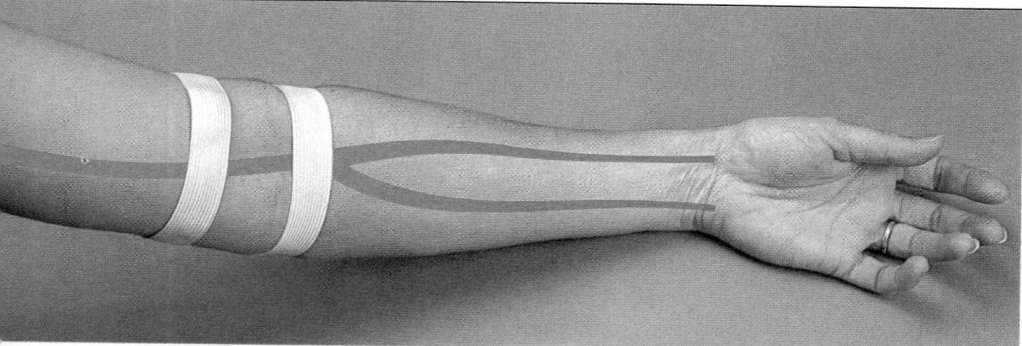

1. ADJUSTING THE STRAPS
Sitting in a chair with one arm resting on a table, slip two elastic straps over the arm, one just above the elbow, one just below. On the inside of the elbow locate the arm's main artery (indicated here in red) above the point where it branches along the forearm. This artery has a faint pulse, which you can usually detect with a finger.

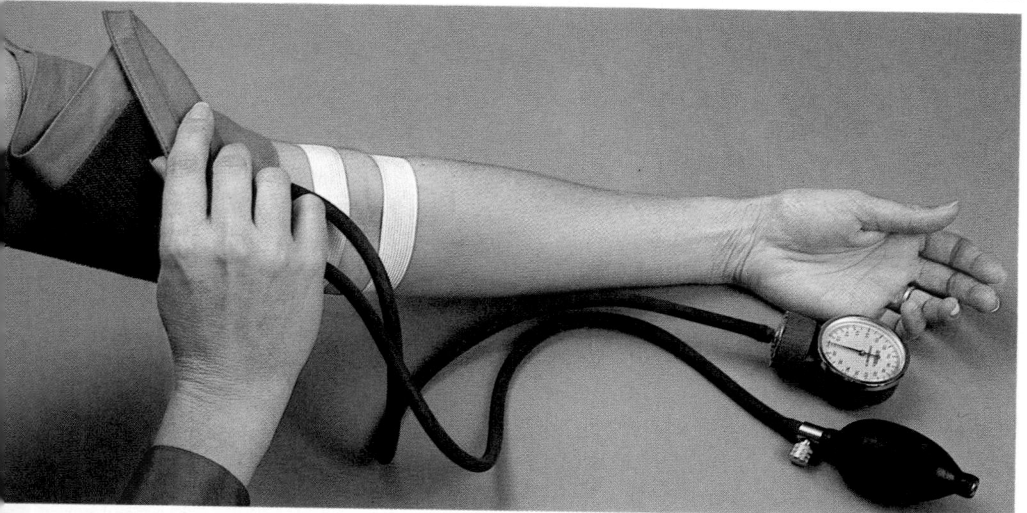

2. FITTING THE CUFF
Wrap the sphygmomanometer cuff around your upper arm firmly but not tightly, and secure it with the built-in fasteners. The inflatable bag in the cuff should lie on the inside of the arm over the artery located in Step 1; the bottom of the cuff should be about an inch above the elbow.

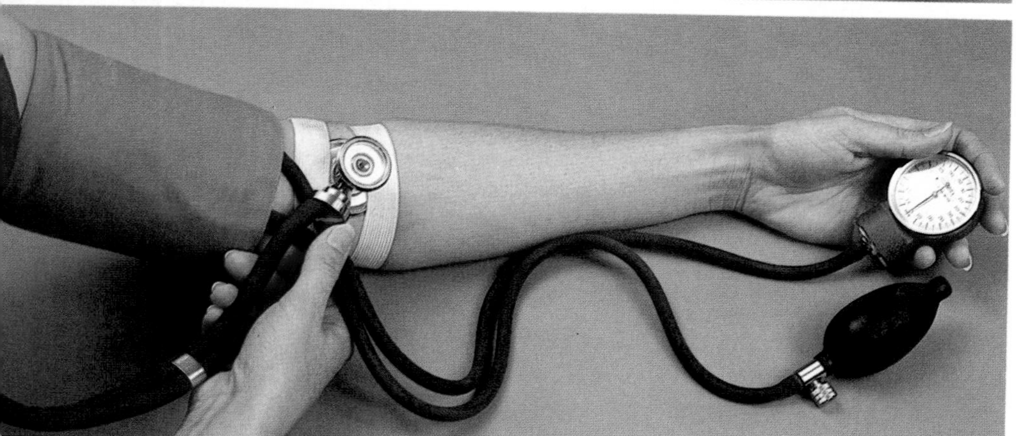

3. ATTACHING THE STETHOSCOPE
Insert the single end of the stethoscope, the diaphragm, under the elastic straps and right over the artery; set the double ends in your ears. Listen for a steady thump of blood in the artery. Take the pressure gauge in your hand for easier viewing.

4. STOPPING THE FLOW OF BLOOD
Close the valve of the bulb and pump steadily until blood flow ceases (drawing) and you no longer hear the thump of blood in the artery. Keep pumping to raise the gauge reading about 30 more points.

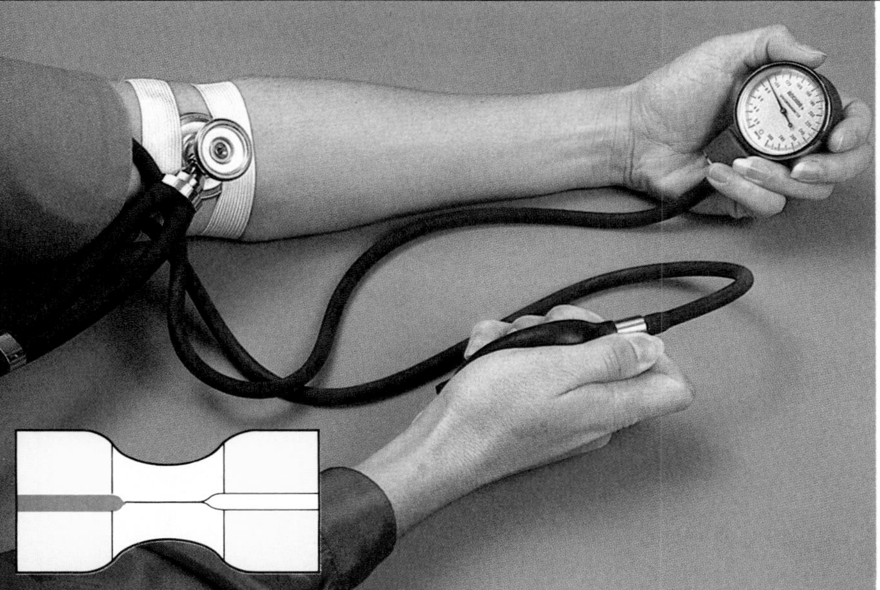

5. RESTORING THE FLOW OF BLOOD
Gently loosen the valve with your free hand, and monitor the gauge closely. The pressure in the cuff, as indicated on the gauge dial, should drop slowly—no more than five points per second.

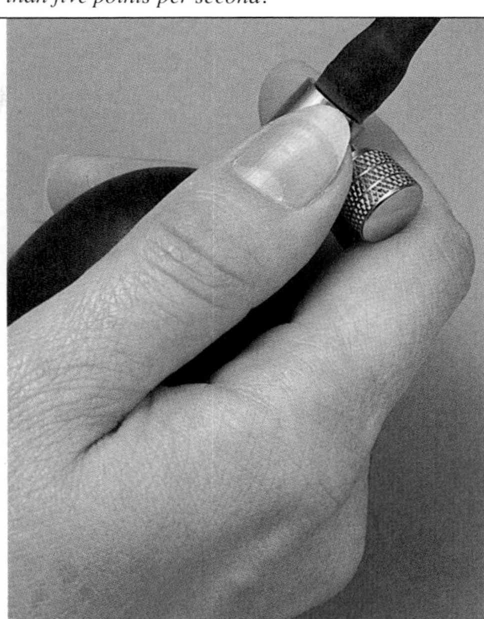

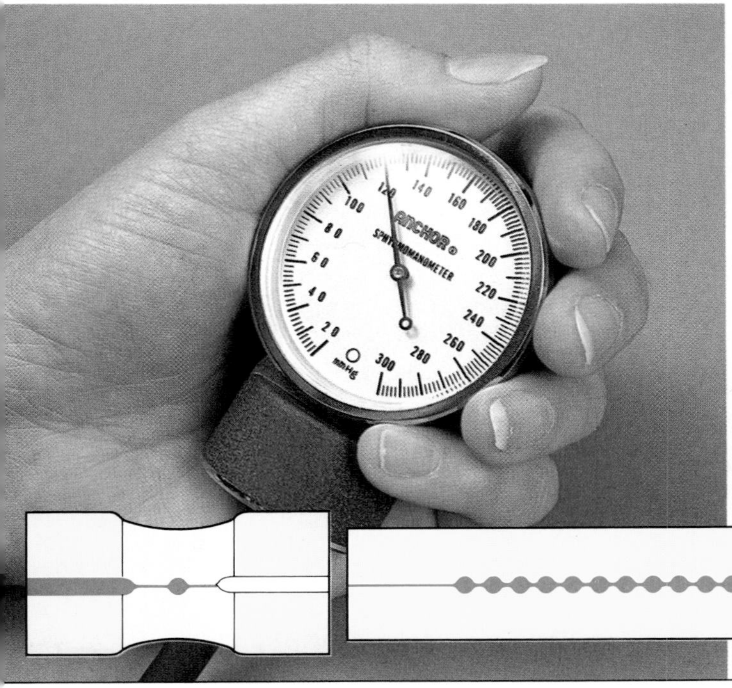

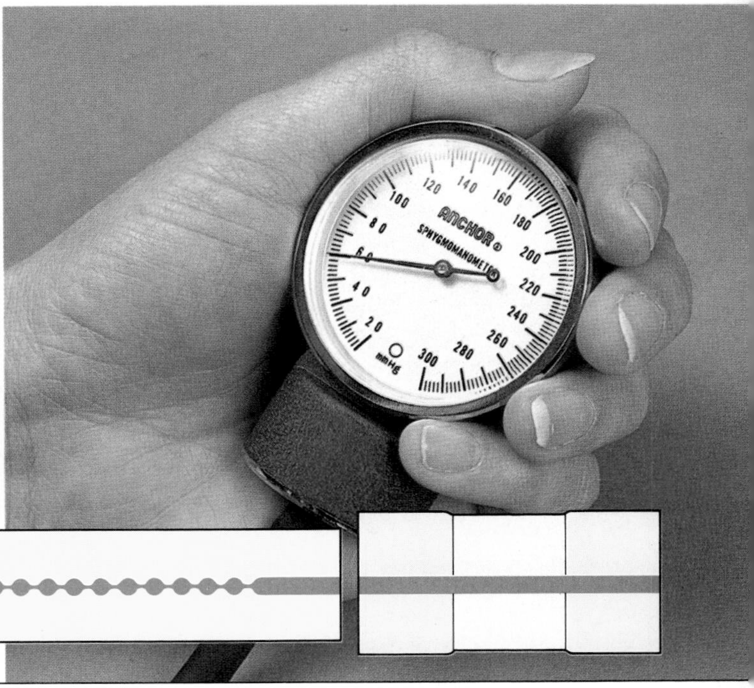

6. TAKING THE READINGS
Listen for a strong thump, which means that a surge of blood has been forced through your artery (drawing, left). At the first thump, note the reading on the gauge: This is your systolic reading—the pressure of your blood when your heart pumps. Continue listening; you will hear progressively lighter thumps, then silence. At the moment the thumps cease, read the gauge again: This is your diastolic pressure, recorded when your heart is between beats (right). The readings shown here, 120 and 60—expressed as "120 over 60"—are normal for adults. The systolic figure is more important—high pressure can lead to serious problems—but both figures tell much about health (overleaf).

Interpreting the numbers: what blood pressure readings mean

Your blood pressure is not one pressure, like air pressure in a tire, but a range of pressures, constantly changing from its diastolic minimum to its systolic maximum as your heart expands and contracts. Thus it is specified by two measurements, one at either limit of the range *(preceding pages)*. Even this range varies from day to day, hour to hour, and moment to moment. Physical exertion or nervousness can drive the range up; a cold or simply rising to your feet can push it down. Only continued high or very low readings of either pressure are cause for concern, which is one reason your doctor may want a log of pressures over time.

In the two graphs below, the normal, healthy diastolic and systolic pressures are charted by the horizontal tan bands. So long as diastolic pressure stays in the lower band and systolic in the upper, both are satisfactory. The range within these acceptable limits varies from person to person—some people have blood pressures of 140/50, others 110/80, without suffering harm. Only if either figure falls outside the satisfactory limits is disease suspected.

The actual pressures of the average person, however, differ alarmingly from those considered healthy. The blood pressure of adults in industrialized nations tends to climb with age *(below, right)*. Many people with satisfactory blood pressures at the age of 20 or 30 develop dangerously high pressures by 40 or 50.

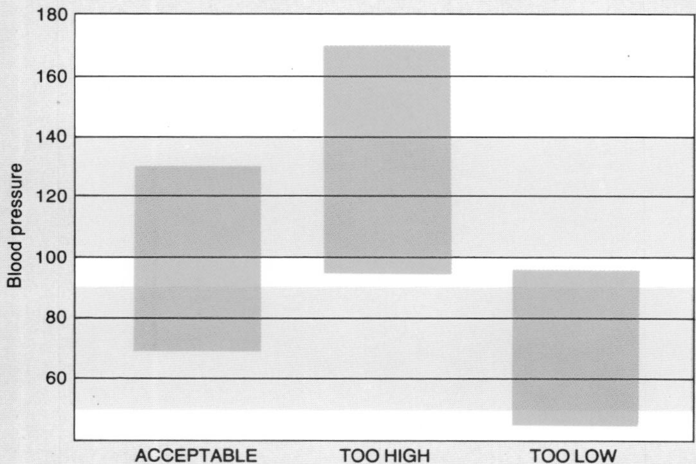

PRESSURES: NORMAL AND ABNORMAL
The horizontal bands on this chart indicate normal, healthy ranges of systolic (top band) and diastolic (bottom band) blood pressure readings; the vertical bars represent specific readings, normal and abnormal. At left a typical reading for healthy young adults is about 130/70. The bar at center suggests serious high blood pressure, with a reading of 170/95. A person with repeated high readings needs medical care for hypertension. The pressures in the right-hand bar, 95/45, though found in a very few healthy people, ordinarily would alarm a physician, suggesting shock or internal hemorrhaging.

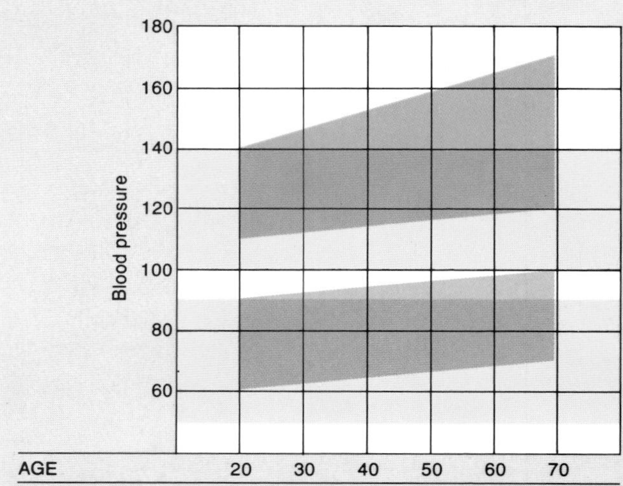

INCREASING AGE, RISING PRESSURE
As in the chart at left, the horizontal bands in this chart represent satisfactory systolic and diastolic readings. The diagonal bands indicate the actual systolic (green) and diastolic (blue) ranges of American men and women at different ages. By the age of 70 many Americans—like most industrialized peoples but unlike some still living in traditional cultures—require medical treatment to reduce blood pressure.

apy. The extra evidence, reported in 1980, came from a six-year study conducted by the National Heart Foundation of Australia. The researchers screened about 3,400 residents of Melbourne, Perth and Sydney who suffered from mild high blood pressure, which the Australian team defined as a diastolic reading between 95 and 110. The subjects were then divided into two groups: One group was given active pressure-reducing drugs; the other, placebo tablets—medically inactive tablets.

At the end of the study, Australians in the actively treated group had suffered 50 per cent fewer strokes—and of those who suffered strokes 50 per cent fewer died—than those given placebos. The overall death rate from cardiovascular disease was two-thirds lower in the drug-treated half than in the placebo half. Projected nationwide, the results of the study indicated that drug treatment of mild hypertension could reduce cardiovascular disease in Australia by 7,000 cases per year and stroke deaths by 2,000.

Thus, the case is strong for using drugs when simpler means of reducing high blood pressure fail. Luckily, half of all hypertensives can be helped by the least objectionable of the drugs—diuretics. These force the body to excrete more water and sodium than usual, reducing the total blood volume—and thus the blood pressure. Diuretics such as chlorothiazide and furosemide sometimes can lower high blood pressure by themselves. Quite often, however, diuretics are used in combination with other medications.

The choice of additional drugs depends on the degree of hypertension. It also depends on how the patient reacts to the drugs. A doctor treating a hypertensive patient may start with a low dose of one drug, increase the dose somewhat if it is ineffective, then step up to a second drug, and so on, continuing up a ladder of higher doses and different drugs until effective control is achieved.

One category of drugs often used in combination with diuretics is made up of vasodilators, such as hydralazine and diazoxide. These medications act directly on the muscle walls of blood vessels, relaxing them and causing them to enlarge. This reduces resistance to the flow of blood, and thus lowers the blood pressure.

The other major group of antihypertensive drugs, the sympatholytics, acts on the nervous system, interfering with the chemical nerve messengers that help control blood pressure. One of the oldest such drugs is the tranquilizer reserpine, which inhibits nerve messages to the adrenal glands, making them secrete less of their pressure-raising hormones. Newer sympatholytics include guanethidine, clonidine and a very promising class of drugs known as beta blockers.

Beta blockers, such as propranolol and metoprolol, obstruct nerve endings called beta receptors. Some of these receptors help control the release of the pressure-regulating hormones; others affect the power and speed of the heartbeat. When these nerve receptors are dulled by beta blockers, blood pressure drops.

If your doctor prescribes any of these drugs to lower your blood pressure, you should resist a common temptation—to stop taking the medicine once pressure has been brought under control. That is almost always a grievous error on two counts. Stopping some of these drugs may produce harmful side effects. For example, if clonidine is discontinued suddenly, blood pressure may zoom above the original high reading. But in addition, most people who need a blood pressure drug require lifelong treatment. If you stop taking the drug, you give up the protection it provides against a trio of cardiovascular diseases that hypertension can bring on: congestive heart failure, coronary heart disease and, perhaps most demonstrably, stroke.

Stroke: an accident inside the brain

A link between high blood pressure and brain-damaging stroke is to be expected because hypertension strikes hard at the delicate blood vessels that bring nourishment to the brain. The added force of the blood roughens the sensitive inner walls of these vessels, causing fatty plaques to accumulate on them quickly. The higher pressure also overstretches the normally elastic vessels, making them lose their ability to expand and contract. These conditions impede flow, increasing the likelihood of a sudden interruption of the brain's blood supply—a stroke. Medically termed a cerebrovascular accident (cerebro, for brain; vascular, for blood vessels), it can occur in a number of equally pernicious ways.

Some causes of stroke are relatively rare: These include head and neck injuries, inborn deformities of the blood vessels, and the effects of diseases such as syphilis, meningitis and leukemia that sometimes attack and weaken the walls of the cerebral arteries. A very small number of strokes have even followed visits to a chiropractor; vigorous manipulations of the neck can damage the vertebral arteries. In a few bizarre cases, individuals have actually suffered strokes when they twisted their necks to look behind them while driving a car in reverse.

However, most strokes result from one of the three distinct types of arterial damage not clearly linked to injury or infection. Cerebral thrombosis occurs when a clot, or thrombus, plugs one of the vessels that delivers blood to the neck and head, such as a carotid artery, or blocks an artery in the brain itself. Cerebral embolism occurs when such an artery is plugged by an embolus, a clot that has traveled from some other part of the body. Either way, part of the brain's blood supply is cut off.

The third major cause of stroke, cerebral hemorrhage, is like the bursting of a pipe. A defective artery, usually weakened and made inelastic by a combination of hypertension and atherosclerosis, ruptures or tears, leaking blood into the brain. (An aneurysm—a special kind of arterial weak spot resembling a blister—can burst, also producing cerebral hemorrhage.) Not only is the portion of the brain previously fed by the artery deprived of blood, but the escaping blood forms a clot that can press against other blood vessels or on part of the brain itself.

The body occasionally gives off two early warnings of possible stroke. The first, obviously, is high blood pressure. The second signal is one or more brief episodes that mimic the symptoms of a real stroke. Caused by a temporary oxygen shortage in some part of the brain, these false strokes are known as transient ischemic attacks—TIAs for short. (Ischemia means a localized shortage of blood.)

Most TIAs last less than 20 minutes and occur when a person is awake and active. Vision may be blurred; the face may become numb; an arm, a hand or a leg may feel as if it is asleep; speech may be slurred. In a few cases the TIA symptoms are alarmingly like those of a fairly severe stroke—paralysis, memory loss or inability to speak. But they are always short-lived.

One description of a TIA was made by science-fiction writer Robert A. Heinlein. After a period of strain from overwork, he went on a cruise with his wife. "We were taking a walk on Moorea, Tahiti," he said, "when I turned my head to look at a mountain peak—and something happened." Heinlein told his wife that he thought he had suffered a stroke. "I'm seeing double," he said, "and my right side feels paralyzed." Back aboard the cruise ship, the symptoms disappeared. A doctor on board diagnosed what had happened—a transient ischemic attack.

Some people—even some doctors—tend to shrug off a TIA as merely a harmless dizzy spell. That is a mistake. In one group of men and women in the Framingham study of heart and blood-vessel diseases, strokes followed TIAs in 39 per cent of the subjects, usually within six months. In Heinlein's case, stroke did not follow within six months, but he did develop other, less serious circulatory problems.

Once alerted to a TIA, a physician may be able to determine its origin. About 65 per cent of the time, a partially blocked carotid artery is at fault. If so, the artery sometimes can be cleaned out in an elaborate surgical procedure, or a new pathway to the brain can be constructed in an operation called a brain bypass.

Most of the time, surgery is not called for; doctors rely instead on an arsenal of drugs to help prevent stroke. Antihypertensives constitute the first line of defense. Anticoagulants—drugs that reduce the blood's ability to form clots—often are the second part of the regimen. And a group of Canadian researchers reported that an anticoagulant found in most household medicine chests—aspirin—may be extremely helpful in preventing stroke.

In a discouraging number of cases, however, stroke hits without warning or in spite of medical efforts to prevent it. At its worst, stroke kills: If too large or too vital a portion of the brain is not supplied with blood, it will die. Stroke is the world's third leading cause of death, taking more than

Drugs—new and old—that protect the heart

Much of the credit for lives saved from heart ailments goes to drugs. Not all are new. The active ingredient from the old wives' remedy, foxglove, is still in use, and that stand-by among medicines, aspirin, has found new use in preventing blood clots. Following are descriptions of drugs that are commonly prescribed for circulatory disorders. They are listed by their generic chemical names, with common brand names beneath (some brands contain two or more drugs); if your prescription label does not include all generic names, ask your pharmacist.

All drugs have side effects. Many medicines may cause nausea, lightheadedness or drowsiness; this can be hazardous when you drive a car or operate machinery. And many react dangerously with alcohol, tobacco, sedatives or even body exposure to heat and sunlight. When you take any drug, pay close attention to the special cautions that apply to it.

DRUG	Intended effect	Minor side effects	Serious side effects	Special cautions
ASPIRIN Many brand names	Prevents blood clots that cause heart attack and stroke	Mild drowsiness in some individuals; upset stomach; ringing in the ears	Kidney damage; liver damage; activation of ulcer	Do not take if you bleed easily, are taking anticoagulants (drugs to prevent blood clots) or have an ulcer. Stop taking one week before surgery.
CHLORETHALIDONE Hygroton	Similar action to CHLOROTHIAZIDE			
CHLOROTHIAZIDE Diuril	Lowers blood pressure	Lightheadedness; increased urination; sensitivity to light; blurred vision; yellow vision	Potassium deficiency; increases the severity of diabetes and gout; affects bone marrow	Increase intake of potassium-rich foods such as bananas and orange juice. Do not eat licorice, which reduces drug effectiveness. Notify doctor of sore throat, bruising or bleeding—signs of bone marrow dysfunction.
CHOLESTYRAMINE Questran	Reduces cholesterol	Constipation; changes in sex drive; weight gain or loss; ringing in the ears	May prevent the absorption of vitamins K, A and D	Vitamin supplements are generally needed.
CLONIDINE Catapres	Lowers blood pressure	Drowsiness; dryness of nose and mouth; constipation; lightheadedness; insomnia; dryness and burning of the eyes	Severe depression; possible congestive heart failure	Do not discontinue drug suddenly—to do so may produce severe reaction. Carry an identification card with name of drug; reactions to it are common. Alcohol may increase the sedative effect. Do not take if you have congestive heart failure or heart block. Notify doctor of shortness of breath, a possible symptom of heart failure.
COLESTIPOL HYDROCHLORIDE Colestid	Reduces cholesterol	Constipation	May prevent absorption of vitamins K, A and D	Vitamin supplements are generally needed.
DIGITOXIN Crystodigin	Controls heartbeat; increases force of heart contraction	Double or blurred vision; changes in color perception	Severe mental confusion	This drug has a narrow margin of safety; space pills exactly as prescribed. Carry an identification card that states you take this drug; reactions to it are common.
DIGOXIN Lanoxin	Similar action to DIGITOXIN			
DIPYRIDAMOLE Persantine	Reduces pain of angina pectoris	Flushing; lightheadedness	May lower blood pressure	In some individuals it may increase the pain of angina pectoris; if so, notify doctor immediately. Smoking and exposure to cold may reduce effectiveness. Avoid overexertion, which may cause heart injury because warning pain is absent.

DRUG	Intended effect	Minor side effects	Serious side effects	Special cautions
DISOPYRAMIDE Norpace	Controls irregular heartbeats	Dry nose, mouth and throat; constipation; blurred vision; may impair ability to urinate	Lower blood pressure; possible congestive heart failure	Do not take if you have had congestive heart failure or heart block. Inform doctor if you have glaucoma, since this drug can increase pressure within the eye. Notify doctor of shortness of breath, a possible symptom of congestive heart failure.
ERYTHRITYL TETRANITRATE Cardilate	Reduces pain of angina pectoris	Flushing; lightheadedness; headache	Lower blood pressure	Inform doctor if you have glaucoma, since this drug can increase pressure within the eye. Smoking and exposure to cold may reduce effectiveness. Avoid overexertion, which may cause heart injury because warning pain is absent.
FUROSEMIDE Lasix	Similar action to CHLOROTHIAZIDE			
GUANETHIDINE Ismelin	Lowers blood pressure	Lightheadedness; weakness blurred vision; nasal congestion; dry mouth; difficulty in urination; loss of scalp hair; impaired ejaculation in men	Affects bone marrow; chest pains; possible congestive heart failure	Notify doctor of sore throat, bleeding or bruising—symptoms of bone marrow dysfunction. Alcohol, tobacco and carbonated drinks react with this drug. Do not take this drug if you take drugs for depression that contain monoamine oxidase (MAO) inhibitor, which causes severe reactions. Avoid overheating, which may intensify lightheadedness. Notify doctor of shortness of breath, a possible symptom of heart failure.
HYDRALAZINE Apresoline Ser-Ap-Es*	Lowers blood pressure	Lightheadedness; nasal congestion; difficulty in urination; constipation	Numbness and tingling in legs; severe depression; confusion; chest pain; changes in blood cell count; liver damage	Smoking increases the possibility of chest pain. Do not drink; alcohol can dangerously lower blood pressure. Notify doctor of sore throat, bruising or bleeding—symptoms of bone marrow dysfunction.
HYDROCHLOROTHIAZIDE Hydrodiuril Esidrix Aldactazide* Ser-Ap-Es*	Similar action to CHLOROTHIAZIDE			
ISOSORBIDE DINITRATE Isordil Sorbitrate	Similar action to ERYTHRITYL TETRANITRATE			
METHYLDOPA Aldomet	Lowers blood pressure	Lightheadedness; nasal stuffiness; dry mouth; weight gain; impaired sex drive	Severe depression; high fever; severe abdominal pain	Do not drink; alcohol may lower blood pressure excessively.
METOPROLOL TARTRATE Lopressor	Lowers blood pressure	Fatigue; overall hair loss; blurred vision	Severe depression; possible congestive heart failure	Do not take if you have heart block or heart failure; it will make these conditions worse. Do not drink; alcohol may lower blood pressure excessively. Notify doctor of shortness of breath, a possible symptom of heart failure.
NITROGLYCERIN Nitrobid Nitrostat	Reduces pain of angina pectoris	Flushing; throbbing in the head; faster pulse; lightheadedness	Blurred vision; dry mouth; severe headache; possible congestive heart failure	Do not take if you have had a recent heart attack, or have severe anemia or low blood pressure. Notify doctor of shortness of breath, a possible symptom of heart failure. Inform doctor if you have glaucoma, since this drug can increase pressure within the eye. Do not drink; alcohol increases the severity of side effects. Smoking and exposure to cold reduce drug effectiveness. Avoid overexertion, which can cause heart injury because warning pain is absent. Use fresh tablets only; this drug becomes ineffective 60 days after the original container is opened.

*Combination drug. Refer also to other active ingredients listed on label.

DRUG	Intended effect	Minor side effects	Serious side effects	Special cautions
PENTAERYTHRITOL	Similar action to ERYTHRITYL TETRANITRATE			
POTASSIUM CHLORIDE Kay Ciel	Prevents or treats potassium deficiency caused by blood pressure drugs	Mild laxative effect	Severe confusion; irregular heartbeat; abdominal pain; excess potassium	Do not take if you are taking spironolactone or triamterene, which make the body retain potassium. Do not use salt substitutes containing potassium.
PRAZOSIN HYDROCHLORIDE Minipress	Lowers blood pressure	Lethargy; weight gain; lightheadedness	Fainting	
PROCAINAMIDE Pronestyl Sub-Quin	Controls heartbeat	Lower blood pressure; itching	Muscular weakness; severe depression; affects bone marrow	Do not take if you are allergic to procain or similar local anesthetics; the drug may have a similar effect. Do not take if you have myasthenia gravis (severe muscle weakness), which is worsened by this drug. Report arthritis-like symptoms to doctor immediately; this is a toxic reaction. Notify doctor of sore throat, bruising or bleeding—symptoms of bone marrow dysfunction.
PROPRANOLOL Inderal	Controls heartbeat; lowers blood pressure; reduces pain of angina pectoris	Fatigue; cold hands and feet; lightheadedness; overall hair loss	Severe depression; increased risk of asthma; possible congestive heart failure	Do not take if you have asthma or seasonal hay fever because it increases risk of asthma. Do not drink; alcohol may cause sedation and severely lower blood pressure. Do not smoke; tobacco reduces effectiveness. Once taking this drug, do not stop suddenly; to do so may cause increased angina or heart attack. Notify doctor of sore throat, bruising or bleeding—symptoms of bone marrow dysfunction. Do not take this drug if you take drugs for depression that contain monoamine oxidase (MAO) inhibitor, which causes severe reactions.
QUINIDINE Cardioquin Cin-Quin	Controls heartbeat	Lower blood pressure; lightheadedness	Fever; affects bone marrow	Inform doctor if you have an acute infection of any kind; infection increases possibility of toxic reaction. Carry an identification card that states you take this drug; reactions are common. Notify doctor of sore throat, bruising or bleeding—signs of bone marrow dysfunction.
SISTEROLS Cytellin	Lowers cholesterol	Diarrhea	None	None
SODIUM WARFARIN Coumadin	Prevents blood clots that cause heart attack and stroke	None	Bleeding	Do not take if you have a tendency to bleed or suffer from ulcers or ulcerative colitis. Carry an identification card that states you take this drug; it increases severity of accidental bleeding and also reacts with other drugs. Do not take vitamin K, which decreases effectiveness. Do not drink; alcohol may alter effectiveness.
SPIRONOLACTONE Aldactone Aldactazide*	Lowers blood pressure	Increased urination; menstrual irregularities in women; enlargement and sensitivity of male breasts; deepening of voice in women	Excess potassium	Do not use potassium supplements or increase intake of potassium-rich foods such as bananas or orange juice. Do not reduce salt intake, which helps counter dehydration.
TRIAMTERENE Dyazide	Lowers blood pressure	Blue urine; increased urination	Affects bone marrow; excess potassium	Do not use potassium supplements or increase intake of potassium-rich foods such as bananas or orange juice. Do not reduce salt intake, which helps counter dehydration. Notify doctor of sore throat, bruising or bleeding—signs of bone marrow dysfunction.

*Combination drug. Refer also to other active ingredients listed on label.

180,000 lives annually in the United States alone. In Japan, a smaller nation with a relatively greater stroke problem, almost 170,000 die each year from stroke; in Great Britain, more than 80,000.

The number of strokes that occur is even greater than these fatality totals indicate, for many stroke victims survive; in the United States the figure is three out of five. Often, however, there are aftereffects. When stroke does not kill, its aftermath depends on how many brain cells were destroyed and in what parts of the brain, on what functions or parts of the body they controlled, and on whether the affected functions can be handled by the surviving cells or by other parts of the brain. Memory can be lost, speech impaired, vision worsened and movement impeded. The effects can range from the

A destructive attack on the heart—myocardial infarction

The slow, methodical way in which the industrialized world's greatest killer—heart attack—brings down its victims is shown below. First, fats in the blood collect inside the coronary arteries, the vessels nourishing the heart. These fat deposits, or plaques, grow and choke the arteries, starving the muscle they serve.

Curiously, a natural lifesaving property of blood makes the plaques worse. Clots form around some of them. If the combination of plaque and clot becomes sufficiently large, the artery is completely plugged and blood flow is stopped. The heart muscle, downstream from the obstruction, thus is killed. This is a heart attack—in medical parlance, a myocardial infarction.

Only 15 to 25 per cent of hospitalized heart attack patients die. About 80 per cent of the survivors are capable of returning to work after several weeks of recovery.

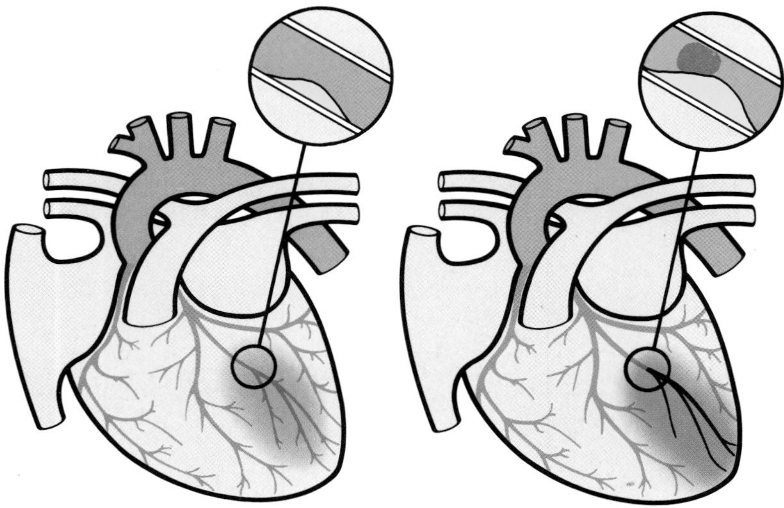

TWO STEPS TO A HEART ATTACK
Green shading in the diagrams above indicates the starvation of the heart muscle by progressive blockage inside the arteries (enlarged details at top). Partial blockage (left) by a fatty lump on an artery wall begins the process, limiting nourishment to a section of muscle (light green). An enlarged lump, plus a blood clot (right), plugs the artery, killing the muscle (dark green).

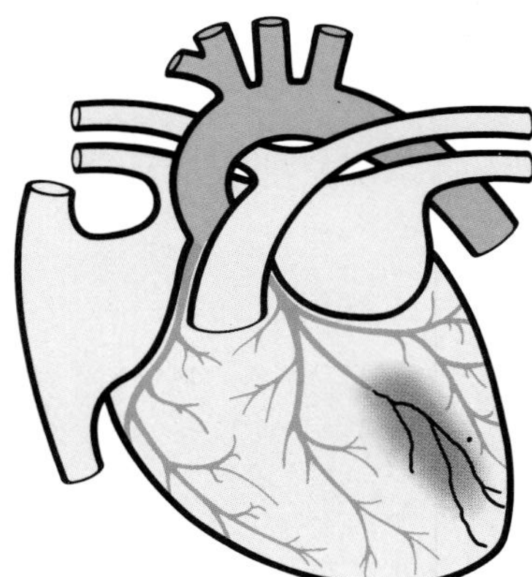

THE HEALING PROCESS
Gray shading on the diagram above represents heart muscle that has been killed by a myocardial infarction. Within three to six weeks, scar tissue replaces the dead muscle while still-healthy heart muscle takes on a bigger work load.

very mild to the very serious—from a slight limp, for example, to total paralysis of one side of the body. In the case of speech, the impairment can vary from a barely noticeable stutter to a total inability to talk. The damage can be temporary or permanent.

In almost all incidents of stroke, doctors prescribe antihypertensives or anticoagulants to help prevent a recurrence. But these drugs occasionally can do more than prevent a second stroke. Primarily by reducing blood pressure, secondarily by limiting clots, they can lessen the risk of attack by the second great cardiovascular menace that hypertension helps cause—coronary artery disease. This killer takes about 650,000 lives each year in the United States alone. In West Germany, nearly 135,000 die annually from coronary heart disease; in the United Kingdom, more than 150,000; in Canada, more than 50,000.

Angina: pain from a starved heart

Because high blood pressure increases the clogging of the coronary arteries with deposits of fat—the condition known as atherosclerosis—the flow of blood through them diminishes. Reduced blood flow can be tolerated by many parts of the body, but not by the heart. It is its own best customer, demanding as much as 20 per cent of the fuel it pumps. And unlike most other parts of the body, which have cross-connecting blood vessels to take over if one vessel is stopped up, the heart has few such backup vessels. The coronary arteries, and the network of smaller vessels that arise from them, are the only supply lines to feed the heart. If one of them becomes too narrowed, the undernourished muscle cells in the heart wall complain.

Despite the heart's appetite for blood, a fairly severe narrowing of a coronary artery—a blockage of 60 per cent or more—is required to bring on the first "heart cries," signs of arterial disease. The first signal may be abnormal fatigue, shortness of breath or an awareness of an irregular heartbeat. But most often atherosclerotic disease introduces itself as an achy, uncomfortable sensation in the midchest, the neck or the arms—particularly during periods of exercise, emotional stress or exposure to cold, when narrowed arteries are unable to meet the heart's increased demand for blood. The medical term for this ache is angina pectoris; it means inflammation *(angina)* of the chest *(pectoris)*. The ailment is called angina for short.

Angina was aptly and colorfully described by an 18th Century British physician named William Heberden. In an article entitled "Some Account of a Disorder of the Breast," Heberden wrote: "They who are affected with it are seized while they are walking (more especially if it be uphill, and soon after eating) with a painful and most disagreeable sensation in the breast that seems as if it could extinguish life if it were to increase or continue; but the moment they stand still all this uneasiness vanishes."

Heberden's description has been much amplified and refined since the 1700s. Usually, explained the 20th Century cardiologist Norman Krasnow, angina is not what most people would describe as pain. "That is," he said, "it's not a sticking or a stabbing kind of feeling that strikes suddenly, like the pain you might get from a poke or a burn. Actually, it's less a pain than a discomfort: a squeezing, constricting, tight or heavy feeling in the chest."

Because angina is less a pain than a feeling of distress, and because it usually disappears in 10 minutes or less, it is easy to downplay as everyday indigestion or heartburn. Many people, especially men who pride themselves on their masculinity, are unable to admit that something is wrong with an organ as vital as the heart. Even some doctors and cardiologists, who certainly should know better, succumb to this inexcusable temptation. And it is inexcusable, because angina is an eminently treatable condition.

Avoiding stressful situations and strenuous exercise keeps the heart's demand for oxygen low, thus limiting the number of anginal episodes. If angina does occur, the drug nitroglycerin—the safe-cracker's explosive, which works in ways not completely understood—can instantly modify the muscle's need for oxygen and bring rapid relief. But nitroglycerin and relaxation treat the symptom—the pain of angina. Other drugs as well as changes in life style can actually help reverse the underlying disease—atherosclerosis. Antihypertensives lower blood pressure, slowing the formation of plaques. Eating less-fatty foods can have the same effect.

Neglecting angina pain is inexcusable not only because the ailment can be treated but, more important, because disregarding it risks more severe heart trouble. For just as a TIA can warn of possible stroke, angina can signal oncoming heart attack.

Angina indicates only that coronary circulation is impaired; heart attack occurs when no blood gets through to an area of heart muscle. The blood-starved part of the myocardium (the heart wall) is killed, or infarcted—which accounts for the medical term for heart attack, myocardial infarction. Angina, by contrast, kills none of the myocardium.

The heart attack

How a heart attack kills heart muscle is the subject of intense medical debate. The majority of doctors believe that the process is parallel to that of a stroke. In the case of a heart attack, though, one or more of the coronary arteries, rather than a cerebral artery, are involved. The vessel becomes narrowed, roughened and almost clogged with fatty plaques. As in stroke, if the artery becomes completely obstructed by plaques and blood clots, blood flow is shut off. The part of the heart muscle formerly sustained by the vessel begins to die. At least, so goes one theory.

This view is challenged by cardiologists who have revived a heart attack scenario introduced some 200 years ago. First suggested by that perceptive British doctor, William Heberden, who described angina, the rival hypothesis states that heart attack occurs when the walls of the coronary arteries go into spasm, pinching the vessels shut. The spasm theory reached a peak of popularity in the 1920s and 1930s, then fell into decline as research revealed the role of atherosclerosis in narrowing arteries. Still, many doctors were puzzled because certain heart attack patients had coronary arteries comparatively free of plaque.

Then, in 1970, a team of surgeons opened the chest of a Los Angeles woman preparatory to open-heart surgery. Before they could hook her up to a heart-lung machine to circulate her blood and breathe for her during surgery, the doctors were thunderstruck to see one of her coronary arteries twitch shut in a spasm, precipitating a heart attack. (The doctors quickly administered nitroglycerin to control the spasm and then proceeded with the planned surgery. Ten years later their patient was in fine health, golfing and gardening in California.)

At about the same time as the Los Angeles incident, Italian cardiologist Attilio Maseri began to look for arterial spasms by making angiograms *(pages 100-101)*, then a newly developed technique for taking X-ray movies of the living heart. He studied more than 200 patients hospitalized for angina, and he found spasms. They could be seen in angiograms made at the moment of an angina attack.

Maseri also found circumstantial evidence that spasms could launch full-fledged heart attacks. One of Maseri's angina patients, a 24-year-old woman, was seized by severe spasms of an unblocked coronary artery during angiography. Two weeks later, the woman suffered a heart attack that killed—coincidentally or not—the part of the heart muscle served by the artery that Maseri had X-rayed in spasm. Seven other patients whose coronary arteries Maseri had witnessed in spasm suffered heart attacks as well. Although these people all had some degree of arterial blockage—unlike the 24-year-old woman—in each case the heart muscle killed by the attack was the part that had been nourished by the artery previously filmed in spasm.

Researchers have suggested several possible causes of coronary spasm, including emotional stress. Stress prompts the adrenal glands to give off adrenaline and noradrenaline. Under some circumstances, the release of these chemicals can be desirable, constricting blood vessels, raising blood pressure and boosting strength to, say, help a mugging victim fight off an attacker. But in heart attack, these chemicals apparently overstimulate key nerve receptors within the walls of the coronary arteries, making the vessels pinch shut in spasm.

The spasm theory suggested that drugs might prevent spasm and thus prevent heart attacks. Several such drugs have been tried. One promising type, the calcium antagonists, apparently prevents arterial spasm by inhibiting contraction of the vessels' muscular walls. These drugs—which

Learning to restart failed hearts with CPR

In medical matters the oystermen and crabbers of Smith Island in Chesapeake Bay are an independent lot. They have to be. Eight miles of water—nearly an hour's boat ride—separate them from the nearest hospital, on Maryland's Eastern Shore.

For medical emergencies the 565 islanders used to rely on mainland helicopters, a visiting doctor or a resident nurse. But one year heart attacks claimed four lives in three months, and the islanders decided they had better learn to cope with such emergencies on their own. At the invitation of the community American Heart Association, volunteers went to the island to teach cardiopulmonary resuscitation (CPR), a set of lifesaving techniques for restarting a failed heart. Some 120 islanders were certified in CPR, and several continued training to become instructors.

The Chesapeake watermen are not alone. In every part of the United States, in Canada and in Europe, firemen, ambulance attendants and ordinary citizens are learning CPR. In the United States the program hopes to train 20 per cent of the population—a goal already surpassed on solitary Smith Island.

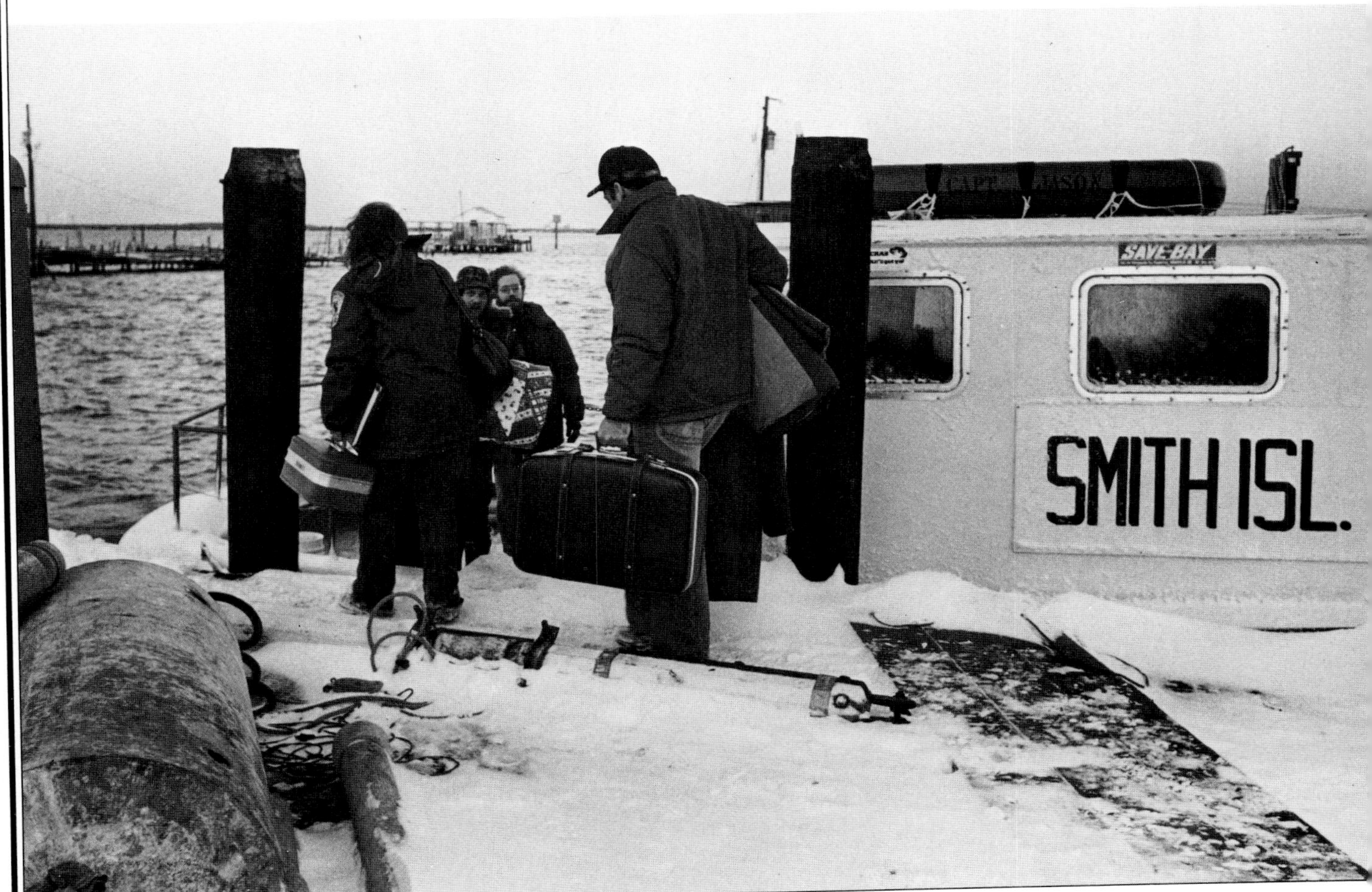

CPR instructors board a snow-crusted ferry after training Smith Islanders to revive heart attack victims.

Using a manikin, two students learn CPR techniques as an instructor (center) supervises. One breathes for the victim mouth to mouth, inflating the lungs every five seconds. At one-second intervals the other presses hard on the victim's breastbone with both hands to force the heart to pump blood. Careful training is necessary for CPR; the pressing can cause internal injuries.

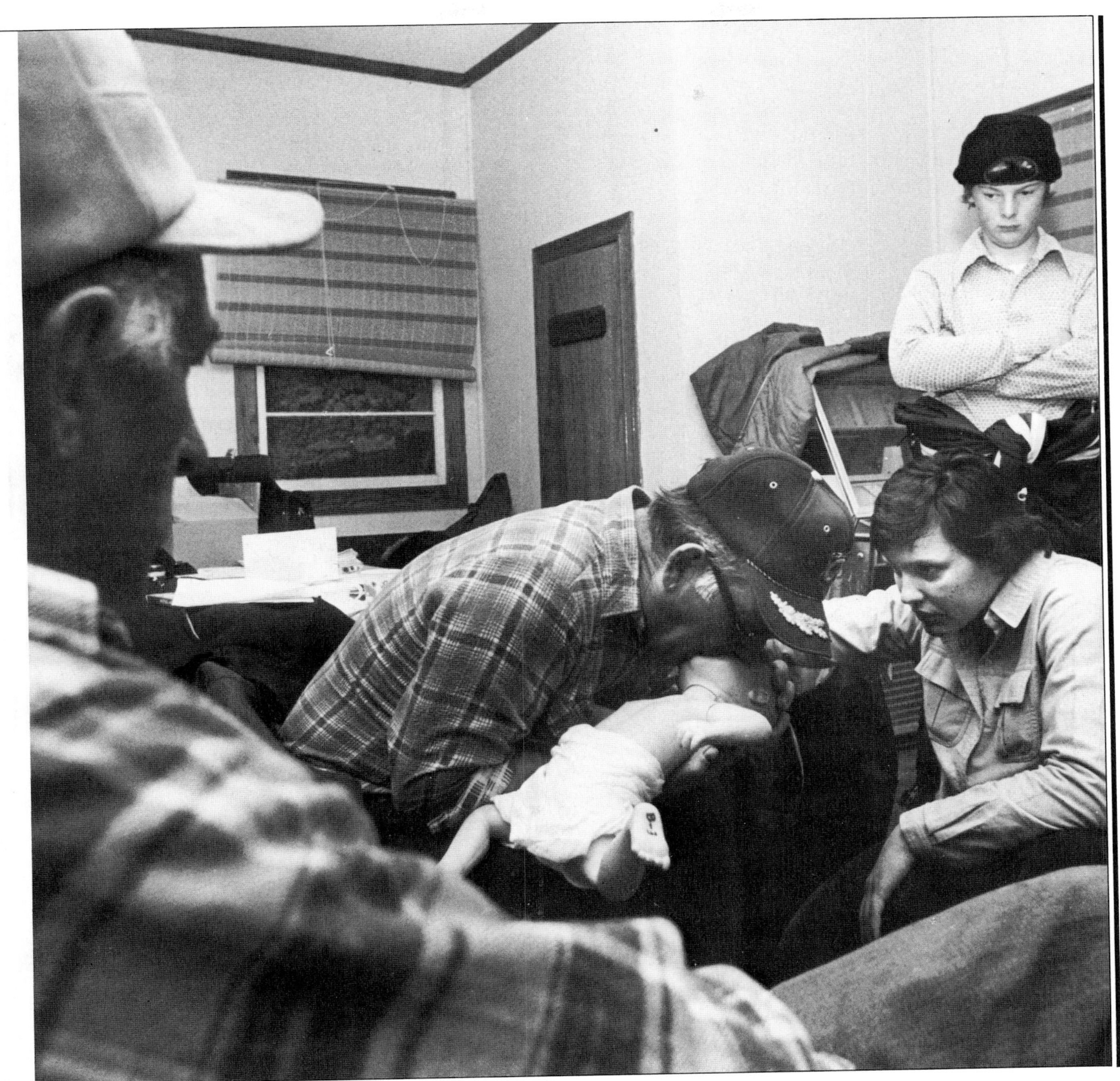

An islander practices the special methods required for children. The rescuer covers the manikin's nose and mouth with his mouth and forces comparatively shallow breaths into the lungs once every three seconds, rather than once every five. Breastbone compression is also less vigorous than for an adult—one hand for a child, finger tips for an infant.

include verapamil, diltiazem and nifedipine—have achieved a success characterized by Dr. Eugene Braunswald of Harvard Medical School as "nothing short of spectacular." In one United States trial of nifedipine, 127 angina patients were treated with the drug; 80 of them, or 63 per cent, gained total control of their angina. In an Australian trial of verapamil, 15 of 17 angina patients responded to treatment.

In an effort to resolve the clog-versus-spasm controversy, Harvard's Dr. Braunswald has suggested that there is a spectrum of coronary artery disease. At one end are patients who get angina and heart attacks solely because their coronary arteries are clogged by atherosclerosis. At the other end are those whose arteries are "clean" and who have trouble solely because of spasm. Most patients fall somewhere in between. If the arteries are almost totally blocked, it takes only a minor spasm to cause angina or to bring on a heart attack; if the arteries are relatively free of fatty plaques, a larger spasm is required.

Whatever the cause of heart attack, the result is always the same: the death of heart muscle, which can cause the death of its owner. Thus, it is obviously even more important to seek immediate help at the onset of a heart attack than for angina. For this reason, it is wise to do some advance planning if you or any member of your family suffers angina or has a history of other cardiovascular problems such as high blood pressure. To prepare for a possible cardiovascular emergency, you should:

- Keep lists of emergency phone numbers—hospital, ambulance, doctor—close at hand. Have one list at work, another at home, and one in your wallet.
- Find out which nearby hospitals have coronary care units (CCUs), sections with sophisticated equipment and specially trained personnel to monitor heart attack patients around-the-clock. Not all do. Know the route to these hospitals from home and from work.
- Make sure you and your family know the signs of a heart attack and what to do when they appear.

The last bit of advice is often the most difficult to follow. Heart attacks can be hard to recognize. If a victim previously has had angina, a mild heart attack may seem little different, with one key exception: A heart attack lasts longer than 10 minutes. Frequently the symptoms of a heart attack are more intense than those of angina. The squeezing sensation may mount to excruciating pain. The pain is likely to radiate to the arms, neck, jaw or back. In addition to the chest sensations, which an individual might deny, there will be other signs, which are visible: heavy sweating, pallor, weakness, nausea, possibly even vomiting.

Blisters in the circulatory system

When a blood vessel is weakened—by birth defect, disease or accident—it can give way to the pounding pulse of its fluid cargo, and bulge. Doctors call this bulge an aneurysm.

If an aneurysm in the brain ruptures, brain cells die from lack of nourishment or from pressure—a type of stroke. The bulges can be equally serious in major arteries or the heart *(below)*. Occurring in 5 to 10 per cent of heart attack survivors, heart aneurysms—areas of weak scar tissue—bulge when the heart contracts, and less blood is pumped.

Doctors can repair many aneurysms. They cut out the weak tissue and either sew the hole closed or, if the hole is too large to be closed, stitch on a patch.

A BULGE THAT COULD KILL
Green shading shows the swelling of an aneurysm in one of the heart's ventricles. Unless it is repaired, such a bulge can reduce pumping power, forcing the heart to work harder and fail; or it can burst, causing death within hours.

The need for speed in recognizing a heart attack and securing medical attention is crucial. The average heart attack victim waits a dangerous three hours before deciding to seek help. More than half who die from heart attack succumb before they reach a hospital; most of these die within two hours of the first symptoms.

If you are with someone who seems to be suffering a heart attack, ignore such all-too-common protests as "It's probably just indigestion" or "It'll go away if you let me sit down." Get the victim to a hospital—fast. If you have been trained in the technique called cardiopulmonary resuscitation (CPR), you may be able to save a victim's life on the spot. CPR training enables you, first, to recognize whether someone who collapses suddenly (or whom you discover unconscious) has merely fainted or is suffering a possible heart attack; then, to tell whether the heart has stopped or is beating in such an uncoordinated fashion that it is no longer pumping blood. If the heart has stopped or is beating inefficiently, a combination of mouth-to-mouth breathing and chest massage can get it working again. CPR is relatively easy to learn. Courses are widely available, and they are generally inexpensive or free *(pages 85-87)*.

The severity of a heart attack depends largely on which section of the heart muscle is destroyed. If the infarction kills a part of the heart muscle that helps regulate the heart's electrical activity, the heartbeat may stop altogether or an irregular pumping rhythm, called ventricular fibrillation, may occur. A fibrillating ventricle flutters ineffectually, pumping little or no blood.

Irregular heart rhythms are probably the leading cause of sudden death from heart attack—those attacks in which the victim literally "drops dead" or dies within hours of the first symptoms. Such deaths are cruelly unfortunate, particularly in the case of those victims who have ignored initial clues, because many hospitals and rescue squads have electrical tools, called defibrillators, that can shock a stopped heart back into action or return a fluttering one to a normal pumping rhythm.

The other major determinant of a heart attack's severity is the amount of heart muscle killed. In a mild infarction, perhaps 20 per cent of the heart muscle dies; in a severe one, perhaps 60 or 70 per cent. There are many heart attack victims alive today whose hearts pump at 30 and even 20 per cent of their original capacity. But if too large an amount of heart muscle is destroyed, the body's pump fails. Blood and other fluids collect in the extremities and pool in the lungs. The whole circulatory system backs up, or congests, with blood that is not being pumped efficiently. This condition is called congestive heart failure, and until quite recently it almost always caused invalidism or death.

When the pump fails

When a heart attack causes congestive heart failure, one or both of the main pumping chambers—the ventricles—have been so badly damaged that they do not empty of blood with each beat. This can happen because too much of the heart muscle has been killed and cannot pump, or because of a fairly common complication of acute heart attacks: ventricular aneurysms, weak spots in the ventricular walls. These occur when extensive tissue damage or destruction leaves the wall so damaged that it balloons out, creating a flaccid sac. The sac absorbs much of the force of the heart contractions. With each heartbeat, some blood fills the sac instead of being pumped into the lungs or out into the body. The ventricle tries mightily to rid itself of the extra blood, but over time it weakens and may fail.

If the left ventricle is the one that fails, the blood it normally would pump out of the lungs and into the body backs up. The lungs become logged with blood, and breathing may be labored and uncomfortable. If the right ventricle fails, blood that the heart would normally drain out of the veins stays there, never reaching the lungs. Congestion fills and distends the veins. The increased pressure forces a clear watery fluid—blood minus its red cells—to ooze into the tissues, most often of the feet and ankles. The ankles, for example, may swell to the size of small tree trunks. The common term for this fluid-swollen condition is dropsy; the medical term, edema.

Congestive heart failure can result from causes other than heart attack. There are a whole host of disorders that can

Defects babies are born with

One baby in every 100 is born with a malformed heart—it has a hole, a pinched vessel, crossed connections or several of these congenital defects combined *(right)*. Many defects are not serious and may go unnoticed for a lifetime. Others heal themselves. But some are life-threatening and must be mended by surgical techniques ranging from simple suturing to replacement of malfunctioning parts with man-made substitutes.

One major defect usually becomes apparent in the delivery room: Oxygen-rich blood mixes in the heart or major vessels with deoxygenated blood. The result is an infant with a bluish complexion—a blue baby. The combination of defects that produces most blue babies is called the tetralogy of Fallot *(opposite, top)*, because it was first identified in 1888 by a French physician named Étienne-Louis Arthur Fallot. Until surgery to correct these malformations was perfected in 1954 by Dr. Walton Lillehei and his associates at the University of Minnesota and the Mayo Clinic—the first of the massive heart-rebuilding operations to prove successful—the disease was an almost certain sentence of death.

In only 3 per cent of the cases can doctors identify the cause of an inborn heart defect. Frequently, abnormalities in genes controlling inheritance are at fault. But more often, doctors point to environmental factors—especially the pregnant mother's exposure to viral illness and drugs. German measles can cause a pregnant woman's baby to develop heart defects, and many other viruses are suspect. It is also dangerous to unborn babies when the mother smokes, drinks or uses drugs, medicinal or recreational. Many doctors, as a precaution, advise pregnant women to refrain from taking all drugs, even aspirin.

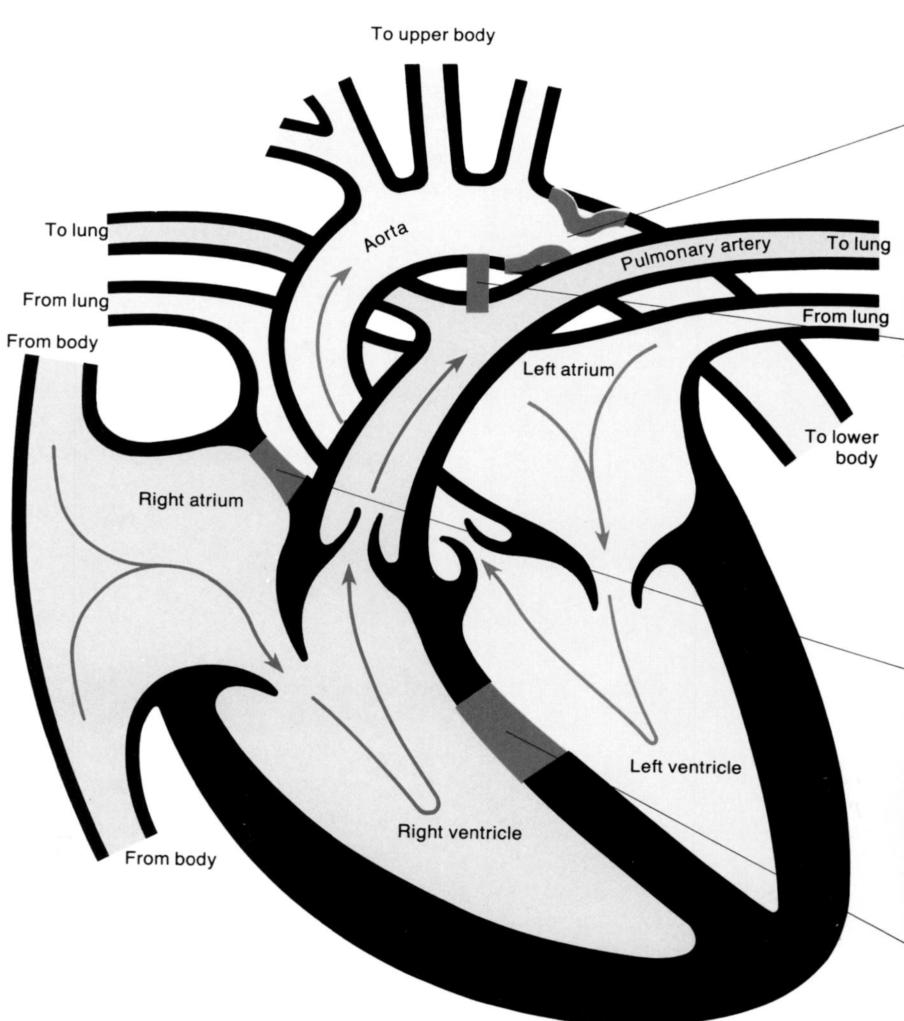

THE LIKELIEST FAULTS OF CONSTRUCTION
Arrows on the diagram above indicate the flow of blood—red for oxygenated and blue for deoxygenated—in a healthy heart, while green shading shows four common congenital defects. These flaws, described at right, affect the heart's internal dividing walls or its great vessels, the aorta and the pulmonary artery.

BOTTLENECK IN THE AORTA
The pinching of the aorta, commonly called coarctation, forces the left ventricle to pump harder and consequently causes blood pressure to rise in the upper body. Unless the narrowed segment of the aorta is removed—a synthetic graft often is inserted as its surrogate—blood vessels in the neck and brain may rupture.

A VESSEL THAT FAILS TO SHUT
In this defect a blood vessel needed by the unborn baby only before birth fails to close. In the womb this vessel channels blood from the baby's pulmonary artery to the aorta, bypassing the lungs, left atrium and left ventricle. If the connection stays open after birth, enriched blood on its way to the body leaks back into the pulmonary artery, forcing the left ventricle to pump harder to supply the body.

A LEAK BETWEEN THE ATRIA
This malfunction is simply a hole in the wall between the atria. Because blood pressure in the heart's left side is normally higher than in the right, blood usually leaks through the hole from left to right; this leakage adds more blood to the amount that the right side of the heart must handle, placing a potentially lethal strain on it.

A LEAK BETWEEN THE VENTRICLES
Like the abnormality above, this defect—the most common—is a hole in one of the heart's dividing walls, but in this case it occurs between the muscular pumping chambers, the ventricles. It can cause a similar strain on the heart's right side.

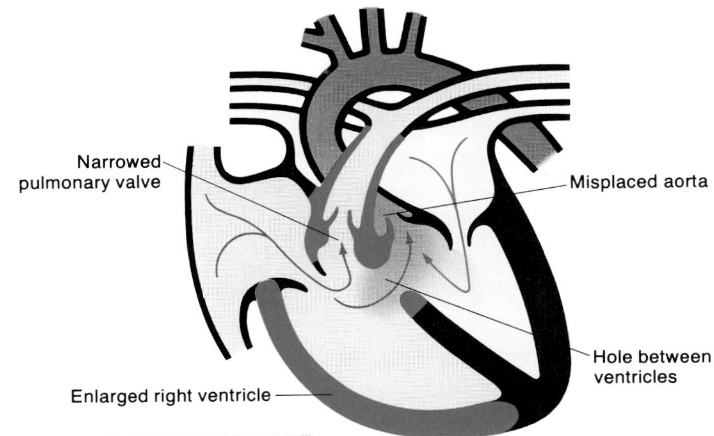

TETRALOGY OF FALLOT
Green shading indicates defects combined in most blue babies: a narrowed pulmonary artery, an enlarged right ventricle, a hole in the wall between the ventricles, and an aorta that is open to blood from both ventricles. These defects cause spent blood to be pumped into the aorta, where it mixes with oxygenated blood.

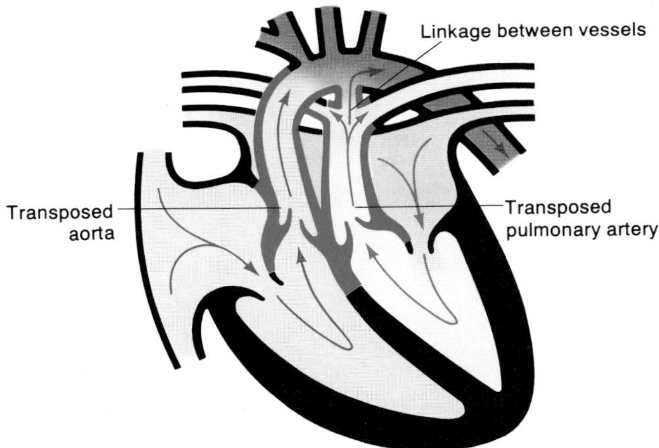

TRANSPOSITION OF THE GREAT VESSELS
This defect occurs when the aorta and pulmonary artery connect to the wrong ventricles. Thus spent blood circulates through the body, while oxygenated blood shuttles between heart and lungs. Only if another defect, such as a passage between aorta and pulmonary artery (above), mixes the blood can the newborn live.

make the heart fail—prolonged drug addiction or alcoholism; certain bacterial or viral infections, referred to as cardiomyopathies, that destroy the heart muscle; and most notably, that seemingly catch-all cause of heart trouble, hypertension. High blood pressure forces the heart to pump against greater arterial resistance. Gradually and insidiously, the muscle weakens and eventually it gives out. Fat-clogged arteries similarly offer increased resistance to the heart, occasionally producing heart failure.

If high blood pressure is the culprit, antihypertensives—particularly diuretics—may be prescribed. At the same time, depending on his physical condition, the patient may have to either reduce his physical activity in order to limit the demands made on the heart, or increase it in order to strengthen the muscle so it is capable of greater effort. Drugs such as digitalis, norepinephrine, dopamine and glucanon may be prescribed to reduce the frequency of heartbeats but increase the power of each contraction. If a ventricular aneurysm is the source of the trouble, drugs may be the first line of defense; if they prove inadequate, surgery to remove the aneurysm can be performed.

Two of the most prevalent causes of heart failure—heart attack and hypertension—afflict middle-aged and older adults almost exclusively. Unfortunately, congestive heart failure does not so restrict itself. Infants, children and younger adults can be stricken too. When they are, the causes of their conditions and hence the treatments may be radically different from those of older victims.

The first contributors to congestive heart failure in young people are present even before birth. In some babies the marvelously intricate combination of chambers, valves and vessels making up the heart and circulatory system fails to form properly before birth or fails to undergo certain necessary changes soon afterward.

Such irregularities are called congenital heart defects. Holes exist where walls should be solid, tubes that should close remain open, vessels are misconnected, the heart's chambers are narrowed or misshapen, a great artery is pinched and almost shut, valves are malformed and leaky—there are almost unlimited possibilities for problems and combinations of problems. In fact, one such combination has a name all its own; called the tetralogy of Fallot, it involves four separate abnormalities and was first identified by a French physician, Étienne Fallot *(pages 90-91)*.

The origins of inborn heart defects, like those of most birth defects, remain essentially unknown. Drugs taken by the pregnant mother, such as LSD and thalidomide, cause some abnormalities. Others are linked to rare genetic disorders. But there is no uncertainty about one major cause: rubella, or German measles, in the mother during the first 12 weeks of pregnancy. The chances are better than 1 in 12 that an afflicted mother will give birth to a baby with a defective heart, usually one with an abnormal connection between the aorta and the pulmonary artery.

Some congenital defects are so severe that the infant is stillborn. Others spare life but limit the amount of oxygenated blood that reaches the child's tissues, sometimes so drastically that the skin and lips are literally blue—the so-

Heart valves that stick and leak

Like parts in a man-made pump, the heart's four valves can malfunction. Because of injury, infection or inborn defect, a valve may fail to open fully or close tightly. Either condition forces the heart to work harder and may ultimately cause it to fail.

A common source of valve trouble is rheumatic fever, caused by a streptococcus infection but named for its symptoms—fever and rheumatic pain in joints and muscles. The infection, which generally starts as strep throat in children aged five to 15, damages the heart about half the time. The valves on its left side—the mitral and aortic valves—usually are stricken. Left scarred and puckered, they narrow or leak later in life. Another common heart infection, bacterial endocarditis, which inflames the inner part of the heart, often damages the tricuspid valve, on the right side.

If the damage is severe and not manageable with medicine, surgery often is required. Fortunately, the repairs are now almost routine. Doctors may choose to fix the damaged valves or to replace them outright—inserting substitutes that are manufactured from metal and plastic or transplanted from cadavers or from animals such as pigs.

called blue-baby syndrome. Almost all defects place a strain on the child's heart in one way or another. Assume, for a moment, that a congenitally leaky valve lets a single drop of blood drip backward from the aorta into the left ventricle with each beat. If the heart beats a fairly average 80 times per minute, in two minutes about two teaspoonfuls of blood will have dripped backward; in an hour or so, a glassful or more. Although the heart tries to rid itself of the extra blood, the time comes when it can no longer handle the overload, and congestive heart failure results.

The incidence of congenital heart defects is fairly high—about one out of every 100 babies. But until medical science knows more about what causes the defects, little can be done to reduce the risk—with one key exception: Vaccinations against German measles can all but eliminate the congenital abnormalities arising from that potent cause. Yet, though prevention of most inborn defects remains impossible, treatment has become remarkably successful. Better diagnoses, drugs and surgical techniques have enabled many children with defective hearts to avoid heart failure, overcome their handicap and lead normal adult lives.

Even more serious than congenital defects as a cause of congestive heart failure in the young is the childhood illness rheumatic fever. Though the disease usually strikes children between the ages of five and 15, the heart failure it can produce normally appears later in life—in the twenties, thirties or even in the forties. This delayed reaction takes place because the damage started by rheumatic fever often continues to scar certain heart valves over time.

Valves damaged by childhood fever

After hypertension and atherosclerosis, rheumatic heart disease is the most widespread cardiac ailment in the United States. Approximately 1.8 million Americans suffer from it, and each year more than 10,000 of them die. As prevalent as the illness is in the United States, it is even more so in the

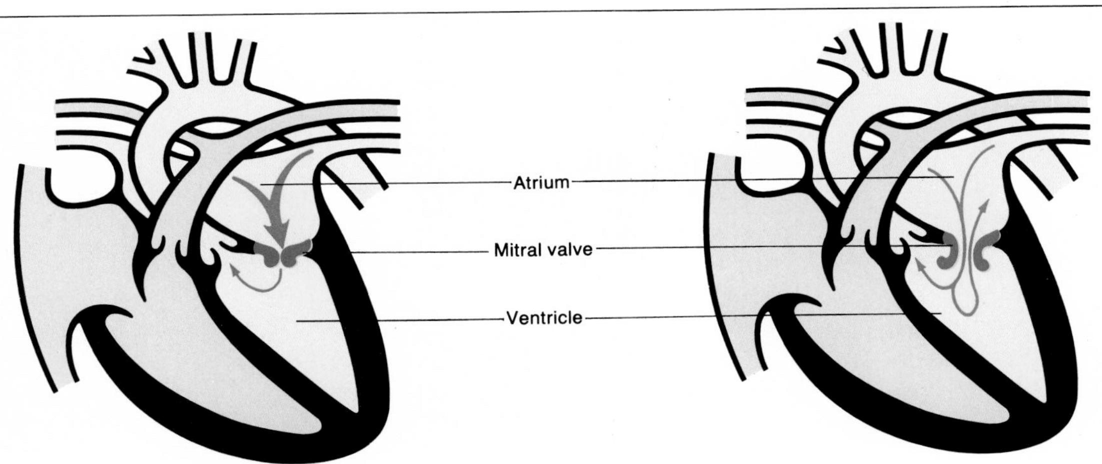

A VALVE THAT STICKS CLOSED
This abnormality, stenosis, is characterized by thickening and narrowing of a heart valve. Above, an afflicted mitral valve (green) cannot open fully, restricting blood flow (arrows) and increasing the pressure of oxygenated blood (red) behind the obstruction. If uncorrected, the condition can be fatal.

A VALVE THAT STICKS OPEN
Failure of a valve to close properly produces regurgitation, or leakage. Here, a leaky mitral valve (green) permits oxygenated blood (red) to flow back and forth (arrows) between atrium and ventricle, reducing the amount of vital oxygen supplied to body tissues. Most victims resume normal lives after surgery.

How an electrocardiogram analyzes a heartbeat

If you have never had an electrocardiogram —a recording of heart activity—you may find your first experience eerie. It seems the nurse is about to wire you up for a mad scientist's experiment. She spreads electrically conductive jelly on your arms, legs and chest, then, as at right, uses straps and suction cups to attach wires from a device that hums, blinks and makes a wavy line on a graph.

Alarm is unwarranted. No electricity flows into your body during an electrocardiogram (called ECG or sometimes, after the German spelling, EKG). The flow is in the other direction. The electrodes pick up electricity put out by your own body: minute voltages transmitted to the skin surface when nerve centers generate the charges that cause the heart to contract and relax during one beat *(pages 12-13)*. These voltages are amplified to activate the stylus that traces their strength on the paper. Peaks and dips in this graph of voltage tell much about the heart (a normal, healthy ECG is explained at right).

Extra wiggles, or changes in position or shape of a peak or valley may indicate specific defects. They even enable a doctor to recognize that the patient has unknowingly suffered a heart attack in the past.

ECGs often give false readings, however, particularly if made on a patient at rest, as most are. More informative are ECGs taken after exercise *(pages 134-135)*.

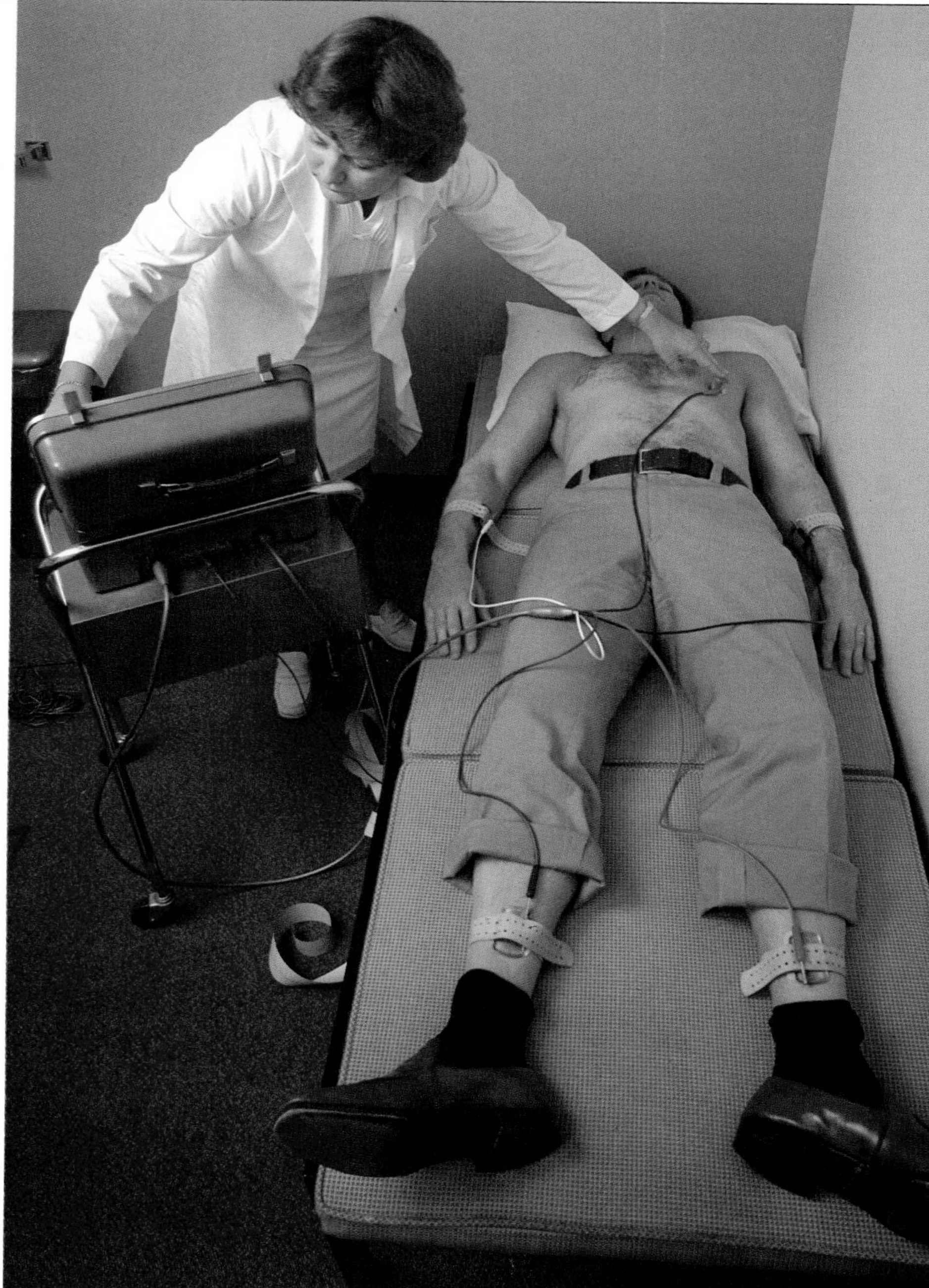

A technician scans an electrocardiogram as she holds an electrode against the patient's chest. For routine ECG, about a dozen tracings are usually made, each with the chest electrodes—only one is used here—in different positions.

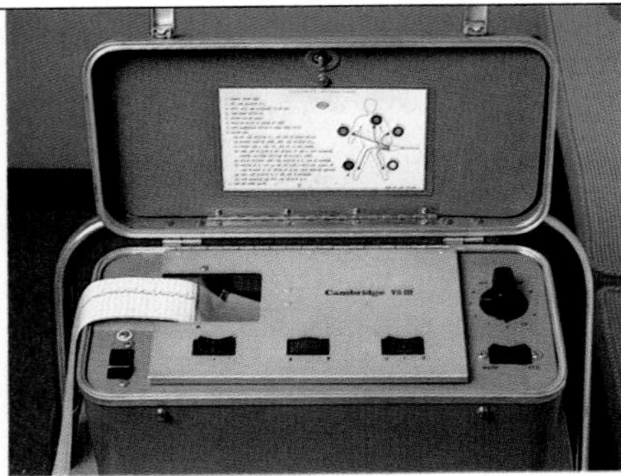

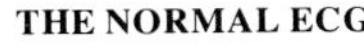

THE NORMAL ECG

Electricity generated during a heartbeat is picked up (opposite), then recorded by the instrument at left to produce an ECG graph (below). Each variation, termed a wave and given a letter name, arises as depicted in the following diagrams, in which electrical activity is colored the same as the resulting ECG.

THE P WAVE

To start a heartbeat, the pacemaker nerve center fires a negative charge (red, far left) to the atria—receiving chambers—causing them to contract from their relaxed shape (dotted lines) and push blood to the ventricles. This contraction causes the P wave (left) in the ECG; the gradual rise and slightly steeper drop to horizontal shows healthy rhythm and good blood supply.

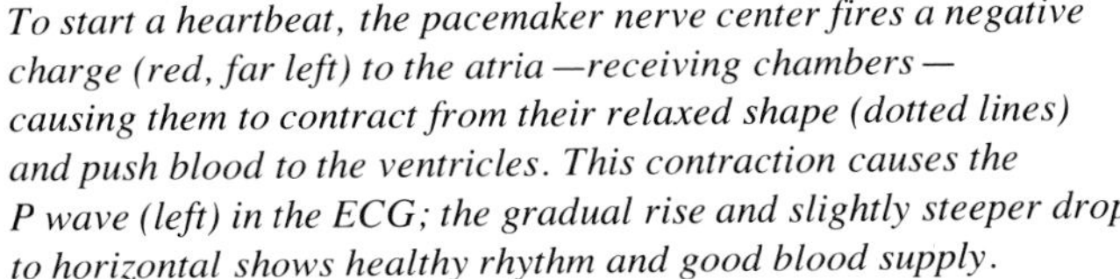

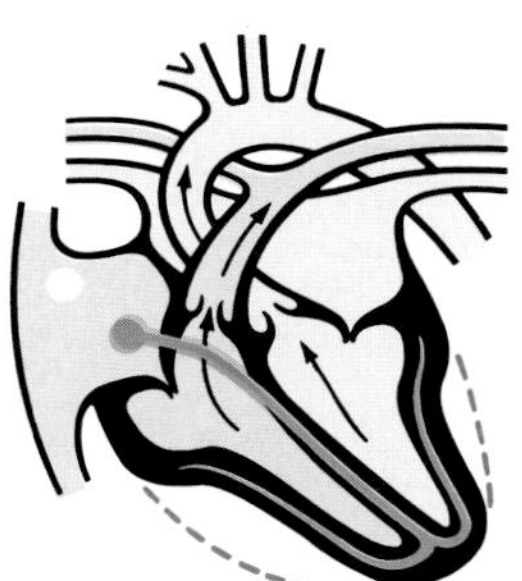

THE QRS COMPLEX

To make the ventricles contract from their relaxed shape (dotted lines) and force blood throughout the body, a second center, the atrioventricular node, transmits the impulse from the atria to the ventricles (dark green, far left), causing them to contract. When they do, the ECG records the sharp peaked tracing that is known as the QRS complex. The form depicted here indicates healthy pumping. But if this wave group is located at an irregular distance from the P wave or is missing, the actions of the atria and ventricles may not be properly coordinated. A wider QRS can suggest malfunction of the heart's electrical system.

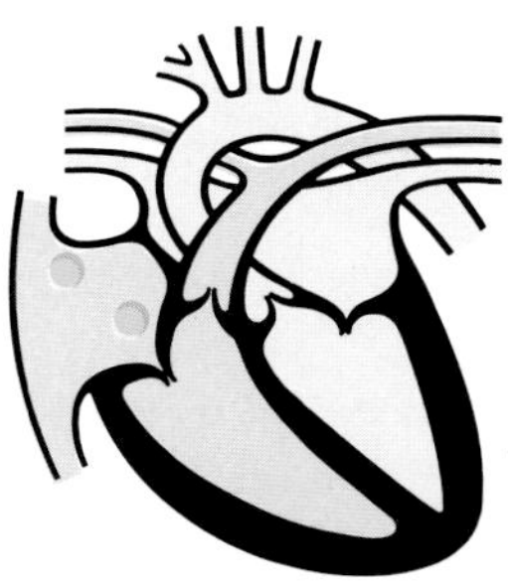

THE T WAVE

As the ventricles relax after pumping, the negative charges that were generated by pumping disappear. Nerve centers and heart muscle revert to a positive charge (yellow, far left). This "repolarization" generates the T wave. An inverted T wave—pointing down instead of up—may indicate blocked arteries.

developing countries. In India, rheumatic heart disease is said to be the No. 1 heart problem.

The reason for a higher incidence in the developing world can be traced to the roots of the disease. Rheumatic fever is preceded by an infection of streptococcus bacteria, as in strep throat. The overcrowded living conditions found in many poorer nations encourage the communication of the strep infection. What is more, the antibiotic drugs that have helped control rheumatic fever in affluent countries are less widely available in the Third World.

The damage done by rheumatic fever is caused by an adverse reaction to streptococcus bacteria. Strep can strike in any of three ways: It can injure the heart muscle; it can affect the heart's lining—the endocardium—especially around the heart valves; or it can damage the sac of tissue in which the heart is suspended, the pericardium. Worse, the infection sensitizes these tissues so that the heart valves become vulnerable to further damage later in life if the individual is reexposed to streptococcus. (That is why children and adults who have had the disease are advised to remain on long-term antibiotic therapy.) The disease can leave the overlapping parts of the valve, called flaps, scarred and distorted. These flaps can progressively thicken so that they lose their flexibility, causing the valve either to obstruct the flow of blood or to leak, or both.

The mitral valve, between the left atrium and the left ventricle, is the valve that is most frequently harmed by rheumatic heart disease. The diseased valve usually sticks partially shut, allowing less blood than normal to flow from the atrium into the ventricle. Blood volume, and thus blood pressure, builds in the left atrium, forcing the right ventricle to work harder. In time, the right ventricle fails. If, on the other hand, the damaged mitral valve sticks open, blood is free to flow back and forth between left atrium and ventricle. This inefficiency forces the left ventricle to pump the same blood over and over, and this overwork eventually produces congestive heart failure.

Obviously, the best way to treat rheumatic heart disease, and thus to avoid the heart failure it can bring, is to stop the illness before it starts. Although few strep infections are followed by rheumatic fever, any suspected strep infection, particularly strep throat, calls for prompt attention. The illness should be treated with antibiotics for at least 10 days. If rheumatic fever does set in, a similar regimen of antibiotics can eradicate the underlying streptococcus while aspirin eases fever and body aches. In a great many cases, drugs called steroids will be given to diminish inflammation of heart and other body tissues. Prolonged bed rest used to be part of the regimen as well. Nowadays, the treatment is shorter and the patient is advised to be more active; he thus avoids many of the physical and psychological problems of lengthy confinement.

If, in spite of all efforts to avoid and control it, rheumatic heart disease is severe, the heart may be scarred dangerously. If it is, surgery may be required to repair or replace damaged valves and thereby ward off congestive heart failure.

Clearly, whether it is brought on by heart attack, hypertension, congenital defect, rheumatic heart disease or other, less prevalent maladies, congestive heart failure is no longer as ominous as it once was—nor as final as the words sound. In the first place, it is usually avoidable. Second, if heart failure does occur, it is treatable—either with medicines that stimulate or strengthen the weakened pump, or with surgical procedures that repair it.

Similar progress has been made in dealing with the other major diseases of the heart and blood vessels—high blood pressure, stroke, coronary artery disease—and with a host of lesser ones as well. One of them, intermittent claudication—occasional pain and limping brought on by narrowing of arteries in the leg—can be treated by any of several surgical techniques. In one of these, called balloon angioplasty, the doctor inserts and then inflates a small balloon inside the damaged artery in order to widen the vessel. In another procedure, the surgeon takes a section of a vein from a different part of the body and grafts it onto the diseased artery so that a new pathway for blood is created.

Veins, too, are subject to disease. The unsightly and often painful bulging blue striations of varicose veins afflict one out of every five women and one out of 15 men. They result from a failure of one-way valves in the leg veins to keep blood from draining downward. Sitting or standing for long periods of time, or wearing tight-fitting garters or shoes, or doing anything that tends to reduce the circulation in the legs may predispose an individual to varicose veins. So may a family's medical history: Many doctors now believe that varicose veins run in families. If you develop varicose veins, your doctor may advise you to stay off your feet as much as you possibly can or to wear elastic support hose, which, by squeezing areas of the leg, prevent blood from draining downward and distending the veins. In very severe cases, surgery may be required to tie off or strip away the diseased portions of the veins.

A more serious affliction that strikes blood vessels in the legs is thrombophlebitis, a blood clot accompanied by inflammation. Thrombophlebitis can be fatal if untreated. The clot can break off from its position in the leg, travel through the bloodstream and lodge in a coronary artery or in a cerebral artery, causing a heart attack or a stroke. Doctors normally prescribe anticoagulants to treat thrombophlebitis; but if drugs do not prove effective, surgery to remove the clot may be required.

Yet, whether medical or surgical, whether aimed at the great killers or at the lesser maladies—all of the modern treatments for cardiovascular disease depend on one thing: accurate diagnosis. In identifying ailments, today's physicians have an enormous advantage over their colleagues of only a few decades ago.

To the basic diagnostic tools—the stethoscope *(page 9)*, invented in 1816 by the French physician Réné Laënnec, and the electrocardiograph recording of the electrical signals emitted by the heart *(pages 94-95)*, developed in England in the late 19th Century—has been added a panoply of innovative procedures. Many of these new techniques are nothing short of fantastic, combining electronics and nuclear science to yield detailed pictures of the heart at work—and malfunctioning. Equipped with these new medical tools, physicians can eliminate much of the guesswork from diagnosis, so that the treatment and cure of cardiovascular disease is now more successful than it ever has been *(pages 98-105)*.

A venturesome probe into the heart

When Werner Forssmann, a 25-year-old intern at a small hospital outside Berlin, proposed in 1929 that he insert a long rubber tube—a catheter—through a vein into his own heart, his superiors, aghast, forbade the experiment. Forssmann went ahead anyway—and transformed cardiac medicine.

Working in secret, he exposed a vein with a scalpel and then very slowly inched the catheter through the vein and into his heart. Had the heart wall been irritated and the rhythm of the heartbeat thrown off, Forssmann would have died almost instantly. Nevertheless, he performed the catheterization eight more times, including one time in which he injected a fluid visible in X-rays directly into his heart.

In one bold stroke, the young intern had invented angiography—the means of X-raying the heart and its arteries, and blood vessels elsewhere in the body—a technique that led to such lifesaving operations as bypass surgery, the implantation of pacemakers and the removal of blood clots from the lungs. Forssmann became a small-town physician—he died in 1979—and did not continue his pioneering work. But 27 years after his dangerous journey of discovery, Werner Forssmann shared in the Nobel Prize for Medicine.

A 1929 X-ray shows the rubber catheter threaded by Werner Forssmann into his arm, and its looping route to his heart.

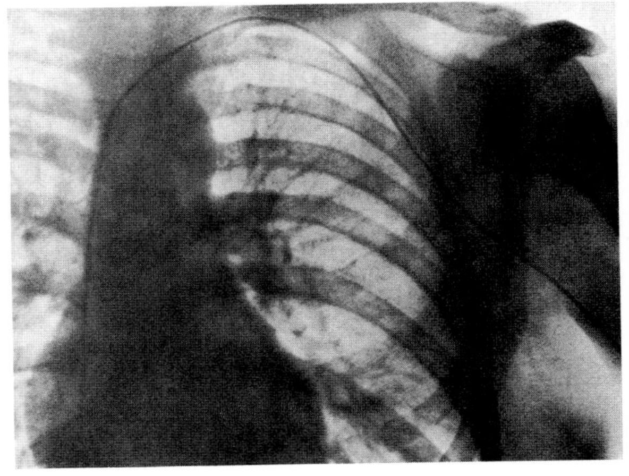

Getting a look at the problem

Until recently, physicians tracking down the causes of an ailing heart were stymied by an inescapable fact: The heart is ordinarily invisible. Secured inside the rib cage, it cannot be exposed to direct view without major surgery. Diagnoses had to be made by shrewd deduction from sounds heard with a stethoscope *(page 9)* or from graphs of signals recorded in an electrocardiogram *(pages 94-95)*. Even X-rays were of little help; they clearly revealed the solid bones of ribs and spine but showed only dim outlines of the soft tissue making up the circulatory system.

But now this has changed. Space-age surgical techniques, ultrasonics and nuclear science have brought the living, beating heart into view and enabled doctors to see what is wrong—or right *(opposite)*. In many cases the patient can see, too.

The most widely used method of viewing the heart was invented in the mid-1950s, when the development of open-heart surgery made clear images essential. The technique involves X-rays, but made in a special way. A long, thin plastic tube, or catheter, is threaded through a vein or artery to the patient's heart so that dye can be squirted into it. The dye is harmless but, unlike the tissues of heart and blood vessels, is opaque to X-rays. When these structures are filled with dye, they block X-rays as bones do, casting shadows to be recorded on the film. The shadow images—called angiograms—reveal blockages in arteries, holes in the heart walls, enlargements, constrictions and misconnections. Still pictures or X-ray movies can be made this way.

Angiograms proved to be such a valuable diagnostic tool that their use quickly became standard for heart-surgery prospects. However, the technique is of the kind that doctors call invasive: The patient's body must be cut, and breached by the catheter. This surgery is minor and reasonably safe—in a good hospital the mortality rate for angiography is less than two per thousand—but even such a small risk is not easily countenanced when the procedure is undertaken not to cure the patient but simply to find out what is wrong with him.

In an effort to reduce the number of angiograms performed, researchers have been trying to develop safer ways to look at the heart—noninvasive (nonsurgical) methods. And they have been eminently successful. In one technique, called echocardiography *(pages 102-103)*, sound waves are beamed at the heart and the echoes are used to draw its picture on a screen like a television screen. In another innovation, nuclear scanning *(pages 104-105)*, radioactive materials are injected into the bloodstream—without surgery—and the radiation from the blood-filled heart is picked up by a detector that constructs a vivid picture of the organ.

Angiograms generally are required only before surgery. The newer and noninvasive methods such as nuclear scanning and echocardiography are applied only to the relatively few patients who cannot be diagnosed by simpler means. In most cases, perceptive interpretation of sounds heard through a stethoscope and of electrical activity recorded in an ECG tells the doctor all he needs to know. An unexpected swish of surging blood reveals a hole in an interior wall of the heart; extra thumps suggest unsynchronized valves; subtle variations in the peaks and valleys of an ECG indicate restricted blood flow.

The value of such basic sound and electrical techniques in diagnosis has also been enhanced by modern improvements. Until recently, for example, a patient had to sit or lie in one place for an ECG, and it recorded only a few seconds' worth of heartbeats; now there are portable units that a patient wears strapped to his chest to record every heartbeat for as much as 24 hours. Other ECG devices transmit heart data by radio *(page 147)* so that recuperating heart attack victims can be monitored as they walk hospital hallways. As for the stethoscope, it has been supplemented by the addition of a sensitive microphone and amplifier to pick up and record, as squiggles on paper tape, sounds so faint that a doctor might easily miss them with his own ears.

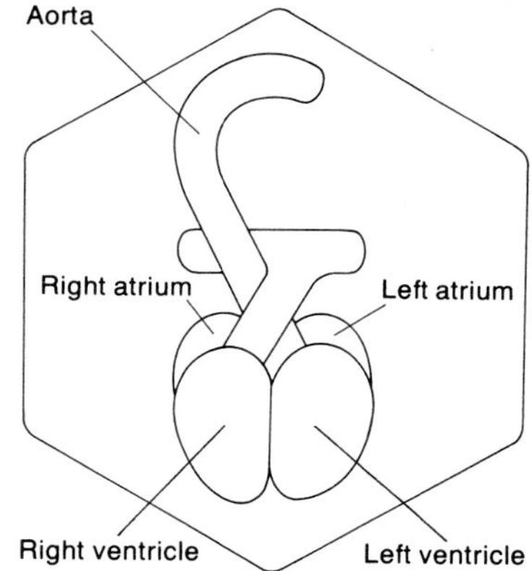

In brilliant hues at right—a computer creation based on emissions from an injection of radioactive technetium—the color yellow outlines the chambers of a heart and its aorta (diagramed above). Overlapping circles trace the left ventricle at its largest and smallest, revealing how much that chamber contracts as it pumps blood into the aorta.

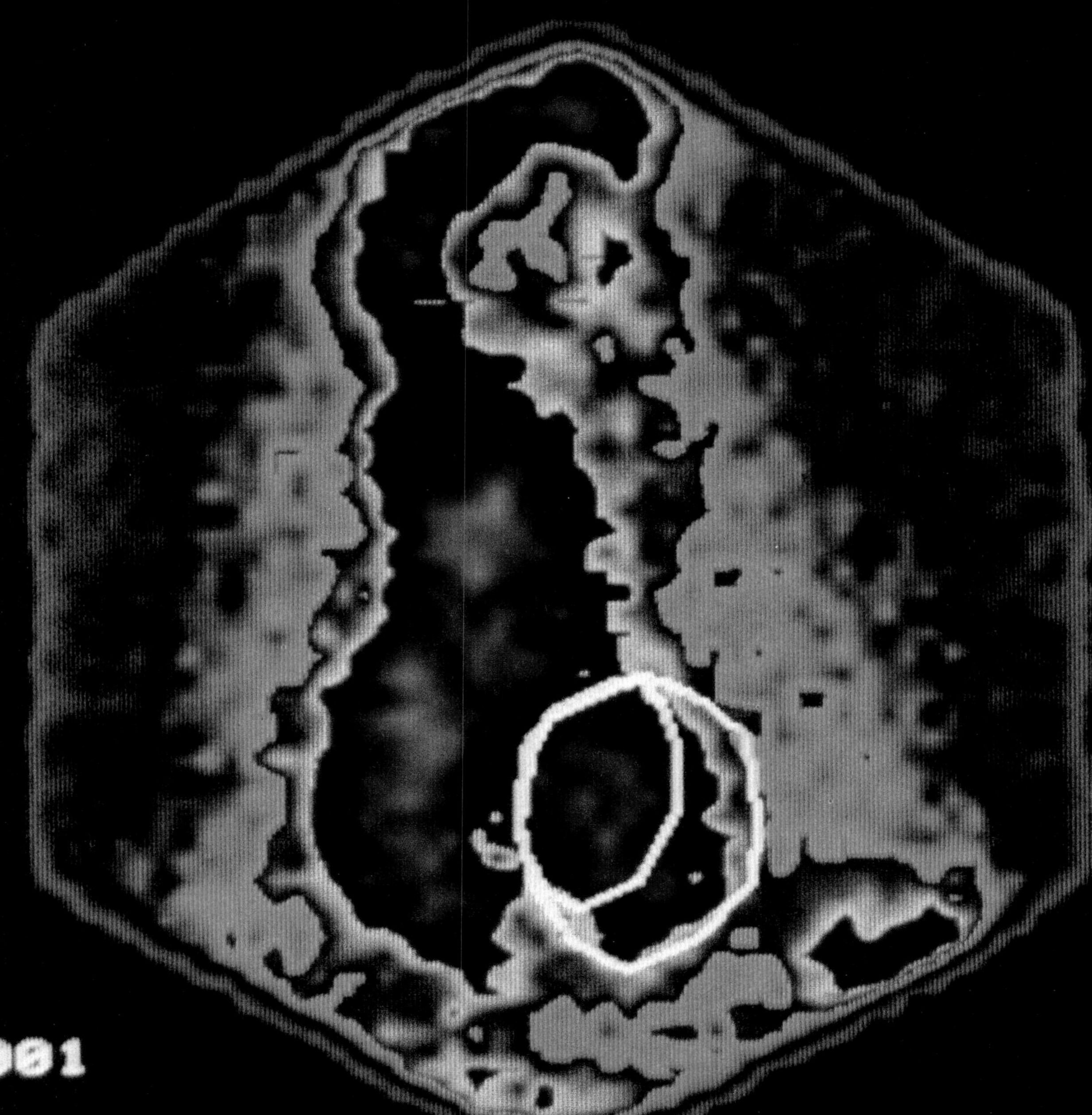
0001

Injecting dye to bring defects into X-ray view

When a doctor schedules a patient for angiograms—X-rays of the dye-filled heart—he has usually found something amiss through other tests. Arteries may be blocked, valves malfunctioning or, especially in children, a structural defect may have reduced the pumping capacity of the heart.

These problems generally can be corrected surgically, but a surgeon must first pinpoint the difficulty. Angiograms give the best pictures of the situation; and, where arteries are narrowed by clogging, the only reliable ones.

Before angiograms are made, the patient usually is hospitalized for preliminary examinations. Then he is given a local anesthetic and an incision is made in a vein and artery at his elbow or groin. As many as three catheters are threaded through the cuts toward the heart so that they stop near the parts of the heart the surgeon wishes to see. Finally, dye is injected through the catheters. Most people feel no more than a tickle as the catheters are inserted or a hot flash as the dye is injected, and patients usually go home the day after the test.

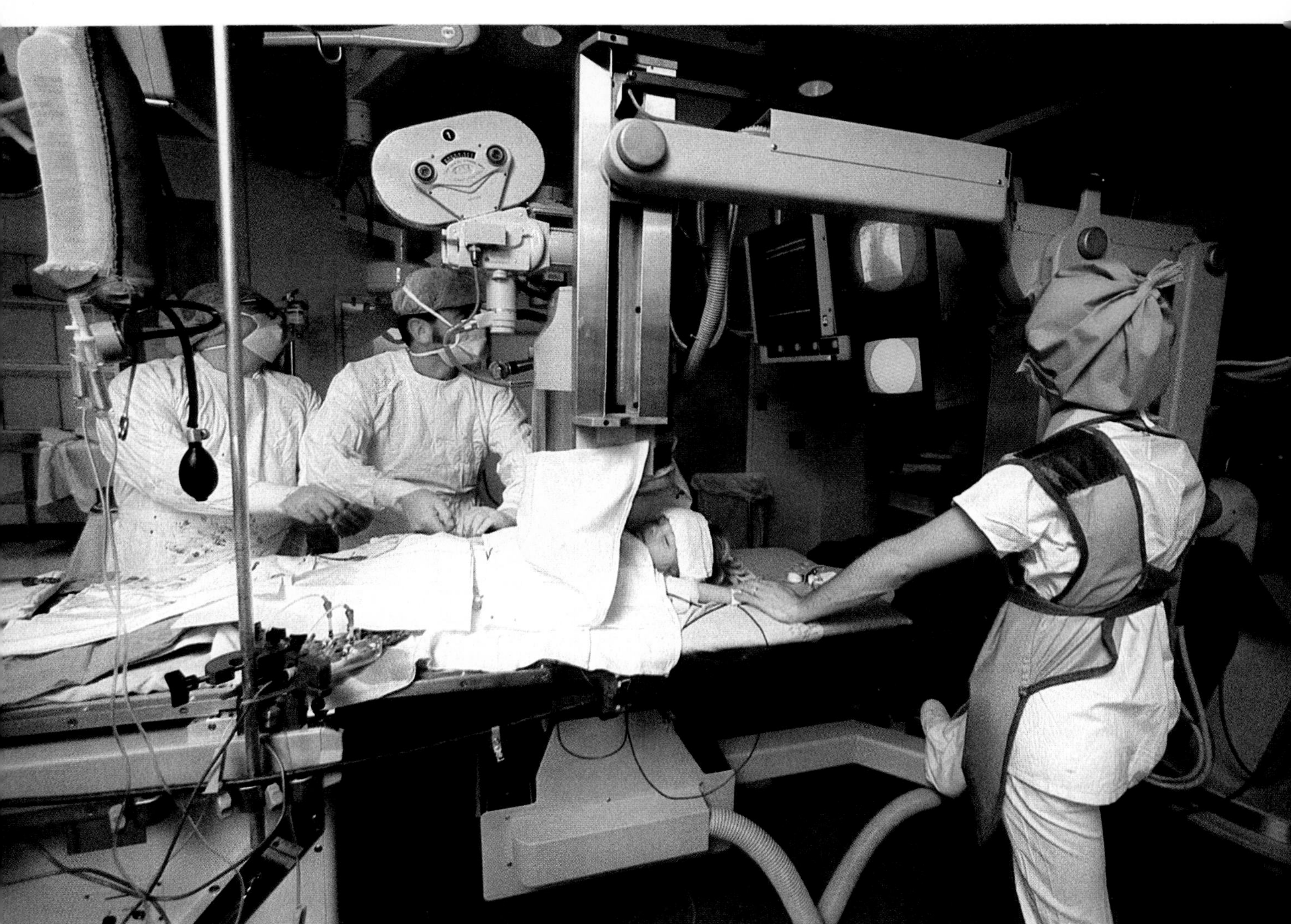

Following their progress on the upper fluoroscope screen, two doctors guide catheters into the heart of a six-year-old girl who, because of her age, is mildly sedated and is comforted by a nurse. The movie camera above the child will make an X-ray film of her heart during the fleeting seconds before the dyes injected through the catheters are flushed away by the flow of blood.

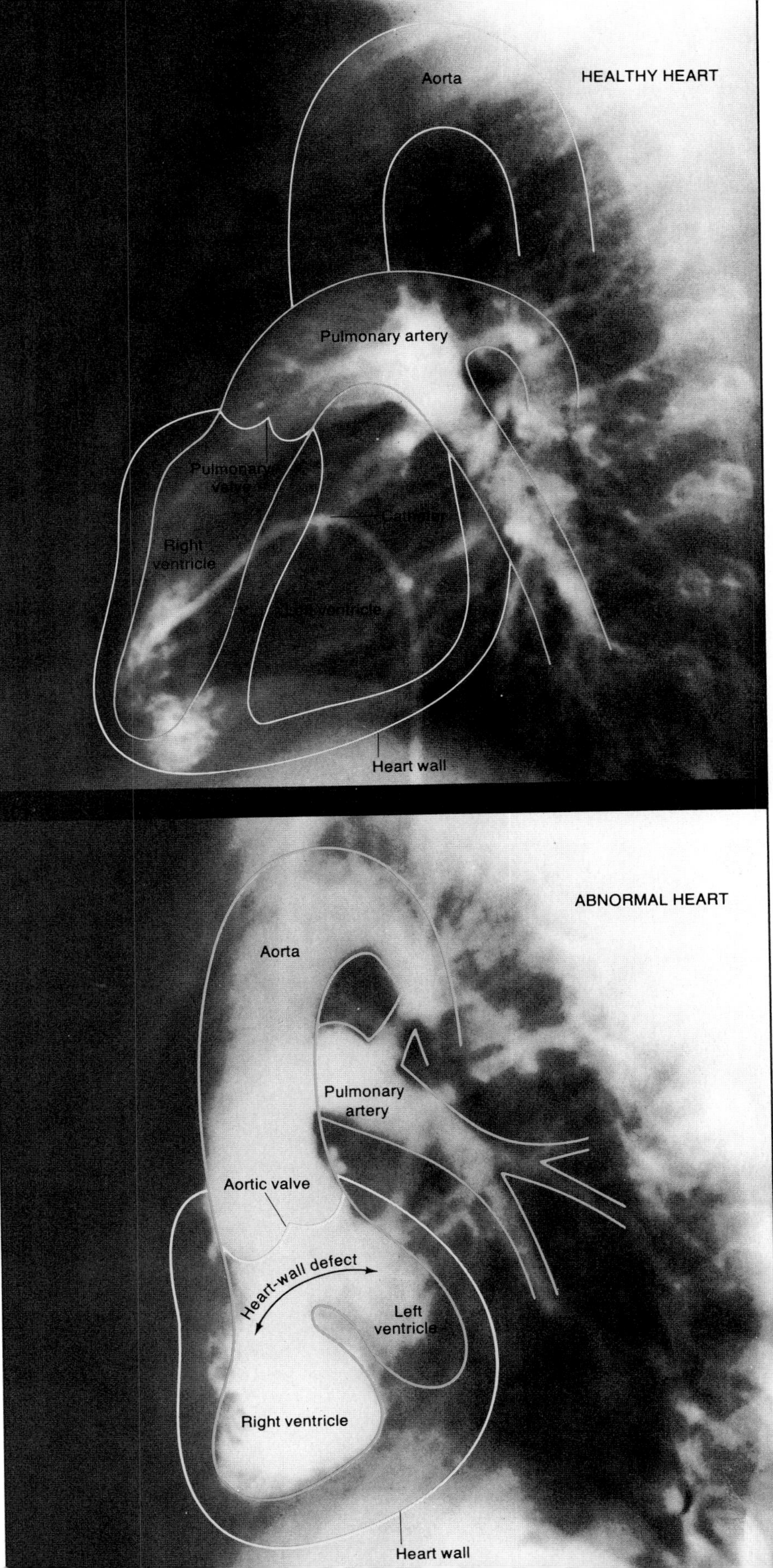

Green outlines superimposed on this X-ray angiogram delineate the parts of the heart revealed when dye is injected into the right ventricle (other structures of the heart are outlined in yellow). The T-shaped, light area inside the green outline shows the dye flowing from the ventricle, through the pulmonary valve and artery, and on toward the lungs. Other light areas and streaks, except for the prominent curve of the catheter, are structures of the body that are irrelevant to the test.

A heart with a congenital defect like that afflicting the young patient at left is pictured in this angiogram, which was taken at a different angle from the one above and does not show the catheter. Dye injected into the heart has not only filled the right ventricle and the pulmonary artery as in the healthy heart, but it has also leaked through a hole in an interior wall (arrow), into the left ventricle and from there on through the aortic valve into the aorta.

Sounding out the faults with ultrasonic waves

Among the safest techniques a doctor has for examining a heart is echocardiography, which is an adaptation of the sonar used to detect submarines. It looks inside the heart with high-pitched, or ultrasonic, sound waves. Inaudible to the human ear, such sounds can be aimed and focused like light. They penetrate certain tissues of the body but are bounced back by other structures, such as the heart and the blood vessels. These ultrasonic echoes are detected and converted into an image on a screen.

With the most advanced echocardiography equipment, a technician directs a thin, fan-shaped pulse of sound toward the heart, taking care to miss the bones and the air-filled lungs, which would cause extra reflections. When sound reaches the heart, part of the sound is reflected back, first by one exterior wall, then by internal structures and finally by the opposite exterior wall. The echoes received by the instrument create a shadowy cross section of the heart and reveal to an expert that organ's innermost secrets.

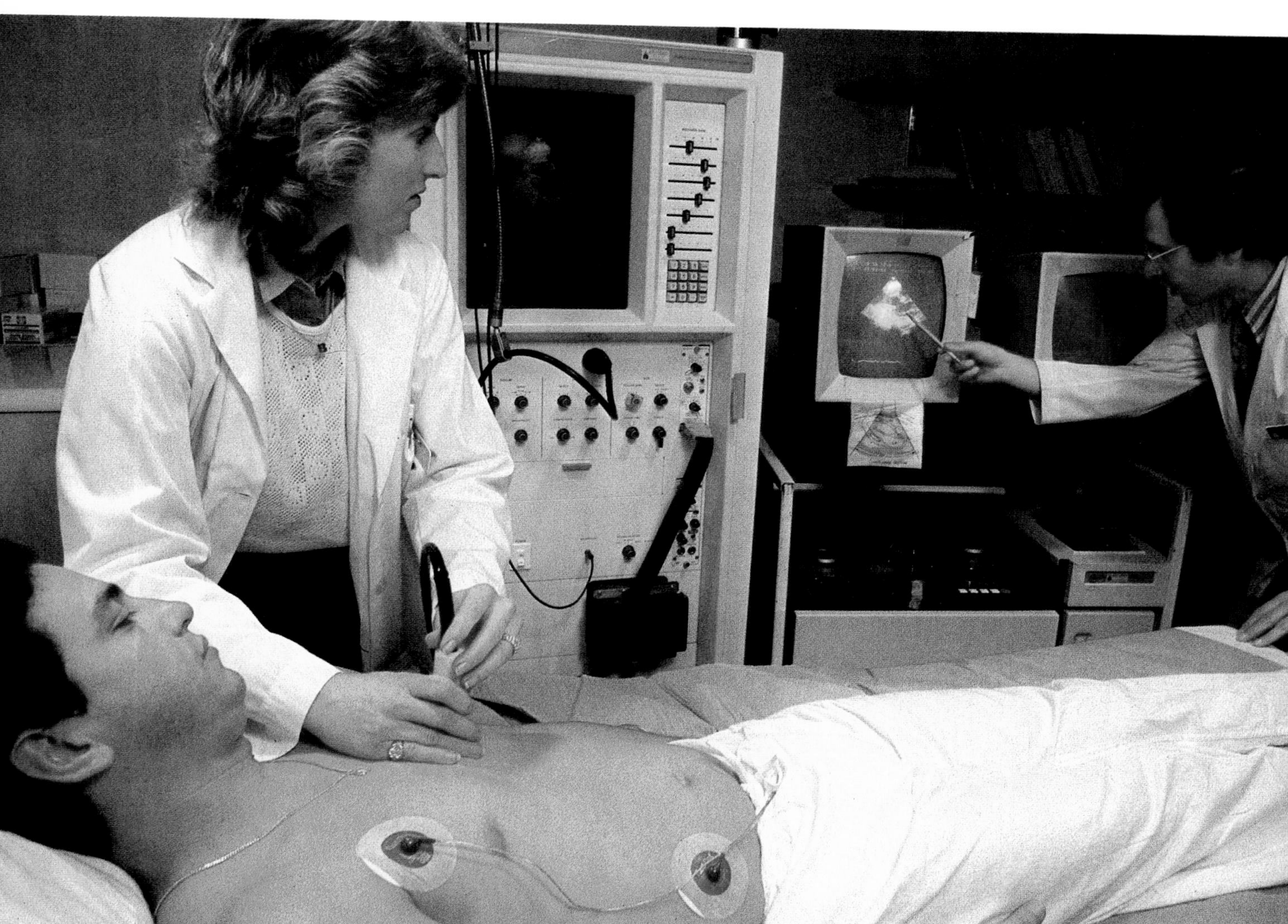

A nurse holds an echocardiography transducer—which both transmits and receives sound—so that its signals create the image of the heart on the television-like screen in the background. Electrodes taped to the patient transmit an electrocardiogram (ECG), which tells whether or not the heartbeat is normal.

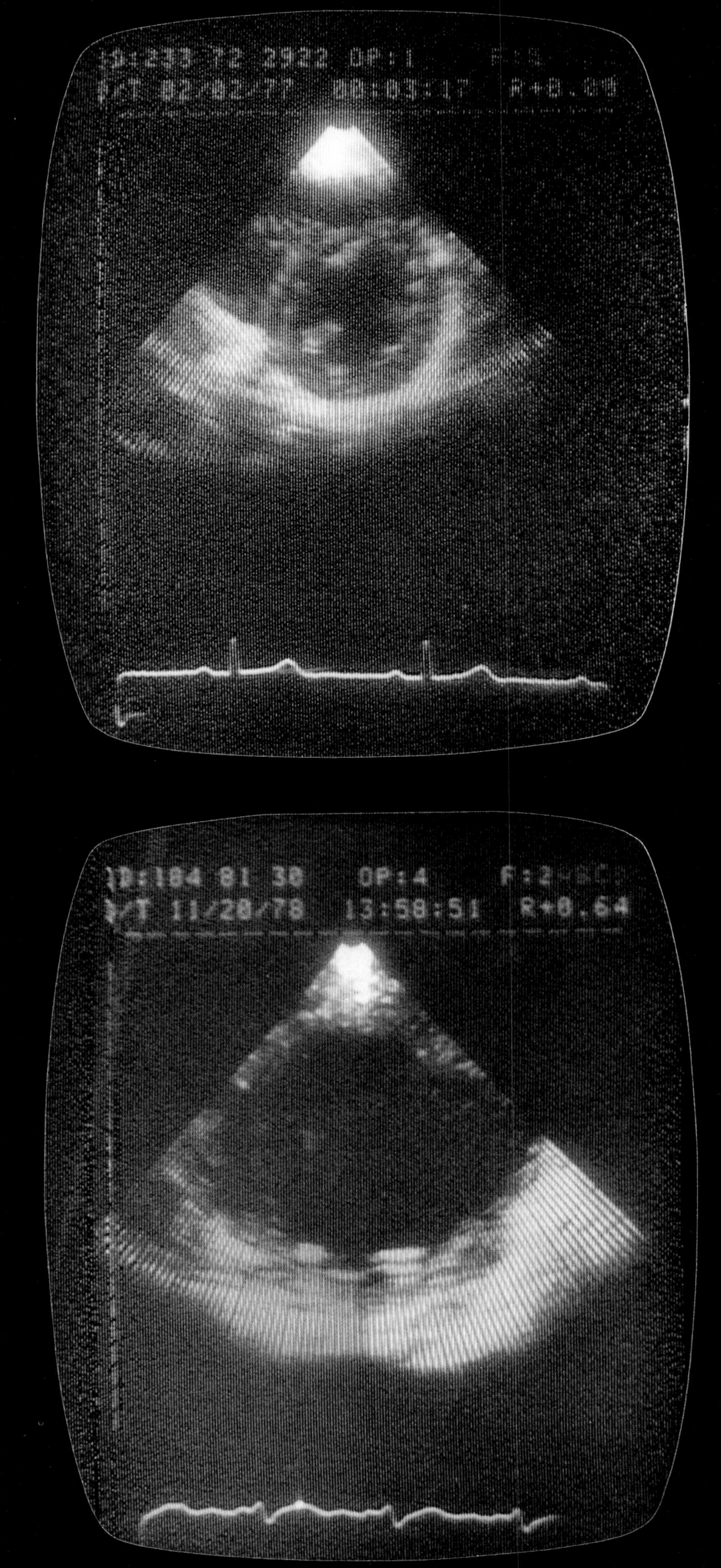

HEALTHY HEART
In the picture at left, echocardiography faintly outlines a cross section of most of a healthy heart as seen from below. The oval in the center of the screen is the left ventricle; part of the right ventricle is visible to the left. Two small light areas at the bottom of the oval are part of the mitral valve, between the left ventricle and left atrium. The ECG tracing along the bottom of the screen shows no irregularities.

DAMAGED HEART
In this cross section of another heart, the left ventricle is more than twice the size of the one above, completely dominating the screen. A misshapen ECG tracing reveals the cause—damage from heart attack. Though this view is similar to the one above, the mitral valve is not seen here because the transducer was held a little lower on the patient's chest to make the picture.

Scintillating pictures from radioactivity

Nuclear science now gives doctors a picture of the beating heart much like an angiogram made with catheters, dyes and X-rays, but without requiring surgery. To make the heart visible, doctors simply inject into a vein or an artery of an arm or a leg a small quantity of a slightly radioactive material.

This substance, constantly emitting radiation, collects temporarily in the heart; precisely where depends on the substance employed. The radiation it emits is picked up by a detector and then is converted electronically into an image, called a nuclear scan or sometimes a nuclear angiogram.

Technetium, the radioactive substance that was used for the pictures on the opposite page, collects in red blood cells; because they fill the chambers of the heart, the image created by the radiation they emit shows the heart's movements as it beats. Other radioactive substances pass from the blood into the heart muscle and reveal whether any parts of the heart are starved for blood or have died as a result of a heart attack.

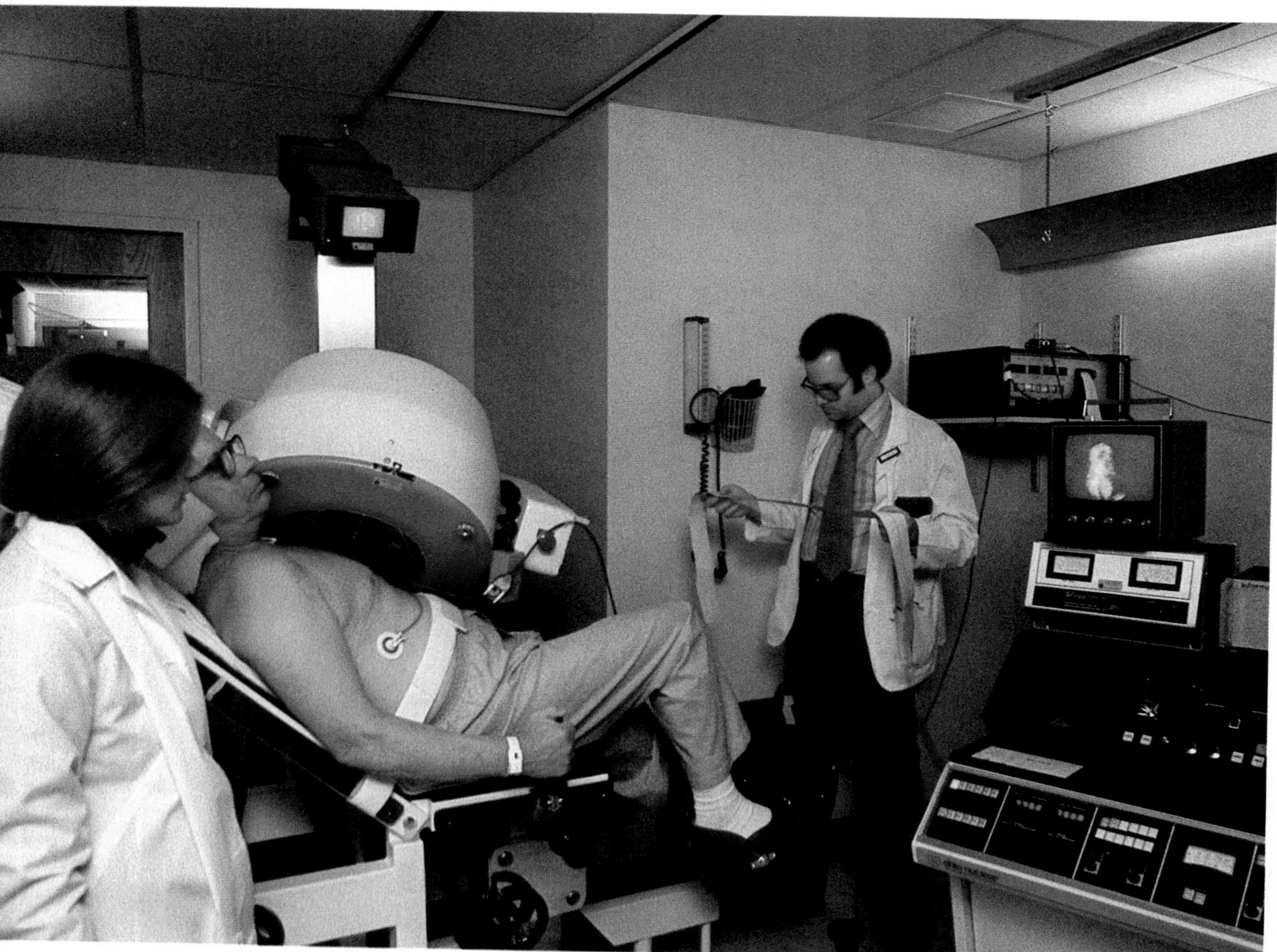

Under the dome of a camera that is making a nuclear scan, a patient pedals a stationary bicycle as the physician testing him examines an ECG for dangerous heartbeat irregularities. Behind the doctor, where the patient can watch, is a screen that displays the beating of his damaged heart.

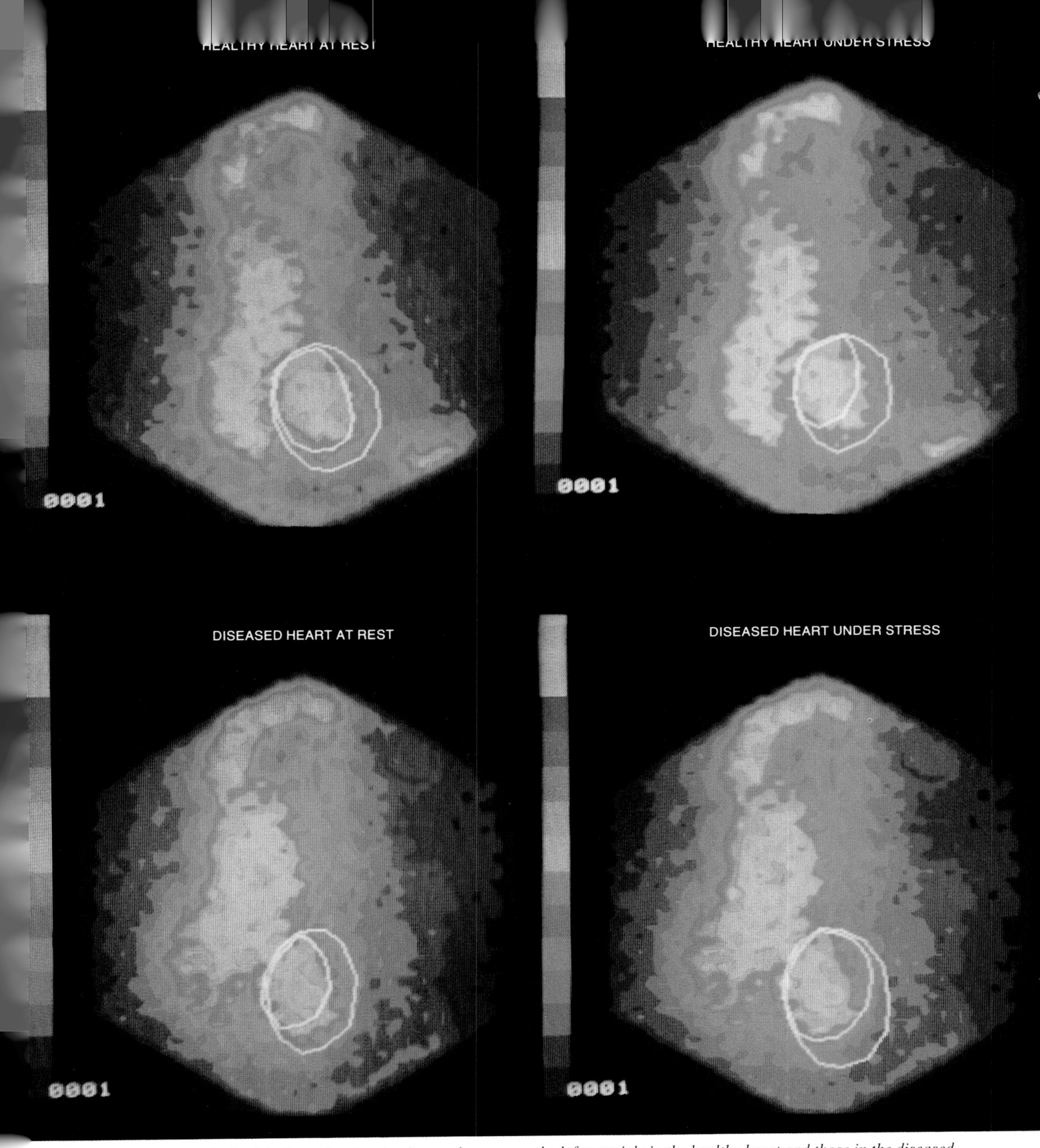

In these nuclear scans of a healthy heart (top) and a diseased one (bottom), white circles drawn by technicians outline the left ventricle at its largest, when it is filling with blood, and at its smallest, as it pumps blood to the body. At rest (in the pictures on the left), the slight differences between the contractions of the left ventricle in the healthy heart and those in the diseased heart are not significant. But under stress the diseased ventricle (bottom right), even though it overexpands to fill with blood, cannot contract enough to pump as much blood to the body as the healthy ventricle does under the same conditions.

CHAPTER 5

New-found prowess of the surgeon

Learning how to stop the heart—safely
The crucial tests
From test to bypass
Greatest miracle of all—the transplant
The drama of the operating theater
Surfacing in the recovery room

Early one spring morning, during vacation time at Stanford University in California, freshman Sam Poole headed south along the Pacific coast with a carload of friends, a surfboard strapped to his trunk. Six feet tall, sun-blond and deeply tanned, Sam seemed hardly different from any of the hundreds of other college students who thronged the beaches that spring.

But Sam was different, and profoundly so. A tiny pacemaker, an electronic device that regulates the beat of the heart, had been embedded in the flesh near his left shoulder. Very few 20-year-old surfers wear pacemakers. That was not all. Down the center of Sam's chest, scarcely noticeable as he stripped off his shirt and paddled his board into the waves, ran a thin, neat scar. It extended from the base of his neck almost to his navel, and it was the signature of another, quite extraordinary medical fact. The heart that pulsed within Sam's athletic frame was not the heart he was born with. It was a surgical transplant.

The replacement of one individual's heart with that of another was unthinkable not so long ago. The ability to remove a vital organ from the body and to replace it with an equivalent part from another human being represents a latter-day miracle of surgery. The procedure demands the most delicate and complex operating-room techniques, a pharmacopoeia of exotic drugs, and a battery of testing and monitoring machines. The patient's abdomen or chest must be sliced open, and the sick organ exposed and cut out. Its replacement, brought still living from the donor to the recipient, must be set into place. Minute blood vessels must be matched up and stitched back together. Once implanted, the new organ must be protected from assault by the recipient's own natural bodily functions—his immune reaction, which responds to the arrival of this alien object by trying to repulse it.

Today, various parts of the body are transferred almost routinely from one individual to another: patches of skin, slivers of bone, the cornea of the eye and, since 1954, even the kidneys. But none of these surgical transplantations is as daring or dramatic as that of the human heart—the seat of life itself.

Cutting deep into the heart poses a unique surgical problem. If the heart is invaded, it can no longer pump blood through the body. When circulation of blood ceases, the brain begins to die. The patient's cells are deprived of oxygen, their functioning stops and they begin to break down. Within two to three minutes the brain cells start to go. Within five minutes the patient is dead. This mortal risk created the greatest single problem of modern heart surgery: finding a way to attack the heart without murdering its owner. There are in fact many ways—most of them far simpler than transplant surgery—that suffice to cure numerous heart ailments.

Certain types of heart surgery can be performed while the heart is still pumping blood—indeed, a great majority of heart operations carry none of the risk that is associated with a transplant. They treat valve defects, accidental injuries, some forms of arterial damage and malfunctioning of the

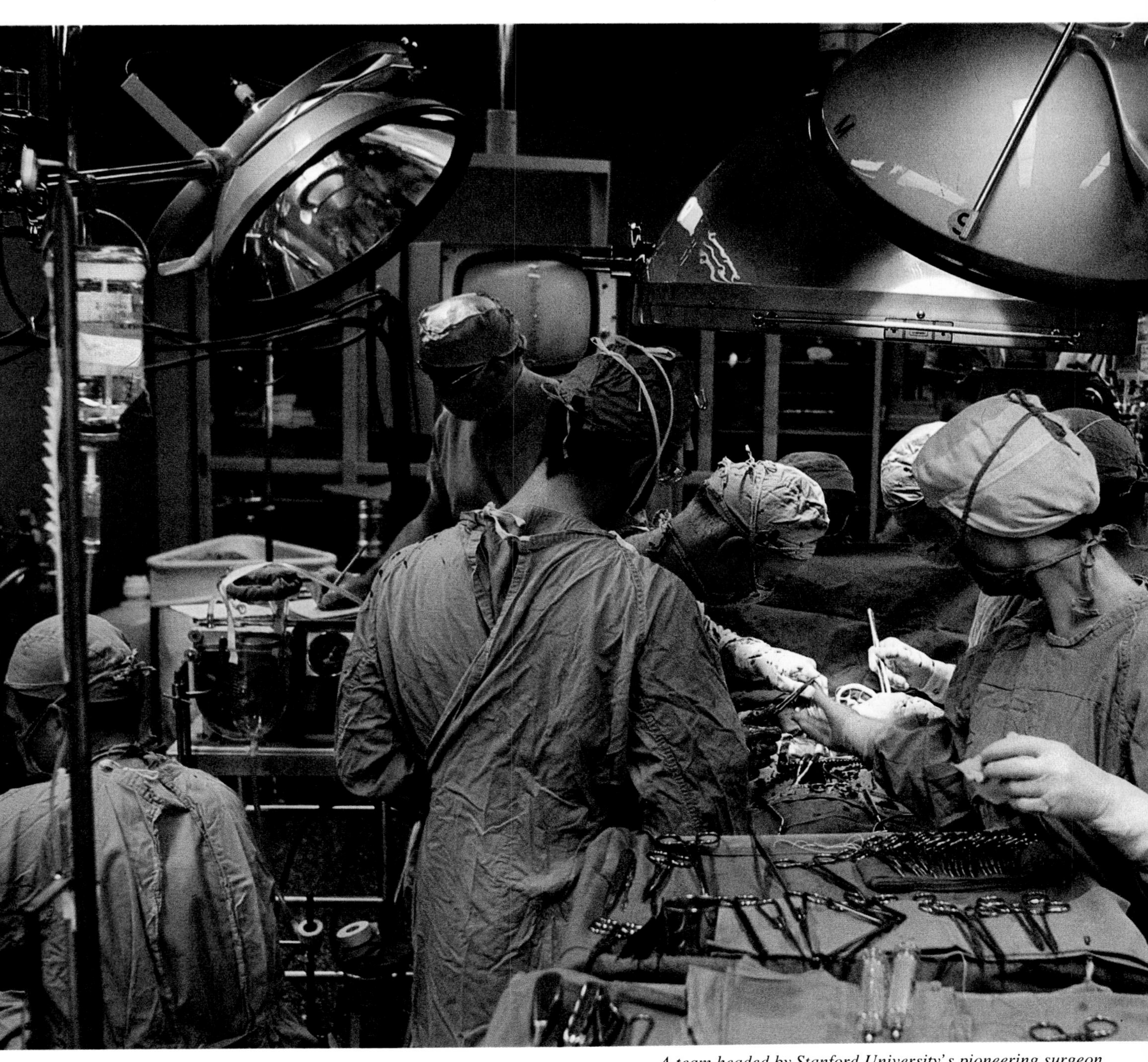

A team headed by Stanford University's pioneering surgeon Norman Shumway (right center, with scalpel) performs open-heart surgery: the replacement of a damaged valve with a man-made substitute. The team includes two assistant surgeons, two anesthesiologists, an intern, a nurse and a heart-lung technician whose machine pumps blood and breathes for the patient.

heart's control system. Many of these operations are performed without even opening the chest; instead, a flexible probe called a catheter *(page 19)* is used. The artificial pacemaker implanted near Sam Poole's shoulder is one example of closed-chest heart surgery.

The natural pacemaker that is part of the normal heart, the nerve center in the upper corner of the right atrium, sends out electrical impulses that control the heartbeat. To begin a beat, this so-called sinoatrial node shoots a signal across the atria—the chambers that receive blood—causing them to contract and force blood into the pumping chambers, called the ventricles *(page 9)*. The signal continues down an avenue of muscle fibers into the ventricles, and these clench up to pump their contents into the bloodstream. Should anything occur to interrupt this rhythm—severe shock, malfunction of the nerve center, damage to the heart muscle—the heartbeat will become irregular, sometimes dangerously so.

A pacemaker *(page 109)* is in essence an auxiliary nerve center. It is a small assemblage of batteries and transistors that monitors the recipient's natural heartbeat; should the pulse rate drop below a set normal rate—usually 68 beats per minute—the electronic pacemaker takes over until the pulse returns to normal. It is implanted inside the body underneath the skin, near the shoulder or the abdomen; this operation can usually be performed with a local anesthetic. It is no more difficult or hazardous than removing an appendix. In the most common pacemaker-implant technique a catheter, which carries an electrode at its tip, is directed into the right side of the heart through a vein in the left or right arm. Then a slit is cut into the torso near the armpit, and a pocket opened to hold the pacemaker box. The catheter is hooked to the box, the pocket is sewed up and the operation is finished. There is no more to it.

Thereafter the recipient will have to take certain precautions. He will have to check his pacemaker at regular intervals according to his doctor's instructions; the newest batteries last about 10 years. After that time he may need another operation to implant a new pacemaker with a fresh battery. And he must avoid such electronic gadgets as microwave ovens, which broadcast electromagnetic waves that could disrupt the pacemaker. But it should cause him no other inconvenience or discomfort. He has joined an informal club of pacemaker recipients that annually grows by 100,000 new members around the world, over 65,000 in the United States alone. He may, should he wish, keep abreast of pacemaker news and technology in national magazines such as *Pulse* in the United States, *Stimucoeur* in France and *Souri Elettci* in Italy.

Another modern, relatively simple operation, called balloon angioplasty, is sometimes prescribed to relieve coronary heart disease as a less traumatic alternative to open-heart surgery. It employs a special catheter that is tipped with a small rubber balloon. The catheter is guided up through an artery of the groin and into the heart's main artery, the aorta; it is then manipulated into position near a clogged segment of the coronary artery. There the balloon is inflated, forcing the artery to dilate and opening the blockage. A similar technique sometimes offers relief to potential stroke victims. The catheter is inserted into the neck and directed up through one of the two carotid arteries, which are located behind the ears and feed blood to the brain. These two vessels are common sites for clogging deposits of fat, but unblocking them does not call for the long and circuitous route of a heart angioplasty. The surgeon simply slides the catheter directly up to the point of blockage, fills the balloon with fluid and opens the passageway.

Angioplasty and pacemaker implantation are but two techniques in the surgeon's broad repertoire of procedures for repairing a damaged heart without stopping its beat. In many of them the heart is actually cut—but the incision is so small and is closed so quickly that the vital pumping action is not interrupted.

A number of these procedures correct inborn congenital defects *(pages 90-91)*. Sometimes, for example, a baby is born with a narrowing in his aorta, a coarctation, that interferes with the flow of blood to his abdomen and legs. To repair the aorta, a surgeon places a clamp above the constricted area, quickly cuts the area out and sews the two healthy, remaining sections of aorta back together—all without stopping the heart. Another operation can save the life of a so-called blue baby, whose ghostly azure skin betrays a lack of oxygen in the blood. Often the cause is a misalignment of vessels at the heart, sending blood from the veins directly into the aorta without allowing it to pass through the lungs to be oxygenated. Again, the surgeon rearranges the ducts while the heart is still beating.

In adults, too, certain defects can be mended with very fast and very skillful surgery that does not interfere with the pumping of blood. Tumors and cysts on the surface of the heart can be excised. Stab wounds and other injuries can sometimes be sewed shut. An aneurysm of the aorta or other major artery, in which part of the vessel weakens and bulges outward, can sometimes be clamped off and replaced with a plastic tube.

Although these procedures do not cut so deeply into the heart that it stops beating, all of them qualify as major operations: The chest must be breached and the heart exposed. They are relatively simple because the heart can continue to function while it is being repaired and the blood can continue to circulate to keep the body alive. Until the mid-1950s, all cardiac surgery fell within this closed-heart category—including a number of ingenious techniques for entering the beating heart itself.

Restoring the heartbeat's normal rhythm

The normal heart beats because unique cells within it create electrical signals in rhythmic impulses that stimulate heart muscle to contract. If these pacemaker cells fail to keep their rhythm, either the beats become erratic or the heart stops altogether. To counter this dangerous arrhythmia, an electronic timekeeper such as the one at right is implanted inside the body and wired to the heart. The first was installed in a patient in 1958; two decades later almost a million were in use worldwide.

Most man-made pacemakers, powered by lithium batteries, function six to 12 years before they need replacement. They are generally set for 70 beats per minute, enough for normal activities.

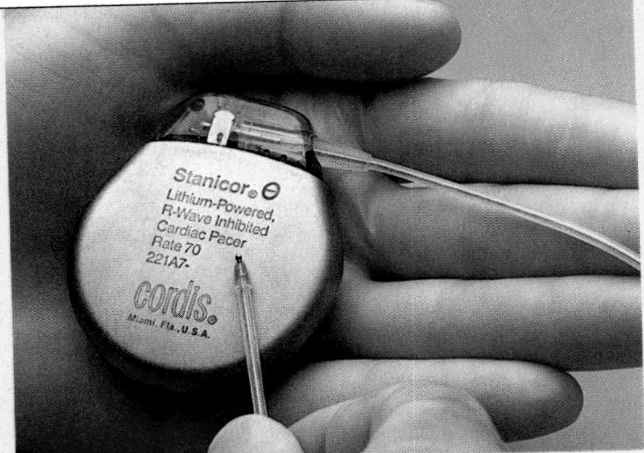

AN ELECTRONIC TIMER FOR THE HEART

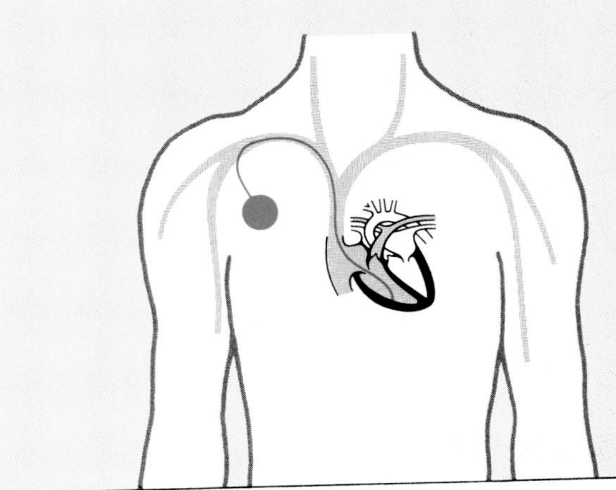

IMPLANTING A PACEMAKER IN THE SHOULDER
Surgeons prefer—because the operation requires only local anesthetic—to embed the pacemaker in shoulder tissue and then thread its connecting wire (red) through a vein (blue) into the right ventricle; the electrical impulses stimulate the heart lining.

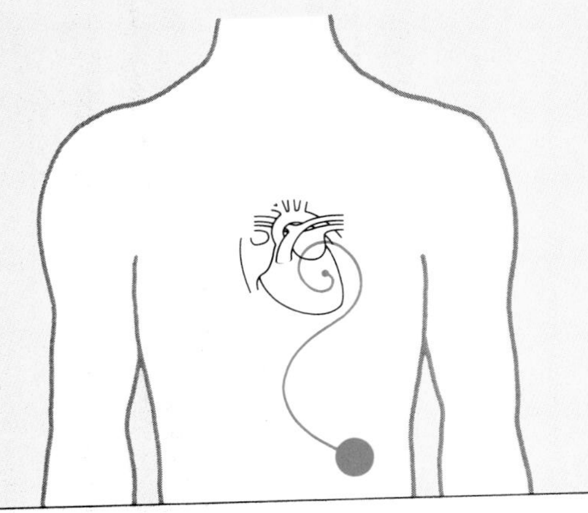

IMPLANTING A PACEMAKER IN THE ABDOMEN
When veins are too small or damaged by disease to accept the connecting wire, surgeons screw or press it into the outside wall of the heart, or epicardium, and then loop the wire loosely to a pacemaker that is placed alongside the abdominal sac.

Among the most demanding of such operations is the repair of defective heart valves. Any number of mishaps may cause a valve to misfunction, one of the most common being a bout of rheumatic fever in childhood. In approximately half of all rheumatic fever patients, the heart valves become inflamed; as the disease subsides the valves of some of these patients are left hardened and scarred. The damaged valves leak, or they freeze up so that blood cannot flow in full volume.

One of the first successful surgical attacks on a hardened valve was aimed at the mitral valve, which governs the flow of blood from the left atrium to the left ventricle. The technique is a monument to the surgical ingenuity of Dr. Henry Souttar of London Hospital. At the top of the left atrium a small, nipple-like protrusion, about the size of a finger tip, juts out, making a perfect entry point to the mitral valve. A row of stitches was run around the base of the node, creating a drawstring. Dr. Souttar cut a hole in the tip of the protrusion, thrust his finger quickly inside and immediately pulled the drawstring snug so that little or no blood escaped. Working with part of his finger inside the beating heart, he then probed straight down into the mitral valve, loosening its flaps and enlarging the opening, breaking up the scar tissue, tickling the valve back to life. The procedure is still in use, and with refinements in technique, it poses no more danger than the removal of a gall bladder. (It does not suffice for all valve operations; some require the more complex, heart-stopping surgery involved in transplants.)

The simple type of surgery that ameliorates many valve defects was the first applied to the greatest heart crippler of all, coronary heart disease. Here the possibilities were more limited, the difficulties far greater—and early efforts suggest a frenzied, trial-and-error desperation. Surgeons scraped the heart surface with their scalpels and sprinkled it with talcum powder, in hopes that such physical insults would provoke the heart to grow new arteries.

In one operation that still enjoys a limited vogue, one of the two internal mammary arteries is diverted from its normal route to the chest and grafted onto the surface of the heart, a shift that can be accomplished while the heart continues to beat. Within six months or so, the relocated artery begins to generate its own network of coronary vessels. Internal mammary implantation is performed only on relatively few patients today, primarily because of the long period of time that it takes for collateral vessels to sprout. During those six months, the patient could die. In addition, the blood supply provided to the heart by these collateral vessels may not be as great as the blood supply provided by veins grafted by the coronary bypass operation.

Learning how to stop the heart—safely

For all their variety and ingenuity, the possibilities of these closed-heart operations are limited. They can be performed while the pumping heart continues its work, sending oxygenated blood through the body and brain, but for a major operation—one that profoundly involves the structure of the heart or removes it entirely—the heartbeat must stop. Circulation must be maintained by other means.

The accomplishment of this feat—stopping a patient's heart while still keeping him alive—represents a well-nigh miraculous surgical breakthrough. For a number of years, doctors had known how to slow down a patient's heart by injecting drugs into it and by drastically lowering body temperature. The cooled state, known as hypothermia, induces a kind of hibernation that retards the operation of the body and diminishes its need for blood. Perfecting a technique for inducing hypothermia was an important step, but it did not go far enough.

The turning point came with the development of a remarkable device, the heart-lung machine, which performs two amazing jobs simultaneously. It takes over the roles normally filled by both the heart and the lungs. First, it pumps a patient's blood outside his body, bypassing his own heart. Second, it charges the blood with the oxygen necessary to sustain life while removing such waste products as carbon dioxide; then it pumps the freshened blood back into the body to circulate it.

The origins of the heart-lung machine date back to the turn of the century, when scientists in Germany and England, studying the effects of drugs on animal organs, contrived

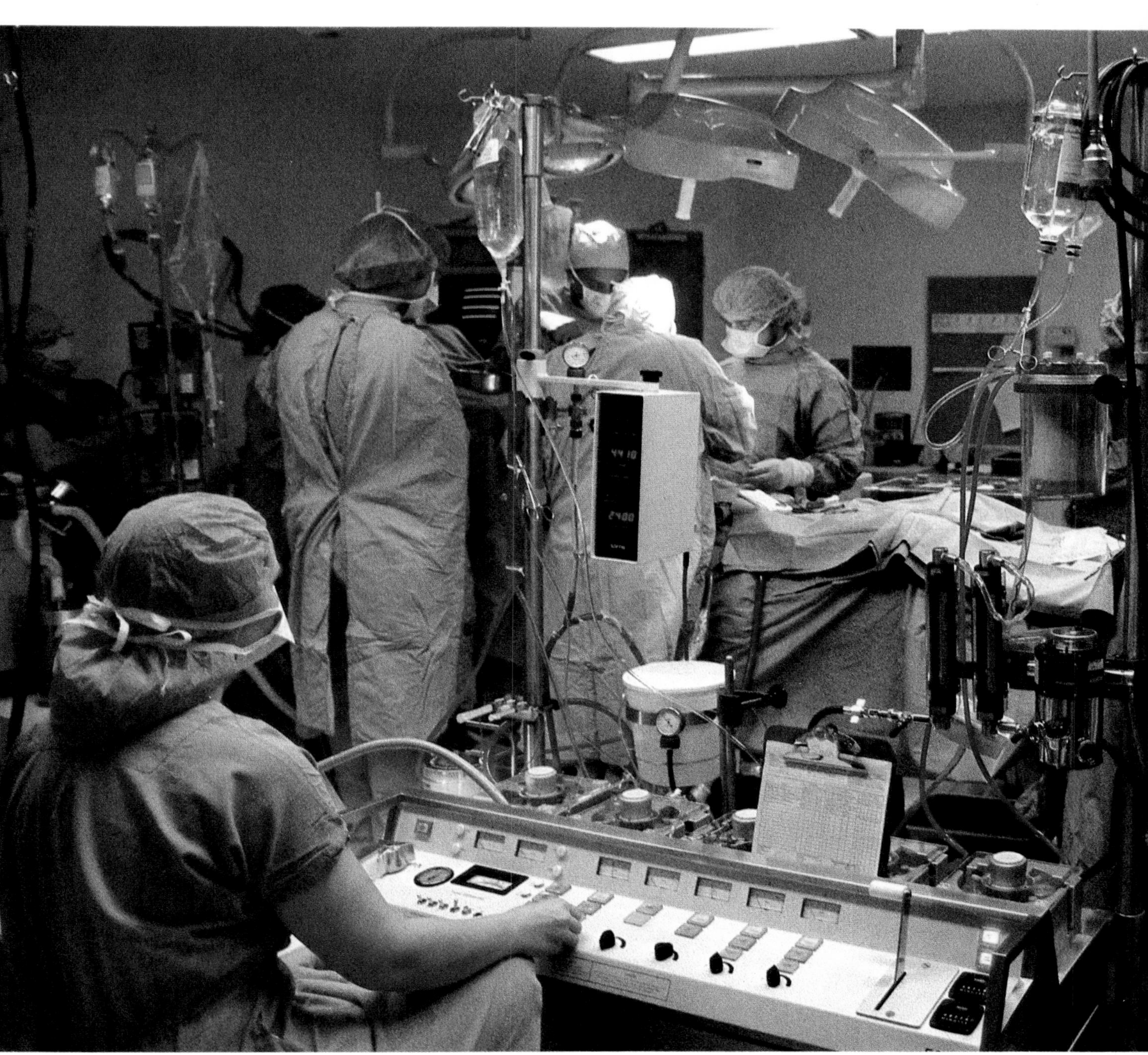

The technician and machine in the foreground substitute for a patient's heart and lungs while his heart is stopped for surgery. The heart-lung machine diverts used blood from his body to a chamber where oxygen bubbles are introduced, producing a chemical reaction that releases carbon dioxide. The oxygen-replenished blood is defoamed and pumped back into the body.

Shopping for a surgeon

If ever a medical procedure required a second opinion, open-heart surgery does. After one cardiologist has recommended surgery and the surgeon to perform it, another specialist may have persuasive reasons for suggesting a different surgeon—or a different course of treatment, such as further medication or a lesser operation.

When a coronary bypass or other type of open-heart surgery is decided on, the qualifications of the surgeon become critical. The more he has performed a particular operation, the better. "And to maintain his skill," says Dr. Oscar Roth of the Yale University Medical School, "he should do at least three such operations a week."

A 2 per cent mortality rate for an appreciable number of operations is good, Dr. Roth adds, for bypass surgery and similar operations. Most patients show some reluctance to ask a surgeon about his mortality rate for an operation. However, a surgeon who becomes indignant at questions about his surgical record disqualifies himself: Every patient has a right to the information.

pumps and syringes to bathe livers and kidneys with mixtures of blood, air and chemicals. There were problems at the beginning. For one thing, mechanical agitation tended to change blood composition and damage blood cells. For another, the researchers could not find a way to combine oxygen and blood without causing clots or air bubbles. They tried washing the blood over metal screens or plastic sheets, aerating it through thin membranes, even shunting it through the lungs of dogs and monkeys.

Eventually the kinks were shaken out. In 1953 Dr. John Gibbon of Jefferson Medical College in Philadelphia performed the breakthrough operation. He connected the blood system of an 18-year-old woman to a complex pump that drained her blood, oxygenated it across a stainless-steel mesh and returned it to her body. For 26 minutes the woman's blood ran through the device while Gibbon opened her now-stilled heart to sew up a hole in the wall separating the two atria. A new age in cardiac surgery had arrived.

The mechanics of the heart-lung machine, and the techniques for applying it, have been refined to the point where its use has now become almost routine. It opened the way not only to transplants like that given Sam Poole, but to an impressive variety of lifesaving procedures. Today clogged arteries are replaced, misconnected vessels shifted, holes patched and defective valves removed so that substitutes can be installed.

Consider, for example, the problems of operating on the valves of the heart. No longer does a surgeon have to grope and poke at the accessible valves and leave the inaccessible ones alone. Today patients with heart valves scarred by fever or misshapen because of faulty genes find relief under the knife. With the heart open and circulation maintained by a heart-lung machine, the surgeon simply cuts away the defective valve and stitches in one selected from a catalogue of available models.

There are man-made valves of plastic and metal that work reasonably well, though the plastic sometimes irritates the heart tissue or generates blood clots. With improved design, these problems are being alleviated. Even so, many surgeons prefer to use natural components of various types—snips of thigh tissue or pericardium, or valves taken from a donor heart. Among the most popular valve substitutes is one taken from the heart of a pig, which closely resembles its human counterpart.

Valve operations are only a minority of the new operations made possible by the heart-lung machine. The most common of all heart diseases—atherosclerosis, with its excruciating pain and constant threat of heart attack—is now regularly treated by open-heart surgery. "We're doing things now that were undreamed of in surgery ten years ago," says Dr. Denton Cooley, the great heart surgeon of St. Luke's Episcopal Hospital in Houston. "Patients who were completely incapacitated or at death's door are now completely rehabilitated. It's an entirely new world."

The crucial tests

Three years before Sam Poole's surfing vacation, hope seemed to have run out for him. His condition had developed slowly, but inexorably. The previous Christmas, Sam had contracted a racking cough, accompanied by a sense of queasy lassitude. These were strange symptoms for Sam, a star athlete at school. The family doctor listened to his chest but could find no explanation. He ordered a chest X-ray, and the result was alarming: Sam's heart had enlarged to perhaps a third again its normal size.

A person's heart may swell for any of several reasons, some of them perfectly healthy. A professional athlete, for example, will build up his heart muscle beyond normal proportions; so, too, will someone who lives continuously at very high altitudes, such as an alpine ski instructor or a Peruvian copper miner. But sometimes the heart grows larger because of disease. A virus may attack the heart muscle, causing it to weaken and distend. Generally the heart shrinks back to its normal size after the virus has receded, but in some cases it is left permanently damaged and enlarged. Such a condition, called cardiomyopathy, is rare but it can be extremely grave.

During the next several months, Sam's condition continued to worsen. His energy plunged, and by midsummer he could not rise from a chair or walk across a room without extreme fatigue. Every meal was likely to end in a bout of vomiting. All through these months, a series of tests kept track of Sam's decline, and the evidence added up to a grim diagnosis: cardiomyopathy.

Several of the tests Sam took are standard for all heart patients. The first and simplest was an electrocardiogram, or ECG *(pages 94-95),* a recording of bodily electrical charges that reveals the rhythm of heartbeats and the exact strength and sequence of contraction in each atrium and ventricle.

Sam's first ECG was a puzzling surprise. The rhythm of his heartbeats was normal.

The next test proved far less encouraging. It was an echocardiogram *(pages 102-103)*—a recording of sound waves reflected off the heart. The technique gives a more vivid portrait of the heart in action than does an ordinary X-ray, and in Sam's case the picture was not a healthy one. It revealed that the distention of his heart resulted not from extra muscle, but from the opposite condition—an ominous deterioration of the heart wall.

The final verdict was provided by the third test, an angiogram *(pages 100-101).* In this test, administered to virtually all candidates for heart surgery, a dye opaque to X-rays is injected into the heart, and X-ray pictures are taken.

An angiogram is a type of surgery in its own right, and it takes place in a hospital. On the day of the test, the patient is given a sedative and wheeled into the angiography room. A number of specialists attend him there: the cardiologist, who will thread dye-injecting catheters through the body into the heart, an X-ray specialist, and various nurses and technicians, all clad in surgical cap and gown. The patient is helped onto the X-ray table and canvas straps are passed across his body; these hold him comfortably in position as the table is tipped and rotated to provide several different picture angles.

Then, pain prevented by local anesthetic, a large needle called a trocar is placed in a main blood vessel, usually the femoral artery, in the right or left thigh. The trocar provides an entry for the catheters. The physician inserts the first one, following its progress on an X-ray screen as he guides it up through the artery, past the pelvis and abdomen, and into the heart itself. At the patient's request the screen may be placed so that he, too, can watch.

The experience of seeing the thin, flexible tube of the catheter snake through the body to invade his heart can fill a patient with awe. Dr. Harold Lear, a 53-year-old urologist who had suffered a heart attack and was a candidate for surgery, viewed the start of his angiogram with a cool professional eye. "Oh, yes," he thought, as the tube wound up through his chest, "that's the arch of my aorta." Then, still watching as the tube looped down into a shadowy chamber, he lost his composure. "My God," he thought, "this cavity is my heart! I am looking at the inside of my heart! It was like . . . what? Like seeing God?"

In the last phase of the test the dye is injected. As it squirts through the catheter, in carefully measured doses, the patient feels a sudden hot flush, as though an oven door has opened. In a few rare instances there is a spasm of nausea. These sensations usually last no more than 60 seconds, and they are a small price to pay for the next moments of insight directly into the heart and its workings. On the X-ray screen, as the dye flows through the heart and its arteries, the physician can see virtually every abnormality. Should a valve malfunction, the dye will show it. Should there be a leak in the wall between the atria—a common congenital defect—its exact position will become clear. The test is particularly valuable in diagnosing coronary heart disease. The dye can be sent through suspect arteries, outlining their locations and shapes on the screen. The physician has an instant reading on the position and severity of the blockage.

Often this is a moment of decision: open-heart surgery, or not? If surgery is called for, the angiogram becomes an essential first step in the operation itself. By studying the test pictures, recorded on video tape, the surgeon will know just where to cut, saving critical minutes on the operating table. The angiogram may in fact be the only test used to pinpoint a patient's problem, and it may be an immediate prelude to surgery.

From test to bypass

Consider the case of Dr. William Nolan of Litchfield, Minnesota. Dr. Nolan was himself a surgeon—the only surgeon at the county hospital—and he carried a heavy work load of perhaps 500 cases a year. Like many men in his profession, he was an energetic, competitive perfectionist—a textbook example of the so-called Type A, coronary-prone personality. He was also athletic. During a racketball match Dr. Nolan felt a strange shortness of breath, accompanied by a burning sensation in his chest and throat. When he took a short break, the burning subsided and he finished the match without further discomfort.

These brief symptoms brought Dr. Nolan no sense of alarm. He had felt no deep pain, nor was there the agonizing flash in the left shoulder or arm that often accompanies the classic angina of a heart attack. But during the next few weeks, the burning returned whenever he exercised. Reluctantly, Dr. Nolan made an appointment with an internist. An ECG was normal at rest, but indicated suspicious irregularities when his pulse rate rose above 122 beats per minute.

Dr. Nolan checked into a hospital for an angiogram, which requires only a few hours. But he did not leave the hospital that day. The test showed that two of his coronary arteries were almost totally blocked. On the strength of these findings, he was whisked into the operating room. Two weeks later he was home, and after another month he was back in an operating room—his own. He soon went back to performing major surgery and scrambling to fit a daily game of racketball into his schedule.

The operation that gave Dr. Nolan this miraculous new hold on life was a coronary bypass. The first one was done in 1962, and within a few years the bypass became the most common of all open-heart operations. By 1970 about 2,500 had been performed and a decade later the total number was more than 115,000 in the industrialized world—100,000 in the United States alone.

The results are dramatic. Cardiac sufferers so crippled by the pain of angina that they could barely climb a flight of stairs leave the hospital to resume a virtually normal life *(pages 122-137)*. Nine times out of 10 the pain decreases markedly or simply disappears. Follow-up studies strongly imply that the threat of death from a heart attack also declines; the five-year prognosis for a successful bypass patient comes close to that for the population as a whole.

Such spectacular success predictably has brought abuses. Coronary bypass surgery became fashionable and was recommended for some patients who stood to benefit little, if at all, from the operation. The prestige that accrued to hospitals offering the service also helped intensify the pressure to perform more bypasses.

The potential for such abuses demands alertness and some knowledge on the part of the patient and his family. Bypass surgery is generally considered essential only for certain disorders of the coronary arteries: "left-main disease"—a blockage in the left main coronary artery—or severe angina not treatable with drugs. Most authorities do not advise it for coronary artery spasm, for irreversible damage to the heart muscle as a result of heart attack, or for widespread atherosclerosis in the branches of the coronary arteries.

If a bypass is suggested, a second, independent opinion

To replace a defective heart valve with this plastic-and-metal substitute—one of many types (page 116)—the surgeon guides it into position with a long holder. It will be snugged into the artery when the web of threads, already sewed around the opening, is stitched to a ring on the replacement and then pulled tight.

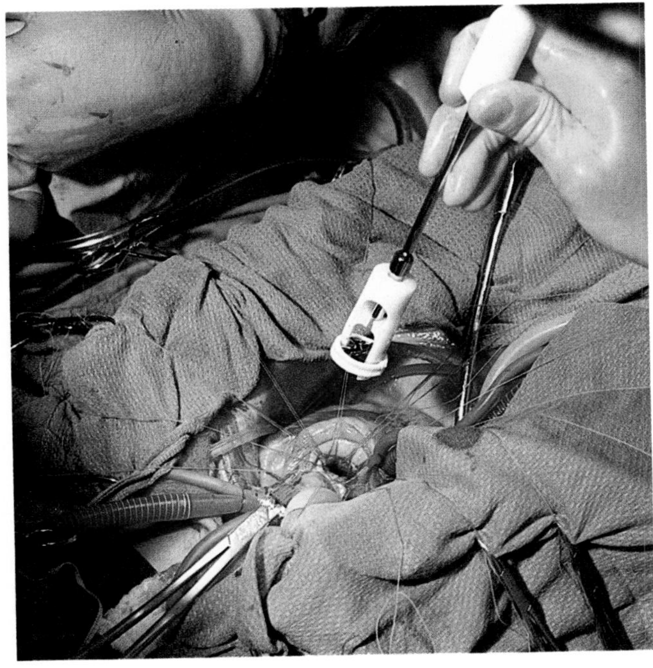

from a specialist in heart diseases is advised. Most physicians welcome such outside advice from an authority. In the American system of private medical practice, finding an expert consultant is not always easy. Some local medical societies maintain lists of specialists; the names of professors and chiefs of cardiology departments can be obtained from university medical schools and hospitals, although numerous inquiries may be needed. Many professors of cardiology treat no private patients, but their offices generally suggest other experts who do.

Even more care is necessary in deciding on the surgeon who will perform the operation *(page 112)*—a choice that is greatly influenced by the character of the hospital in which he works. A bypass operation requires not just one pair of very skillful hands but an entire surgical team that must work together smoothly and efficiently: usually two nurses, a technician to run the heart-lung machine, a monitoring technician, an anesthesiologist, two assistant surgeons and the chief surgeon *(page 107)*.

A well-drilled team is essential. The best are found in hospitals that routinely perform many bypass operations. A report in *The New England Journal of Medicine* concluded: "Hospitals in which 200 or more of these operations were done annually had death rates 25 to 41 per cent lower than hospitals with lower volumes."

It is easy to understand why so much depends on the choice of surgeon and hospital when you learn what is involved in a bypass operation.

A heart bypass is one of the most exacting of all surgical procedures. Segments of vein, most often extracted from the patient's calf or thigh, are grafted between the aorta and an unblocked section of the coronary artery, bypassing the blockage. If more than one artery is clogged, additional grafts are made—as many as nine have been done on one patient. Thus two operations proceed simultaneously: one on the leg to "harvest" the veins that will become substitute arteries, the other on the heart itself. Since coronary arteries run down into the heart tissue itself, the patient's heart must be stopped during the operation and his circulation maintained by a heart-lung machine.

And that is not all. The grafting of a vein to a coronary artery calls for the most delicate surgical touch. Each of the two vessels may be as thin as a pencil lead and, drained of blood, they are limp and fragile. Yet as many as 20 almost-microscopic stitches may be needed to bind the two together *(page 119)*. The only relatively easy part is harvesting the vein from the leg (an operation often performed to correct a case of varicose veins). As the leg wound heals, veins closer to the bone take over the job that had been handled by the one removed.

Like all major open-heart surgery, bypass operations carry some risk. Operations of any type deliver a shock to the system, particularly when a patient's heart is weak. There is a chance, despite all precautions, that the patient may suffer a heart attack while on the operating table. A clot or an air bubble may enter his bloodstream and move to his heart or brain. Sometimes, when the clamps are removed and the blood flows back from the heart-lung machine, the patient's own heart refuses to start beating. Thankfully, these occasions are rare. At major hospitals where bypass surgery is a daily routine, the odds for survival after a bypass operation run as high as 99 per cent.

Greatest miracle of all—the transplant

For Sam Poole, according to the evidence of his angiogram, neither a bypass nor any of the less complex heart repairs would suffice. His heart had stretched so much that its walls were as thin as a child's overexpanded balloon, ready to burst at any time. After the test dye was injected into his left ventricle, most of it simply stayed there. Three fourths of the blood that should have been forced into his aorta with each heartbeat remained behind, sloshing around in the ventricle. There was only one chance for continued life, and that was to remove the entire heart and replace it with a new one—a transplant.

A heart transplant is a last resort. Of all cardiosurgical procedures it is the most hazardous, the most experimental. When Sam Poole became a candidate for the operation, only some 300 transplants had been accomplished. Fewer than 100 patients had survived to leave the hospital, and only one had lived more than 10 years.

The problems occur, for the most part, not on the operating table—the actual surgery is, if anything, less demanding than an ordinary coronary bypass—but afterward. They come from the body's own internal defenses against disease, the reactions of the immunological system. Whenever bacteria or viruses enter the flesh, these defenses go to work immediately. Masses of white corpuscles and other antibodies flood the infected area to battle and expel the intruder. With certain exceptions, almost any matter foreign to the body can prompt this immune reaction: dirt in a wound, a common splinter—or a transplanted heart. The recipient's body interprets the transplant as an invasion, which it tries to repel. Unless the doctors succeed in blocking the body's natural response by suppressing the immune reaction, the new heart fails and the patient dies.

Formidable hazards, these. Yet the ambition to transplant hearts and other organs is as old as medicine itself. A legendary Chinese physician of the Third Century B.C. apparently took credit for swapping the hearts of two soldiers to whom he had slipped knockout drops; three days later the soldiers reported back for duty, none the worse for wear—or so the tale goes.

Better-documented attempts were made over the ages, without success. Then in the early 1900s, researchers at the University of Chicago implanted a laboratoryful of cats, dogs, rabbits and other animals with various inner parts not their own. The groundwork was laid. New surgical techniques were developed and refined, and advances in immu-

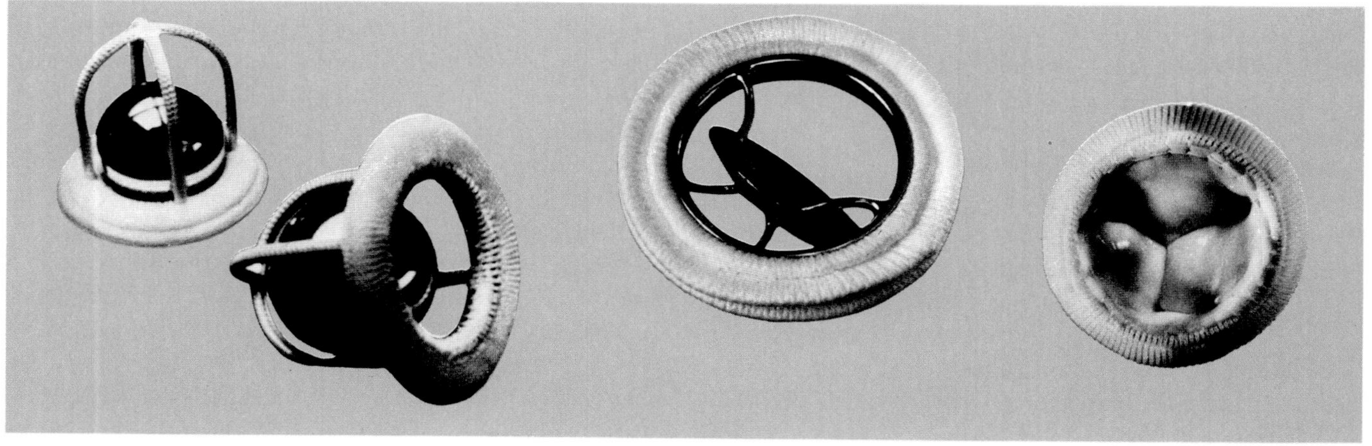

When heart valves are damaged, they can be replaced with spares like these. At far left is a closed ball-and-cage valve; next to it an identical valve is shown open, as if blood were pressing the ball into its cage. In the center model a tilting disk replaces the ball and cage. These substitutes are entirely man-made; at right is one assembled from a heart valve taken from a pig.

nology pointed the way toward taming the body's defense mechanism. In 1954 the first successful organ transplant was performed on a human being: a kidney, installed by Drs. Joseph Murray and John Merrill at Peter Bent Brigham Hospital in Boston, to save the life of Richard Herrick. Today kidney transplants have become routine; an estimated 7,000 are performed worldwide each year.

The heart came next. Three weeks before Christmas of 1967 in Capetown, South Africa, Dr. Christiaan Barnard sewed a heart into the chest of 54-year-old Louis Washkansky. The heart beat 18 days, then quit, a victim of Washkansky's immune system. The day after New Year's, 1968, Dr. Barnard tried again. This time the recipient, a 58-year-old dentist named Philip Blaiberg, lived. Apparently, the dream had come true.

Suddenly cardiac surgeons everywhere, it seemed, were performing transplants. In London and Montreal, in Paris and Warsaw, Bombay and Buenos Aires—in all, a total of 65 teams in 22 countries attempted to duplicate Barnard's tour de force. Dr. Denton Cooley, of St. Luke's Episcopal Hospital in Texas, became so proficient that he could suture a heart into place, it was said, in only 36 minutes.

In the year of Dr. Barnard's apparent success, 101 patients received new hearts. Then, as suddenly as it had started, the flood of transplant operations dwindled. The problem was that postoperative survival rates had begun plummeting. Once the patient was out of the hospital, months or years later, his new heart might, for no apparent reason, be rejected by his body. Nothing seemed able to stop the terrifying inevitability of an immune reaction. Five years after that false dawn of heart transplants, just one of the 101 patients survived.

In view of that discouraging record, only a few surgeons and hospitals persevered. One was Stanford Medical Center in Palo Alto, California. Stanford's chief heart surgeon, Dr. Norman Shumway, was an unquestioned pioneer in transplantations—he had performed the first viable operation, on a dog, in 1959. Now Dr. Shumway turned his hand to staving off the immune reaction, and thus increasing the staying power of borrowed hearts.

The first step was early identification of a rejection crisis. In 1972 Dr. Philip Caves, a member of Dr. Shumway's team, devised a technique for taking heart biopsies. A catheter fitted with a set of pincers at its head is directed into a transplanted heart to snip off a sliver of lining, which can then be checked under a microscope for deterioration. Next, Shumway's team came up with a new immune suppressant. It is a blood serum with the mouth-filling name of antithymocyte globulin, or ATG, which is grown in live rabbits and injected into a patient's thigh in large doses. The injections are appallingly painful, but they seem to be effective. Survival rates for heart recipients began to climb, and other institutions resumed the operation.

There is one problem with heart transplants that no one can easily solve. For every recipient, the heart must be implanted live. In other words, not only should the donor be young and disease free, but he must have died within hours of the operation, in fairly close proximity to the hospital. The cause of his death must have been a failure within the brain that permitted the heart to go on pumping after the brain ceased to function. For practical purposes, donors are limited to accident victims who die in the same area as the transplant center. A potential recipient may wait months on end before getting his new heart.

In the light of these facts, uncertainty clouded the outlook for Sam Poole as he left home with his parents to enter the Stanford transplant program. He signed into the hospital for an intensive round of testing—not just of his heart but of every major organ in his body, for signs of weakness or infection that could jeopardize success. An equivalent scrutiny was focused on his emotional well-being, and that of his parents. "A heart transplant is something you have to fight to get," he was told, "and you have to fight for the rest of your life to keep it." Sam knew this. Months later, when it was all over, Sam said, "You've got to want to live more than anything else in the world."

Sam's determination never came into question. After his tests he moved with his parents to a motel near the hospital, where he waited in constant pain for more than two months, battling to stay alive and gambling that a new heart would be found before his own gave out. Then he received a phone call: Report immediately to the hospital. His heart had arrived, and would be implanted the next morning.

The drama of the operating theater

Although Sam Poole's operation would be an unusually dangerous one, he came to it and out of it by a route that is common for all who undergo heart surgery. Nearly all share similar experiences in their doctors' offices and—except for the surgery itself—in the hospital. By the time surgery is decided upon, the patient is usually under the care of a cardiologist. Generally a different specialist—a surgeon who concentrates on the heart—will take over in the operating room, but afterward the cardiologist will pick up responsibility once again.

If you enter a hospital for heart surgery, the first thing that happens, after you sign in, is yet another barrage of tests and needles: temperature, blood pressure, blood samples for laboratory analysis, a thorough physical examination and perhaps a preoperation angiogram. A stream of white-coated visitors arrives. You should be visited by your cardiologist, the surgeon, the anesthesiologist and several nurses, who brief you—more or less frankly—on what to expect, and what is expected from you. A nurse gives you lessons in breathing and coughing; after surgery, despite your considerable discomfort, you will be urged to breathe deeply to clear fluid from the lungs. The general procedures of the operation will be explained to you, and you will be told what it is like to regain consciousness in the recovery room, your body bristling with wires and tubes, and awash with pain.

These briefings may sound ominous, but they are tremendously important. A heart operation is a shock not only to the body, but to the mind and to the emotions. No other surgery affects people in quite the same way. "It is unthinkable, finally, that one's heart should be cut open," wrote the wife of one bypass patient. "There are other vital organs, but they are vital only to life. This is more. This is other. No high priest ever offered a lung to the gods. No one ever wrote a poem about a gall bladder."

Even medical professionals feel an eerie, irrational unease before subjecting themselves to the scalpel. The most alarming aspect, perhaps, is knowing that the heart will be stopped, its work taken over by a machine. "I know very well how the heart-lung pump works," said one doctor after his recovery, "but I couldn't get out of my mind the fact that although the machine would keep all my vital functions going, I would be, for all practical purposes, dead."

In this light, a patient's doubts and questions had all best be resolved in advance. But the time for briefings and explanations soon comes to an end. If you are to be operated on, you are "prepped" the night before by the hospital staff. Final blood tests are taken. An orderly stops by to shave you from neck to ankles, and your body is painted with pungent amber antiseptic. A shot of antibiotic goes into each buttock. You are told to eat nothing following the evening meal. You are given an enema and a sleeping pill. Next morning, more pills and more needles. First there is a sedative, taken orally, followed by another jolt of antibiotic, then an injection of a drug called atropine, which dries various bodily secretions that may interfere with anesthesia (you become very thirsty). If the operation is to be a transplant, you get a double shot of ATG to combat the immune reaction.

Early in the morning you are wheeled into surgery. In a large hospital you do not go directly into the operating room—you may, in fact, never see it—but to an alcove alongside. Nurses, surgical interns, residents and anesthesiologists attend you there. Tubes for intravenous feeding and drugs are set into your wrists; two or three pints of blood and glucose may be poured through your system during the next few hours, along with drugs and anesthetics. An ECG monitor is hooked up. The anesthesiologist administers his potions and you black out. A catheter is led up one arm into one of the great veins at the entrance to the heart, to measure pressure. A tube is inserted into your mouth to supply oxygen; another drains your stomach. There is a tube in your posterior to monitor body temperature, and one in your bladder to draw off fluid. The nurses envelop you in a cocoon of transparent, sterile plastic resembling food wrap, and drape you with sterile sheets, leaving window-like openings where incisions will be made.

Inside the operating room eight or so masked and gowned figures may hover about—the entire surgical team except for the chief surgeon, who will arrive later to work on the heart after the chest has been opened. Two deputy surgeons begin the operation, one opening the chest, the other assisting (if a bypass is scheduled, they harvest a leg vein). A scrub nurse hands them instruments. The anesthesiologist and assistants administer drugs and oxygen. A technician mans the heart-lung machine, while others attend a battery of electronic monitoring devices that flash vital signs on a screen: temperature, blood pressure, heart and brain waves. A bank of overhead lights bathes the operating table in the center of the room, and canned music may be piped from a public-address system, a standard technique for easing the tension of the surgical team. This is the operating theater. The term is aptly chosen—there may be an audience of medical students watching and learning.

The first incision, a thin red line right down the center of the chest, is strangely bloodless. The scalpel carries an electric current that instantly cauterizes the wound. The surgeon works the scalpel deeper into the flesh, using long careful strokes—each somewhat like that of a glazier scoring a windowpane—cutting down to the breastbone. When he reaches the bone he discards the scalpel and switches to an electric saw to separate it—again, neatly and bloodlessly, his saw a tiny whirling disk mounted in a holder about the size and

The ultimate in fine needlework—grafting an artery

The surgeon who sews a replacement vessel onto a coronary artery uses a technique familiar to anyone who has ever sewed—but his stitches must be extraordinarily fine and regular. The vessels to be joined may taper to the width of a pencil lead, yet the connection must be leakproof against the pounding of pumped blood. Some 20 stitches are required, about 25 to the inch.

Using magnifying spectacles to see and a forceps to grasp tiny needles crimped to both ends of a length of thread, the surgeon first secures the toe of the graft *(below, left)*. Next he places sutures partway around one side of the graft *(center)*, and then sews from the toe around the other side and down to the meeting point *(right)*. There, the ends are tied and the needles snipped off.

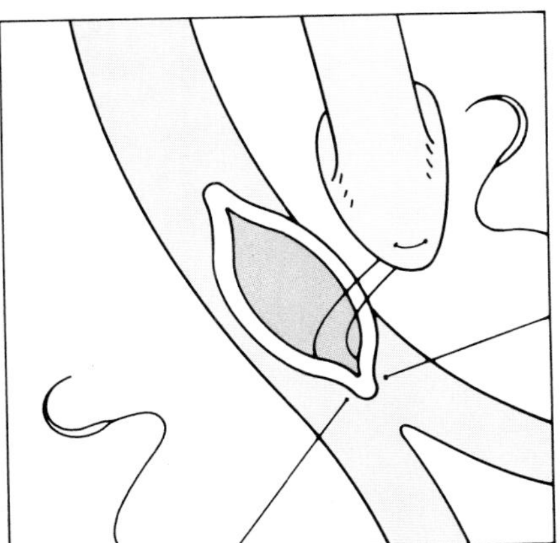

The first stitch is made by passing the needles through the vein (blue), then through the artery (red). The thread is as fine as hair; the needles, ¼ inch long.

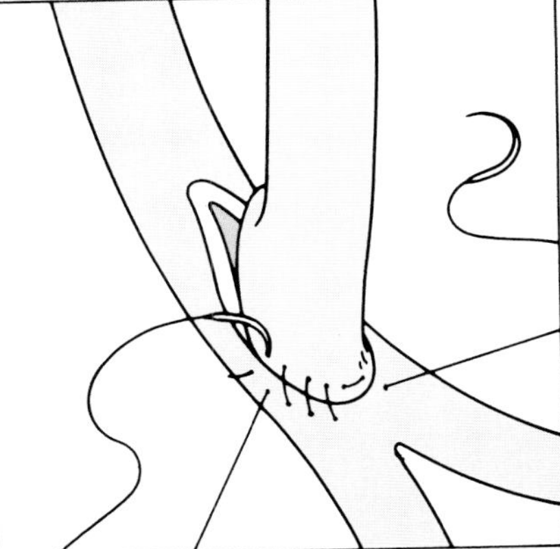

The simple "running stitch" (above) used in embroidery attaches one side of the graft partway. The stitches generally measure about 1/12 inch across.

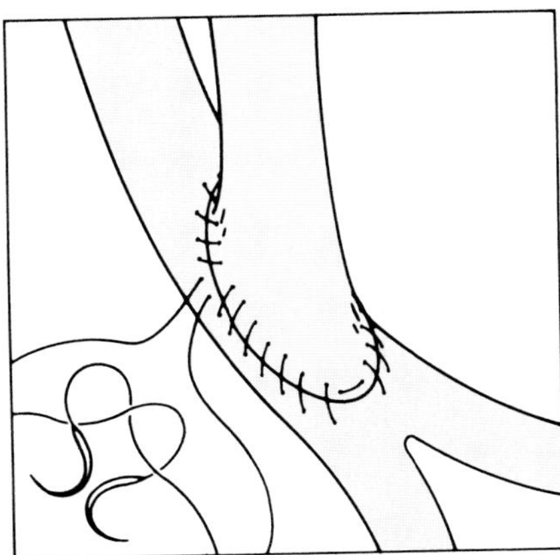

Last, the surgeon sews the other side of the graft, starting at the toe and using the other needle. Tissue slowly grows over the thread, which stays in place forever.

The high cost of repairs

Open-heart surgery demands so much in medical talent and hospital facilities that it is very expensive: In the United States the average cost of a bypass operation is more than $10,000. In most cases, the patient pays only a fraction, for insurance covers most of the expense. Blue Cross/Blue Shield, the medical-insurance organization for 101 million Americans, pays at least 85 per cent of the total, the remainder coming out of the patient's pocket.

In many countries that have comprehensive national health insurance, open-heart surgery costs the patient nothing. Britain's National Health Service, for instance, picks up the entire tab—the surgeon's fee, the hospital room and board, medicine and all.

shape of a small hair drier. A thin glaze of beeswax will serve to protect the raw edges of bone.

A retractor is fitted into the gap in the breastbone, and slowly cranked to pry the rib cage apart, opening a cavity about six to eight inches across. Movement can be seen inside, a steady pulse. As the surgeon continues his downward cut, carefully laying back the folds of flesh, the pulse appears stronger and closer at hand. And then the heart is revealed. Deep gold and mauve inside its crimson cavity, it pumps with a seemingly gallant indifference to what is being done to it. With the draped, anesthetized body inert as driftwood, with the surgeons and nurses indistinguishable behind sterile masks and gowns, in the harsh lighting and amid the gleaming machinery of the operating room, the beating heart seems to hold more life than any other object in the room. At this moment Dr. Michael DeBakey at Baylor College of Medicine has been known to pause and cry out, in hushed reverence, to the students, "Isn't this beautiful! Come and see the human heart!"

The chief surgeon goes to work. Now the heart-lung machine is connected. A pair of cannulae—giant catheters, in effect—are plunged through the heart's right atrium and into the two great veins that carry used blood from the body to the heart. A return cannula is inserted, sometimes into a leg artery, sometimes directly into the aorta. The aorta is clamped shut. Switches are thrown, and blood begins to drain from the heart into the machine. The heartbeat dwindles, stops. On the electronic monitor, the peaks and dips of the patient's ECG tracing diminish; a line jiggles, then goes flat. For the next few hours, the machine will be the body's life line, pumping blood, suffusing the blood with oxygen and removing carbon dioxide. It may, in addition, be adjusted to cool the blood, bringing the body to a state of lowered temperature called hypothermia—perhaps as low as 77° F.—to cool the body tissues and thereby reduce their need for oxygen.

With the heart now quiet, the principal task can begin—whatever it may be. The chief surgeon exposes an artery, just below the surface of the heart, that will receive a bypass. Or he gently slices into the heart wall, opening the organ to replace a valve, to sew up an internal wall, to close off an aneurysm. Or, as in Sam Poole's case, he excises the entire heart and stitches in a new one. He works quickly but carefully; each movement is decisive; not a gesture is wasted. After each cut he bathes the surface with saline solution from a syringe and pats it dry with a gauze sponge. A mixture of cold saline solution and an anticoagulant drug washes through the cavity and drains off through a cannula, cooling and cleansing the area and keeping it free of clots. Sometimes an ice-cold wash of saline solution is injected directly into the coronary arteries along with a potassium solution; together they discourage any tendency for the heart to start beating prematurely.

Then, the repairs completed, withdrawal from the heart-lung machine begins. Temperature is returned to normal. This is a moment of supreme tension. As the blood returns to the mended heart, as the potassium and ice water leave its vessels, the heart should start to beat. If it seems reluctant, the surgeon must jolt it into life with a mild shock from a pair of paddle-like electrodes. Only when the fist of muscle resumes its rhythm, and the level trace on the ECG returns to its customary rise and fall, can the chief surgeon consider his task accomplished.

Once the heart is pulsing regularly, the cannulae connected to the heart-lung machine are removed. The assistant surgeons begin the painstaking task of joining each severed fold of tissue and each parted bone, placing tiny, careful sutures of nylon thread and steel wire. The chest is closed. The operation is over.

Surfacing in the recovery room

As a patient, of course, you would know none of this. You emerge into consciousness groggy from anesthetic, in considerable discomfort, perhaps not knowing who you are or where. But you soon recover your identity and learn your whereabouts: the recovery room.

No prior briefing does full justice to the general disagreeableness of the next few days. Rachel McKenzie, a magazine editor scheduled for surgery to remove a ventricular aneurysm, was warned what to expect in recovery. "It's an open room with four beds and a good deal of equipment," her doctor said. "Bright lights are kept on 24 hours. You can't tell night from day. There's constant activity. You'll wake up with a large tube in your throat—not very comfortable. It's connected to a machine that will be breathing for you. There'll be a good many tubes."

Indeed there were. Most of the wires, catheters, intravenous connections and other plastic cordage that had been inserted before the operation were still attached. A pair of cannulae protruded from under her ribs, left in place after the operation to drain fluid from around her heart cavity. The ECG monitor beside her bed emitted a constant beep-beep. The cord of a respirator snaked down the tube in her throat, carrying oxygen to her lungs. At frequent intervals a nurse replaced it with a suction device that pulled fluid from her lungs. With the tube stuck in her throat she could not talk, though she could hear. She could communicate only with pad and pencil.

All this is perfectly normal. Visitors commonly register shock and dismay when they see their loved ones immobilized in this tangle of equipment. They need not despair. It is an essential part of shepherding a patient through the first critical days of recovery.

Certain hazards unique to open-heart patients must be dealt with during this recovery period as an immediate aftermath of the operation itself. For example, the blood undergoes chemical changes during its course through the heart-lung machine. These changes affect bodily salts that help determine the amount of water the body retains. A build-up of fluid in the chest cavity can stop the heart; in the lungs it can lead to pneumonia or suffocation. Thus the patient is submitted to periodic suctioning of his lungs, and to a constant stream of diuretics, salts and drugs fed through intravenous tubes to redress the blood's chemistry.

Heavy doses of antibiotics are also given, to prevent post-operative infection. Often there is an aching fever, brought on by the shock of surgery and other complications; ice-cold blankets may be wrapped around the body to bring down the temperature. After surgery the heart tends to be, in the cardiologists' euphemism, "irritable," and to beat in wildly fluctuating patterns. Pills are administered every few hours to steady and calm it.

A relay of nurses hovers in attendance throughout these early days of recuperation. They check vital signs every half hour, they may take a daily chest X-ray, and they always make a daily ECG. They weigh you each day to check for the loss or retention of fluids. They badger you to start breathing on your own, without the assistance of a respirator. This is perhaps the most unpleasant challenge of all, but it must be met. Said Dr. Nolan: "Every time you take a breath or—heaven help you!—cough, you feel as if you are going to split in half." This cannot happen of course—the sutures are too secure to break or tear. It just feels that way.

Eventually the pain subsides. The tubes come out—first the one in the throat, then the cannulae in the chest, the catheter in the bladder, the intravenous lines. You are helped to walk around, to eat meals. You are ready to move up to a regular cardiac floor, sometimes as soon as a day or two after surgery.

"Food! I need food!" cried Sam Poole the day after his transplant, "I'm a growing boy!" Then he turned to his mother, standing at his bedside: "See? I can breathe again, and it doesn't even hurt." ❋

A victory in one man's war against heart disease

It started out to be an ordinary Sunday for Jim Sanders, foreman for a Washington, D.C., construction firm. He went bowling in the afternoon and then went home. He walked up the two flights to the family's third-floor apartment and at the top he felt a sharp, heavy pain in his chest. He was badly out of breath. The discomfort and the shortness of breath had occurred before, but never like this. The other episodes, he said, had felt like indigestion; this time he thought he was going to die.

Sanders was 45 and had never had a serious illness. Two days later, however, his family doctor said Sanders had angina pectoris. This crippling pain usually indicates that coronary arteries are so clogged they prevent an adequate blood supply from reaching the heart muscle. Within a week, his agony unrelieved by medication, Jim Sanders sought the care of a heart specialist.

Almost from the outset, the cardiologist suspected the worst. A stress electrocardiogram *(below)*—a graph of the heart's electrical rhythms under strain—indicated a narrowing of the left main coronary artery, the vessel that furnishes 75 to 90 per cent of the heart's fuel. At any moment the artery might be plugged shut; if it was, a heart attack could follow within a day.

Facing that grim prospect, Sanders entered the Washington Hospital Center for more extensive tests and treatment. In the days just before he checked into the hospital, and in the weeks thereafter, Sanders was followed by photographer John Senzer, who became his friend and helped him cope with the emotional ups and downs that inevitably accompany intensive medical care.

Sanders' treatment would include a panoply of procedures—some diagnostic, some remedial—during which he would be questioned, observed, poked and probed. His heart would be listened to, injected with dyes, filmed by X-ray and ultimately repaired in modern medicine's most dramatic surgery: an operation on the living heart.

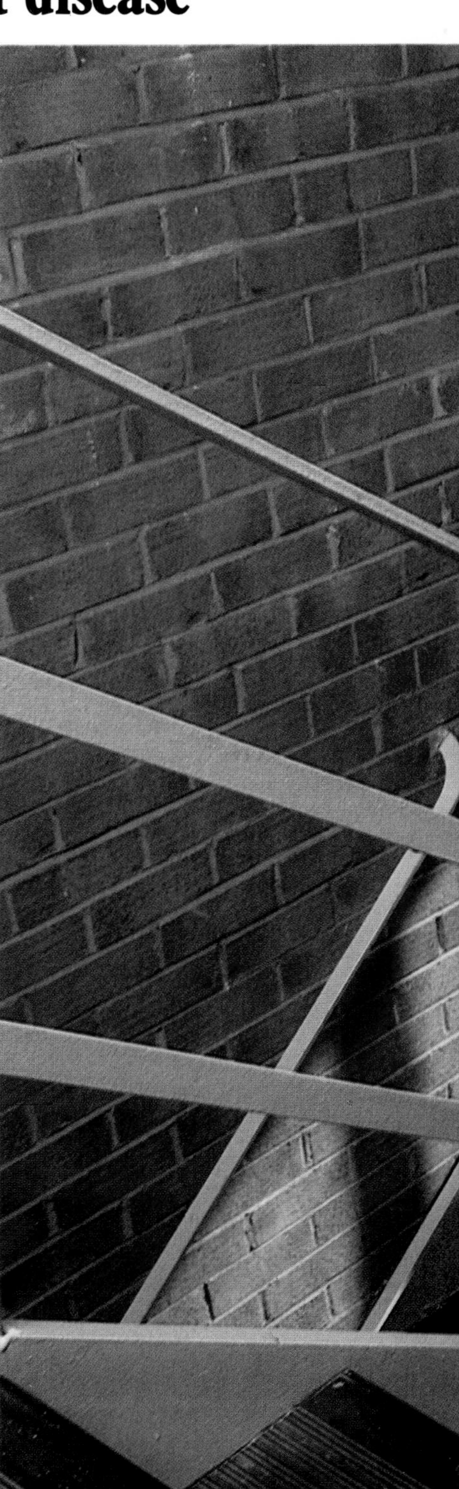

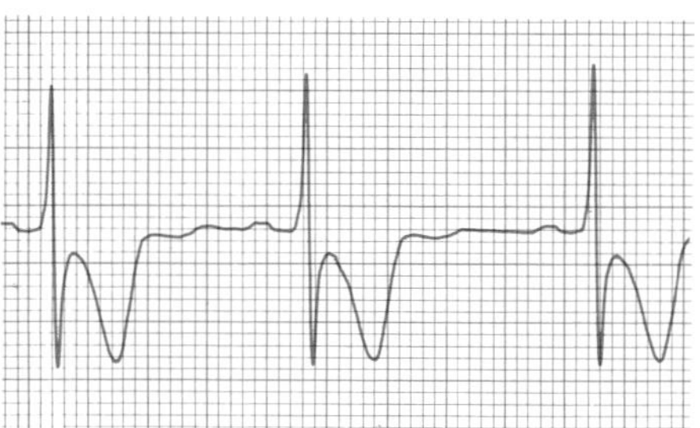

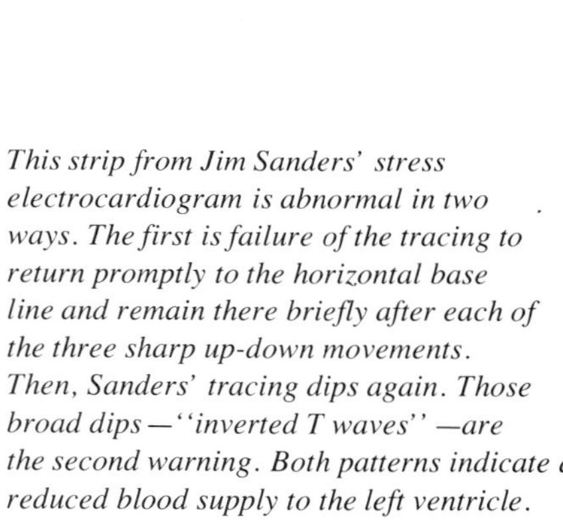

This strip from Jim Sanders' stress electrocardiogram is abnormal in two ways. The first is failure of the tracing to return promptly to the horizontal base line and remain there briefly after each of the three sharp up-down movements. Then, Sanders' tracing dips again. Those broad dips—"inverted T waves"—are the second warning. Both patterns indicate a reduced blood supply to the left ventricle.

PHOTOGRAPHS BY JOHN SENZER

Two days before entering the hospital, Jim Sanders pauses on a landing to catch his breath. His wife, Phyllis, carries the groceries to their third-floor apartment, a chore he would normally do.

Locating the "widow maker"

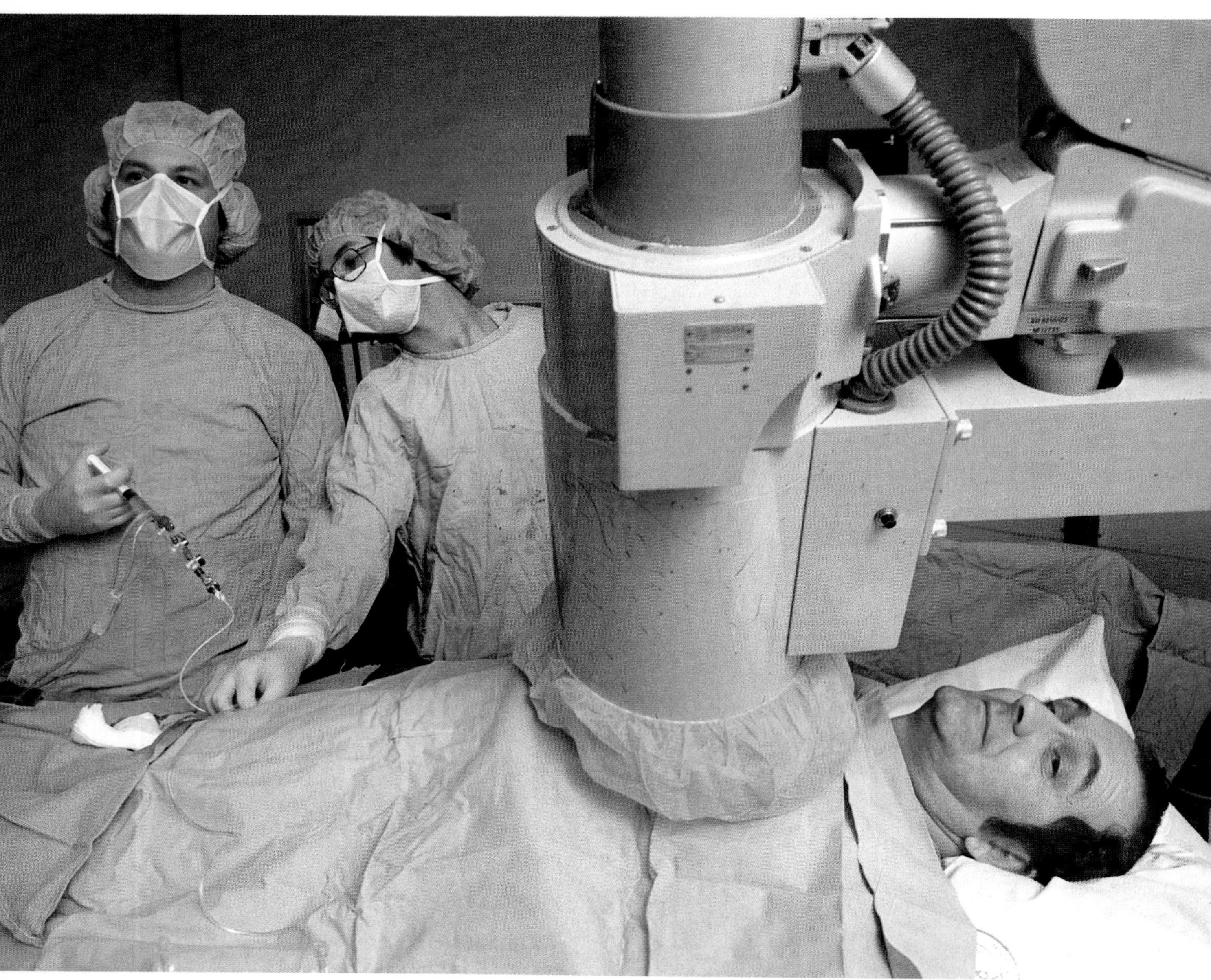

In the hospital Sanders lies sedated but awake during an angiogram. The two cardiologists are injecting dye into Sanders' coronary arteries via a catheter, or thin tube, which they earlier had inserted into a groin artery and snaked up into the heart. The dye shows up on the X-ray movies, its shadow pinpointing arterial blockages. The test takes about two hours.

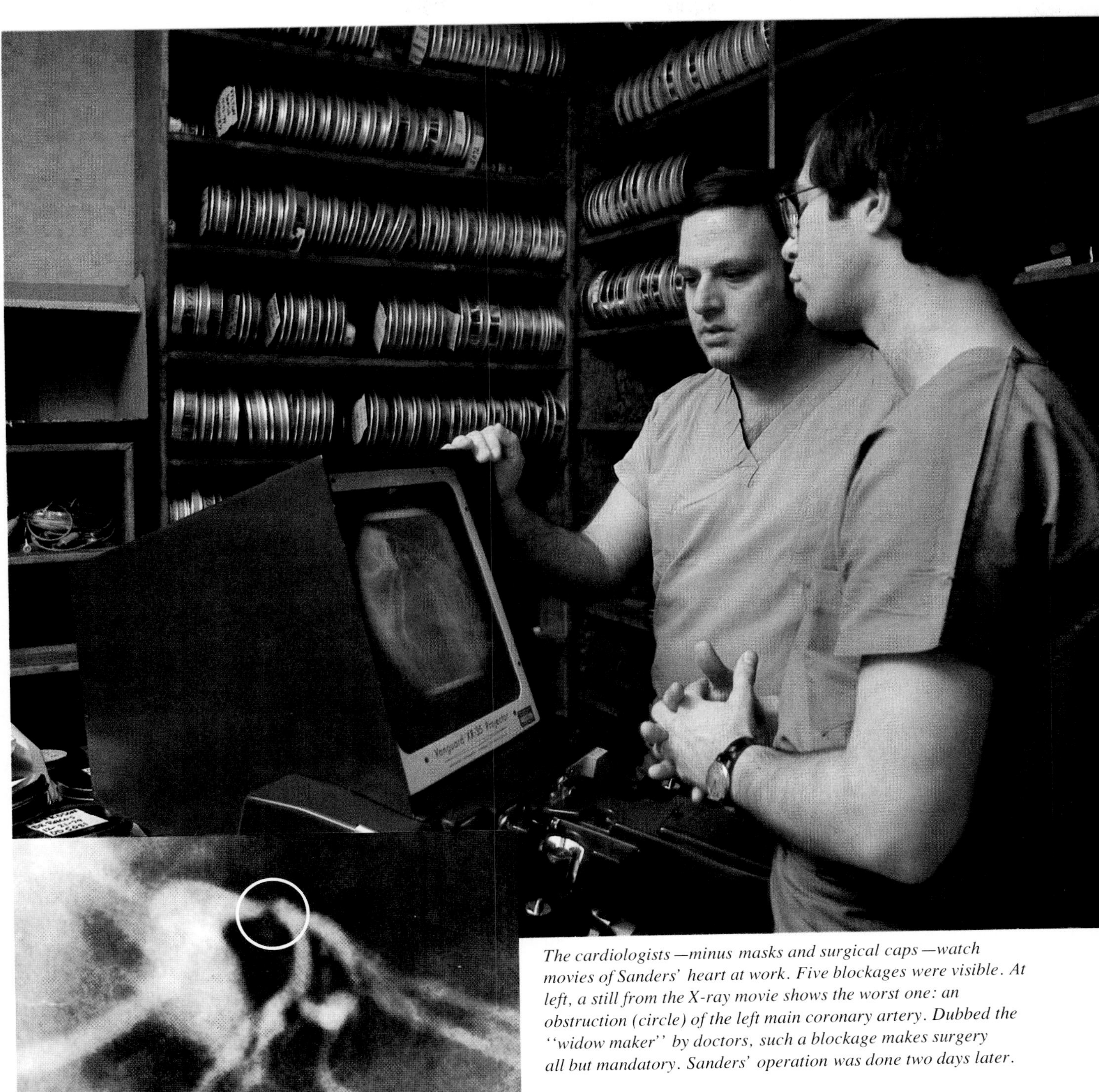

The cardiologists—minus masks and surgical caps—watch movies of Sanders' heart at work. Five blockages were visible. At left, a still from the X-ray movie shows the worst one: an obstruction (circle) of the left main coronary artery. Dubbed the "widow maker" by doctors, such a blockage makes surgery all but mandatory. Sanders' operation was done two days later.

Creating new pathways for blood flow

An operating-room team headed by Dr. Jorge Garcia (left rear) huddles over Sanders at the start of a bypass operation. At this stage the surgeons are "harvesting" two 15-inch vein segments from Sanders' legs. Expendable there, where veins are abundant, the vessels were to be stitched to Sanders' heart to carry blood around the arterial blockages, bypassing them.

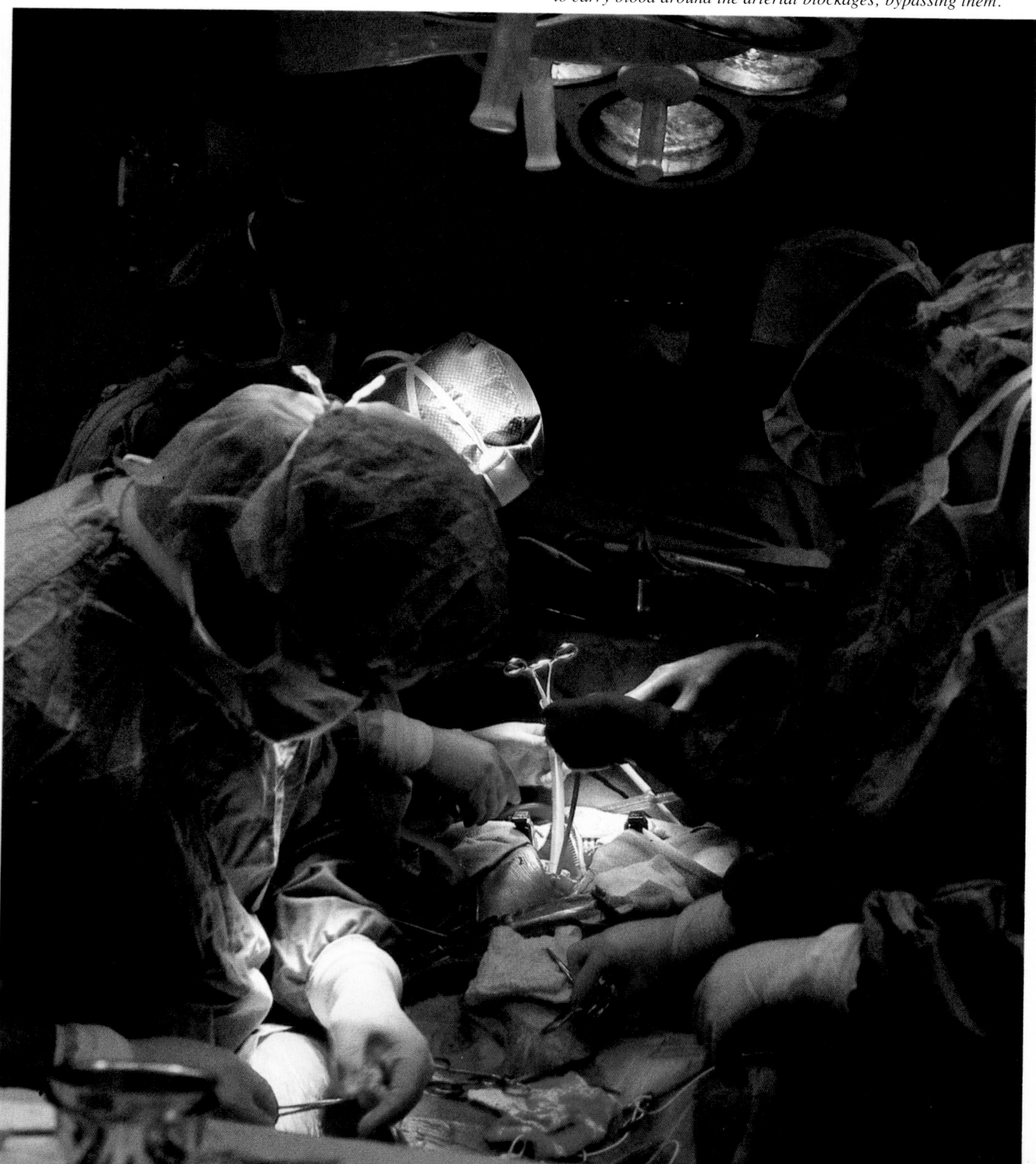

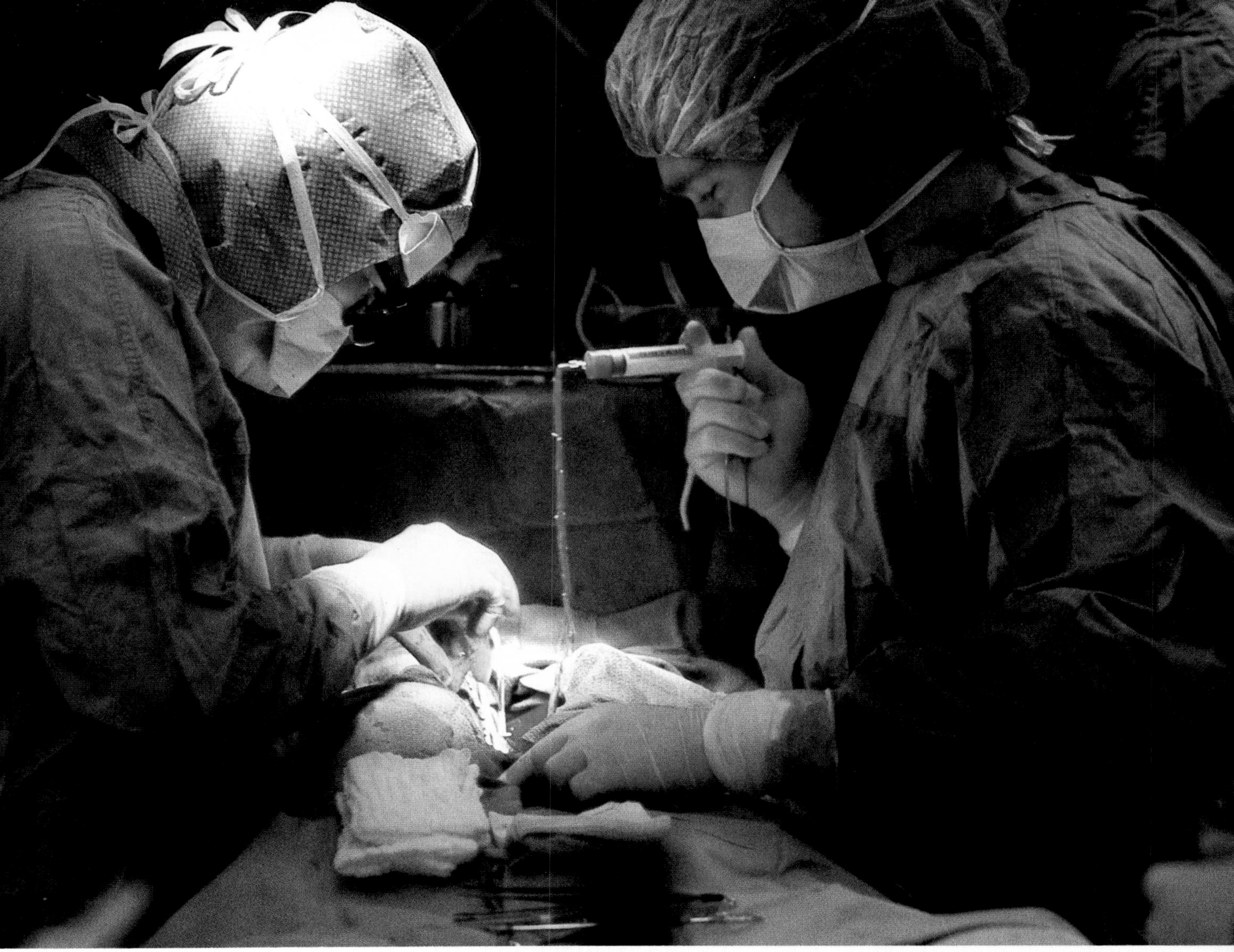

To make sure the vein sections are elastic and free from clots or leaks, Dr. Garcia (left) and an assisting surgeon flush each one with the patient's own heparin-treated blood. The blood flowed through smoothly and evenly, proof the sections were good.

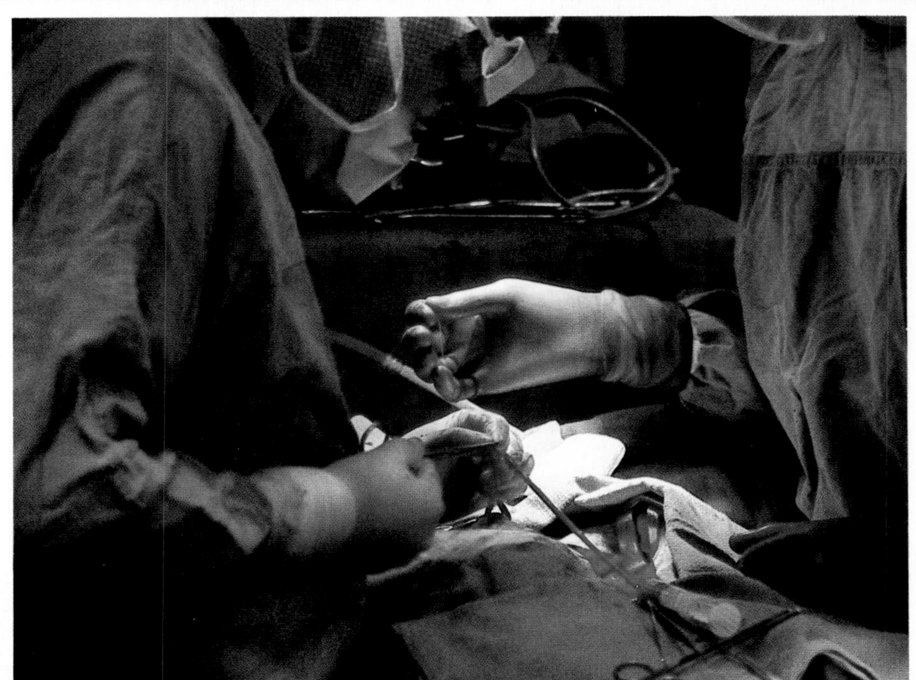

The surgeons measure and cut the lengths of vein they will need, about 20 inches in all. Sanders' chest has been slit and sawed open, and his rib cage has been spread with retractors. His heart has been connected to a heart-lung machine, so the doctors can stop his heart, yet keep him alive while the decommissioned pump is repaired.

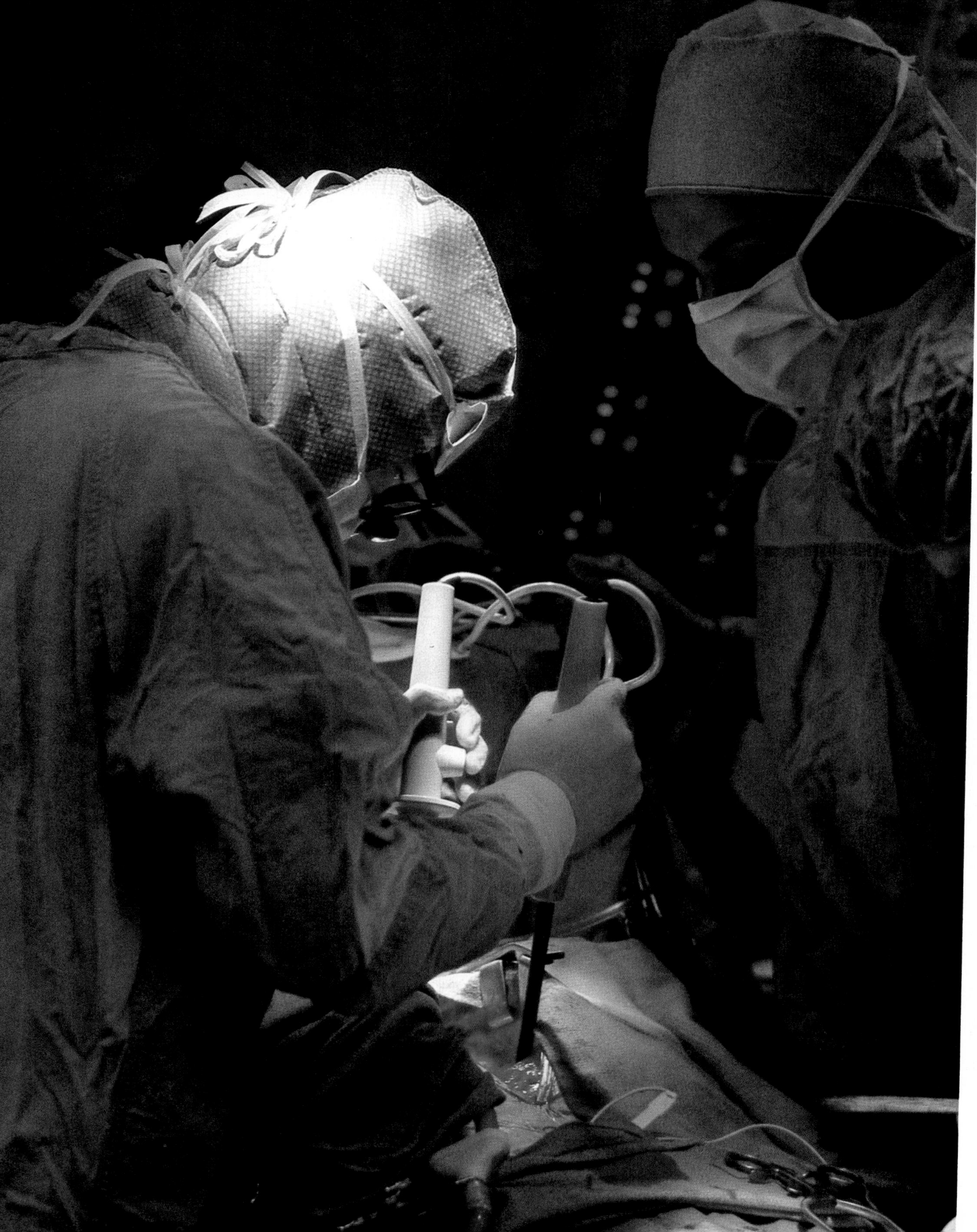

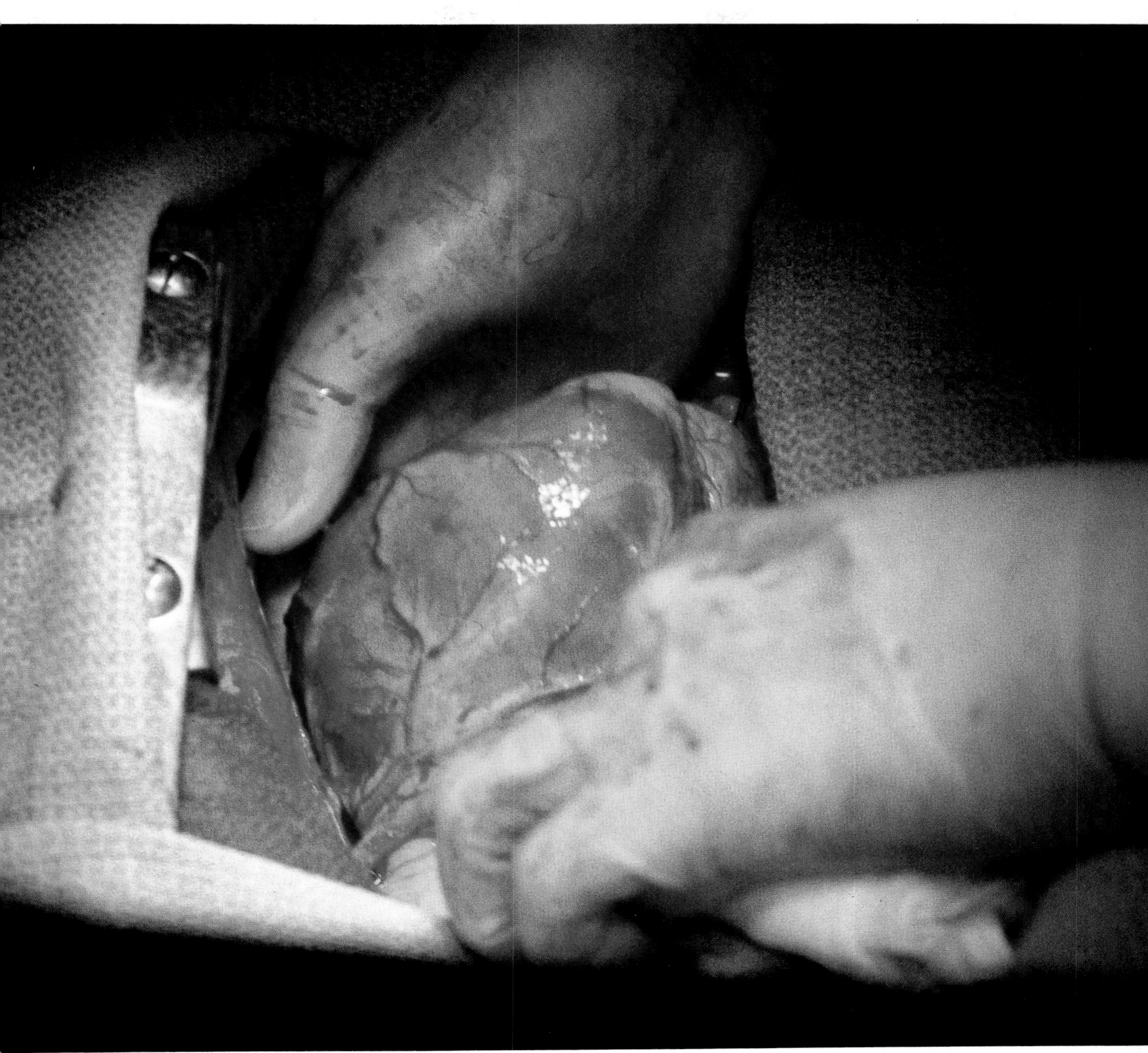

In the climax to the surgery, Dr. Garcia places two electrodes on Sanders' still heart. Voltage from a defibrillator shocks it back into action, and it pumps blood through the newly grafted veins. At this tense stage, as throughout the surgery, taped harpsichord music played in the background, creating a relaxed atmosphere for Dr. Garcia's crack surgical team.

Holding Sanders' beating heart in his hands, Dr. Garcia examines the connections for leaks and kinks. When the chief surgeon was satisfied, an assistant sutured Sanders' leg incisions while Dr. Garcia and another surgeon stitched together the pericardium, or heart sac, and sewed up the chest. Sanders' operation, an uneventful quintuple bypass, took four hours.

Bouncing back for a quick recovery

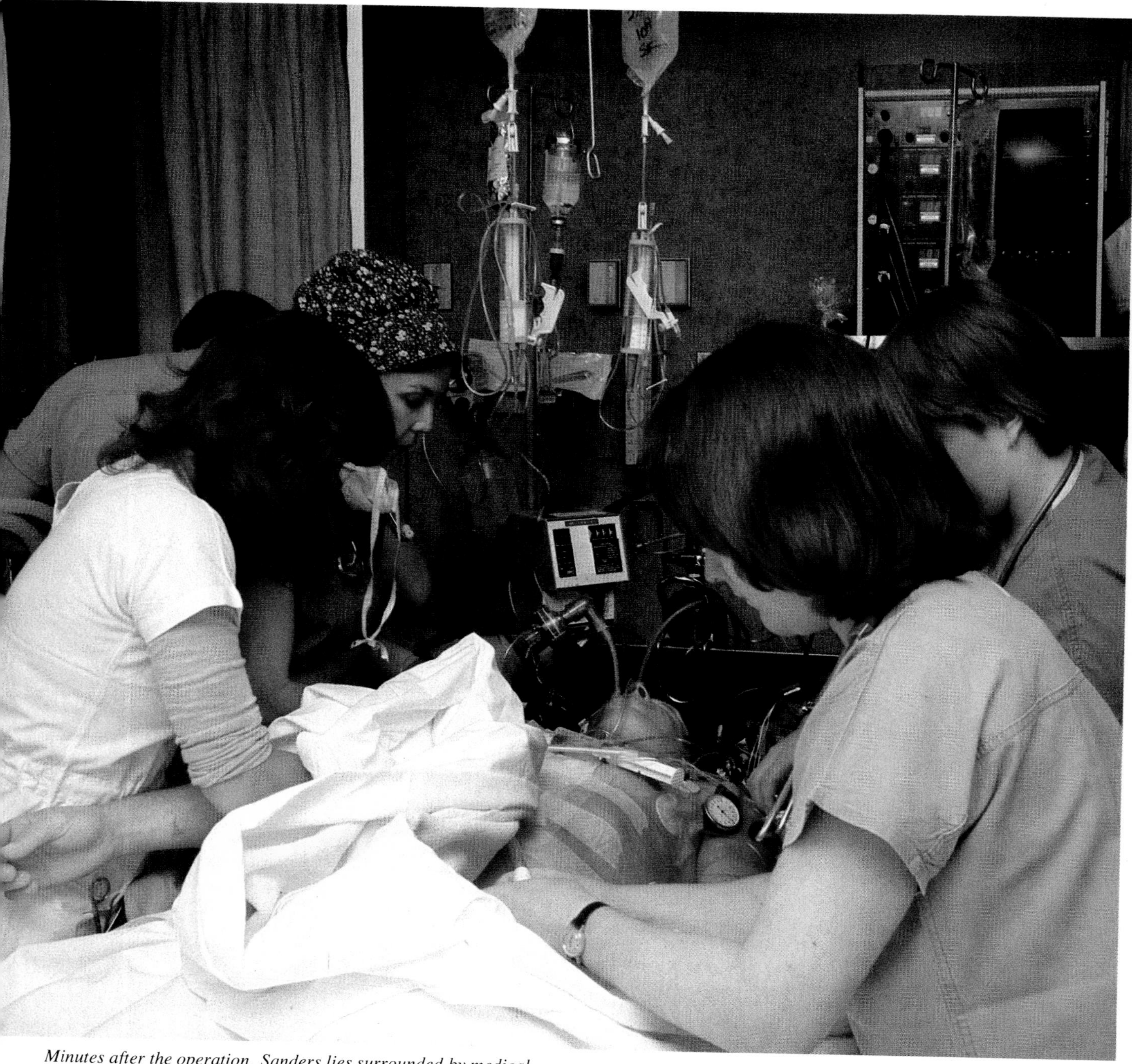

Minutes after the operation, Sanders lies surrounded by medical personnel and monitoring equipment in the intensive care unit. He remained there for two days, hooked up to an assortment of computerized devices that kept track of blood pressure, pulse, temperature and respiration. Until his vital signs stabilized, a nurse checked on him every 15 minutes.

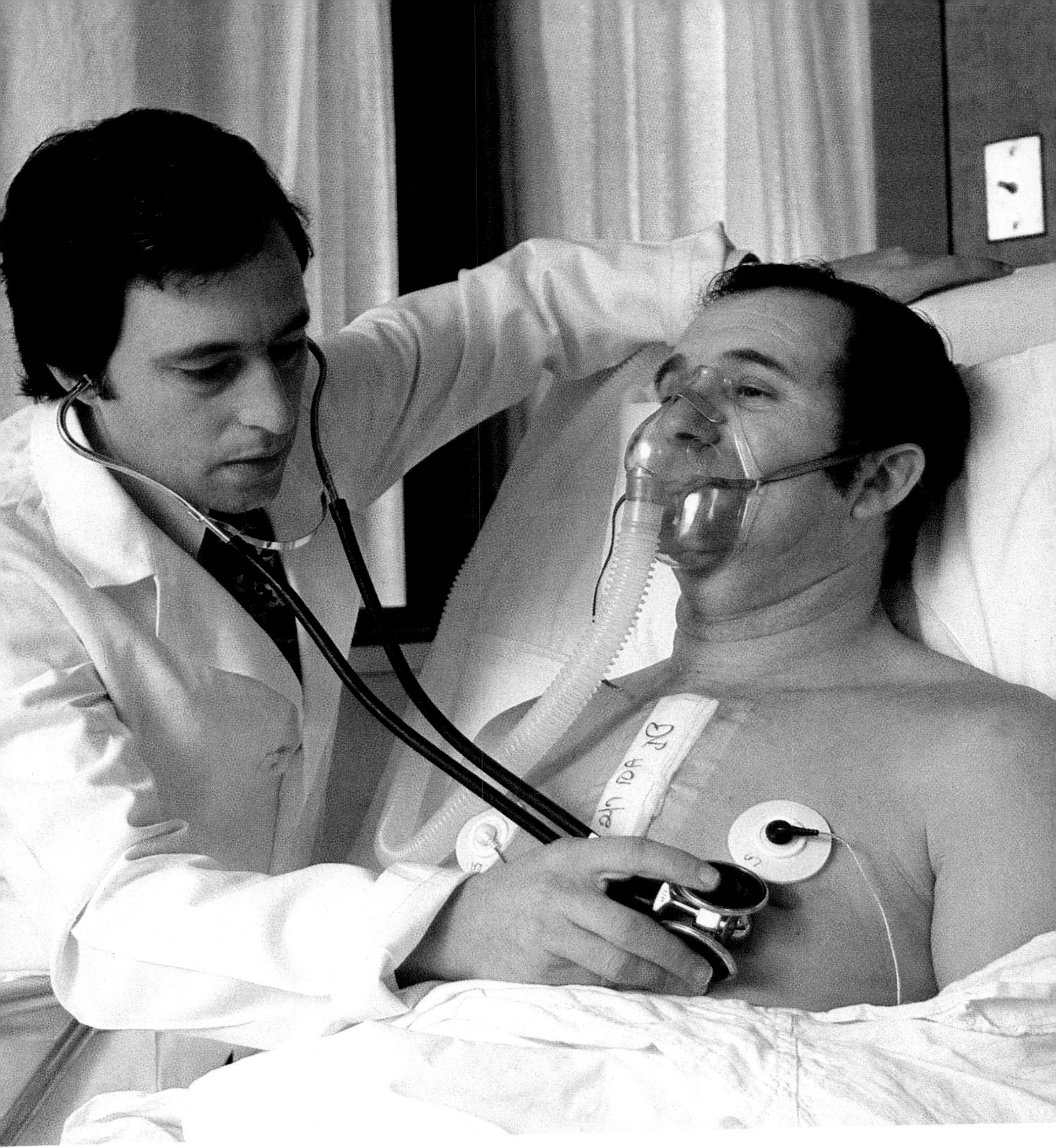

The day after surgery, Sanders, his face partly covered by the mask of a machine that helps him breathe, sits up in bed while his cardiologist, Dr. Gary Fisher, listens with a stethoscope to the sounds of the mended heart. "I was aching and sore," recalled Sanders of his first recuperative day, "but my spirits were good. The doctors said everything had gone fine."

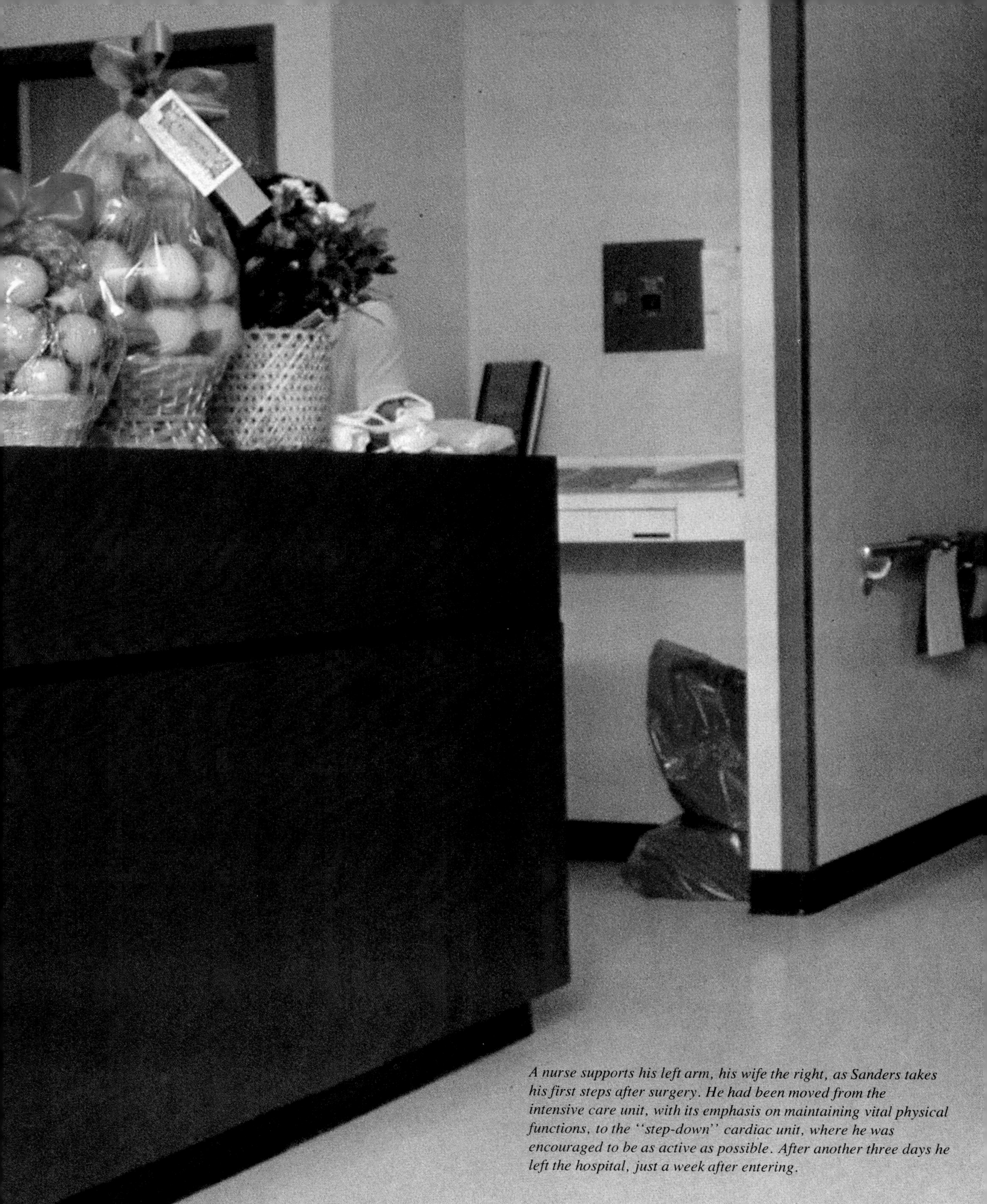

A nurse supports his left arm, his wife the right, as Sanders takes his first steps after surgery. He had been moved from the intensive care unit, with its emphasis on maintaining vital physical functions, to the "step-down" cardiac unit, where he was encouraged to be as active as possible. After another three days he left the hospital, just a week after entering.

Checking out the rebuilt system

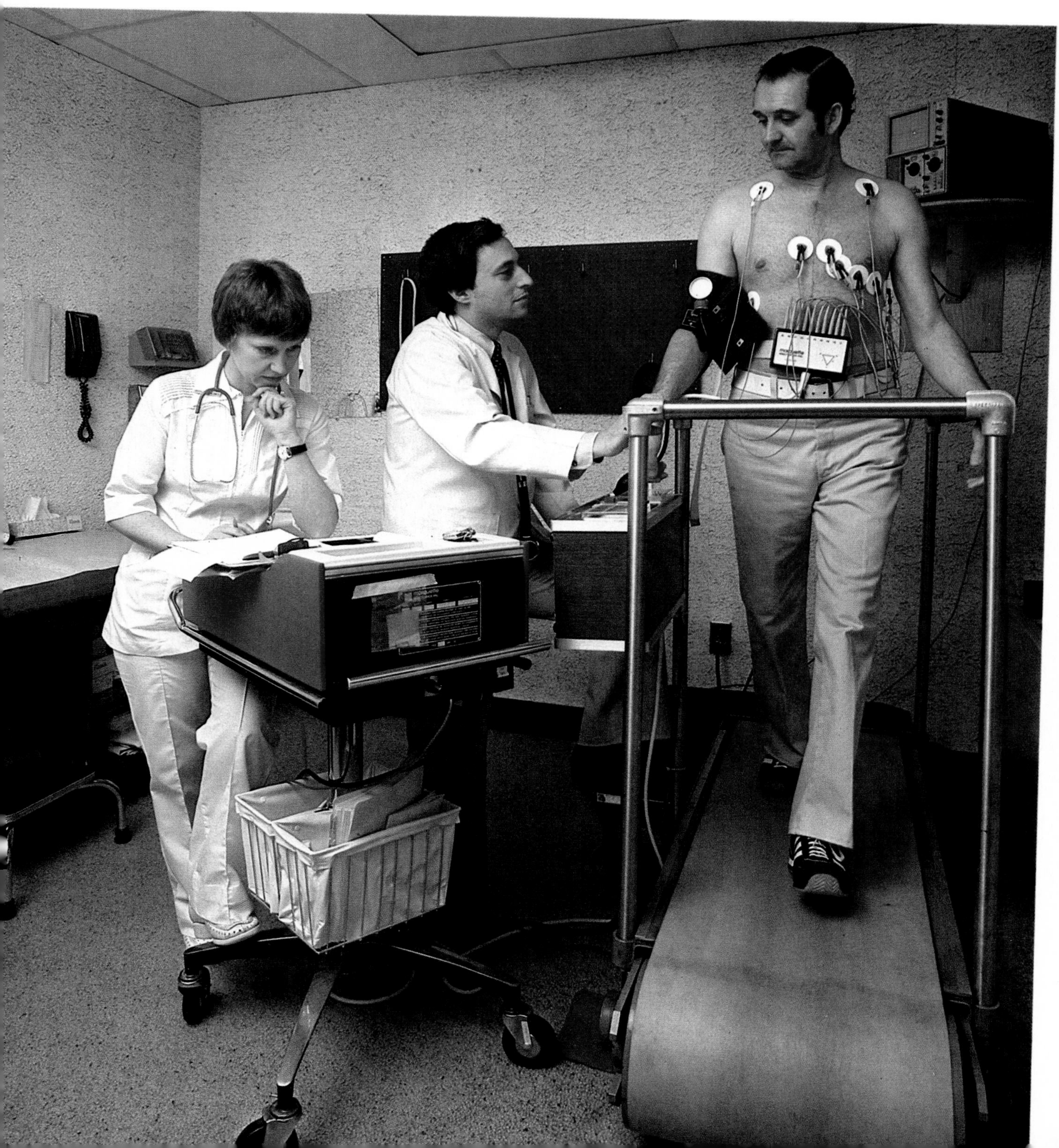

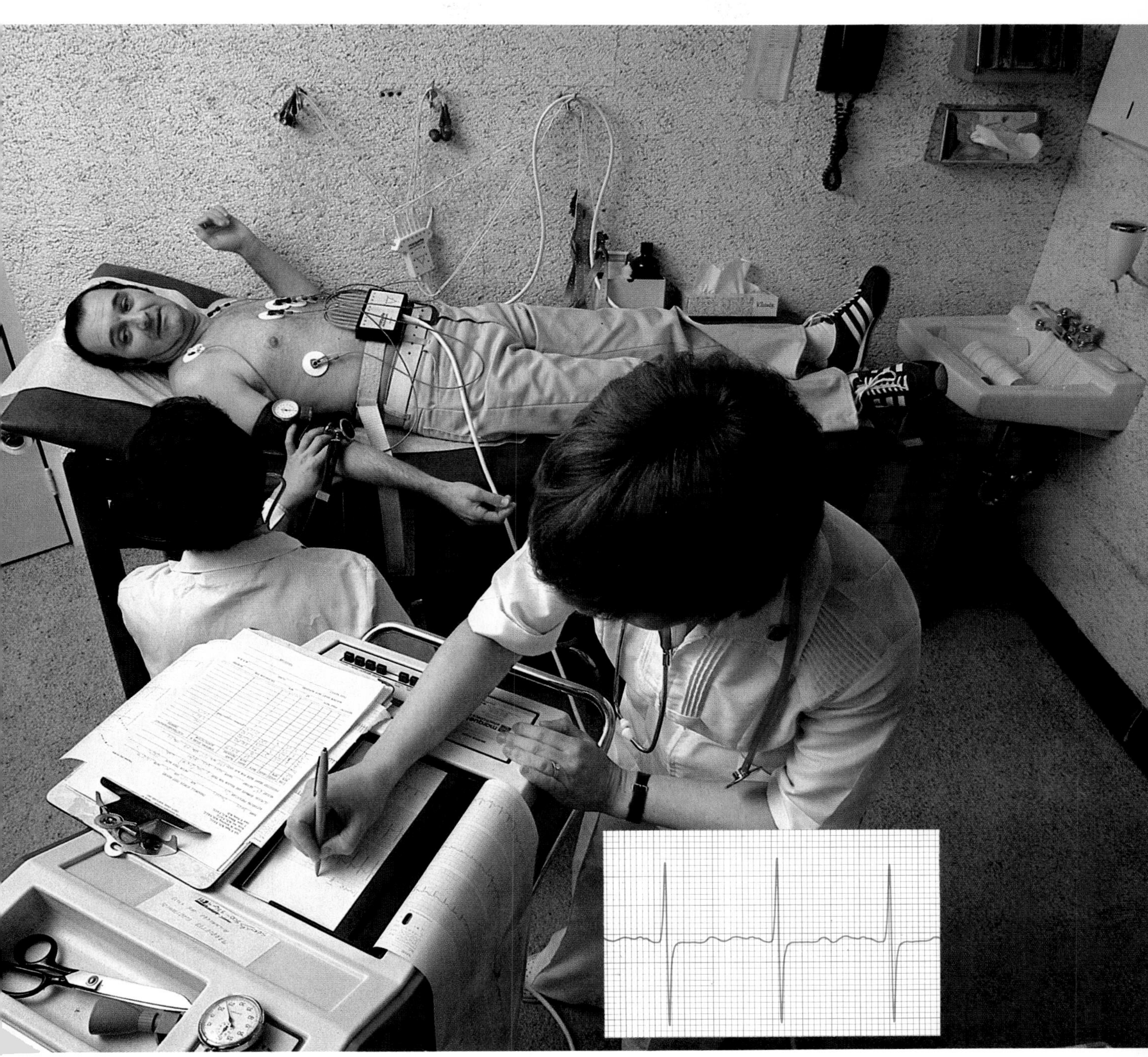

Walking three miles an hour on a treadmill, Sanders takes a stress test at Dr. Fisher's office six weeks after the operation. The doctor watches for any visible indications of distress and takes a reading of Sanders' blood pressure; the nurse monitors the pattern that the patient's heartbeat produces on the electrocardiogram, the sensors of which are attached to his chest.

A second set of blood pressure and electrocardiogram readings is taken immediately after Sanders leaves the treadmill. The resulting graph (inset) differs from the presurgery counterpart, seen on page 122. Now the tracing returns completely to the base line after its sharpest fluctuations; the inverted T waves have disappeared. Sanders' heart is now receiving adequate blood.

Three months after surgery, Jim Sanders, back on the job, lifts a heavy metal pipe. He had won a battle against heart disease, but had to continue to fight a war. He was required to keep to a low-cholesterol diet and exercise regularly. "I get out and walk a lot," he said. "I'm up to two miles a day, at a pretty good clip, and I don't have any of the old chest pain."

CHAPTER 6

How to get over a broken heart

The first step: staying alive
A quick return to activity
A fresh start at home
A lifelong course of medication
The need for exercise
Sex after a coronary

On vacation in Denver in 1955, President Dwight David Eisenhower was awakened one night with severe chest pain—a heart attack. He recovered to serve a second term. Bo Schembechler, head football coach at the University of Michigan, had a heart attack at the age of 40. He underwent coronary bypass surgery at 47 and continued a coaching career that brought Michigan 104 victories and 19 defeats over a span of 10 years. In June 1953 Prime Minister Winston Churchill suffered his fourth stroke in four years. Three months later he resumed full control of the government. Dmitri Shostakovich, the celebrated composer, suffered a heart attack in 1964 but recovered to continue composing for more than a decade.

Like these famous examples, uncounted numbers of ordinary folk now survive severe, life-threatening attacks of circulatory disease to continue active, productive careers. Not only may such serious attacks be prevented—by sensible living habits, drugs or surgery—but if they occur they can be treated successfully. Neither heart attack nor stroke causes immediate death so frequently today as it once did—if skilled care is provided fast. But there is more to surviving than not dying. In the past, people who had managed to live through a cardiovascular attack were condemned to semi-invalidism. New knowledge and new treatments have now demonstrated that prolonged life and productivity depend on quick return to essentially normal work and play.

This radical turnaround in outlook is the result of two developments. The first is a remarkable improvement in emergency and hospital care. People thought to be dead in the street can now be resuscitated on the spot *(pages 85-87);* specially trained and outfitted ambulance crews can maintain the faintest spark of life to bring a victim to the haven of a hospital *(pages 154-165);* once inside a well-equipped hospital, a stricken patient stands a very good chance that he will, within about two weeks, walk out on his own. Of the 460 heart attack victims brought alive to the Washington Hospital Center in the District of Columbia in a typical year, 436 recovered to go home.

The second development in the care of patients with heart-related ailments is a radical change in treatment after the danger of sudden death has been minimized. At one time, prolonged bed rest was a strict prescription for most victims of heart attack. Now a regular exercise program—sometimes beginning as soon as two days after an attack—is recognized as an important step to recovery. Further changes have come in the growing awareness of the emotional needs of patients and their families. "After a heart attack," said one heart specialist from the Netherlands, "more problems rest in the mind than in the heart." Doctors specializing in cardiac psychology found that a patient's negative feelings—anger, depression and loss of self-esteem—are a normal and predictable accompaniment to the disease. Once acknowledged by the patient, these feelings, like the disease itself, can be addressed and brought under control.

Local hospitals and heart associations can now wheel up a battery of support in the form of therapy and rehabilita-

Composer Dmitri Shostakovich
Choreographer George Balanchine
Judge John Sirica
Prime Minister Winston Churchill
Actor Peter Sellers
Pitcher John Hiller
President Lyndon Johnson
Actor Walter Matthau
Coach Woody Hayes
Author James Michener
Astronaut James Irwin
Director Alfred Hitchcock
Actress Patricia Neal
Musician Count Basie
Choreographer Bob Fosse
President Dwight Eisenhower

Heart attacks and strokes no longer condemn victims to lives of inactivity, as the post-illness careers of these 16 celebrities prove. All of them survived attacks to resume demanding work, some aided by pacemakers (Sellers) or surgery (Balanchine).

tion programs. Thanks to these revolutions in care, four out of five of those victims who reach the hospital alive after a heart attack can now expect to return to the occupations they had before their attack. For those felled by stroke—the other major circulatory killer, and an insidious thief of both physical and mental capabilities—the odds in favor of recovery are comparable.

But even the most sensitive therapists and up-to-date technology can take a heart or stroke patient only so far. Patients must make a contribution of their own—matched by support from their families. The first, and perhaps most crucial, step in the journey to recovery is to believe in one immutable fact: Anyone stricken by circulatory disease is permanently afflicted. The affliction is not unmanageable but—unlike an infection, or even the life-threatening consequences of a skull fracture—it will never go away. Most of the problems that beset postcardiac patients and their families spring from a failure to accept this reality. Those who have had a heart attack or stroke must, for example, give up smoking—completely and permanently. And they must discipline themselves to manage stress, weight and cholesterol levels in the blood—a discipline that will remain, literally, a matter of life or death.

The first step: staying alive

The long-term need for a disciplined life style is usually far from the thoughts of the victim of a sudden attack. He is concerned about surviving the next few minutes. He is probably disoriented and unnerved by a siren-screaming ride in an ambulance. In the hospital emergency room he may feel abandoned.

Emergency-room attention, though generally prompt, is far from constant. One heart patient recalled that, after he had been treated and sedated in the emergency room, "I began to feel pretty good and closed my eyes. The next thing, I looked around and no one was there—it was as if a vacuum cleaner had sucked all the people out. I wanted to get up and run away. It was spooky as hell."

In a first-rate emergency department, this apparent abandonment of a patient may, paradoxically, be a good sign—virtually the only time well-trained doctors and nurses hover over one patient is when matters are critical. And recent standardization of emergency care for heart attack and stroke victims generally gives these cases top priority.

Regrettably, only a few hospital emergency departments are considered first-rate. "Basic errors of assessment and treatment are reported with disturbing regularity," according to six authorities on emergency medicine, writing in the *Journal of the American Medical Association* in 1979. In some emergency rooms, lack of attention may be dangerous neglect. If you accompany the victim of a heart attack or stroke to the hospital, do not be shy about demanding immediate attention for him, and try to stay alongside him until you see that he is in good hands.

Emergency treatment for the heart attack victim is generally more elaborate than for those suffering sudden onset of other cardiovascular diseases. Even before reaching the emergency room, the victim of a heart attack has probably received some treatment, in the form of drugs, intravenous fluids and oxygen. In the hospital, the oxygen generally continues, and the number and variety of fluids and drugs expand. Treatment to restore normal heart function is now fairly standardized. If the patient's blood pressure is low and the heart is beating too slowly, atropine is given to speed the heart rate and restore blood pressure. Lidocaine is administered to regulate a heart that is beating irregularly and too fast, and if this condition degenerates into the disorganized and ineffective beating called fibrillation, it is countered with the electric defibrillator. Blood pressure is recorded frequently to see if there is any danger of shock.

Electrocardiograms monitor heartbeat to detect any dangerous variations in rate that may signal the onset of another attack or even cardiac arrest, the stopping of the heart. These ECGs may be displayed on a TV-like monitoring screen that is visible to the emergency-ward staff. If the heart should stop or beat erratically, the doctor can shock the heart into action or control its beat by applying electric defibrillator paddles to the patient's chest.

A battery of other drugs, instruments and procedures also comes into action. When the heart stops, so does breathing.

The emergency-room team inserts a tube into the patient's windpipe to restore his oxygen supply, using either a hand-operated bag-valve system or a mechanical respirator. To alleviate acidosis, an abnormally acid condition that is caused by the decrease in oxygen supply and that affects the response of the heart, an antacid such as sodium bicarbonate is given. Some of the other drugs used for cardiac arrest include epinephrine and isoproterenol, both of which make the heart beat faster and contract more forcefully. Calcium chloride is also administered to improve the responsiveness of the heart muscle, to make the heart beat more forcefully after normal rhythm is restored, to increase blood pressure and to improve blood flow to the brain. Many of these medications follow a patient throughout his stay in the hospital and after he is discharged. Taking his medicine will become a part of his contribution to his own recovery.

The stroke victim's experience in the emergency room is considerably different from that of the heart attack victim. There is relatively little that the emergency-room staff can do to help him. Treatment consists of maintaining his breathing, blood pressure and fluid levels if any of these are failing. Most stroke victims will be moved from the emergency room onto a regular floor of the hospital, or to a special stroke care unit if the hospital has one. But those who have suffered a significant loss of brain function may be transferred immediately to the intensive care unit, or ICU, where any patient who is in mortal danger—accident survivor, surgical patient or disease victim—is surrounded by the hospital's most skilled nurses and its most elaborate life-preserving machinery.

A victim of a severe heart attack may also go to the ICU, but in most cases he moves from the emergency ward to the coronary care unit, or CCU *(pages 143-145)*, where he remains for three or four days. The specialized care delivered in the CCU is credited with reducing hospital mortality for heart attack patients worldwide from 30 per cent to 20 per cent. In the CCU, the patient is still surrounded by tubes, screens and machines, yet he feels a sense of deliverance. The CCU is not so impersonal as the emergency room, and it is less like a scientific laboratory than the ICU. Patients are generally in the recovery stage and are alert to their surroundings. There is food to eat instead of synthetic nutrients dripped into a vein, even if the food is bland, with fats and salt reduced nearly to the vanishing point. Hot, regular meals—which begin within 24 hours of a patient's admittance to the CCU—have a reassuring effect.

Although still in danger, patients in the CCU are considered well enough to be left in relative peace—to nap, perhaps to read a bit, and to start to take hold of their lives again. Much of this peaceful, encouraging atmosphere is accomplished by the CCU nurses, who, as one patient described their work, "do everything for you except brush your teeth." Another saw the nurses literally as angels of mercy, "gentle and good," plumping his pillow and saying, "This will make you feel better." Most important, they touched him, "flesh to flesh."

A quick return to activity

The person lying in the CCU needs every shred of this encouragement, for he is likely to be frightened and depressed. Though some of the anxieties brought on by a recent heart attack are eased by tranquilizers or sedatives, the patient may be conducting an inner debate: "I may live—but what will I have to give up to stay alive? No more smoking? How about drinking? Sports? Social life? That's not living." Partly to combat such anxieties, many hospitals begin rehabilitation while the heart attack patient is still in the CCU. Step by step the patient moves from the enforced stillness of the immediate postattack period to a degree of mobility that allows as much time out of bed as possible. He may even be required to climb stairs.

At Georgia Baptist Hospital in Atlanta, for example, a recovering heart patient performs a mixture of three kinds of activities at each of eight graded steps in the rehabilitation process, which takes from nine to 14 days in the hospital. The three activities called for at Step 2 (Days 3 and 4), for instance, are sitting in a bedside chair for 20 minutes, lying in bed and moving the limbs through their full range of motion in such actions as swinging the arms up over the head, and talking with a therapist or reading. In Step 6 (Day 10) the schedule includes a tub or shower bath, lateral bending exercises and the beginning of a craft project involving work with the hands.

Physical and psychological therapies are also critical in the hospital treatment of a stroke victim. He may be despondent, yielding to emotional upsets that pour out with little control—crying easily, laughing at inappropriate times. These outbursts are only temporary aftereffects—not symptoms of personality disorders or mental degeneration—and are to be expected.

More than heart attack victims, stroke patients are likely to require physical rehabilitation. Most of those who survive the early crisis are afflicted with lingering disabilities, including speech handicaps and paralysis. Their sense of touch may be lost or impaired, making them unable to feel pain or to tell the size or weight of objects. They may also lose the ability to sense movement.

By moving the limbs for a patient, the physical therapist can help prevent joints from stiffening and muscles from shortening and atrophying. These early corrective measures are essential to the success of more extensive rehabilitation later, when the patient is helped to retrain both brain function and muscles. Meanwhile, there are things even untrained family members can do to help the patient cope with the immediate effects of his condition. For example, a paralyzed arm may be entirely without sensation, but its shoulder may hurt from the stricken arm's weight; a pillow to prop the arm will help. It is also important to keep the patient's fingernails trimmed so they will not score the palm of a paralyzed hand that remains clenched.

If a member of your family has reached this stage of the immediate aftermath of a stroke or heart attack, you may find your early visits to the hospital unsettling unless you recognize that his morale and self-esteem are likely to be low. To counter this understandable reaction to illness and confinement, let the patient know that he remains an important member of the family and society. When visiting an ailing spouse, dress your best to point out that you—the healthy partner—still care enough to want to appear physically attractive. Involve the patient in easy decisions about his life: who on his job should be informed of the illness, how much they should be told, who among them would be welcome visitors. Encourage children to communicate—to write postcards, draw pictures of themselves and their school activities, and visit if they are old enough.

Leaving the refuge of the CCU

The last segment of the hospital stay takes place in a convalescent room, which in a modern hospital may look much like a motel room. The life-supporting machinery and tubes are gone. The patient, moving steadily further away from the threat of sudden death, is encouraged to step up his physical activity.

At this stage many people become anxious and edgy about leaving the more visible security of the CCU. Some may reject the plain fact of their illness—not in words, but by actions. They may skip scheduled medication or disobey a doctor's orders and sneak a surreptitious smoke.

Some patients respond to their transfer from the CCU to a convalescent room with irritability. They may snap at family members and make petulant demands, an indication that they are feeling left out of their families' busy lives. The convalescent phase thus is a good time to tell the patient more about what is going on at work and at home. Gradually increase his participation in decisions—about filing health insurance claims, for example, or about making the arrangements for a return home. Encourage friends to visit, but make sure the number and frequency of visitors meet with the doctor's approval.

From the emergency department, through the CCU, to the convalescent room, the momentum of recovery mounts. By the happy day when the patient is scheduled to be released from the hospital, both he and his family—it is hoped—will have been well prepared to continue that vital progress at home.

A fresh start at home

The obstacles are many. They include a vulnerable psychology and the adjustment to changes in habits such as smoking and eating. But perhaps most painful is the fear, similar to

Computerized life support in the CCU

A red light blinks on a console panel, the number of a nearby room appears on a screen, and electrocardiogram (ECG) data spew from a printer. In seconds, nurses and physicians are at the bedside of a patient whose heartbeat tripped the alarms—perhaps without his even knowing he needed attention. An array of machines *(pages 144-145)* begins helping him breathe and medicating his heart.

This is a coronary care unit (CCU). Its electronic life-support system is mainly intended to keep patients on the mend for the critical three to five days during recuperation from heart attack, but it is also used to monitor patients with other circulatory trouble requiring close surveillance. It generally serves fewer than 20 patients, in small rooms encircling the monitoring console. Glass walls permit the nurse at the console to see the patients. In the most modern CCUs, a computer does much of the watching; it never blinks, observing every second, 24 hours a day. Electrodes attached to each patient's body constantly feed the computer such information as pulse rate, heartbeat rhythm, and in some cases blood pressure, temperature, breathing rate and other vital signs. It compares these data with previous data on the patient and sounds the alarms when serious deviations occur.

The effectiveness of such facilities shows in the statistics. When the first CCU was installed, in Bethany Medical Center, Kansas City, Kansas, in 1962, about 30 per cent of those treated for heart attack in hospitals died there. By 1978 more than two thirds of the American hospitals with more than 400 beds had CCUs—and in them the in-patient death rate had been cut in half.

A nurse monitors a CCU console in Georgetown University Hospital, Washington, D.C. The screen at left displays several electrocardiogram patterns simultaneously; next to it are printers that can produce ECG tracings. The two screens at right display computer data on patients' progress, including two graphs showing different irregularities in rhythm.

Anatomy of a coronary care unit

MONITOR SCREEN
The screen displays the patient's heart electrical signals—his ECG—and also can graph his blood pressure. Pulse rate appears below the screen on a digital panel.

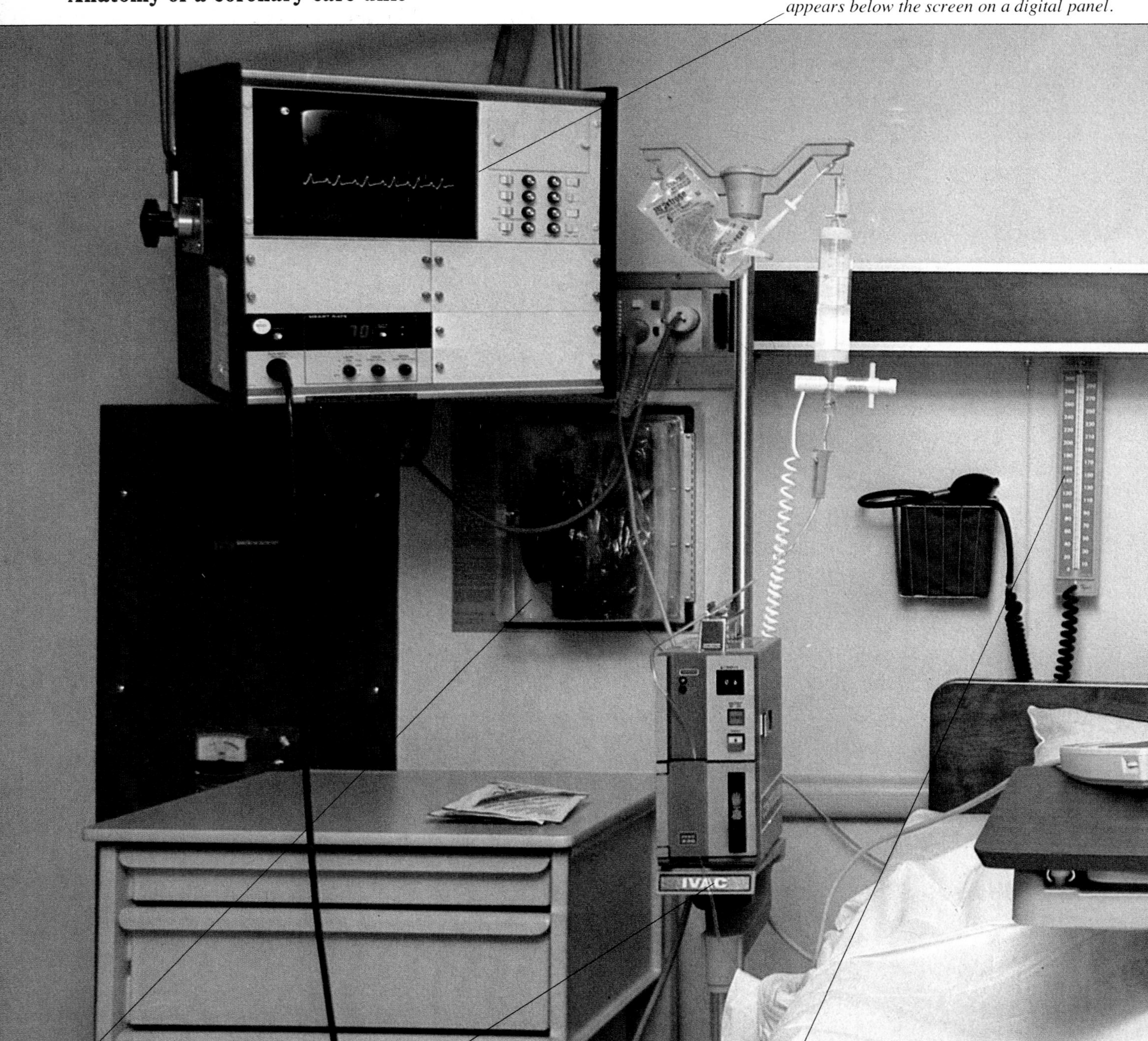

MANUAL RESUSCITATOR
Generally known by its trade name, this Ambu bag serves as a manual respirator to fill the patient's lungs with room air or with oxygen from the taps at upper right.

INTRAVENOUS METER
This mechanism can be adjusted to regulate the rates at which different kinds of medicine flow through intravenous tubes and into the patient's bloodstream.

BLOOD PRESSURE CUFF
A traditional sphygmomanometer is kept near the patient's bed for general use. More accurate, continuous readings can be made by an electronic device.

STOMACH PUMP
To prevent the vomiting that can accompany heart trouble, this device, plugged into a vacuum pipe, sweeps food and liquid from the stomach into a diposable chamber.

OXYGEN TAPS
Two outlets, one an emergency backup, can dispense life-sustaining oxygen to a patient through a mask or through two tiny tubes inserted in the nostrils.

SUCTION DEVICE
Plugged into a vacuum pipe in the wall, the tube can clear the patient's throat and upper lungs of mucus that would hamper breathing and could lead to pneumonia.

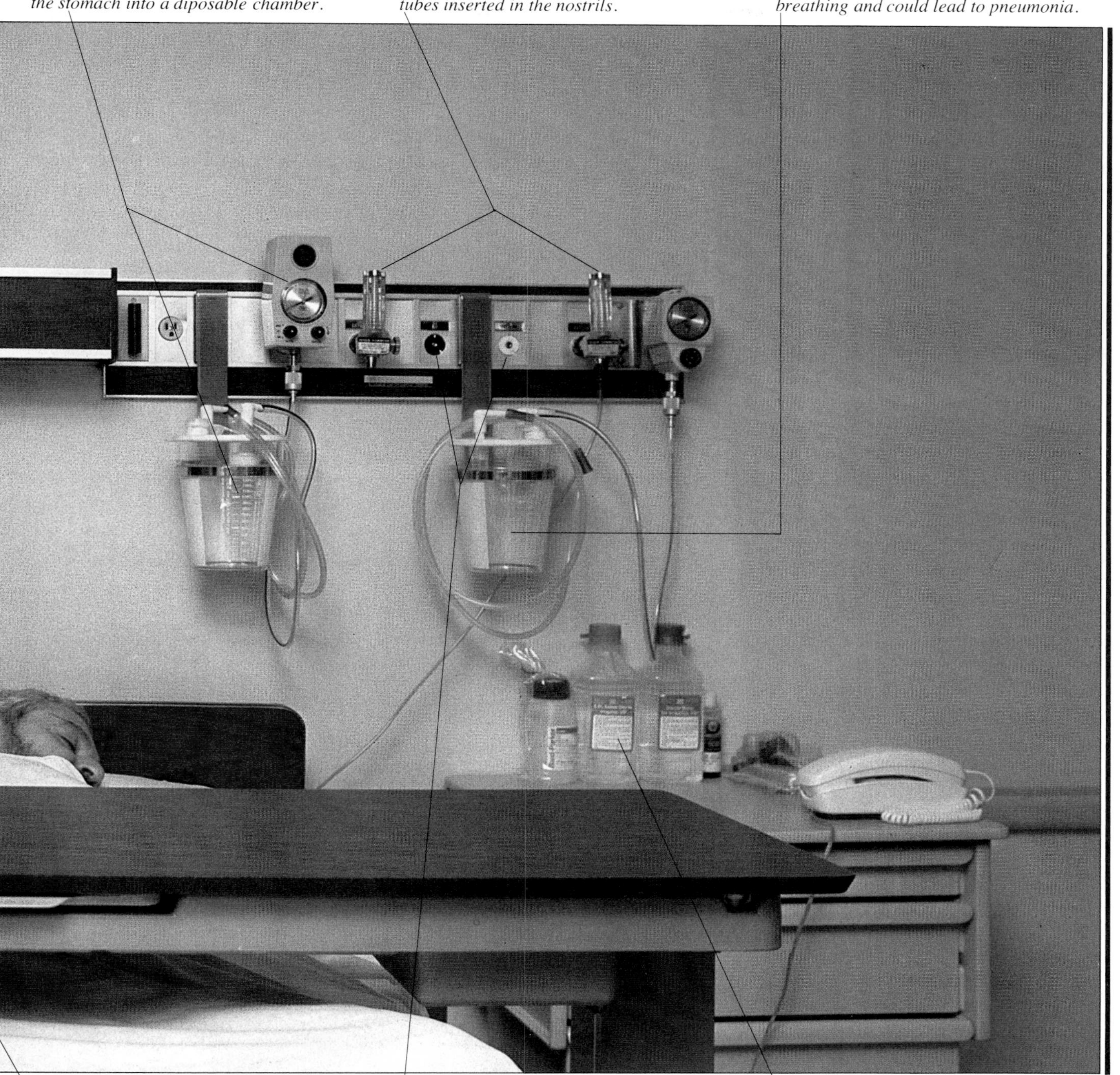

NURSE'S SIGNAL
Pushing one button summons a nurse by turning on a light on the nurses' console. Other buttons control the TV set, which is an aid to the generally bored patient.

AIR AND SUCTION SOURCES
The outlet on the left supplies air, sometimes preferable to pure oxygen in helping a patient breathe. The connection to its right provides a backup source of vacuum.

BEDSIDE BOTTLES
The smaller bottle contains sterile water to humidify air or oxygen for patients. The others contain saline solution to be used to irrigate the lungs and dislodge mucus.

that following the transfer from CCU to convalescent room, of being away from medical help in an emergency. In San Pedro, California, San Pedro and Peninsula Hospital established a hot-line telephone system for discharged patients. A nurse at the hospital stands by in a control center where the patient's chart is within reach. On leaving the hospital, patients are instructed to call the hot line not just any time they sense an emergency but every day for the first four weeks, weekly for the next month, and monthly from then on.

In its first year of operation, the San Pedro hot line handled 2,500 routine calls and 87 emergency calls. Paramedic teams were summoned from the hospital to handle 11 of the emergencies, and 22 other patients were sent to the hospital emergency department. The rest needed only reassurance or notification to their doctor of a minor change in their condition. Such a system enables the cardiac patient to attend directly to his own needs, and this sense of taking the initiative is essential. But the patient's family can also help, particularly in the areas of smoking, medication and diet.

In *Heartsounds,* Martha Lear described the subterfuges she used to avoid smoking in front of her husband, a former smoker who was recuperating at home after open-heart surgery. She hid cigarettes in pillow cases and once in a soup tureen. Her husband had started to filch cigarette butts while still in the hospital, getting the most smokable from the visitors' lounge after hours. When he got home, he found her caches of cigarettes and helped himself. He also picked butts out of the gutter.

One day, "while seeming to tie his shoelace near a parked car," Martha Lear wrote, he happened "to glance up and catch his image in the car's rear-view mirror; and to look down and see the butt he had just picked up, the yellow stain of dried saliva on its edge.

" 'You are disgusting,' he said to the mirror image. 'You disgust me.' And began to cry."

A lifelong course of medication

After a heart attack or stroke a patient may have to take a variety of drugs regularly. Among them are:

- *Heart strengtheners.* These may be needed to regulate and buttress the heartbeat and to forestall heart failure as fluids back up and progressively impair pumping action. Digoxin and digitoxin are common forms of the classic heart strengthener digitalis, derived from the dried leaves of the foxglove plant *(page 21).*
- *Heartbeat regulators.* These drugs control heart rhythm by stabilizing the electrical activity of the heart. The most common generic names are disopyramide, quinidine, procainamide and propranolol.
- *Pain relievers.* Two distinct types are used, beta blockers and vasodilators. Both relieve angina by reducing the work load of the heart. Beta blockers interfere with the normal response of the beta-type receptor cells in the nervous system. They lower the oxygen requirement of the heart by reducing the force of its contractions. Propranolol is the beta blocker that is most often prescribed. Vasodilators lower blood pressure by enlarging the blood vessels, thus reducing the resistance they offer to blood flow. This also alleviates pain by increasing the flow of blood to the heart. Prazosin and hydralazine are two commonly prescribed vasodilators, along with nitrates such as nitroglycerin and isosorbide dinitrate.
- *Tranquilizers.* To help the patient relax and rest, diazepam (Valium), chlordiazepoxide (Librium) or meprobamate (Miltown) are prescribed to relieve anxiety.
- *Preventives.* These drugs act to forestall another heart attack or stroke by lowering blood pressure, by preventing the formation of blood clots, or by reducing blood levels of fats such as cholesterol. The blood pressure pills are the standard ones—diuretics such as hydrochlorothiazide, beta blockers such as propranolol, or vasodilators such as hydralazine. One common anticoagulant drug is coumadin, and aspirin is also often prescribed. Drugs that reduce blood fats include clofibrate and cholestyramine.

Many of these drugs may have to be taken routinely for years; most victims of a heart attack or stroke must resign themselves to using them on schedule for the rest of their lives. Many patients cannot. The medicines often cause unpleasant side effects; their benefits (and the ill effects of not taking them) are seldom obvious. But heart patients and their families should understand one thing clearly: Failure to take prescribed drugs, or taking them in the wrong dosages or at the wrong times, may confer a sentence of death. Family members can help ensure a heart patient's compliance with his medication regimen at home by setting up a log of times and other particulars—including the state of the drugs' supplies. The log helps make sure the patient takes the drugs as prescribed, and it is also useful to the doctor when prescriptions need revising.

For some people, even more difficult than taking medicine or quitting smoking is following the heart patient's diet. Low in saturated fat, cholesterol and salt (or sodium), it generally tastes much different from the meals common in the Western world. A dietician, usually available at the hospital or through a local heart association, can supplement the doctor's dry orders with appetizing menus and meal plans. Whoever does the shopping and cooking for the household may have to change methods to ensure that meals conform to the doctor's requirements; instructions can be found in many pamphlets and specialized cookbooks.

Getting open-air exercise safely, two cardiac patients walk and jog in a hospital parking lot (background) while an electronic receiver (foreground) monitors their heart rhythms. On their chests the patients wear electrodes that pick up heart signals, and portable transmitters that radio these signals to the receiver.

Even the way that food is eaten may have to be altered. People who have attacks of angina or who suffer congestive heart failure are advised to eat more slowly than they ordinarily would and to eat a number of small meals during the course of the day rather than three large ones. Both of these practices will spare the heart from exerting too much effort to aid the digestive system. The consumption of alcohol must be watched very carefully as well, since alcohol causes the heart to beat faster and acts to raise triglyceride levels in the blood.

Family cooperation at home with diet and medication is essential to the rehabilitation of both heart attack and stroke victims. Yet more vital to the comfort and dignity of those who have been paralyzed or severely weakened by stroke is the opportunity to do as much as possible for themselves. Some simple mechanical devices can make day-to-day life more convenient for them. Secure handrails generally are needed in hallways and bathrooms. Other devices to ease life for the stroke patient include eating utensils that can be used with a single hand, shoes that need not be laced and specially constructed elevator toilet seats that lift or lower the user*(page 152)*.

The need for exercise

Family cooperation also may be necessary in helping the victim of a stroke or heart attack to exercise. For a person who has suffered a stroke, regaining the use of his muscles can be a slow and painful process. He may need someone to help him simply move his arms and legs around or to support him as he resumes walking. For the heart attack victim, encouragement may be all that is required. In any case, those recovering from either type of ailment must exercise as much as they are able.

There is now considerable evidence that regular exercise not only rebuilds and strengthens a stricken body, but can prevent another attack. One study in Toronto counted heart attack recurrences and deaths among postcoronary patients on a regular exercise program and compared these statistics with similar data on patients who did not exercise. Those in the group that did not exercise were 20 times as likely to suffer subsequent heart attacks and had a death rate three times as great.

The Toronto research and other similar studies spurred Dr. Terence Kavanagh to begin a program at the Toronto Rehabilitation Centre that guides heart attack victims in vigorous exercise. Patients enter the program as early as six weeks after their attacks. Following tests to be certain that they will not be harmed by the effort, they are started walking or jogging for half an hour five times a week. Subsequently, the time is expanded to one hour. The exerciser's first objective is a 36-minute, three-mile jog; the long-term goal is to reach six miles in 60 minutes. Some veterans of the program have actually competed in the Boston Marathon *(pages 149-151)*.

One of the five sessions each week is held at the center. Dr. Kavanagh supervises this session—and participates himself. His involvement, he believes, enables him to be on the lookout for inept or frightened exercisers who are likely to give up, supercompetitors who often overexert themselves, and those who deny indications of trouble such as angina pain. The other four sessions are unsupervised. Independence is fostered partly to encourage self-discipline—the patient is required to file a report on exercise activities every two weeks—and also to reduce the drop-out rate, a problem that plagues similar programs. Participants must agree to remain in the program for at least one year, and a two-year participation is recommended.

Physical rehabilitation of heart patients is an established practice in most parts of the world. In New Zealand, patients leaving the hospital join follow-up clinics that include group exercise programs and "coronary club" sports centers. In West Germany, many sanatoriums and spas have been converted to cardiac rehabilitation hospitals. At one modern facility, Klinik Hohenreid on Lake Starnberg in Bavaria, some 450 coronary patients—plus an additional 150 men and women judged to be at high risk of coronary disease—are supervised in spirited group activities including rowing sessions on the lake and hiking in the mountains. The details of the physiological aspects of exercise for heart patients are still being weighed and the advantages debated. But the psychological benefits that exercise confers—the lifting of fear and depression, the restoration of self-confidence—make exercise a vital factor in returning heart patients to normal life.

Getting back to work

With care from physicians, friends and family, a patient can resume a normal life and return to his regular job. In some areas, work evaluation programs help determine how much a patient can do, and how soon. At Montefiore Hospital in New York City, the TOWER Program (the letters stand for Testing, Organization, Orientation and Work Evaluation in Rehabilitation) uses one kind of test job to represent other occupations in the outside world. (For example, jewelry making, easily set up in the hospital rehabilitation rooms, stands for jobs such as television repair and metalworking.) The patient's productivity and accuracy are measured against industrial standards, while his heart is monitored to see how it responds to the demands of the work. Similar vocational testing goes on at Benedikt Kneutz Klinik in Bad Krozingen, West Germany, where the topics of job-retraining sessions range from metalwork to advanced executive training.

Elsewhere, a more realistic evaluation is made on the job. Many hospitals can outfit a patient returning to work with a carry-around monitor that tape-records heart rate and rhythm for as long as 24 hours. At the end of the day the tape can be played back at the hospital. Other devices worn by patients can radio vital signs to the hospital. After such evaluation, one man, an accountant, was found to be better off at work than at home, where he was bored and anxious. Monitored as he did carpentry work around the house, the man had an elevated pulse rate and abnormal ECG readings. When he was allowed to go to the office, his pulse rate was lower and his ECG normal.

Prompt return to a normal work routine may not be advisable, however, for the heart of the intense, stress-prone Type A individual. In one study, which examined heart attack victims at intervals of four and a half and eight and a half years after their attacks, researchers found that Type A

Running with "the sickest track club in the world"

On April 15, 1973, more than 900 exhausted runners slogged across the finish line of the annual Boston Marathon, exactly 26 miles 385 yards from their starting point in the little town of Hopkinton, Massachusetts. Among the finishers were seven middle-aged Canadians who called themselves "the sickest track club in the world."

They were certainly the most amazing and courageous club. All of them had suffered heart attacks, and in running the marathon they dramatically disproved the doctrine that such victims are condemned to a life of solicitous inactivity. The marathon runners were trained by a physician who had never subscribed to that doctrine, Dr. Terence Kavanagh, head of the Toronto Rehabilitation Centre. On the day of the marathon, Dr. Kavanagh paced his wards throughout the race and monitored every participant at checkpoints along the route. None of them suffered anything worse than sore feet.

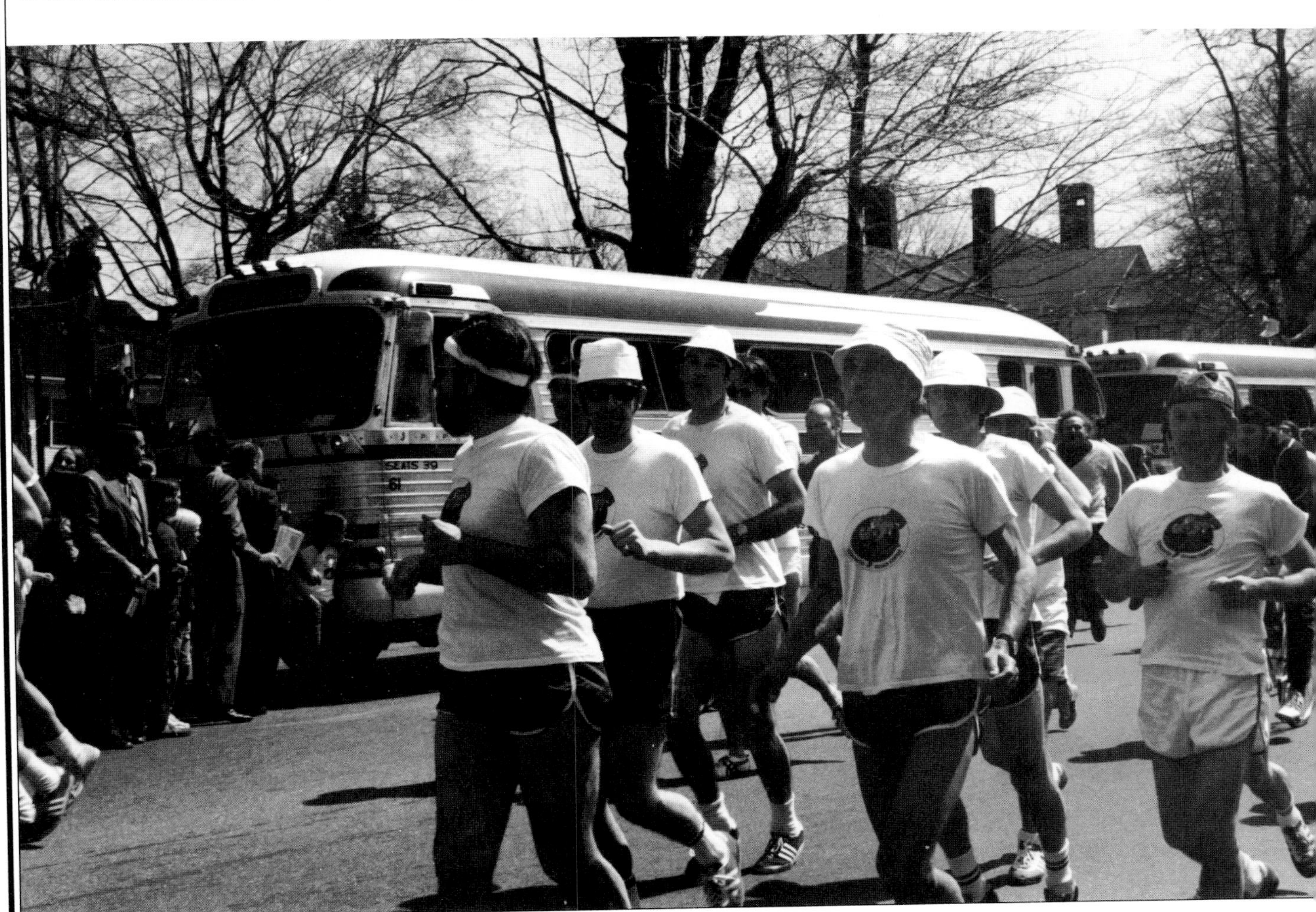

Wearing headgear to protect them from the near-80° heat, heart patients of the Toronto Rehabilitation Centre track team begin their historic marathon. On their T-shirts is a drawing of Superman with an outsized cracked heart, created by Canadian designer Ken Smith—himself a heart attack victim.

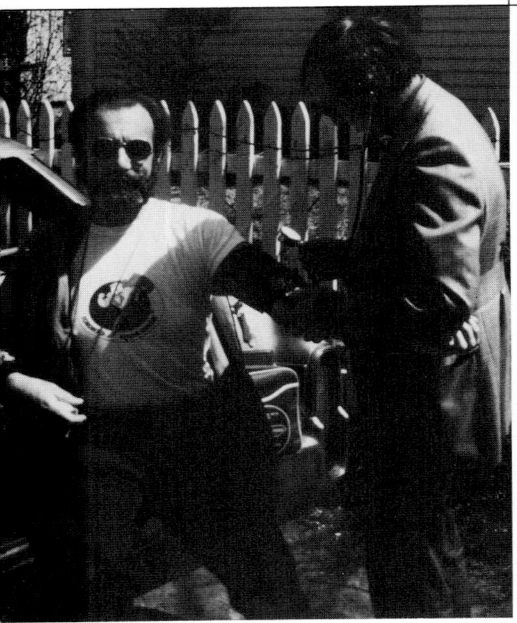

Dr. Kavanagh checks the blood pressure of a marathon runner during the race. The doctor, a nurse and a medical technician drove along the course of the race to check their patients' body weights, measure blood pressure, record electrocardiograms, and take blood and urine samples.

Four miles from the finish line, runner Herman Robers pounds up the ironically named "Heartbreak Hill," a three-and-a-half-mile stretch of the route where all but the fittest fade and drop out. Robers ran the race in a respectable 4 hours 32 minutes—and in a subsequent marathon pared his time to 3 hours 11 minutes.

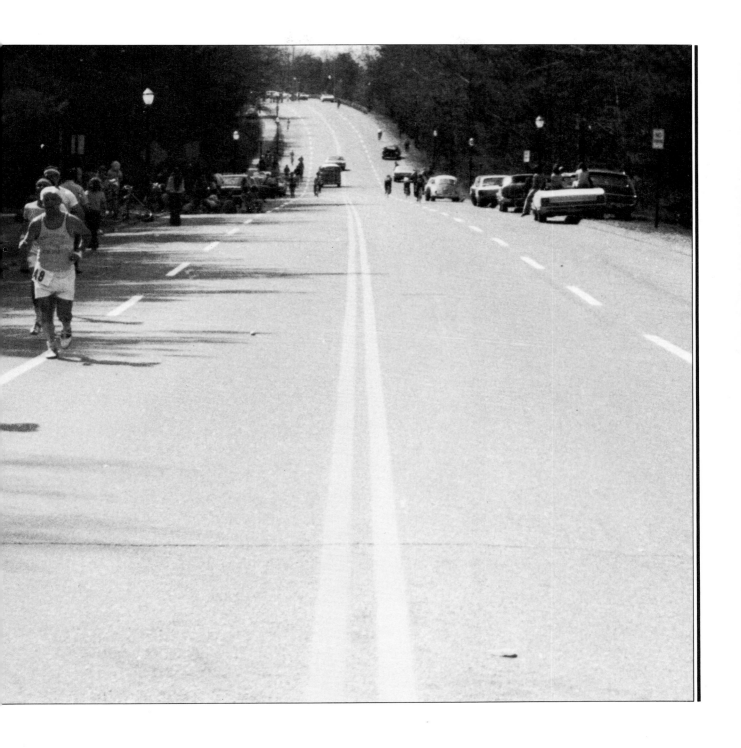

A house that helps a stroke victim

Anyone whose physical mobility is impaired by a stroke can be helped by minor modifications to his home. Most of the structural modifications are simple ones that require a minimum of skill and no special tools; they involve only the installation of readily available hardware.

To guard the stroke victim against trips and falls, substitute flush doorway thresholds for the raised sills used in many older houses. On stairways the regular balustrade or handrail can be complemented by a second, wall-mounted handrail on the opposite side, and slippery wooden steps can be covered with plastic treads or strips of traction tape. Handrails in hallways are also helpful. Throughout the house remove loose rugs; their edges may trip a disabled person by catching a cane or a foot.

To compensate for the impaired dexterity of many stroke victims, replace small lamp switches, which may be hard to reach beneath a lamp shade, with oversized switches mounted on the cord or with old-fashioned pull-chain switches. The standard wall-mounted toggle switch for ceiling fixtures can be replaced with an illuminated rocker switch, which turns on or off whenever its plate is touched. Doorknobs are often too small and slippery for a stroke victim to grasp; you can build them up by winding them with foam-rubber tape or, better still, replace them with large lever latches. Modern push-button door locks can be installed on exterior doors in place of hard-to-work key locks. You also can fit exterior doors with delayed-action door closers; such a device will hold the door open for a while, giving a person time to walk through, and then will pull it firmly shut.

Kitchens and bathrooms create special problems. Storage shelves and closets often must be rearranged and remodeled to accommodate someone who cannot reach as high or as far as he once could. To protect a stroke victim who has lost sensation on one side of his body and might unwittingly scald himself at a sink, bathtub or shower, install thermostatically controlled faucet valves that automatically limit the water temperature. Chairs and low counter tops in the kitchen and bathroom permit a stroke victim to cook, shave or apply make-up sitting down, eliminating the fatigue of standing for long periods.

In the shower or bathtub, install a waterproof seat and a shower head mounted on a flexible rubber hose. And throughout the bathroom—particularly in the shower and alongside the toilet and bathtub—provide sturdy grab bars, very securely installed, which will alleviate the strain of sitting down and standing up.

men suffered recurrences of coronary disease about two to four times as often as those subjects with the relaxed Type B personality.

Sex after a coronary

For most people recovering from circulatory ailments, a return to normal activities implies a return to sexual activity. Not everyone is able to manage this. Research into sexual activity after a heart attack is limited, but among male coronary patients it appears that as many as half taper off sexual activity or give up sex altogether. The reasons are several: fear of a second coronary, feelings of inadequacy leading to impotence, or the onset after intercourse of such symptoms as angina or erratic heartbeat. Marital problems often result, with obvious ill effects on the course of recovery. Yet the fears are largely groundless, so long as certain precautions are understood and followed.

Over the long haul, a heart attack should have little influence on sexual ability. The physical strain is far less than might be imagined—the equivalent of walking briskly for two blocks or climbing a couple of flights of stairs. This holds true as long as the sexual activity is with a spouse or partner of reasonably long standing. Death seems to overtake cardiac patients more often when they are with extramarital or casual partners. Presumably, the excitement of forbidden pleasure increases the burden on the heart.

As with vigorous exercise, a basic precaution is timing. Beginning sex too soon after a heart attack can put undue strain on healing heart muscle. Six weeks is a common waiting period. Another normal requirement is that the patient be able to walk 10 blocks or the equivalent; since the effort involved in sexual activity is about the same as that involved in walking *two* blocks, there is an ample margin for safety. Other precautions include:

• Waiting about three hours after a heavy meal—particularly one that includes alcoholic drinks. The heart is already working hard to aid in the digestive process.
• Postponing sex if either partner is angry or tired. Under the stress of such feelings the heart beats faster, and sex would add another burden.
• Avoiding muscular fatigue (such as may result from leaning on the arms), which may raise blood pressure unduly.
• Taking nitroglycerin to ward off chest pains during intercourse. If severe angina occurs, sexual activity should stop and a doctor should be called. (In most cases, assuming that the pain subsides, the doctor may be consulted the following day.)

An additional precaution applies to women who were taking oral contraceptives before their heart attacks. A change in birth-control method may be advisable. The Pill can act to increase blood pressure, and can heighten the tendency of the blood to clot—dangerous side effects for a recuperating heart patient.

Someone to talk to

Such cautionary advice, simple and sensible though it may be, often adds to fears. Despite reassurances offered by authorities, some people find difficulty after a heart attack in reestablishing normal sexual activity—and this puts extra strain on the most intimate of the many personal relationships that are disrupted by severe circulatory ailments. A spouse, however loving and sympathetic, is not always able to deal singlehandedly with the complex of feelings that beset a recovering patient. This need is often better served by an organization that brings together a group of patients who help one another in their attempts to return to normal living.

One effective group is made up of the participants in the Toronto Rehabilitation Centre exercise program, who meet once a week with the medical staff to air their problems. More specifically geared to heart surgery patients is an organization called Mended Hearts, Inc., founded in 1951 by four patients who were recovering from surgery in a Boston hospital. From this small beginning grew an organization with 100 chapters and about 15,000 members. They visit or telephone surgery patients before and after the operation, and follow up with support throughout rehabilitation. When graduates of open-heart surgery get together at meetings and social gatherings, they reinforce one another's motivation to maintain the life style of the healthy heart patient.

Groups can also be a major resource for stroke patients, who often suffer awkward and painful disruptions of speech and movement. These clubs concentrate on the problems faced not only by the stroke victim but also by members of his family, who may be distraught over physical appearance and behavior that are, in the words of the directors of one club in Butler, Pennsylvania, "not unlike those of automatons—surviving but not living." The club gives these people a chance to learn, from the experience of others, how to live with the problems. In England a similar club for stroke patients emphasizes socializing to encourage people suffering speech impairment to get used to talking again.

These club members acquire the understanding that must come to all who succeed in recuperating from severe circulatory ailments: Once the immediate danger is past, what counts is how the fact of the illness is handled. Dealing with it in the best way—by accepting the condition as unremitting—may be a high price. But the first down payment has already been made with the coronary or stroke, and the sufferer might as well draw as much return on the investment as possible.

One dividend is a new appreciation of the small pleasures of life—jogging before work through the splendor of an early autumn morning, for example. Other changes may be more profound. "Having traveled to the brink and peered over," reported one member of Mended Hearts, "I have become a nicer person. I say 'thank you' more often." Joel Bruinooge, an editor who had both a stroke and a subsequent heart attack at the age of 26, put the matter in this perspective: "In some ways I consider myself very lucky for having had the experience. It's allowed me a chance to sit back and look at my life. I'm happier with the way I live now than I was before. Work is less stressful because I can look at situations that would have produced stress for me before and say, 'That's not a problem—I have had problems.' " ❋

Seattle's heart savers: Medic One

People who have heart attacks in Seattle stand a better chance of survival than heart attack victims almost anywhere else in the United States. The reason is Medic One, an elaborately equipped emergency medical service that scoops up heart attack patients and begins treating them inside the ambulance en route to a coronary care unit in a hospital.

The Medic One teams—all of them fire-department volunteers—are trained at Harborview Medical Center to recognize and minister to every type of heart failure. They work fast. Their five vans are equipped not only with the usual oxygen tanks and intravenous fluids but with devices to restart a stopped heart, to record its action and—most important—to radio vital signs to a physician at the base hospital so that he can tell the technicians what to do for the patient.

How Medic One saves lives can be seen in the remarkable sequence of pictures, beginning at right, that caught on the run the successful rescue of 59-year-old truck driver Clifford Le Beau. The increase in the percentage of lives that have been saved can be seen in the statistics *(graph below)*. By the end of Medic One's first year of operation, 13 per cent of its patients survived; by the end of its first decade, the rate was 30 per cent—one of the highest in the country for this type of emergency treatment. By contrast, survival in surrounding King County was only 6 per cent—until Medic One's services were extended to cover the entire area; within three years the county-wide rate had tripled.

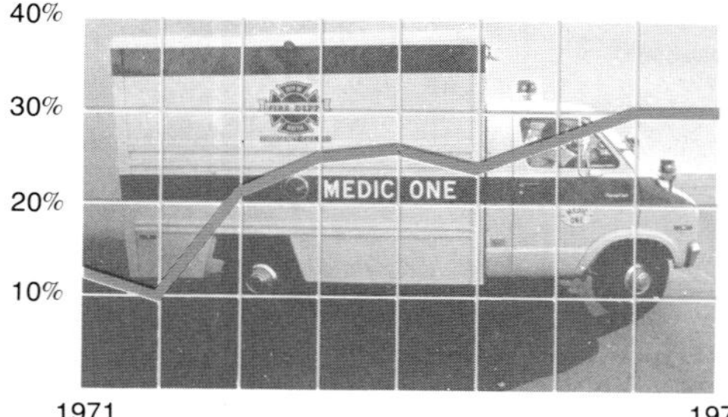

The figures on the vertical scale of this graph indicate the percentages of survivors among the heart attack victims treated by Medic One teams; the horizontal scale follows the first decade of the program.

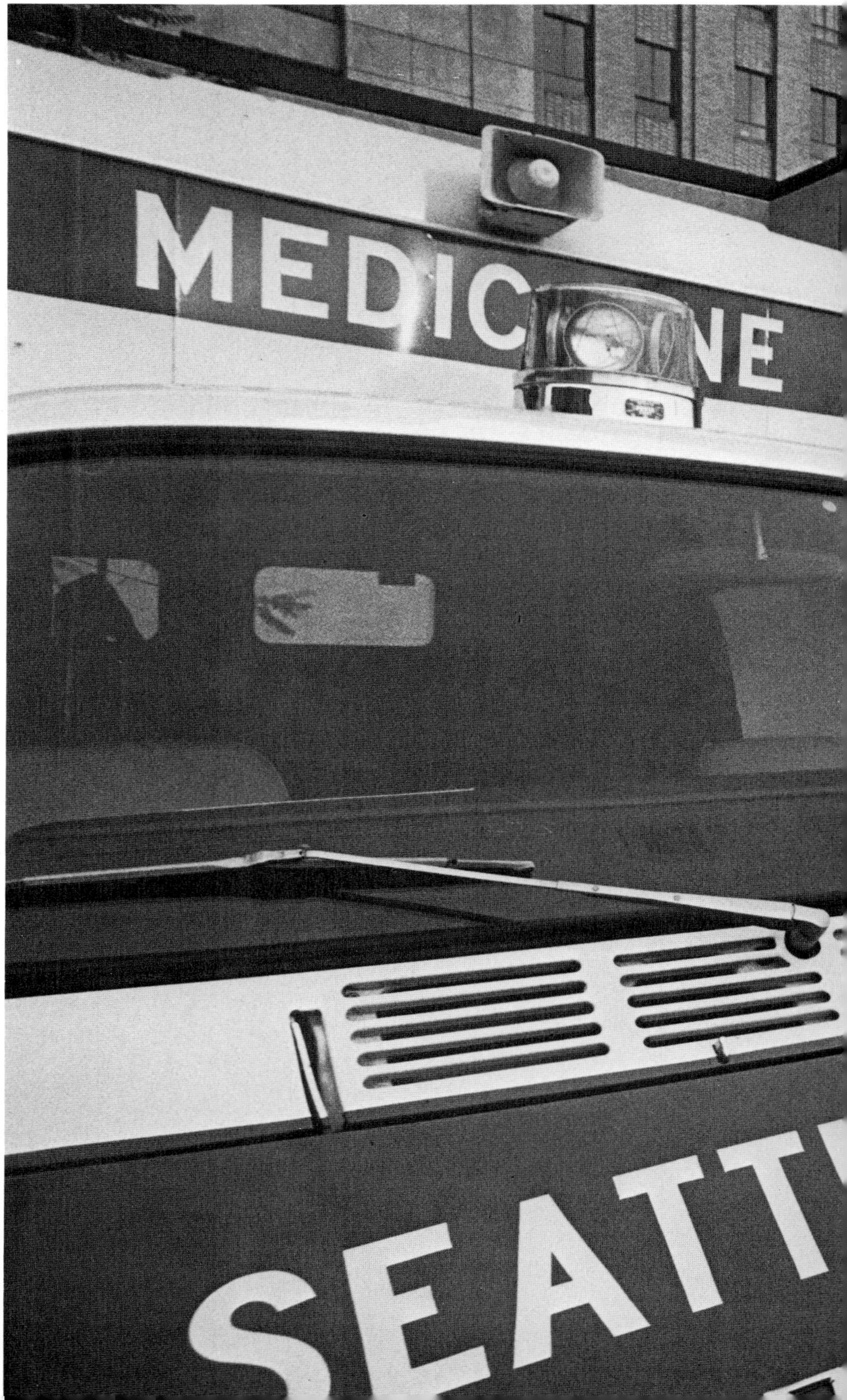

11:20 a.m. *Paramedic Howie Cannon (right) and partner Ray Waugh race from Seattle's Harborview Medical Center, responding to a call that truck driver Clifford Le Beau has suffered a heart attack on the Seattle docks.*

PHOTOGRAPHS BY BOB PETERSON

A quick rescue at the docks

11:23 a.m. *At the scene Waugh (left) unloads a defibrillator, used to regulate the heartbeat. Behind him Cannon removes a kit containing intravenous equipment, syringes, drugs, a blood-pressure cuff; a laryngoscope to ease a tube into the lung, and surgical tools to open an emergency air passage in the windpipe.*

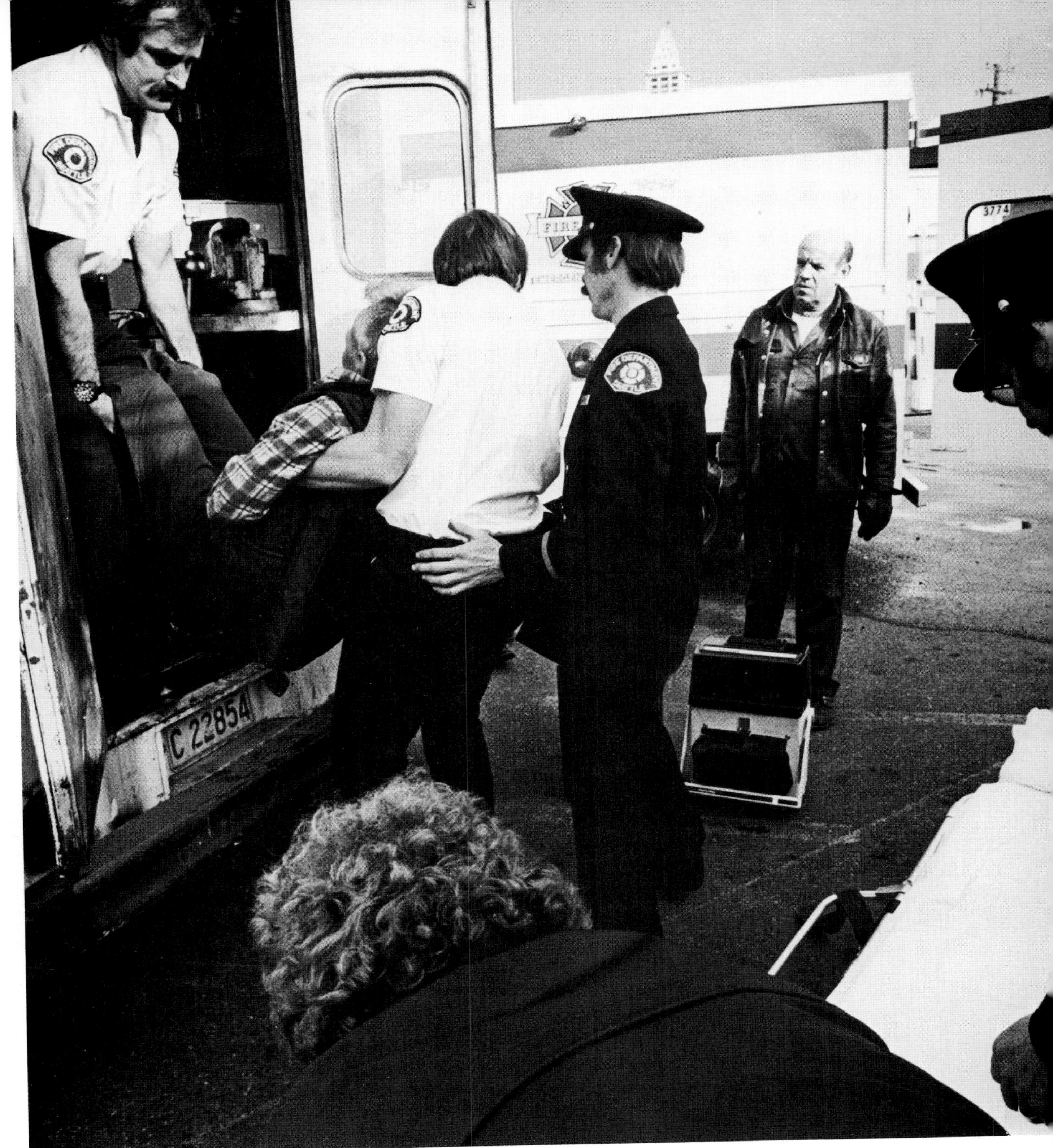

11:27 a.m. *The paramedics pick up Clifford Le Beau as firemen already on the scene assist. "He was sweating, had chest pains radiating into his arms, and he still wanted to walk," said Cannon. "When you have this kind of chest pain, you should sit down, not walk. Your heart's trying to tell you something."*

Treatment on the run

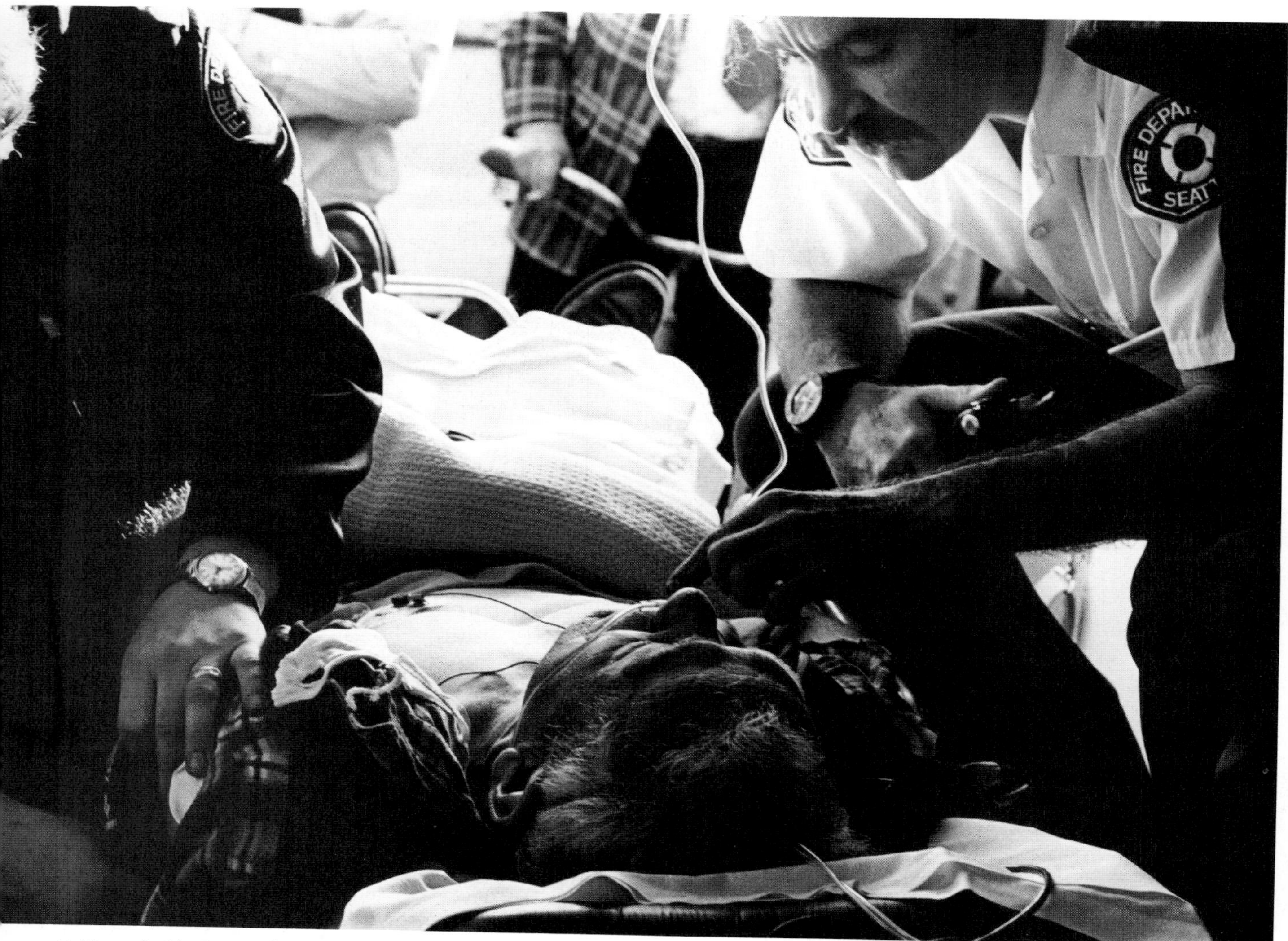

11:32 a.m. *Inside the van the patient receives oxygen and intravenous fluids, while Cannon asks him to rate his chest pain on a 1-to-10 scale. The defibrillator can restart an arrested heart and an electrocardiograph (ECG) records heart activity.*

11:37 a.m. *The patient temporarily relaxed, Waugh discusses the ECG readings with the Medic One cardiologist. The doctor directs him to continue treatment, and to call back if any problems arise. Should the heart stop, Waugh can restart it with the defibrillator paddles (on the floor next to the ECG at lower right).*

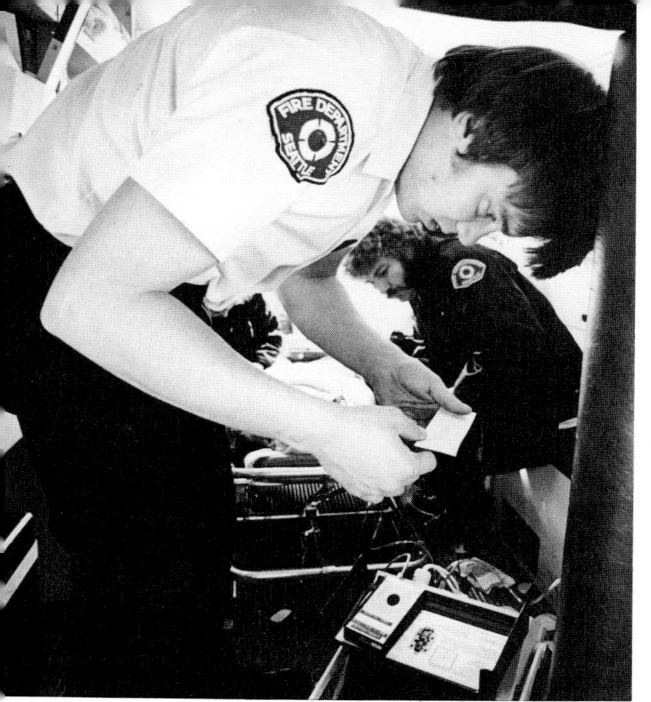

11:33 a.m. *Waugh checks the data of an electrocardiograph (ECG) at lower right — readings radioed to a hospital cardiologist.*

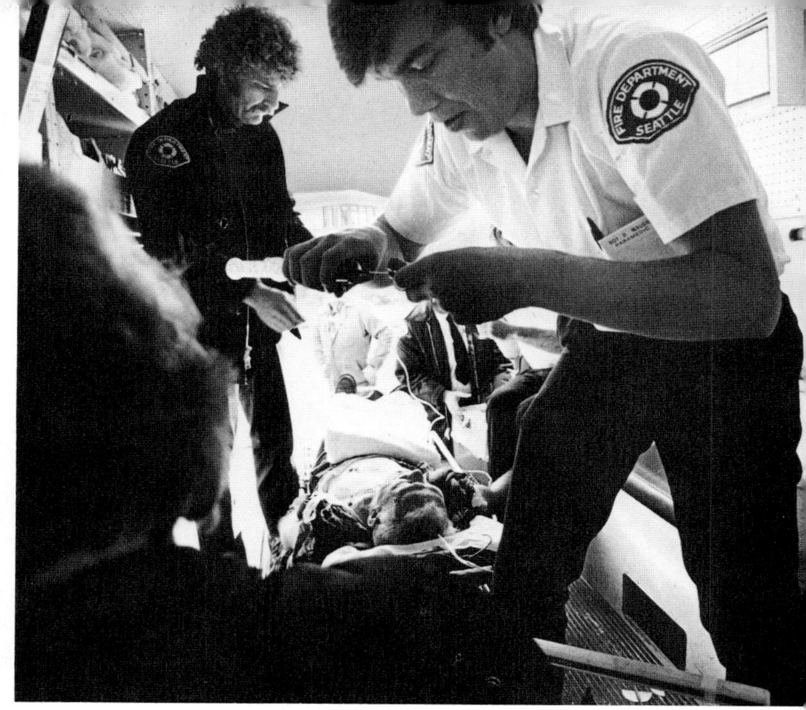

11:35 a.m. *Waugh prepares to inject morphine, which will dilate the patient's arteries and relieve pain and anxiety.*

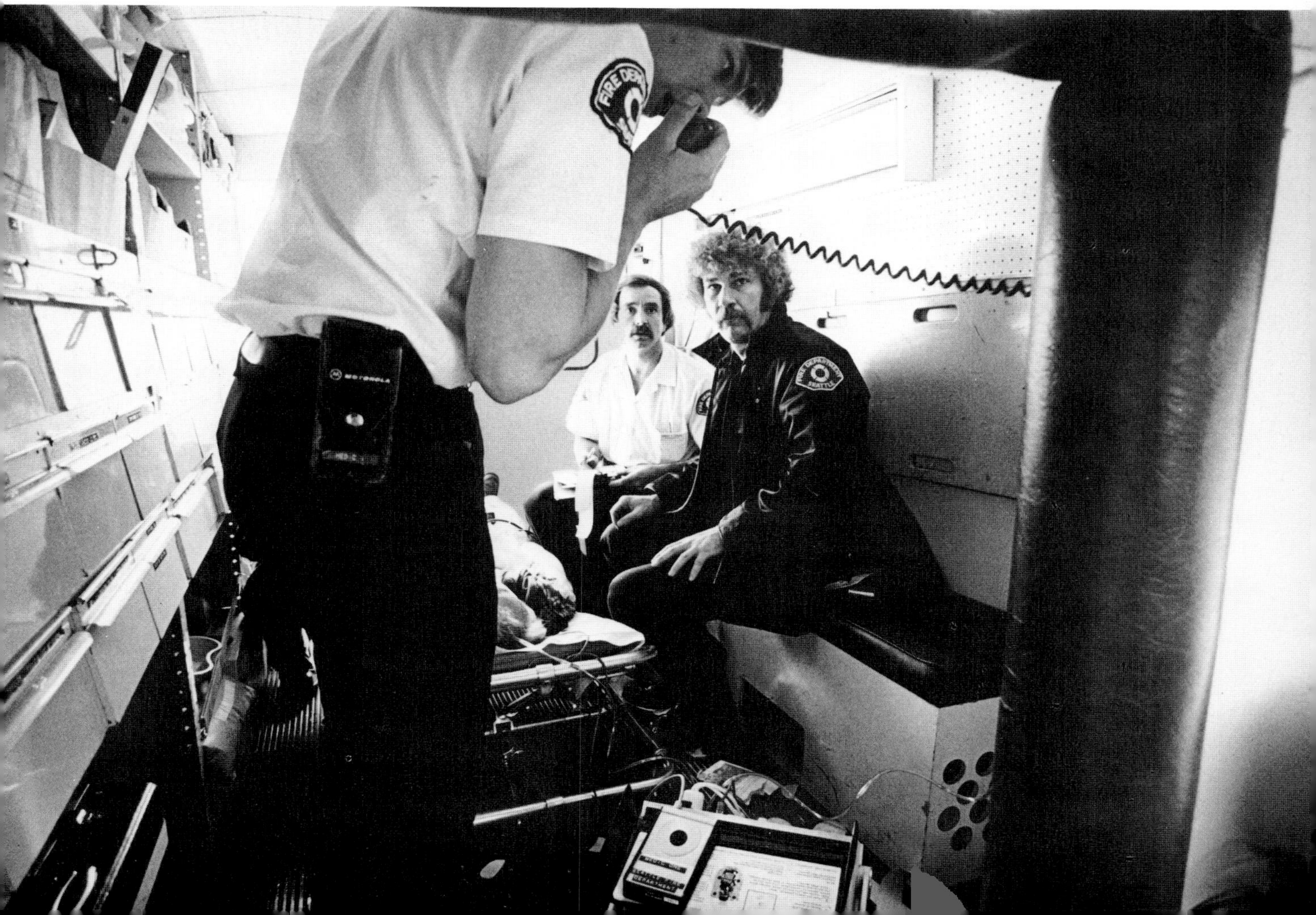

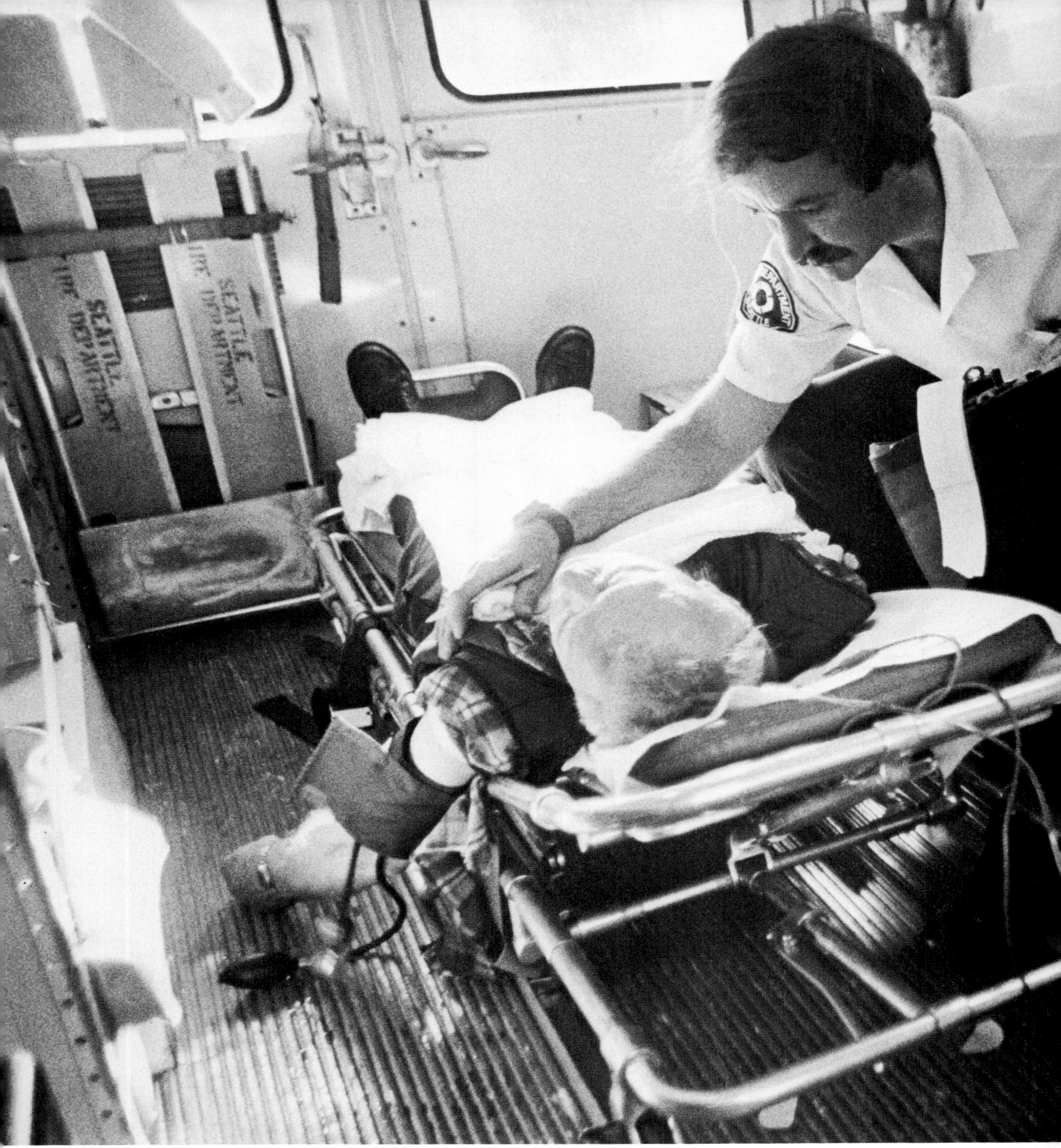

11:40 a.m. *As Waugh screeches around a corner toward the hospital, Cannon holds the strapped-down patient. The monitoring equipment continues to operate under Cannon's supervision.*

SUCTION KIT

At the hospital without a break in care

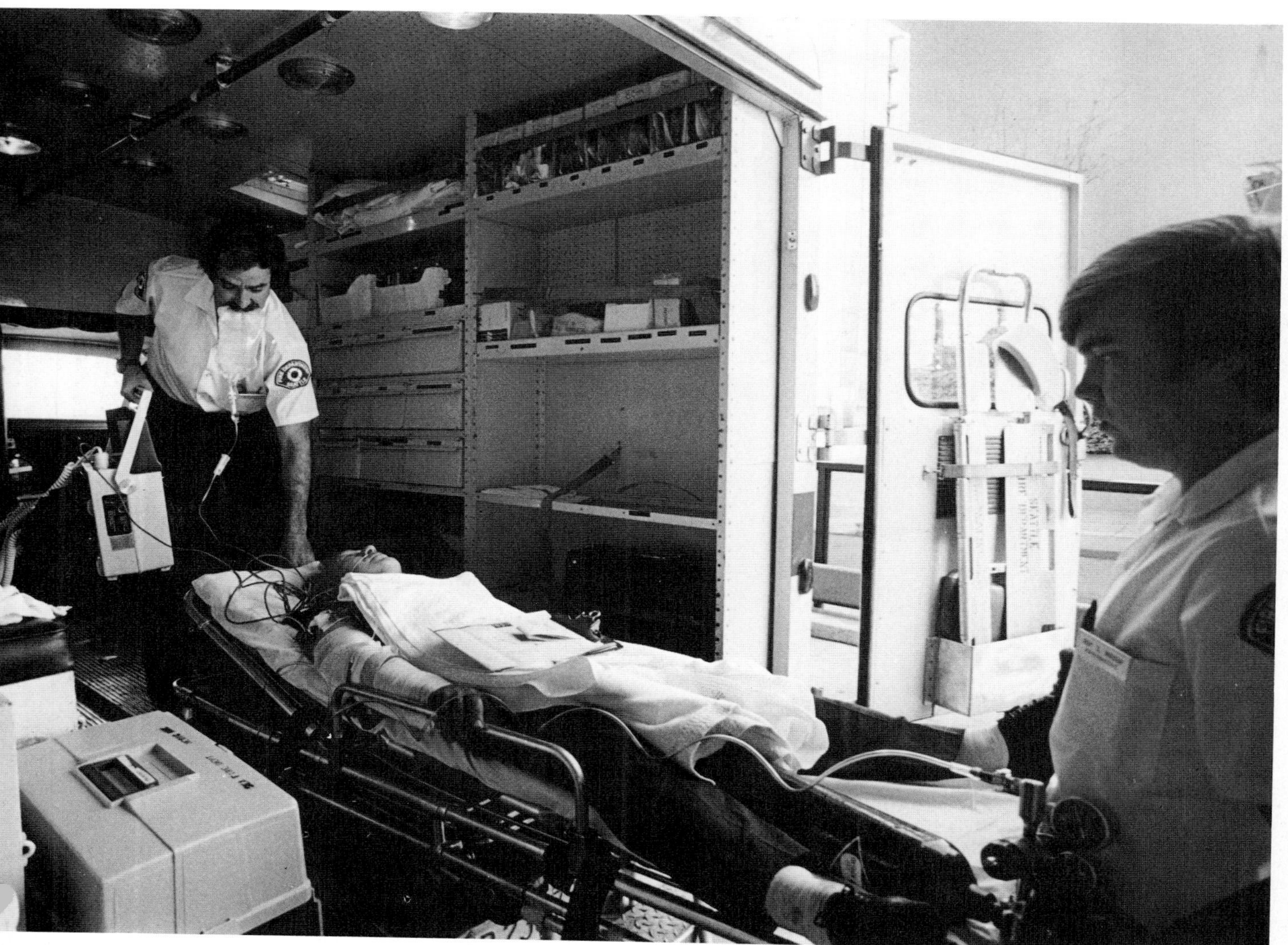

11:45 a.m. *Cannon and Waugh get their patient out of the van in a dazzling display of teamwork. He receives oxygen from the tank at his feet; Cannon holds a fluid bag in his teeth, carries the defibrillator in one hand, and lifts the stretcher with the other, while Waugh pulls the stretcher and bears most of the weight.*

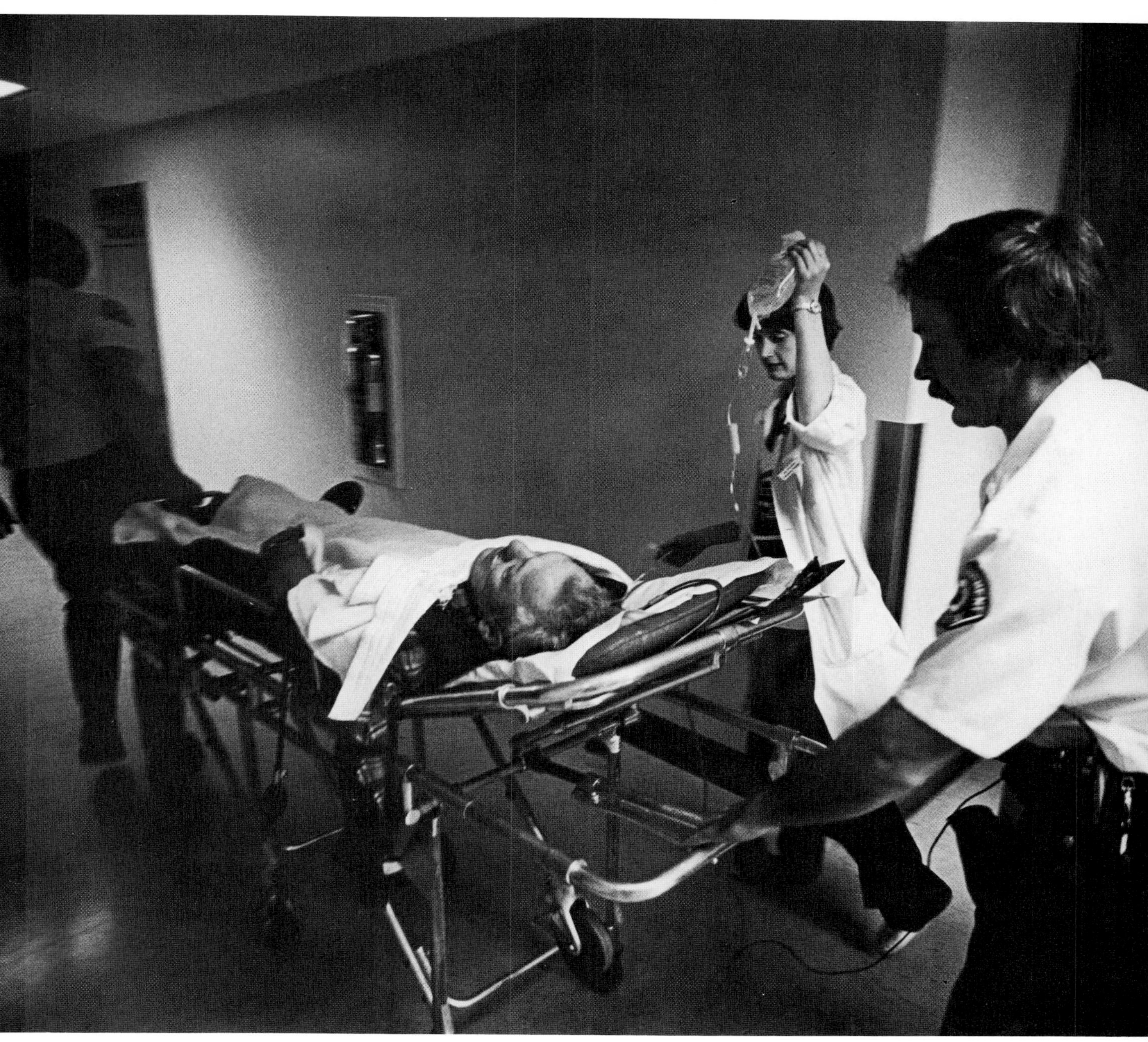

11:50 a.m. *While a nurse carries the bag of intravenous fluids, Cannon and Waugh rush the patient down a corridor to the coronary care unit. Though speed is still important, the prospects for the patient are greatly improved; his heartbeat and other vital functions have been stabilized in the van, and he is about to get the services of a fully equipped hospital and a cardiologist.*

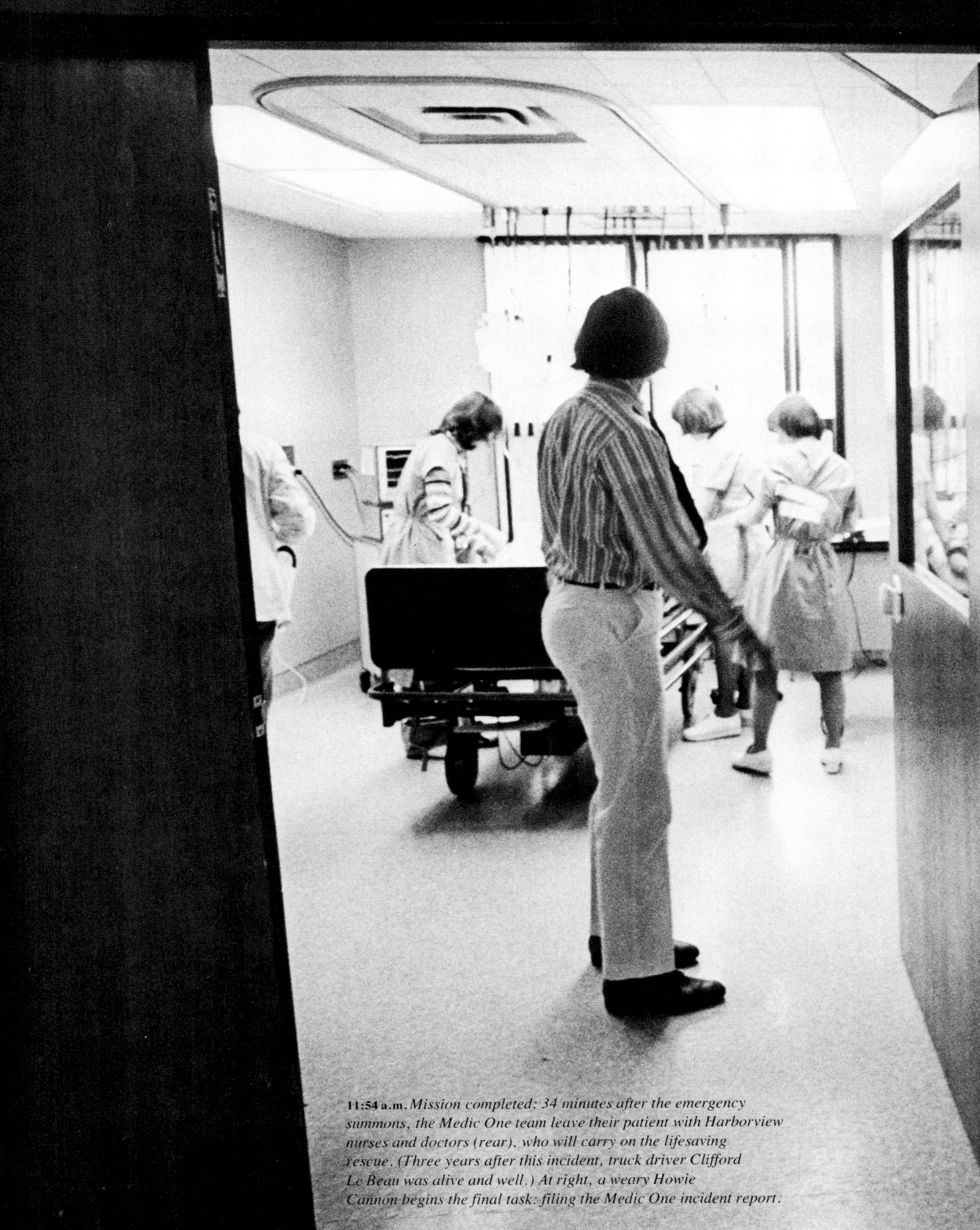

11:54 a.m. *Mission completed: 34 minutes after the emergency summons, the Medic One team leave their patient with Harborview nurses and doctors (rear), who will carry on the lifesaving rescue. (Three years after this incident, truck driver Clifford Le Beau was alive and well.) At right, a weary Howie Cannon begins the final task: filing the Medic One incident report.*

An encyclopedia of symptoms

Heart ailments develop slowly, without obvious warnings. Recognizing subtle signals of trouble ahead is important. And when trouble strikes, it is vital to know when to rush to the hospital and when to wait to visit the doctor the next day. The most common indications of circulatory disorders are described below, listed alphabetically by symptoms that can be felt or seen. The disease that causes each symptom—or, more often, each group of symptoms—is named in small capital letters. These descriptions are simplified; if you have any doubt about the meaning of any symptoms you experience, call a doctor.

BEHAVIOR CHANGES. Behavior changes can indicate anything from insomnia to cancer but they can also arise from blood vessel clogging that changes blood flow to the brain. The type and degree of behavior change depends on the area affected in the brain. Memory, especially for recent events, may be poor. Irritability, wide mood swings, loss of interest and inappropriate emotional responses are common. Changes in appearance and loss of inhibitions often result. Usually, behavior changes occur with other evidence of brain involvement from heart disease, such as dizziness, headache, muscle weakness, and vision and speech disorders.

- **Behavior changes that appear suddenly** may be evidence of a STROKE *(pages 77-83)* or THROMBOSIS (blood clot, *page 78).* Get medical attention as quickly as possible.
- **Behavior changes that appear gradually or periodically** may suggest ATHEROSCLEROSIS *(Chapter three)* without thrombosis; this situation often represents a gradual clogging of blood vessels, and this can lead to more serious disorders. Consult a physician, but you can wait until the next day.

BLUE SKIN (CYANOSIS). Blue or purple skin and mucous membranes can signify either lack of oxygen in the blood or inadequate blood circulation. It is most noticeable when it appears in the hands and face, but it may appear anywhere on the body. Blueness is normal when it follows exposure to extreme cold, high altitudes or bruising injuries. Otherwise it may indicate one or more of the following disorders, many heart-related.

- **Blueness accompanied by severe chest pain** can indicate a very serious condition.

If blue skin is accompanied by viselike, constricting chest pain that is not affected by breathing or movement and lasts longer than 20 minutes, it may indicate a HEART ATTACK (ACUTE MYOCARDIAL INFARCTION, *page 82).* Get medical attention as quickly as possible. Other symptoms may be shortness of breath, sweating, paleness and a sense of impending doom.

If blue skin is accompanied by constricting chest pain and severe shortness of breath that awakens you and leaves you gasping, you may have CONGESTIVE HEART FAILURE or PULMONARY EMBOLISM *(pages 89-92).* Get medical attention as quickly as possible. The symptoms are usually made better by sitting up. Swelling of the hands and feet and an irritating cough may also occur.

- **Blue skin with a weak pulse,** mental confusion, cold and moist skin, paleness and fatigue may mean that you are in shock. Get medical attention as quickly as possible.
- **Frequent blue skin and shortness of breath after exertion** are common in CONGENITAL HEART DISEASE *(pages 90-91),* a disorder present at birth, and in several lung diseases such as EMPHYSEMA. Consult a physician, but you can wait until the next day. Continued exercise makes the blueness worse. Swelling of the finger tips (CLUBBING) is also common.
- **Blue skin localized in one area of the body** can be an early symptom of inadequate circulation, sometimes dangerous and sometimes trivial.

If localized blueness and pain are sudden and severe and occur with numbness and coldness, you may have a blocked blood vessel *(page 97).* Get medical attention as quickly as possible.

If localized blueness in the lips and cheeks occurs with paleness of the rest of the face, you may have MITRAL STENOSIS *(page 93),* a narrowing of a heart valve. Consult a physician, but you can wait until the next day.

If localized blueness in the fingers and toes follows paleness and occurs after emotional upsets or exposure to cold, it may indicate BLOOD VESSEL SPASMS (RAYNAUD'S PHENOMENON). Consult a physician, but you can wait until the next day. Other symptoms include numbness, tingling or burning.

If localized blueness, without pain, of hands and feet is aggravated by cold and relieved by warmth, you may have ACROCYANOSIS caused by spasms of small arteries. Hands and feet will also be persistently cold and sweating. No medical treatment is necessary.

BREATHLESSNESS: ***See SHORTNESS OF BREATH***

CHEST PAIN. Chest pain is common and can arise from causes as diverse as indigestion and muscle strain. It usually does not indicate heart or blood-vessel trouble. But when it does, its significance must be understood promptly.

Two simple criteria sometimes help in identifying true heart pain. One is the effect of body position. Heart pains generally are eased somewhat by sitting up; rarely does lying down help. The second key is the size of the area that hurts: If you can cover the pain with one finger, it is unlikely that it originates in the heart.

Outlined below are simplified descriptions of common chest pains—some serious, some not so serious, some heart-related, some not. Any of them can be caused by anxiety or emotional tension rather than by a physical ailment; however, serious symptoms should not be ignored, even if you think they are more psychological than physical.

• **Viselike constricting pain,** centered somewhere over the front of the chest but sometimes felt in the abdomen and shoulders, is a signal of any of several serious heart-related ailments.

If such a squeezing pain is very severe, lasts longer than about 20 minutes, is not affected by breathing or moving, is not necessarily brought on by exertion and is not relieved by rest, it may be caused by a HEART ATTACK (ACUTE MYOCARDIAL INFARCTION, *page 82*). Get medical attention as rapidly as possible. Other indications of heart attack are pains that go up the neck toward the jaws, to the back or down the arm—either or both arms, but usually the left one. Heart attack pain may be followed by perspiration that makes the skin cold and moist, by nausea or vomiting, and by a feeling of weakness and impending doom.

If the basic squeezing chest pain occurs with severe shortness of breath—despite lack of exertion—or with shortness of breath that awakens you suddenly in the night and leaves you gasping, you may be suffering from CONGESTIVE HEART FAILURE *(pages 89-92)*. Get medical attention as quickly as possible. The pain and shortness of breath may be accompanied by an irritating cough or, in certain cases, by swelling of the limbs, especially the hands and feet. The pain is not usually affected by movement.

If the basic squeezing pain resembles that of a heart attack but can be affected by deep breathing or changing position, it may be caused by a PULMONARY EMBOLISM, a clot in an artery of the lung. Consult a physician immediately. Such a clot may also cause you to cough up fluid and blood, or to become breathless.

If the basic squeezing chest pain occurs after exertion but usually subsides with a few minutes' rest, it probably indicates ANGINA PECTORIS *(pages 83-84)* rather than congestive heart failure or a heart attack. Angina is not an emergency but is a symptom of a potentially serious deficiency in blood supply to the heart. Consult a physician, but you can wait until the next day.

• **Sharp, stabbing chest pain** can indicate either of two serious heart defects. However, it is seldom a symptom of heart attack or congestive heart failure, and is more commonly associated with ailments that do not involve the circulatory system.

If the stabbing pain can be made better or worse by deep breathing or changing position, it may be caused by PERICARDITIS, inflammation of the heart lining. Consult a physician immediately.

If the stabbing pain is affected by movement, like pericarditis pain, but also extends over much of the chest and through the back, it may indicate a DISSECTING AORTIC ANEURYSM, a tear in the lining of a main artery. Consult a physician immediately.

If the stabbing pain is spasmodic, not steady, and occurs on the right side just under the ribs, you may have a GALLSTONE. You may also suffer generalized pain in the right shoulder, break into a cold sweat and feel an urge to move the bowels. Consult a doctor.

If the stabbing pain is in the lower chest and radiates up the esophagus, you may have a HIATAL HERNIA, a tear in the diaphragm. Hiatal hernia pain is made either better or worse if you eat or drink something or simply swallow hard. Consult a physician.

• **Burning pain behind the breastbone** generally originates in the digestive system—simple INDIGESTION or an ULCER. If it recurs with any frequency, consult a physician.

• **A steady ache or catching pain** on one side of the chest may be caused by STRETCHED OR TORN CHEST MUSCLES. Unlike the pains of heart ailments, muscle pains generally are relieved by the application of heat or by change in position; they usually do not require professional treatment.

COUGHING. Coughing, which protects the lungs and windpipe from excess fluid that might endanger breathing, can sometimes signify a serious heart-related disorder.

• **Coughing and shortness of breath** that occur on exertion or awaken you at night, causing you to sit up gasping, may be evidence of CONGESTIVE HEART FAILURE *(pages 89-92)*. Get medical attention as quickly as possible. Such coughing may bring up frothy pink sputum and may be accompanied by swelling and sweating.

If coughing occurs with hoarseness, difficulty in swallowing, shortness of breath and chest pain, it may be an indication of AORTIC ANEURYSM *(page 109)*, a bulge in the main artery. Get medical attention as rapidly as possible.

If dry coughing occurs with radiating chest pain that is relieved by sitting up and leaning forward, PERICARDITIS may be the cause. Consult a physician immediately. Fever, chills, weakness and anxiety are accompanying symptoms.

CYANOSIS: *See* ***BLUE SKIN***

DIZZINESS. Dizziness is usually sudden and brief, lasting only a few minutes. It is normally not heart related, but when it is, it signals a reduction in blood flow that can be serious.

• **Dizziness that occurs with fatigue,** shortness of breath on exertion, and angina-like chest pain that lasts less than 20 minutes and is relieved by rest may be an indication of AORTIC STENOSIS, a narrowing of the valve through which blood flows out of the heart. Get medical attention as quickly as possible.

If dizziness follows a fluttering or irregular, throbbing heartbeat—sometimes accompanied by paleness, nausea, weakness and fatigue—your heart is in ARRHYTHMIA *(page 109),* an irregular beating pattern that can be caused by a heart attack. Get medical attention as quickly as possible.

If dizziness follows movement of your arm or head, you may have an artery narrowed or blocked by ATHEROSCLEROSIS *(Chapter 3).* Consult a physician, but you can wait until the next day.

If dizziness occurs when you assume an upright position after lying down, it is often the result of ORTHOSTATIC HYPOTENSION, a lowering of blood pressure that may be heart related. Consult your physician, but you can wait until the next day.

DROPSY: *See SWELLING*
DYSPNEA: *See SHORTNESS OF BREATH*

EDEMA: *See SWELLING*
EXHAUSTION: *See FATIGUE*

FAINTING. Because fainting, a temporary loss of consciousness, is a serious condition by itself and can also be a symptom of heart disorder, it is wise to consult a doctor about any episodes.

• **Fainting with severe chest pain** may signal either of two dangerous heart-related disorders.

If fainting occurs with viselike, constricting chest pain that is not affected by breathing or movement and lasts longer than 20 minutes, it may be caused by a HEART ATTACK (ACUTE MYOCARDIAL INFARCTION, *page 82).* Get medical attention immediately.

If fainting occurs with stabbing chest pain that extends through the back, you may have DISSECTING AORTIC ANEURYSM, a tear in the lining of a main artery. Get medical attention immediately.

• **Even without pain, sudden fainting** accompanied by pallor but few other warning signals may constitute an emergency.

If sudden fainting follows exercise, you may have STENOSIS, a narrowed heart valve or a muscular obstruction beneath the valve; or SUBCLAVIAN STEAL SYNDROME, a blocked artery in the arm. Get medical attention as quickly as possible. Unconsciousness may last as long as 30 minutes and convulsions may occur.

If sudden fainting at rest or with little exertion is followed by redness in the face on recovery, it may indicate ARRHYTHMIA (irregular heartbeat, *page 109),* or HEART BLOCK (a stoppage of the heartbeat). Consult a physician immediately. Twitching may occur 15 to 20 seconds after unconsciousness. If such fainting occurs during sleep, the only symptom may be redness and warmth in the face.

If sudden fainting occurs after head or neck movement, you may have either an AORTIC ARCH SYNDROME, a blockage of the main artery, or CAROTID SINUS SYNCOPE, a disorder of a neck artery. Consult a physician immediately. Temporary blindness, loss of speech and memory, and loss of feeling in one side of the body may also occur. However, this type of fainting may be caused by nothing more than a too-tight collar.

If sudden fainting occurs when you sit or stand up, it indicates POSTURAL HYPOTENSION, low blood pressure caused by a change in posture. Consult a physician, but you can wait until the next day. Such episodes, though frequent, may or may not be heart related.

• **Sudden fainting with slow recovery** that leaves you with a headache, sleepiness and mental confusion may be a symptom of EPILEPSY. Consult a physician immediately. Other symptoms include facial color that does not change, upturned eyes and jerking body movements.

FATIGUE. More than 80 per cent of the time, extreme lassitude is caused only by anxiety. But if it comes on suddenly, accompanies other symptoms and is not relieved by rest, it needs attention.

• **Sudden, severe fatigue without exertion** may indicate rapidly developing CIRCULATORY FAILURE or KIDNEY FAILURE if accompanied by severe shortness of breath, swelling in legs and arms, and rapid heartbeat. Get medical attention as quickly as possible. Other signs of heart failure may follow. If instead of these accompanying symptoms you suffer muscle aches, fever and an overall feeling of illness, the fatigue may be caused by an ACUTE INFECTION. Consult a physician, but you can wait until the next day.

• **Frequent fatigue after mild exertion** is a common early sign of developing heart disease, particularly if other symptoms are involved: shortness of breath, blue skin, unexplained weight gain and swelling of arms or legs. Typically, the fatigue is relieved by rest and you awaken refreshed by a night's sleep but become profoundly tired as the day progresses. Consult your physician, but you can wait until the next day or so.

• **Frequent fatigue that is not related to exertion,** is not relieved by rest, seems worse in the morning and gradually improves during the day may be caused by ANXIETY or EMOTIONAL STRESS. You should suspect an emotional cause if fatigue is associated more with some activities than with others of equal physical stress, and is accompanied by insomnia, nervousness, headaches, shortness of breath, loss of appetite and depression. Consult a physician, but you can wait until the next day or so.

FEVER. Body temperature above normal (98.6° F.) is by itself not a primary indication of heart disease, but it can be significant when other symptoms are present.

• **Fever that occurs with viselike constricting chest pain** that is not relieved by rest may be evidence of a HEART ATTACK (ACUTE MYOCARDIAL INFARCTION, *page 82*). Pallor, sweating, nausea and restlessness may also be noticeable. Get medical attention as quickly as possible.

If fever occurs with shortness of breath, a throbbing heartbeat, fatigue and chest discomfort, you may have MYOCARDITIS, an inflammation of the outer lining of the heart. Get medical attention as quickly as possible.

If fever is accompanied by chest pain—pain that is relieved by sitting up and leaning forward—as well as a dry cough, weakness and restlessness, it may be caused by PERICARDITIS. Consult a physician immediately.

If fever goes up and down and you have muscle pains, look for nodules on the finger tips and red blotches on palms and soles—you may have BACTERIAL ENDOCARDITIS *(pages 92-93)*, an infection of the inner lining of the heart. Consult a physician immediately.

INSOMNIA. Only rarely does sleeplessness indicate circulatory trouble. Other symptoms are more significant.

- **Sleeplessness combined with shortness of breath** can be serious. If shortness of breath awakens you and is made better by sitting up and worse by lying down, it may be caused by HEART DISEASE or LUNG DISEASE. Consult a physician immediately.
- **Sleeplessness that makes you disturbingly aware of your heartbeat** may be an indication of AORTIC INCOMPETENCE, a leaking of the valve through which blood leaves the heart. Consult a physician immediately.

IRRITABILITY: ***See BEHAVIOR CHANGES***

JOINT PAIN. Pain that appears suddenly in the ankles, knees, elbows and wrists may signal RHEUMATIC FEVER *(pages 93-96)*—an allergic-type reaction that can damage the heart severely—if you also have a rapid pulse and chest pain that is relieved by sitting up and leaning forward, but is made worse by breathing or coughing. Consult a physician immediately. The joint pain of rheumatic fever is destructive. The pain commonly travels from one joint to another and also strikes shoulders, hips and small joints of the hands and feet. Other symptoms include fever, a red rash, painless nodules on the joints and, rarely, jerking muscle movements.

- **Joint pain that occurs without chest pain,** and joint pain that appears in several joints at one time may be evidence of OSTEOMYELITIS or RHEUMATOID ARTHRITIS. Consult a physician, but you can wait until the next day or so. Other symptoms may be similar to those of rheumatic fever.

LANGUAGE DISTURBANCES. Sudden changes in the ability to speak, write or understand language frequently indicate STROKE *(pages 77-83)*, caused by changes in blood flow to the brain. Vision changes, muscle weakness, confusion, headache, pallor, dizziness and other symptoms of heart involvement may also occur. You may be unable to understand spoken words (WORD DEAFNESS), to understand written words (WORD BLINDNESS), to write (AGRAPHIA) or to express your thoughts (CORTICAL MOTOR APHASIA). You may be unable to utter words or sounds correctly and fluently (DYSARTHRIA), or to control the loudness of your voice (DYSPHONIA). If you have any combination of the above language disturbances, consult a physician immediately.

LUMP: ***See NODULES***

NAUSEA. Nausea is seldom significant unless other symptoms are also present.

- **Severe nausea that occurs with viselike, constricting chest pain,** shortness of breath, indigestion and rapid heartbeat may indicate a HEART ATTACK (ACUTE MYOCARDIAL INFARCTION, *page 82*), especially if symptoms are not relieved by vomiting. Get medical attention immediately. Symptoms of heart failure may follow.

If severe nausea occurs after eating and is accompanied by pain like that of a heart attack but the nausea and pain are relieved by vomiting, you may have a PEPTIC ULCER. Consult a physician, but usually you can wait until the next day.

NERVOUSNESS: ***See BEHAVIOR CHANGES***

NODULES. Nodules are solid lumps, no larger than a pea, that appear under the skin. They are a secondary symptom common to many disorders, including two heart-related diseases.

- **Painless nodules on ankle, elbow, knee or wrist joints,** accompanied by chest pain that is relieved by sitting up and leaning forward but made worse by breathing or coughing, can be an indication of RHEUMATIC FEVER *(pages 93-96)*. Consult a physician immediately. Rheumatic fever can cause permanent damage to the heart. Other symptoms may include painful and swollen joints, fever, painless red rash and, rarely, jerking muscle movements.

If tender nodules on the tips of fingers and toes appear with fever that rises and falls, chills, loss of appetite, and a feeling of illness, the cause may be ACUTE BACTERIAL ENDOCARDITIS *(pages 92-93)*, an infection of the heart lining. Get medical attention as quickly as possible. Other symptoms include large red spots on the palms of the hands and the soles of the feet.

If painless nodules appear on joints without chest pain but with morning stiffness and joint pain and swelling, the cause may be RHEUMATOID ARTHRITIS. Consult a physician, but you can wait until the next day or so.

NUMBNESS. This pins-and-needles sensation can occur when heart disease reduces the flow of blood to the central nervous system. It appears most often in the legs, arms and face.

• **Numbness, pallor and chills within fingers and toes** following severe pain may be an indication of a BLOCKED ARTERY *(page 96)*. Get medical attention as quickly as possible.

If a hand or foot gets numb periodically and you experience brain-related symptoms such as minor difficulties in speech, double vision, dizziness, confusion or muscle weakness, you may have ATHEROSCLEROSIS *(Chapter 3)* or the early symptoms of a STROKE *(pages 77-83)*. Consult a physician immediately.

If fingers and toes feel numb and turn blue or pale after emotional upsets or exposure to cold, the cause may be BLOOD VESSEL SPASMS (RAYNAUD'S PHENOMENON). Consult a physician, but you can wait until the next day.

PAIN: *See CHEST PAIN AND JOINT PAIN*

PALENESS. Paleness is a common symptom, which can indicate any of several medical emergencies.

• **Sudden paleness, if it occurs with severe, constricting chest pain,** shortness of breath, sweating, nausea and fatigue, may indicate a SEVERE HEART DISORDER or SEVERE LUNG DISORDER. Get medical attention as quickly as possible.

If sudden paleness is accompanied by fatigue, a weak pulse and cold, moist skin that is blue in the hands and feet, you may be developing shock. Get medical attention as quickly as possible.

If sudden paleness in legs or arms is accompanied by severe pain, chills and numbness in fingers or toes, you may be suffering from a BLOCKED ARTERY *(page 96)*. Get medical attention as quickly as possible.

• **Frequent paleness** is, in many cases, an early symptom of circulatory disorders.

If frequent facial pallor includes blue cheeks and lips, it may indicate MITRAL STENOSIS *(page 93)*, a narrowing of a heart valve. Consult a physician, but you can wait until the next day.

If frequent paleness in fingers or toes follows emotional upsets or exposure to cold, it may indicate BLOOD VESSEL SPASMS. Consult a physician, but you can wait until the next day. Often this pallor is followed by blueness, then redness, before the skin color returns to normal. You may also have numbness, tingling or burning.

If frequent paleness occurs in legs or arms when they are raised and disappears when they are lowered, it indicates poor blood vessel function. Consult a physician, but you can wait until the next day.

• **Continuous paleness** with fatigue may indicate anemia or a nutritional deficiency. Consult a physician.

SHORTNESS OF BREATH (DYSPNEA).

Shortness of breath can be an important symptom of heart disease or the natural result of exercise. Because normal breathing seems so effortless, any difficulty in breathing is disturbing but may not be serious. Mild shortness of breath associated with overexertion, obesity, pregnancy and hearty eating is normal.

• **Severe shortness of breath** is, in many cases, an indication of heart-related disorders.

If severe shortness of breath occurs with viselike, constricting chest pain that lasts longer than 20 minutes, is not relieved by rest and is not affected by movement or breathing, it may be caused by HEART ATTACK (ACUTE MYOCARDIAL INFARCTION, *page 82*). Get medical attention as quickly as possible. Other symptoms may be perspiration that makes the skin clammy and moist, nausea, vomiting, fatigue and a feeling of impending doom.

If severe shortness of breath occurs, with or without squeezing chest pain, when you have not exerted yourself—it may awaken you suddenly at night, causing you to sit up, gasping for air—you may have CONGESTIVE HEART FAILURE *(pages 89-92)*, particularly if the pain and shortness of breath are eased by sitting up. Get medical attention as soon as possible. Other symptoms include coughing that brings up frothy pink fluid, swelling in legs and arms, blue skin color and rapid heartbeat. Breathing in may sound like grunting; breathing out may take longer than normal.

If severe shortness of breath occurs with squeezing chest pain that lasts less than 20 minutes and is relieved by rest, it probably indicates ANGINA PECTORIS *(pages 83-84)* rather than a heart attack or congestive heart failure. Angina is a symptom of a potentially serious lack in blood supply to the heart. Consult a physician but if the symptoms do not recur repeatedly during the day, you can wait until the next day. Recurrent anginal symptoms may indicate impending heart attack, and they require immediate medical attention.

If severe shortness of breath occurs after strenuous exertion, with severe chest pain that is worse when breathing in and is not relieved by rest, you may have a COLLAPSED LUNG (PNEUMOTHORAX). Get medical attention as quickly as possible. A hacking cough may also be present.

If severe shortness of breath occurs with fever, shaking chills and sharp, stabbing chest pain that is made worse by coughing and deep breathing, you may have PNEUMONIA. Consult a physician. Other symptoms may include nausea, vomiting, coughing that brings up rust-colored fluid, and a grunting sound when you exhale.

If severe shortness of breath occurs with faintness and chest pain or tightness but it follows irregular or deep, sighing breaths, you may be HYPERVENTILATING—breathing too deeply or rapidly. Hands and feet may also tingle. Although the symptoms may seem like those of a heart attack, hyperventilation is not an emergency and is usually caused by anxiety. Symptoms may be relieved by breathing into a paper bag and rebreathing the exhaled air. Consult a physician if hyperventilation recurs frequently.

- **Periodic shortness of breath** that occurs more and more often after less and less exertion can warn of a serious disorder.

If periodic shortness of breath is accompanied by overall body swelling, fatigue and unexplained weight gain, you may have early symptoms of HEART FAILURE, particularly if you have to prop yourself up with pillows in order to breathe while sleeping. Consult a physician, but you can wait until the next day.

If periodic shortness of breath occurs with wheezing, chest pain affected by breathing, and a cough that brings up fluid, you may have TUBERCULOSIS or another lung disease. Consult a physician.

SKIN DISCOLORATION: ***See BLUE SKIN***

SLEEPLESSNESS: ***See INSOMNIA***

SWELLING (EDEMA, DROPSY). Any unexplained weight gain, tightness of your shoes or clothing at the end of the day, a taut feeling to your skin, or a puffiness in your face, ankles or hands is a sign of swelling, a common early warning of heart failure. When you press a swollen area with your thumb, the indentation may remain for a while.

- **Overall body swelling, particularly in the legs, arms or abdomen,** accompanied by shortness of breath, chest discomfort, fatigue, rapid heartbeat and a cough, may be caused by CONGESTIVE HEART FAILURE *(pages 89-92)*. Get medical attention immediately.
- **Overall body swelling that appears in the abdomen,** accompanied by fatigue, weight loss, loss of appetite and yellow skin color, may be an indication of LIVER DISEASE. Consult your physician.

If overall body swelling is related to menstruation and produces large daily changes in weight, you may have IDIOPATHIC CYCLIC EDEMA. This condition is seldom serious.

- **Swelling in one area** is usually caused by an obstruction of a vein or by an allergy.

If swelling in a leg is accompanied by pain, inflammation and blue skin color, it is probably caused by an obstruction of a vein (VENOUS THROMBOSIS, *page 97*). Consult a physician.

If one area of your body becomes swollen, tender and inflamed, the cause may be an allergy. Consult a physician, but you can wait until the next day.

TEMPERATURE: ***See FEVER***

VISION CHANGES. Sudden blindness—usually in one eye but sometimes in both—blurred vision, double vision (DIPLOPIA), jerking eye movements (NYSTAGMUS) and drooping eyelid (PTOSIS) can each result from an inadequate blood supply to the brain or eye. These changes are normally temporary, but can be an early warning signal of a stroke. Get medical attention immediately.

- **Any vision change accompanied by other symptoms**—chest pains, shortness of breath, fainting, headache, dizziness or speech disorders—can be a more serious indication of heart-related disease. Consult a physician immediately.

WEIGHT GAIN. Increases in weight, if not related to normal growth or to a change in eating or exercise habits, may be a result of overall body swelling that accompanies heart or kidney disease. If severe, such swelling can be indicated by the indentation that remains when you press your skin with your thumb.

- **If weight gain occurs with periodic shortness of breath,** and fatigue after mild exercise, you may be in the early stages of heart disease. Consult a physician, but you can wait until the next day.

If such weight gain is related to menstruation and fluctuates daily, it may be caused by IDIOPATHIC CYCLIC EDEMA.

Bibliography

BOOKS

Adams, Catherine, *Nutritive Value of American Foods in Common Units.* U.S. Department of Agriculture, 1975.

Alpert, Joseph S., *The Heart Attack Handbook: A Commonsense Guide to Treatment, Recovery, and Prevention.* Little, Brown, 1978.

American Heart Association, *Heartbook: A Guide to Prevention and Treatment of Cardiovascular Diseases.* E. P. Dutton, 1980.

Benson, Herbert, *The Relaxation Response.* Avon, 1975.

Brecher, Edward M. and the Editors of Consumer Reports, *Licit and Illicit Drugs.* Little, Brown, 1972.

DeBakey, Michael, and Antonio Gotto, *The Living Heart.* David McKay, 1977.

Farquhar, John W., *The American Way of Life Need Not Be Hazardous to Your Health.* Norton, 1978.

Federation of American Societies for Experimental Biology, *Evaluation of the Health Aspects of Sodium Chloride and Potassium Chloride as Food Ingredients.* Food and Drug Administration, 1979.

Freidman, Meyer, and Ray H. Rosenman, *Type A Behavior and Your Heart.* Knopf, 1974.

Havlik, Richard J., and Manning Feinleib, eds., *Proceedings of the Conference on the Decline in Coronary Heart Disease Mortality.* U.S. Department of Health, Education, and Welfare, 1979.

Johnson, Stephen L., *The History of Cardiac Surgery, 1896-1955.* Johns Hopkins, 1970.

Kannel, William B., and Tavia Gordon, *The Framingham Study: An Epidemiological Investigation of Cardiovascular Disease,* Sections 1, 27, 28 and 30. Superintendent of Documents, 1974.

Keys, Ancel, *Seven Countries: A Multivariate Analysis of Death and Coronary Heart Disease.* Harvard University Press, 1980.

Lear, Martha Weinman, *Heartsounds.* Simon and Schuster, 1980.

Levy, Robert I., Basil M. Rifkind, Barbara H. Dennis, and Nancy Ernst, eds., *Nutrition, Lipids, and Coronary Heart Disease: A Global View.* Raven Press, 1979.

MacKenzie, Rachel, *Risk.* Avon, 1975.

Mayer, Jean, *Overweight: Causes, Cost, and Control.* Prentice-Hall, 1968.

Nolen, William A., *Surgeon Under the Knife.* Coward, McCann & Geoghegan, 1976.

Phibbs, Brendan, *The Human Heart: A Guide to Heart Disease.* C. V. Mosby, 1979.

Poole, Victoria, *Thursday's Child.* Little, Brown, 1980.

Steinfeld, Jesse, William Griffiths, Keith Ball, and Robert M. Taylor, eds., *Smoking and Health,* Vol. 2, Proceedings of the Third World Conference on Smoking and Health, U.S. Department of Health, Education and Welfare, 1975.

Thompson, Thomas, *Hearts: Of Surgeons and Transplants, Miracles and Disasters Along the Cardiac Frontier.* McCall, 1971.

U.S. Department of Health, Education, and Welfare:
The Health Consequences of Smoking for Women: A Report of the Surgeon General. Office on Smoking and Health/Public Health Service, 1980.
Healthy People: The Surgeon General's Report on Health Promotion and Disease Prevention. Superintendent of Documents, 1979.

Zohman, Lenore R., and Jerome S. Tobis, *Cardiac Rehabilitation.* Grune & Stratton, 1970.

Zohman, Lenore R., Albert A. Kattus, and Donald G. Softness, *The Cardiologists' Guide to Fitness and Health Through Exercise.* Simon and Schuster, 1979.

PERIODICALS

Ernos, William, et al., "Pathogenesis of Coronary Disease in American Soldiers Killed in Korea." *Journal of the American Medical Association,* July 16, 1955.

Fuley, Ruth, et al., "Cholesterol Content of Foods." *Journal of the American Dietetic Association,* Vol. 61, 1972.

Kannel, William B.:
"Risk Factors in Coronary Disease—Update (Part 2)." *CME Medicine,* 1979.
"Status of Coronary Heart Disease Risk Factors." *Journal of Nutrition Education,* Vol. 10, January-March 1980.

"Margarine the Better Butter?" *Consumer Reports,* February 1979.

McMichael, John, "Fats and Atheroma: An Inquest." *British Medical Journal,* January 20, 1979.

McNamaria, Judson, et al., "Coronary Artery Disease in Combat Casualties in Vietnam." *Journal of the American Medical Association,* May 17, 1971.

McQuade, Walter, "Good News from the House on Lincoln Street," *Fortune,* January 14, 1980.

"Overweight Adults in the United States." *Advancedata,* No. 51, August 30, 1979.

"Stress: How It Can Hurt." *Newsweek,* April 21, 1980.

"Why Is High Blood Pressure More Common in Blacks?" *Urban Health,* March 1978.

OTHER PUBLICATIONS

"British Study Shows Biofeedback May Reduce Heart Disease Risk." American Heart Association, November 14, 1979.

"Controlled Clinical Trial of a Diet High in Unsaturated Fat." American Heart Association, No. 25, 1969.

"Diet and Coronary Heart Disease." American Heart Association, 1978.

"Exercising Your Right to Know: A Consumer Guide to Choosing and Using Exercise Training and Stress Testing Facilities." Exercise Committee of New York Heart Association, Inc., 1980.

Food and Nutrition Board, "Toward Healthful Diets." National Academy of Sciences, 1980.

"The Framingham Heart Study: Habits and Coronary Heart Disease." Superintendent of Documents, No. 1515, 1966.

"Heart Facts." American Heart Association, 1980.

Jenkins, C. David, "Social and Behavioral Risk Factors." American Heart Association, 1980.

"The Smoking Digest." U.S. Department of Health, Education, and Welfare, October 1977.

Zohman, Lenore R., "Beyond Diet—Exercise Your Way to Fitness and Heart Health." CPC International, 1974.

Picture credits

The sources for the illustrations that appear in this book are listed below. Credits for the illustrations from left to right are separated by semicolons, from top to bottom by dashes.

Cover: Mike Mitchell. 7: Henry Groskinsky, courtesy The American Museum of Natural History. 9: Henry Beville, courtesy Walter Reed Medical Museum. 11-14: Fil Hunter, drawings and sculptures by Nicholas Fasciano. 17: © Lennart Nilsson, from *Behold Man,* Little, Brown and Co., 1974. 19: Chart by Walter E. Hilmers Jr., HJ Commercial Art. 21: Henry Beville, courtesy Museum of History and Technology, Smithsonian Institution. 22, 23: © Lennart Nilsson. 24: © Lennart Nilsson, from *Behold Man,* Little, Brown and Co., 1974—diagram by Walter E. Hilmers Jr., HJ Commercial Art. 25: © Lennart Nilsson—

diagram by Walter E. Hilmers Jr., HJ Commercial Art. 26-29: © Lennart Nilsson, from *Behold Man,* Little, Brown and Co., 1974—drawings by Walter E. Hilmers Jr., HJ Commercial Art. 31: National Heart, Lung, and Blood Institute at National Institutes of Health. 32: Chart by Walter E. Hilmers Jr., HJ Commercial Art. 35: National Aeronautics and Space Administration. 37: Ira Wexler. 38: Parcourse, Ltd. 40: Fil Hunter. 42: Drawing by Joan S. McGurren. 44-53: Al Freni. 55: © Lennart Nilsson. 57: National Institutes of Health. 58: Drawing by Joan S. McGurren. 63: Dr. R. D. Shaffer, Nairobi, Kenya, courtesy Dr. G. V. Mann and the African Medical and Research Foundation and also the National Livestock and Meat Board. 64: Drawing by Joan S. McGurren. 67: Drawing by Stan Hunt, © 1959 The New Yorker Magazine, Inc. 69: Csaba L. Martonyi, Department of Ophthalmology, The University of Michigan. 70: Drawing by Joan S. McGurren. 73-75: Fil Hunter. 76: Chart by Walter E. Hilmers Jr., HJ Commercial Art. 82: Drawings by Walter E. Hilmers Jr., HJ Commercial Art. 85-87: Ken Heinen for *The Washington Star*. 88-93: Drawings by Walter E. Hilmers Jr., HJ Commercial Art. 94: Al Freni. 95: Al Freni—drawings by Walter E. Hilmers Jr., HJ Commercial Art. 97: Norbert Nordmann, from *Klinische Wochenzeitschrift,* Nov. 5, 1929, courtesy Bonn University. 98: Diagram by Cynthia T. Richardson. 99, 100: Richard Anderson. 101: Courtesy Johns Hopkins Cardiovascular Diagnostic Laboratory, outlines by Cynthia T. Richardson. 102-105: Richard Anderson. 107: Stanford University Medical Center. 109: Cordis Corporation—drawings by Walter E. Hilmers Jr., HJ Commercial Art. 111: John Senzer. 115: Pegasus. 116: American Edwards Laboratories; Shiley Incorporated; Hancock Laboratories Incorporated. 119: Drawings by Walter E. Hilmers Jr., HJ Commercial Art. 122, 123: Cardiology and Internal Medicine Professional Association; John Senzer. 124: John Senzer. 125: John Senzer—courtesy Washington Hospital Center. 126-134: John Senzer. 135: John Senzer, insert, Cardiology and Internal Medicine Professional Association. 136, 137: John Senzer. 139: Camera Press-Pix, London; Keystone; Wide World—Peter C. Borsari; The Detroit Tigers Baseball Club; Library of Congress; Peter C. Borsari—Wide World; © Steven Landis; National Aeronautics and Space Administration; Alfred J. Hitchcock Productions, Inc., Universal City Studios—UPI; O'Brian, courtesy J. F. Kennedy Center; *All That Jazz,* courtesy Twentieth Century Fox-Columbia; Library of Congress. 143-145: John Senzer. 147: Kim Brace, courtesy National Hospital for Orthopedics and Rehabilitation. 149-151: Toronto Rehabilitation Centre, Post-Coronary Exercise Program. 154, 155: Photo © Bob Peterson, chart by Walter E. Hilmers Jr., HJ Commercial Art; © Bob Peterson. 156-165: © Bob Peterson.

Acknowledgments

The index of this book was prepared by Barbara L. Klein. For their valuable help with the preparation of this volume, the editors wish to thank the following: Edward Ahlquist, Adelphi, Md.; American Heart Association, Dallas, Tex.; Nancy Anderson, Washington Hospital Center, D.C.; Pat Bader, Johns Hopkins Hospital, Baltimore, Md.; Dr. Charles F. Bahn, University of Michigan, Ann Arbor; Dr. Henry Blackburn, University of Minnesota, Minneapolis; Don Bradley, National Heart, Lung, and Blood Institute, Bethesda, Md.; Dr. H. Bryan Brewer Jr., National Heart, Lung, and Blood Institute, Bethesda, Md.; Edward Brooks, Edwards Laboratories, Santa Ana, Calif.; Dr. Frank L. Brown Jr., Washington Hospital Center, D.C.; Michael F. Calhoun, Parcourse, Ltd., San Francisco, Calif.; Howard Cannon, Bothell, Wash.; Kathy Clatanoff, Shiley Sales Corp., Irvine, Calif.; Dr. Leonard A. Cobb, Harborview Medical Center, Seattle, Wash.; Barbro Dal, Albert Bonnier's Forlag AB, Stockholm, Sweden; Dr. Fred Epstein, University of Zurich, Switzerland; Dr. Manning Feinleib, National Heart, Lung, and Blood Institute, Bethesda, Md.; Dr. Victor Ferrans, National Heart, Lung, and Blood Institute, Bethesda, Md.; Dr. Gary Fisher, D.C.; Dr. Samuel M. Fox, Georgetown University, D.C.; Jan C. Glover, National Hospital for Orthopedics and Rehabilitation, Arlington, Va.; Dr. Murray Goldstein, National Institute of Neurological and Communicative Disorders and Stroke, Bethesda, Md.; Paul Goldstein, Cordis Corp., Miami, Fla.; Mr. and Mrs. Hartley Grey, Smyrna, Del.; David L. Gunner, Warren Museum, Boston, Mass.; Dr. Pablo A. Guzman, Johns Hopkins Hospital, Baltimore, Md.; Carol Haines, National High Blood Pressure Education Program, Bethesda, Md.; Michael R. Harris, National Museum of History and Technology, D.C.; J. Lee Hendricks, Hancock Laboratories Inc., Anaheim, Calif.; Carter Huff, Johns Hopkins Hospital, Baltimore, Md.; Everett Jackson, National Museum of History and Technology, D.C.; Dr. Larry K. Jackson, Georgetown University, D.C.; Dr. William Kannel, Boston University, Mass.; Lucinda Keister, National Library of Medicine, Bethesda, Md.; Nancy J. Keneipp, Germantown, Md.; Robert S. Kohansky, *Sports Illustrated,* New York, N.Y.; Dr. George P. Leitl, Baltimore, Md.; Robert H. Levenson, American Pacemaker Corp., Woburn, Mass.; Lilka Lichtneger, John F. Kennedy Elementary School, West Babylon, N.Y.; Dr. James W. Long, National Science Foundation, D.C.; Alf McCreavy, Belfast, Ireland; June Martinez, The American Museum of National History, New York, N.Y.; G. W. Meredith, Washington Hospital Center, D.C.; Lori Mintz, Washington Hospital Center, D.C.; Dr. Michael Mock, National Heart, Lung, and Blood Institute, Bethesda, Md.; Virginia Mock, Johns Hopkins Hospital, Baltimore, Md.; Linda A. Morgan, Pulse, Atlanta, Ga.; Dr. Gary Nelson, National Heart, Lung, and Blood Institute, Bethesda, Md.; York Onnen, National Heart, Lung, and Blood Institute, Bethesda, Md.; James O. Page, ACT Foundation, Baskingridge, N.J.; Dr. Gerald H. Payne, National Heart, Lung, and Blood Institute, Bethesda, Md.; Susan W. Plaster, Cardiac Pacemakers Inc., St. Paul, Minn.; Dr. Basil M. Rifkind, National Heart, Lung, and Blood Institute, Bethesda, Md.; Dr. Jean-Michael Roland, Children's Hospital, Buffalo, N.Y.; Lorraine Rose, D.C.; Dr. Joel Rosenberg, Washington Hospital Center, D.C.; Dr. Russell Ross, University of Washington at Seattle; Richard Rowcroft, John F. Kennedy Elementary School, West Babylon, N.Y.; Mari Schaarschmidt, International Association of Pacemaker Patients, Inc., Atlanta, Ga.; Jerome H. Schiffman, John F. Kennedy Elementary School, West Babylon, N.Y.; Dr. Eric Schreiber, Baltimore, Md.; Dr. Stuart Seides, Washington Hospital Center, D.C.; John Slowikowski, Smith Island CPR Group, Silver Spring, Md.; Nancy Smith, Parkville, Md.; Jane P. Snyder, Washington Hospital Center, D.C.; Dr. Jeremiah Stamler, Northwestern University Medical School, Evanston, Ill.; Thomas Thom, National Heart, Lung, and Blood Institute, Bethesda, Md.; Roy Waugh, Seattle, Wash.; Dr. James Weiss, Johns Hopkins Hospital, Baltimore, Md.; Dr. Edward R. White, AFIP Medical Museum, D.C.; Michael F. White, National Heart, Lung, and Blood Institute, Bethesda, Md.; Dr. Robert White, Johns Hopkins Hospital, Baltimore, Md.

Index

Numerals in italics indicate an illustration of the subject mentioned.

Printed in U.S.A.